Successful Career
Soft Skills and Business English

Personality Development and Career Path

Successful Career
Soft Skills and Business English
Personality Development and Career Path

Varanasi Bhaskara Rao

Business English by
Y. Kameswari
MA(English) B.Ed.,

BSP BS Publications
An Imprint of **BSP Books Pvt. Ltd.**
4-4-309/316, Giriraj Lane,
Sultan Bazar, Hyderabad - 500 095

Successful Career Soft Skills and Business English
Personality Development and Career Path
by **Varanasi Bhaskara Rao**

Third Reprint 2024

Published by:

BSP BS Publications
An Imprint of **BSP Books Pvt. Ltd.**
4-4-309/316, Giriraj Lane, Sultan Bazar,
Hyderabad - 500 095
Phone: 040 - 23445688
e-mail: info@bspbooks.net
www.bspbooks.net

Printed at
Repro India Limited.

Price: Rs. 695.00

ISBN: 978-81-7800-239-2 (Paperback)

A. Prasanna Kumar
(M.A.Hons Ph.D.,)
Director, Centre for Policy Studies
(Former Rector, Andhra University)
47-7-23 Dwaraka Nagar 4th Lane
Visakhapatnam.

FOREWORD

In this age of awesome technological power man's capacity to invent and innovate has been growing at a furious pace. When Joseph Nye coined the term 'Soft Power' almost two decades not many foresaw the range and impact of that power. Experts classified power as soft and hard and even culture too as pull(soft) and push(hard). Materials, weapons and laws come under hard culture category while ideas, creative work and culture belong to the realm of soft culture. Soft skills have assumed considerable importance in both the academic and administrative worlds, in teaching and research and in daily practice as well. Indian youth endowed with soft skills are a national asset and their skills are recognized in advanced countries too.

Interestingly India is 'a super power' in English language, so crucial for modern computer-dominated technology. No country in the world has so many English knowing people as India has and that is one of India's major strengths today. Soft skills are considered vital for the development of human personality and professional excellence. Soft skills include communication skills, courtesy, manners and values. Knowledge is power. But culture is a shock absorber for both the individual and the institution in which he or she works. The teaching of soft skills is, therefore, vital for quality education which many top universities and educational institutions are vying with one another to provide for the benefit of the younger generation.

Shri V. Bhaskara Rao, a retired bank official with vast experience in the field of banking, management and modern finance has authored a number of articles and books during the last two decades for the benefit of those in service and also those appearing for competitive examinations. All his publications have been extremely useful and the latest one on **Successful Career Soft Skills and Business English : Personality Development and Career Path** will, I am sure, be very useful to those in service, both public and private, and also to those seeking to join them. The book containing eleven chapters on important themes is timely and welcome and I congratulate Shri Bhaskara Rao on making yet another useful contribution to the subject.

PREFACE

This book is meant to help people to help themselves using their present resources and develop knowledge, skills, and values by moulding their career paths to reach their life goals rather than just land a job.

A number of career profiles of people from diverse disciplines and vocations have been included, with special emphasis on the Indian scene. By studying these real life stories, the students can learn from others' experiences rather than hypothetical situations.

There are many books on career success and job seeking. Most of them come from the West. They write for their own audiences with their own case histories. Whereas concepts are the same, the context and culture make a huge difference.

It is hoped that the case histories from the book help the trainer/teacher in the classroom to explain the concepts and present precepts. The teacher can form groups and engage them in group discussions, select skills the students need to perfect to secure a selection. He may also give them writing assignment using the cases for identifying the concepts involved in each case.

The real-life career paths presented give the teacher an opportunity to discuss how students can plan for their entire future keeping in mind change of jobs, careers, and change of industry. They may even quit and pursue their personal interests. Lifelong learning is the theme of the book, personality development, free, frank, and independent life, thrown in.

The student should be prepared for the unexpected changes, economic crises in the dynamic interconnected multi—level reality.

The textbook touches a broad spectrum of areas, from discovering in which you are to conduct career researches, how to prepare and present yourself for opportunities and choices.

This book is not a quick-fix answer to get a job to eke out a livelihood. This is to help people focus on moulding their career paths to fit their larger life goals.

The book is not a mere presentation of concepts and precepts. The case histories of real people–diverse people–in the Indian context who have worked hard at shaping their careers. At my request these people spared time and agreed to share their personal profiles beneath which lie their personality, their values, motivations, abilities, in-born or acquired, their striving and struggles, etc.

Some of them have the experience in interviewing and selecting people for jobs through campus selections or otherwise. Their experiences and ideas throw light on the mismatch between what the employers want and what the candidates present.

The students' focus is more on careers than on the skills that contribute to success in careers. They may think that the academic success guarantees career success. This is far from true. People in higher education have also noticed that the rankers in competitive examinations had been dull students in the classroom. Similarly the employers have found that rank holders in higher education perform poorly because they lack what has come to be known as soft skills.

Moreover the employers, who have been trying to shape the new entrants to suit the immediate job requirements as well as future responsibilities through their training establishments, have come to the conclusion that it is better to recruit the 'finished products' with all the features in tact—the hard or job specific skills and also the soft skills which are most needed as they move up the career ladder.

Buck passed on to Educational Institutions

With the result the buck of training the students or preparing the students or laying the foundation for a successful career both for the benefits of the individual and that of organization; eventually the society is the ultimate beneficiary, is passed on to educational institutions. Producing the right men and women for careers has become a joint responsibility of the educators and the employers.

Therefore, there is a move in the universities to include such subject like soft skills in the curricula. Hence this attempt is to highlight career success as function of soft skill.

The *CAST*

I have *CAST* the structure with *Cases, Appendices* and *Acronyms, Snippets, and Titbits.* The sources are personal accounts, expository writings, on subjects which demand separate study in books (popular and scholarly) and print media. Cases are intended for class-room learning using case method; acronyms for memory; snippets for quoting authorities; and finally titbits for developments in the world around.

The acronyms are more than mementos. They remind you to test the validity of the concepts by practical results, pragmatic in true sense. They appear as foot-notes at the bottom of the pages in which the concepts appear. It is hoped that both the teacher and the student will avail of the acronymic reminders for study purposes and examinations point of view.

The reason why they are not highlighted in the running test is two-fold: too numerous and at times inhibit the rapid comprehension as figures and tables do. I had the general reader in mind when this decision to relegate them to the foot-notes was taken.

- Authors

Acknowledgement

It was an experience true to my thesis outlined in the book. It was one Mr.Ravindranath who is in the publishing field who persuaded me to write a textbook on soft skills based on the syllabus of MBA of one university.

He had to persuade me because I stopped writing for over a year; I had no inclination but had plenty of time. The lack of inclination was more due to symptoms of senility!

There is now a change in my attitude for which I am extremely grateful to Ravindranath.

I set forth on writing the book about which I had only vague idea. I had not written any textbook before. I approached B.S. Publications who published two of my books – 'Communicative Competence' and 'Personal and Emotional Competence', who were too glad to publish whatever I write. They said I am like a member of their family. This was a wonderful gesture from a publishing house which has been a tower of strength. I am grateful to them. Then I read a couple of books published in the West. I am thankful to the authors and their publishers who gave me ideas to go ahead. Inspiration to Indianize the presentation came from these Western books.

The rest of my reading was confined to my dailies – The Hindu and their 'Business Line'–and their supplements. I acknowledge and thank their indirect support. My uniqueness– my strengths – is that my mode of learning is more from the print media than electronic media. I enjoyed reading using all the techniques of rapid and reflective reading about which I had covered in my earlier books. I must thank Francis Bacon who wrote, 'Reading maketh a full man, Conference a ready man, and Writing an exact man'.

I believed in 'Net working' and I began talking about my project with my friends and ex-colleagues and relatives. I began collecting the career profiles from friends, colleagues, and relatives, senior citizens as well as others who are at different stages of their careers who volunteered to spare time to sit and write and supply them to me. I am thankful to all of them for their first person accounts which gave me new insights. It is a pilgrimage.

A friend who has been collaborating with me in the training programmes Mr.K Seetaram, retired General Manager from a Public Sector Oil Company, who supported me in the work with ideas, suggestions, and material, asked me to prepare the structure of the book first for discussion along with Mr.Vinay Vardhan another expert engaged in placement and training.

I could not come to any conclusion on the structure for months. My thesis – uniqueness – has always been brainstorming on paper, writing freely, randomly, and leave the structure to emerge on its own–heuristic approach, the approach ideal for career success. However much we try to follow an algorithm, that is ultimately what happens. The chance happenings make most of our careers. I am inspired by the writings of Stefan Zweig. In the foreword to his book 'The Tide of Fortune', he wrote:

'Like nature herself, history, which is spiritual mirror of nature, assumes infinitely diversified and incalculable forms'.

Personal histories are no exception.

'It laughs at method, and contemptuously disregards laws. Now, like water, it seems to flow towards a goal; at another time it pursues chance happenings that are the sport of the wind.' Stefan Zweig.

Precise goals are OK when the environment is stable and benevolent. When there are depressions, recessions, job-cuts, chaos all around, it is a sport; which way the wind blows you do not know. I am indebted to Stefan Zweig for the 'pair of glasses' he gave me to glean through the career paths of the volunteers and the titbits, choicest morsel of morning news.

My thanks are to my kith and kin who were silently observing change of behaviour in me – regular, moderate, sometimes intense, activity leading to better health and stalling or even reversing the process of senility.

Last but not the least, I must thank my cousin V. Rama murthy's support, who vetted and edited the work without which I would not have even ventured to take up writing a work worth publication. We are a team in the true sense of the term. It is simple but sincere thanks whose meaning is known to both of us.

There is one more team member Ms. Padma Lakshmi who typed my hand written manuscript with admirable accuracy. She helped me through organizing, revising, correcting, re-organizing the several drafts I had to make. I cannot imagine completing the task without her.

Varanasi Bhaskara Rao

I am deeply indebted to Sri. Varanasi Bhaskara Rao garu, who initiated me into writing Part B of this book. His sane advice and the many discussions we had have been a great help to me.

While collecting the material, I referred to a number of authors whose works have churned and channelized my thoughts (reference given after each chapter). There are many more authors not mentioned but who influenced my thought process indirectly. I thank every one of them from the core of my heart for providing me with this interesting learning experience.

My thanks also go to the first reader of all my writings, a strong critic but a staunch supporter, my husband, without whose encouragement I would not have completed this part.

Y. Kameswari

17th June 2010

CONTENTS

Foreword .... (v)
Preface .... (vii)
Acknowledgement .... (x)

PART A : SUCCESSFUL CAREER AND SOFT SKILLS

Introduction 1

Section I : From Nowhere To Somewhere

Ch 1 Set Forth the Journey 37
Ch 2 Unique Path 79

Section II : Wherefore You Know Where

Ch 1 Choice of Career 139
Ch 2 Control of Careers 179
Ch 3 Enterprise, Enterpreneurship and Ethics 209

Section III : Where on – To Weather, Not Wither

Ch 1 Steering Through, Soaring High 247
Ch 2 Swerve and Sever 277

Section IV : From Here To Eternity

Ch 1 Fitness 295
Ch 2 Utility 311
Ch 3 Legacy 327
Epilogue 337
Appendix I 339
Appendix II 343
Appendix III 349
Appendix IV 361
Appendix V 367
Appendix VI 371

PART B : BUSINESS ENGLISH

Section V : British Legacy – Use of English

Ch 1 Where does Indian English stand? 377
(a) Common errors in English 378
(b) From local to global 393

Ch 2 Communication – Written and Oral 408
(a) Oral communication 408
(b) Written communication 409
(c) What makes one an effective writer 410

Ch 3 Conversations in writing 432
(a) The substance and spirit 433
(b) Layout of a business letter 446
(c) Other forms of business communication 453
- Curriculum vitae 453
- E-mail 457
- Memorandum 459
- Fax 464

Ch 4 Report writing 479

PART – A

SUCCESSFUL CAREER AND SOFT SKILLS

INTRODUCTION

This is first time I am writing a text book.

> 'A text must conform to minimum standards… courses and syllabi should preferably not to be mere repetition. We must think of new ways of projecting the subject reflecting inter-disciplinary methods of investigating the past history'.
>
> ***Romila Thapar***

This book's stress is on 'Soft Skills'. It has a history that needs to be investigated. It has the present preoccupation with 'Soft Skills'. It's future is predictable–Life skills. It is multi–disciplinary: psychology, sociology, linguistics, engineering, media studies, philosophy, public relations, marketing, humanities, and pragmatism, and so on…

I am no specialist in any one of them. Yet, I venture to present ideas gathered from books and personal experience. I am strengthened by several friends by sharing their own career profiles. Two of my books published earlier were meant for general reading. They were

1. Communicative competence
2. Personal and Emotional competence

The emphasis is on the word competence, meaning self–sufficiency in meeting one's needs and fulfilling wants with confidence and control. They were primarily self-improvement guides. The purpose was to make the reader appreciate the meaning and significance so that the reader will help himself or herself.

The purpose of this book is that it should serve as a textbook, a basis of a course of study for, particularly, the students of Business Management on soft skills. My aim is to make it a book to serve the general reader to cover students of other disciplines of any age at any stage of their lives. Therefore, I have gone beyond the syllabus. Syllabi of different universities appear to be different for acquiring soft skills.

The contents of the two books already in the market cover the topic substantially. The need for this one arose because the soft skills seem to be proliferating–necessitating several of on going studies. Studies on social behaviour have been going on in the west for several decades because employers' demands and employees needs and wants are not matching. Soft skills is old wine in new bottle, buzz words now appearing to yield place to new buzz words–employability skills. Some even suggested, why not life skills. The word skill suggests that people can be trained to acquire them with practice. They are not, necessarily, inherited abilities or gifts or aptitudes.

For example, leadership skill, a soft skill; are leaders born or made is a debate that never ends. 'They are both', that is a safe conclusion. That brings us to personality, potential, actualization, and so on.

My search on Google opened the pandora's box; I was assailed by a swarm of terms. You go on listing, you get tired, and you feel like closing the box. Skimming through it you find such diverse things like honesty and integrity, cluster of personality traits, willingness to learn, working under pressure and so on.

I turned to the definition of hard skills, because 'hard' and 'soft' are words borrowed from the computer language. It was quite simple, I thought hard skills are capabilities to operate machinery. So it is a motor skill. But then, human body is a machine, and body-language is included in soft skills.

Because of this confusion the word employability skill has become the buzz word now. May be the universities will change soft skills to employability skills in the next round while designing syllabi.

I shall retain the term soft skills throughout this book to mean all those skills the employee must possess to get a job and retain it other than technical or domain skills.

Business English

Business English is included in syllabus under the title soft skill. For more than half a century commerce students were taught this subject as 'correspondence' or 'letter writing'. It was written communication par se.

To-day oral communication, business presentations, listening skills are included. But in my view, an emphatic view, reading skills should have been included. I always stressed that speaking, listening, reading and writing are like four wheels of an automobile; any one wheel missing the 'vehicle' would not run. It is a vehicle of personality development. (Francis Bacon wrote four centuries age–Reading maketh a full man; conference a ready man; and writing an exact man).

> ---The first was English becoming a global language --- The first time that a language has become truly global, and for linguists that is very exciting because of what happens to a language when it becomes global. --- Second thing was the crisis affecting the languages of the world --- Do they die out in the century? --- Third thing was the arrival of the Internet.
>
> ***Prof. David Crystal***

A question of dominance and ownership

> American English still has quite a strong place too in every body's minds --- Speakers of English in the world are about one and half billion --- 250 million speakers of in America --- There are more speakers of English in India than there are in Britain and America combined --- It will become more cosmopolitan language, it already is.
>
> Any living language has to change because its people change, the worse or for the better. It just changes. --- It is growing for over thousand years borrowing words from 350 other languages --- and Indian languages have loaned words to English as well.
>
> So much as adding a new medium --- The written language and spoken language and we have now computer mediated communication, or Netspeak.

With Internet the medium uses new properties of language that do not exist in traditional speech and writing --- In e-mails you have the amazing phenomenon of e-mail framing where you get your e-mail, cut and paste a paragraph, answer it, and the other person can answer that and soon you get an amalgam of messages --- It is dynamic.

It is a technology inspired informality of expression that didn't exist before. So the language has grown through the Internet with an extra dimension of language use being incorporated.

Over the last five years I have sensed a greater care being taken, greater precision in the formulation of e-mail messages. So on the whole I think the Internet is providing us with good language training here and the more I think we get more used to the technology, I think the more it will sharpen our intellect as for as communication is concern.

I have seen the mention of 'work ethic' and 'personal habits' in the Google list. Right culture, therefore, is the crux. Without saying in so many words, the employers seem to want a 'whole man', they want a master of all trades, not simply a jack. That is the significance of ever growing list. Breaking down the 'whole man' into the 'bits and bites' to *reductio.ad absurdum* leading to *ad infinitum.*

Holistic Approach

I, therefore, chose holistic approach to self development in which 'the whole is greater than sum of its parts'.

The soft skills are a means to an end, a successful career, which is a means to personality development, again a means to realizing the full potential, the very purpose of life.

It is like the solution to a jigsaw—puzzle.

The Jig-saw Puzzle

Given below are 5 pieces of a jig-saw puzzle. When we put them together it becomes a 'whole' as is seen in the second picture. Now you don't see bits any longer although they are there. The pieces are not fragments; they are parts of a larger whole. The whole is different, and greater than the sum of its parts.

Fig. 1

Fig. 2

This is the meaning we get in the following verse from Isa upanishad

What is this World?

Purnamadah purnamidam	That is whole; this is whole.
Purnat purnamudacyate;	This whole comes out of that whole.
Purnasya purnamadaya	That minus this is whole
Purnamevasisyate.	Only whole remains.

Om santihm santihm santih --

There is a profound significance and relevance for our discussion. The employee has a personality of his own, as in the case of pieces they are not identical, but distinct and separate. The employer should know that they are taking into their organization a human being, not a machine which has also parts that make up a whole. The machine or robot has no 'will' of its own. It cannot act on its own entirely. It is programmed to do certain actions. It has no freedom, it cannot be independent. It is not an autonomous self, but man is. But man for long has been reduced to mechanical device ever since factory system and slavery came into existence.

Let us take the craftsman in the village

Take the daily routine of a village craftsman; his work involves planning organizing, and control. His physical work has both art and science of it. All this can be reckoned as hard skills or knowledge put to use, in the production. When the customer arrives on the scene, it is his soft skills that manifest... listening, courtesy, speaking, body language, diction, decorum, etiquette, language etc. At the next level understanding customer requirements and concern, negotiating, bargaining, selling, clinching the deal etc form part of the soft skills of higher order.

The craftsman's livelihood depends on both hard and soft skills—they are practically inseperable. It includes interpersonal skills, emotional intelligence, friendliness, mutuality.

There is still higher level, more subtle than all these and the most valuable skill—the learning the essential part of development—enhancing skills and knowledge related to the craft or career. An integral part of learning is creativity, adaptability, flexibility, tenacity.

Paradise Lost

The village craftsman who had his hard skills and soft skills, lives a life of fulfillment, being of utility to the community in which he lived—embedded and eventually left the world leaving behind a legacy-the *CRAFT*[1]. *Creative, Resourceful, Adaptable, Flexible,* and *Tenacious.*

He was a 'whole man' who made things to order useful to the community and lived in harmony. He used his soft skills in meeting the requirement of the proximate customer and satisfying him–listening understanding, making and meeting the dead lines his CRAFT, 5 clusters of soft skills combined with hard skills of his craft. After industrial revolution he chose to become worker in factory where it was labour and not work in the true sense. Hence the suggestion—Paradise Lost.

Paradise Regained

To-day employers want 'whole men' who may be given sufficient autonomy to the individual and integrate them with a small team; small teams integrating with the large teams obeying holism. Soft skills is a part of total personality—it is not a fragment, it is a whole in a whole, an embedded system. A system consists of elements which constitute the whole. Each element is whole and complete. It is in this concept of embedded system should we try to view the concept of personality. We cannot break it into bits of nothings. For the purpose of analysis we may break it into parts; but we must put them together as in a jig-saw puzzle without fail.

Pygmalion Effect

Eliza Do-little who is a flower girl, illiterate slum dweller is perfectly trained in soft skills, a term not known in those days. She is a character created by George Bernard Shaw's drama, Pygmalion. Prof. Higgins taught her English diction, upper class manners and decorum, dignity of behaving like a lady. I called what she was taught soft skills because soft skills are defined as:

---

[1]**CRAFT**: Creative, Resourceful, Adaptable, Flexible, and Tenacious

Sociological term which refers to language skills, social graces, etiquette, communication skill, desire to learn and to be trained among other omnifarious personal habits

Colonel Pickering in the drama meets all her needs, financial and emotional support. He treats her well, a contrast to Prof Higgins who cannot forget that she was a slum girl, an experimental object, a thing, not a human being who has her own PIE, parental programming, internal aspirations, and external factors that shape her personality.

In the last act, Eliza tells the colonel, 'I shall always be a flower girl to the professor, because he always treated me as one. But I know I can be a lady to you because you always treated me as a lady and always will'.

She was perfectly trained and she was willing to be trained. She spoke royal language, pronouncing correctly to everyone's appreciation and delight. The upper class accepted her as one among them little knowing her background. Prof. Higgin's ego was hurt; he blurts out the truth. At once Eliza reacts violently and the angry flower girl in her comes out with the filthy language, proving a poignant point:

'It is not how she behaves', but 'how she is treated' that matters.

It became psychologists rallying point—the Pygmalion effect. Language, dress code, walk, talk, etc are important but not enough. Soft skills training should go beyond to reach the cluster of personality traits that make up a fully developed individual. Developing subordinates, leading them, motivating them are among foremost soft skills of managers who may be beware of Pygmalion effect.

Need

In 1970s there was an attempt at social skills training to the uncultivated, whose aspiration to occupy positions of prestige even though they stopped with school level education, to compete and avail themselves of equal opportunities dictum, are rising.

SST (Social Skills Training)

Social skills are behavioural skill—a skilled behaviour.. efficient and effective social behaviour. Behaviour stems from values, beliefs, motives, and core self–the unconscious self. It is like an onion in each peeling the hidden phenomena surfaces. Who peels the layers? Psychiatrist, or self? Both can be trained to peel the layers to reach the core.

The external agent, the psychiatrist makes the patient lie down on a couch and subject him or her to a series of questions. He probes into the interior of the mind.

Behaviourists think there is a shortcut. Just modify the behaviour without probing because the individual who knows his behaviour which is not effective can appreciate the weakness and willing to learn.

There can be self–directed change. The individual can also probe into the causes of his behaviour through introspection. His motivation to probe into self can come from the desire to succeed in life. This involves in recognising the connection between values and behaviour. For most people it may not be necessary to go deeper than value system and belief system. The reason for so many values–words creep into soft skills vocabulary lies in this link.

Any training for skill development starts with sensitizing or appreciation. It means making the trainee aware of the concept and secondly making him accept the importance and need for learning systematically. He must also accept and access it. There appears to be no attempt to define the term-soft skills. My colleague says 'define before you refine'. But there has been considerable research on social skills training. The following excerpts from the preface to SST training can be our starting point.

> Classically SST essays a robust empiricism whereby skilled behaviour should be observed, recorded and analysed and trainees should imitate models until, with the help of feedback, they can reproduce, as appropriate, the skills originally observed. This model has been criticized as naively positivistic, insensitive to the meanings created by participants and destructively reductionaist in its skill analysis. None the less it continues, like Dr.Johnson's stone, to refute sophisticated critiques: it works and it can be seen to work.

It seems to work.

Both the investigation of social skills and the devising of training programmers need theoretical and methodological sophistication.

The researcher needs a working definition to enable him to observe and record behaviours that satisfy the criteria.

Definition: A social skill is a complex ability to emit behaviours that are reinforced by others as also not emit behaviours that are punished or extinguished by others. It hinges on the ability to influence others to do things that one values positively and also stop them from doing things that are negatively valued. It also includes not to engage in behaviours that result in negative outcomes or outcomes that are not worth while.

There appears to be no such attempt to define Soft Skills.

The case histories of careers, the first person accounts, in particular, must help the reader in the investigation of social skills and also the so called soft skills.

The central thrust of SST is behaviourist. Behavioural data, however, is necessary but by no means sufficient for the understanding of human actions and experience. SST must take more account of internal processes not themselves observable.

Perhaps it is the internal processes that gave rise to coining of soft skills, an euphemism, artificial elegance.

In particular three directions might be followed. First there must be an elaboration of that part of the social skill training model which refers to perception, information processing and the plans which give structure and organization to behaviour. Secondly, as a practical consequence of this, there should be increased emphasis on SST as a focus and stimulus for cognitive remodeling. There are many pointers to the notion that SST succeeds in affecting human behaviour not so much through behavioural practice but through the effect this behavioural practice and, in particular, the sensitization phase, has upon the cognitions and plans of participants. Thirdly more emphasis must be given to the meanings which trainers and trainees attribute to social exchange in real life and in the controlled environment of SST. As an example of this shift of emphasis social skill trainers might conceive their process as an exercise in the reorientation of constructs. Psychometric instruments with a phenomenological orientation, such as the repertory grid test (Kelly, 1955) Refer to the Appendix.

A word about the repertory grid test. This is a very useful method of instruction in the class-room. I had used it extensively with limited facilities available in the staff colleges and training establishments. The trainers of soft skills will profit from trying in their class-rooms.

> Interpersonal exchanges, verbal and non-verbal, occur within boundaries set by physical circumstances, psychological expectations and social norms. The study of social skills in these situations is already under way (Argyle & Eumham, 1980) and should add a further dimension to training procedures.

Probably these studies led to more comprehensive approach– the soft skills approach which is what this book has attempted.

> Bruner (1966) has described education as a process whereby we discover man's distinctive features and strive to develop them. It is a cliché to describe man as a social animal. But endemically communicative and interminably interactive he is. Social skill training helps people to become more effective socially and thus more fully human.

Focus–on Soft Skills, hopefully, makes people realize their potential–more *fully human.*

What are soft skills beyond social skills?

Soft skills as terminology in vogue now will soon pass and may become life-skills in common parlance. Probably we settle there. Soft skills are literally life-skills universal to all vocations, professions and non-professions. They are common to all in human relationships. Acronymically it can be depicted thus :
LIFE: *Lasting, Indispensable, Fine-tuned, Ennobling*[2].

SOFT: *Software, Omnifarious, Flexibility and Transfarability*[3].

1. SOFTWARE

We have software and hardware in computer language which have distinct meanings. There is no confusion. When it comes to skills there is no clarity regarding the terms hard skills and soft skills.

---

[2] **LIFE:** Lasting, Indispensable, Fine-tuned, Ennobling

[3] **SOFT:** Software, Omnifarious, Flexibility and Transfarability.

If machine is designed, originally, on the analogy of human body with all its organs, machine-like parts, with the invention of machine we have better understanding of human body. Machine breakdown and body breakdown are similar. Poor maintenance. Similarly when we designed computer on the analogy of human brain, we have understood the functions of the brain better.

John Lilly, a neuro scientist called human beings as programmable entities–bio-computers. We are all programmable and programmed entities. There is hardware—the central nervous system—and software programs stored and summoned at the 'press of the button', the stimulus from outside or inside.

There are complete pathways established

Like all behavior patterns, interpersonal skills are "hard-wired" in the neuronal pathways of the cerebral cortex. This means that at some point a behavior was repeated often enough that neurons grew dendrites that reached out to other neurons to make the connections needed to make behavior pattern automatic. A myelin sheath coated the cells like electric wire insulation, making the connection extremely efficient.

The end result: these ways of behaving now feel natural, easy and comfortable.

2. OMNIFARIOUS

Or multiplicity of skills responding to triggers. They are habitual or ingrained behaviours. The observable behaviours stem from attitudes which stem from values, beliefs, motives and finally the self concept. In the final analysis our actions matter for our success and not our thinking.

Saying is also action.

Some of our actions are involuntary, unconscious, and automatic. We may say, habits. The best definitions of soft skills is 'personal habits' rather than desires or wishes or willingness, etc. any training in soft skills must address the issue of habits. Habits die hard.

The most pithy definition of soft skills is 'personal habits that are effective, efficient, and ethical (3Es)'.

The habitual behaviour must be effective in the sense that it must achieve set goal. It must be an efficient action, with minimum effort and use of time, money, and other resources—

Finally it must not be devoid of ethics. The sources spell out honesty, positive work ethic, personal integrity, reliability etc as soft skills all of which come under ethics.

If our habits are ineffective, inefficient, and unethical there is a need for correction. Before correction is attempted by an external agent, the trainer, for internal motivation, the individual must become aware of our habits which are involuntary reactions to a stimulus. Next he must admit and be ready to reform himself. Some people say it is too late to rectify. That is where motivation comes in.

Self knowledge must begin with examination of our personal habits—our habitual behaviour. Take punctuality. If we are always late to work or appointment it is behaviour known to others and ;they give their own explanation—irresponsibility. The behaviour, we said, stems from attitudes, values, beliefs, motives, and self concepts. What is your self concept? What do you want from life, work? If you have goals in life, and chose a career and job to reach your goal then to be punctual is not a problem. If on the other hand you've no goal, you have no plans in life, you lead a mechanical, absent- minded random life, then you have no idea about why you should be punctual. You will be punctual if there is a threat of punishment. You are punctual for external reasons not for internal discipline. As Gita puts it, you are your own friend and foe. Lift yourself mounted on yoga (yogarudhasya). There is a lower self from which you have to lift to a higher self. Leave mechanical life and rise to a disciplined life. Then you are your own friend. If you neglect yourself you are your own enemy.

Goal setting responsibility initiating action, with clear perspective of reality, and self confidence—all these fall under soft skills.

Internet search gives us some definition like the one below: (Partly quoted earlier)

> Soft skills is a sociological term which refers to a person's EQ (Emotional Intelligence) and to the cluster of personality traits, personal graces, ability with language, personal habits, friendliness... include communication, listening, negotiation, etiquette, language skills, etc... positive work ethic, positive attitude, desire to learn and be trained... ability to solve problems proactively and create win-win situations... (add) personal qualities plus interpersonal skills...

You really don't know where to stop.

Another click you get, mathematical skills, courtesy, honesty, reliability, dependability, cooperation, collaboration, adaptability, personal integrity, critical thinking, responsibility etc..

You really stop bewildered and physically tired. It is better to look at the opposite—hard skills.

Hard skills vs soft skills.

In the world of work, "hard skills" are technical or administrative procedures related to an organization's core business. Examples include machine operation, computer protocols, safety standards, financial procedures and sales administration.

Sales administration is hard skills, actual selling is a soft skill. At the professional level they are domain skills–accounting, costing, auditing, analyzing, diagnosing, legal acumen etc. Each profession has a set of professional skills–the hard skills.

All the rest is soft skills. From the list we find that they are not skills in the ordinary sense of the term. It is not behaviours or actions either. You find attitudes and values in the list. Learning is a skill but desire to learn or willingness to learn are not skills. They are motives. According to Dennis E. Coates, Ph.D. CEO of Performance Support Systems, Inc.,

By contrast, "soft skills" (also called "people skills") are typically hard to observe, quantify and measure. People skills are needed for everyday life as much as they're needed for work. They have to do with how people relate to each other: communicating, listening, engaging in dialogue, giving feedback, cooperating as a team member, solving problems, contributing in meetings and resolving conflict. Leaders at all levels rely heavily on people skills, too: setting an example, teambuilding, facilitating meetings, encouraging innovation, solving problems, making decisions, planning, delegating, observing, instructing.

The inter-personal behaviour patterns of people who join organization are already ingrained deep seated and programmed. 'They were'nt learned in the class-room. They are learnt 'on the street' at a very early age'. Their mode of learning is observation and imitation. They experience and experiment, 'sticking to what works for them'. So every one enters the company with a portfolio of soft skills, some effective, others cause problems for them and for others. The problem with the skills is that they become personal habits. And habits die hard. They are 'hard-wired' in the neuronal pathways' as programmes or software. They become reflexes, automatic and involuntary – *Natural, Easy, Comfortable, Kinetic energy* – NECK[4] sticks out each time as a response to a stimulus.

Ingrained habits-behavioural patter are entrenched, established, beaten tracks in the brain; however jig jag they are. When these behaviour patterns are ineffective, then there is need to open a new pathway, shorter and better routes to succeed without hassles.

Try another route, if that pathway 'proves to be satisfying' and productive, it is a choice-conscious choice you have to make voluntarily tread that path. It takes time and adequate reinforcement before the old path fades out and new path gets firmly established, treading it as a regimen. Finally a new pattern emerges and the old becomes abandoned route. The significant point to note is reinforcement or reward for the new behaviour is a must for establishing new pathways in the brain. New pathway becomes as super high way.

Ensuring success

> Without this reinforcement, however, the pathways will not establish themselves, and most people will predictably fall back on the old, comfortable patterns they grew up with. Unfortunately, this disappointing scenario happens more often than not. An organization invests heavily in a people skills training program, no plan for reinforcement is in place, and the intervention fails to have the hoped-for result. There is virtually no return on the investment. The money is mostly wasted. This is why a program of lectures, group exercises and handouts—even a week-long course personally conducted by a world-famous celebrity author—cannot by itself provide enough reinforcement to establish the new pathways needed to change ingrained behavior patterns. Without reinforcement, even people who want to change are likely to return to their comfortable patterns, and so dysfunctional behaviors remain the same. If this happens too often, employees may come to feel cynical about people skills programs.

4 **NECK:** Natural; Easy; Comfortable; Kinetic energy.

Frequent reinforcement

What an understanding of the brain teaches us about learning is that the only thing that can create permanent behavioral change is frequent reinforcement over the long term. If someone who truly desires to change an interpersonal behavior is supported by a knowledgeable coach's ongoing encouragement, new patterns can be established. The most useful perspective on people skills training is that it's an essential first step—a necessary "introduction" to the right way of doing things. After that, ongoing reinforcement of desired behaviors has to be there. When a newly trained individual returns to a workplace, he or she needs knowledgeable coworkers to give ongoing feedback, guidance and encouragement.

Now the individual student aspiring for big things has to pay the price, interms of money, minutes, mindful practice. Ten thousand hours of practice!

Let us look at the learning and training of all these attributes, skills, values, or attitudes, whatever we may call them. Can we teach responsibility, productivity, willingness to learn? That is the question? Yes, we can make them understand the cause and effect relationship of so called soft skills to personality development and success in careers. There are skills which can be learned in the SST model. There are values and attitudes to which the individual can be sensitized. There are certain qualities or disciplines which help individuals in their success in careers.

Passion is a quality. Deep interest is a quality. Honesty? Can it be taught? It is a value; one can adopt believing in truth, integrity, and honesty etc will serve in the long term building trust worthiness and predictability. What about spirituality, belief in the ultimate? All are agreed greed and avarice is the root cause of 2008 financial crisis world over. Freedom is not licence. Communication skills, leadership skills, creating win-win situations and both skills are value loaded behaviours. If you take soft skills as personal habits and the training in habit formation, the cultivation becomes very important.

Culture is a better word as the following list suggests:

- *Communication Skills*- meaning manner of speaking, listening, and written language.

- *Research/Analytical skills*- ability to understand the situation, clarity in multiple perspectives, collecting additional information if needed. Making valid assumptions, making logical deductions.
- *Emotional Effectiveness: (Refer to the book, 'Personal and emotional effectiveness'). Appendix 'ARMED' of this book.*
- *Adaptability and Flexibility:* Adaptability to manage multiple assignments and tasks and adapting to changing conditions. Flexibility is to work with changing goals and priorities. It is really taxing on the autonomy of the employee. The changes could be beyond the control of the superiors in the organization. It may be due to customers or due to misunderstanding between customers and decision makers or due to changes in the environments which is beyond both the employers and the customers or it could be because of teammates, subordinates or machine breakdown, erratic power supply; there can be many other reasons that call for adjustment in the schedule. A great deal of patience is required. If you have that patience, then your employer will prefer you.
- *Team playing: Relationship building and leadership skills and inter-personal skills and emotional intelligence, working with people with diverse cultural background, meeting dead lines, organizational skills..*

  The career profiles highlight leadership skills. But not team playing. Prior to becoming leaders, they might have started as team players successfully. They have not thought it fit to state it as an achievement. But it is. There is no leadership without followership which team playing implies. As mentioned before a team player or follower must display the very same qualities like competence, control, commitment, and courage. Besides they need to collaborate and co-operate with other players in the team. With these qualities shown in the preliminary phase, the leadership may be thrust upon you when it becomes child's play to be a successful leader.

Gandhiji and Nehru not only led the freedom movement, but produced or trained millions of leaders at the grassroots level.

Similar leadership—followership can be seen in the business world as well. There are banks in India who have celebrated centenaries in the recent past. They have a continuity thanks to leadership—followership chain. To claim that they have grown to such stature, as is seen, because of one or two visionaries is not correct. At different points of time different visionaries have steered and guided the institution through appropriate strategies depending on the environmental changes. Some of the successes in careers of individuals is more due to top leadership, policies, strategies; our career successes are largely due to our ability to adapt ourselves to the likes and dislikes of top leadership. We must accept the fact with all our humility.

- *Integrity and Investigative skills:* confrontation, problem—solving, probing, trouble-shooting are in this cluster among others.(Integrity is summed up below).
- *Values made visible:* Soft skills without values could be manipulative. Personal values should match with company/employer values. Honesty, integrity, morality.....There are instances where some employees who appeared very sincere and hardworking, working late hours have cleverly defrauded the company and their customers. Banks are vulnerable to this kind of people. If they are truly both honest and hardworking, they can be targets for peer pressure. Behaviour, skilled or otherwise, stems from values. Your values are visible to others through your behaviour. Employability skills and personal values are critical to succeed in the long run in any employment.

Hard and soft skills are like two sides of the same coin—personality development. The coin has another side, the invisible side, to the naked eye. That is values. All the three, the skills, values, and knowledge constitute integrated individual. There is a better name—culture of the person. Culture is the cultivated personality. I have seen among long list (never ending) of soft skills, 'personal habits'. It is totality of behaviour, the visible and the predictable part of the individual identity. In Mahabharata the wise man Vidura tells the blind Dhrutarastra–blind both literally and mentally–that a Pandita is known not by what he thinks or what he says, but by what he does. Your employer is interested in what you do and how well you do. The 'doing' needs both hard skills and soft skills.

- *Enthusiasm:* Positive, resilient, emotional, self reliant.

To sum up the soft skill the culture is CREATIVE[5];

Integrity should be backed by other values

Industry, Not needing supervision, Tenacity, Endurance, Go-getter, Reliability and *dependability, Initiating action, Trying to excel, Yearning* to learn.

Industry: Busy, industrious, and hard-working may all look alike, but a closer observation may reveal the differences to the discerning mind. Busy people can be busy without any purpose. Hard-working are busy with some purposeful activity, not necessarily effective and efficient. Constant, regular, habitual effort and even earnestness are characteristics of hard working people.

But it is the quality of the industrious that makes the difference. The industrious are intelligent, earnest, diligent, and steady in their work. It is said that the Japanese don't work hard but smart. Being intelligent, the industrious are smart in the sense that they have some more attributes. They *schedule* their work, *make a time-table, assign priorities, respond* to exigencies, and are time-conscious. They are free from some negative attributes. They are not hurried, free from anxiety, rarely have to do re-work, and seldom do wrong things.

[5]**CREATIVE:** Communication; Research skills; Emotional intelligence; Adaptability; Team Playing; Investigative; Values made visible; Enthusiasm

To this list the employer invariably adds loyalty. If you are loyal they will overlook all other weaknesses. It is not uncommon for so–called loyal people to defraud the employer. Thus soft skills minus values could be dangerous to the employer and harmful to the employee in the long run. In fact the word integrity means inseparability of values and skills.

There is another hitch about loyalty. Loyalty to whom? To the employers? To the profession? Or to the society? A man of integrity keeps his resignation letter in his pocket ready to sever connection with the corrupt employer. Ethics and morals are integral to both the institution and the individual.

3 & 4 Flexibility and Transferability

'All learning, as far as we know, is subject to transfer to new situations' '.. the essence of the whole process of learning lies in the flexibility with which the ingrained response may find its place and usefulness in relation to relatively new situations'

All the omnifarous skills stored in the brain are transferable and flexible in their usage.

All learning, simple, complex, hard or soft-skills involves transfer. Here is an analogy given by Garden Murphy in his book, 'A introduction to psychology'

> 'an accomplished singer can look at score never before observed and can go forward into his task, taking into consideration the requirements of expression, demands of his audience, the limitations of his accompanists etc. he not only transfers to the new situation what he has learned at an earlier time...but integrates various activities that are called for inorder to sing to the satisfaction of his audience. Indeed most of everyday learning is not recapitulation of steps taken earlier; it involves appropriate transfer of skill to new situations.

Be it a cricket player, musician, a person making a speech, plumber with his tools, or with finesse of social etiquette, a person is transferring earlier habits to new situations *on the basis of analogy.* When you say someone as 'affable' he is transferring an acquired skill or trait to different situations. Both are ingrained.

Many of the people who shared their careers have not articulated the soft skills they possessed or used in their stories. But they transferred with flexibility the omnifarous soft skills stored in their brain. It is upto us to read between the lines to identify their inherent skills that made them succeed in their careers to the extent they narrated.

Autonomy and Soft Skills

Social and educational backwardness leading to governments affirmative action in creating fee concessions and reservations has made it imperative to make education omnifarious and omnibus. It is not enough if system imparts knowledge and hard skills, it should include soft skills along side. Along with quantity there must be quality improvement, the meaning, of employability, currently vogue word.

Without soft skills, there is virtually no employability. How did we come to this impasse, a block to the career path. A peep into the past becomes necessary.

Lost paradise to paradise regained

After the industrial revolution the world witnessed growth of urban population leaving villages impoverished both in natural and human resources.

When the villager, farmer or artisan or labourer, migrated to become a cog in the wheel of factory system or urban life, his life became mechanical routine with little need for thinking and planning for future. The biggest casualty has been loss of autonomy, freedom and independence which was enjoyed for generations. It was a paradise of living within means lost. The result is the notion;

> Material enters the factory and comes out upgraded; man enters the factory and comes out degraded and corrupted.

When you tried to upgrade the man with hard skills without restoring his autonomy to him, the result is the Elia DoLittle phenomenon. Treating the worker with respect is to allow his freedom to *plan, act, check,* and *take corrective actions* (PACT[6]) using this own native talents, interests and cluster of personality traits. Then he would regain his paradise. That should be the essence of soft skills training.

---

[6] **PACT:** plan; act; check; take corrective actions

The first person accounts written in a style are in keeping with the assumption that hitherto hidden thoughts in the sub-conscious mind of the narrator, throw up data for study and analysis in an objective manner. Finding similarity and common thread running through the career beads is what I wish to get out of the data and compare with the research findings of various scholars which may appear at first sight to be an attempt at reinventing the wheel or a generous reader may consider it as something new altogether. The conceptualization of researchers is presented in my own language. My language is acro-mnemonics, a word I have coined to denote an acronym used as mnemonic-memory aid.

Asli Bharat

According to social learning theory, motivation, model, memory, and methodical ways form elements of learning. Accepting this I stress on memorization of concepts as a must for any behaviour change which is what learning is all about. For example I start with TIP- talents, interest, personality characteristics, constitute the individual. Whatever the individual knows about himself is just a tip of the iceberg, nine tenth being the submerged beneath surface. The individual has to work out to fathom the deeper things. They are aspects of 'collective unconscious' as Carl Jung psychologist called it. Simply it means the culture, generations of training which made the behaviour instinctive.

'Know your culture to know about yourself!'

One research decades back investigated and classified vocational personalities into six types based on their interest. Reference to them will be made throughout the book at appropriate places and contexts to hammer the idea home. The repetition is deliberate. It was the work of a westerner based on the lives of westerners influenced by the culture of the West. It is and has always remained a materialistic culture that led to modern consumerism and greed. The modern western educated Indian has been aping the West while the inheritance is pulling them back to tradition of the orientals. The result is they are neither there nor here and therefore confused. Follow Mrk Tully's advice-

'don't ape America. Leave nakli America and grab alsi Bharat.'

Your deeper self, if you can get in touch with it, will crave for asli Bharat.

Not for MBAs alone

When I sent an email to our family yahoo.com, a group address, asking my nephews and nieces in different countries for their personal profiles for inclusion as case studies for this book *'Career planning and personality development'*, a textbook for MBA students in one of the Indian universities, there was no response. After my call I heard from one of them, that they did not reply because they did not hold an MBA degree. I had to clarify and send another email stating that it is no doubt a textbook for the students of MBA based on the syllabus of one paper for 100 marks. It is a subject taught in MBA, but it does not mean it is restricted to careers of mangers holding an MBA degree. In fact, all professionals, engineers, doctors, lawyers, accountants, company secretaries, journalists, bankers, insurance men, scientists, everyone is a manager. Each one has to manage his or her life. What MBA teaches is that they have to plan, organize and control their careers, academic and professional. Though relevant to everyone, the student of management makes systematic and rigorous study of management principles and practices, as a subject.

Non-management students think what they teach in MBA is all commonsense glorified as if it is a science. Sceptitism apart successful people recognize that they did plan, organize, control without attending MBA classes. They are right. What happened to them naturally, does not happen to others because they did not have this natural endowment, or did not grow in an environment congenial and supportive for sound management.

The reason why multi-national companies look for MBA as an additional qualification is because of the knowledge and the training they get from management schools. There are born geniuses, musicians, artists, poets, leaders and so on. They inherited gifts. Even these people need to learn systematically to become outstanding in their chosen field. They have to be encouraged and nurtured. Both nature and nurture are important. The self-made people must be made self-sufficient.

There are cases of office boys of banks eventually becoming the MD of the same bank. A bank peon quit the job and started pan-shop to grow and become real-estate magnate. Some study, acquire qualification, steadily reach the top. Another a government class IV employee becomes Cabinet minister in the union government or governor of a state.

It is also a fact that such things become obvious only when they are stated. Common sense is not so common. What we need to understand is the process of development, the journey, career paths, so that one can discern and notice them in one's own career paths and steer them in the right direction and with the desired speed.

The stress in this book is on the career path on the superhighway of soft skills.

Meaning and significance of personality development and career path to the student

The focus of the text book is preparation for soft skills development as part of total personality development. Career path paves the way for personality development. Two paths run concurrently once the student gets a job.

Everyone is born with enormous potential, which nobody knows at first. Life's aim is to realize the potential fully. Most of it remains un-manifested. Even Einstein, the greatest scientist said that in his entire life-time he could reach only 20 per cent of his potential. William James, the famous professor of Psychology in the Harward University said that the average person can reach only 10 per cent of his potential. You have to be above average, extraordinary. 'Most of us fail because we major in minor things' as one senior citizen put it. There are hurdles and obstructions to the growth and development. First is the lack of education. Education, Plato said, is not giving sight to the blind man, but turning the head of the man who can see in the right direction. Everyone is born with certain inherited qualities, talents, gifts, traits, aptitudes, etc.

> 'Queer little twists and quirks go into the making of the individual. To suppress them all and follow clock and calendar and creed until the individual is lost… is to be less than true to our inheritance… Life, that gorgeous quality of life is not accomplished by following another man's rules'
>
> From the book, 'A Beautiful Mind' biography of a Nobel Prize Winner

We have to live by our own rules

There is a well known story of 7 fools who crossed a river and found one of them missing. Who was missing? The one, who forgot to count himself. The profound meaning of the story is that we should not forget to take care of our own progress.

> 'Lay down your own day, follow it to its own noon, or you will sit in the outer hall listening to the chimes but never reaching high, enough to strike your own'

You must strike your won. How do you strike your own. That's where this book will be of help to you. If you believe in what I have presented so far, then a beginning has already been made. Pat yourself.

Aside, let us recall our own legacy:

On the occasion of his visit to Kumbhakonam in the south, Swamy Vivekananda delivered an address, 'The Mission of Vedanta', after his return home from his great mission in the West.

Swamiji's off quoted exhortation–

'Arise, awake, and stop not till the goal is reached' is from that speech.

We must know in what context he said these famous words. Then only you will appreciate their significance.

> 'An English boy will tell you, "I am an Englishman, and I can do anything." The American boy will tell you the same thing, and so will any European boy. Can our boys say the same thing here? No, nor even the boys' fathers. We have lost faith in our selves. Therefore preaching the Advaita aspect of Vedanta is necessary to rouse up the hearts of men, to show them the glory of their souls…..

Brahmins, if the Brahmin boy has more aptitude for learning on the ground of heredity than the Pariah (Low caste), spend no more money on Brahmins' education, but spend all on Pariahs. Give to the weak, for there all the gift is needed....If others are not born clever, let them have all the teaching and the teachers they want... therefore (they) require to hear and to know what they really are...

Behind the strong and the weak, behind the high and the low, behind everyone, there is that infinite soul, assuring infinite possibility, and infinite capacity of all to become great and good.

It is in this context in emphatic and resonating and penetrating voice did he say–'Let us proclaim to every soul–Arise, awake, and stop not till the goal is reached (translating from Sanskrit). He did not stop with that. Then follows the elaboration often omitted by those who quote him frequently. Now read on.

Arise, awake, and stop not till the goal is reached. Arise, awake! Awake from this hypnotism of weakness. "None is really weak; the soul is infinite, omnipotent, and omniscient. Stand up, assert yourself, proclaim the God within you, do not deny Him! Too much of inactivity, too much of weakness, too much of hypnotism, has been and is upon our race. O ye modern Hindus, de-hypnotise yourselves. The way to do that is found in your own sacred books. Teach yourselves, teach every one his real nature, call upon the sleeping soul and see how it awakes. Power will come, glory will come, goodness- will come, purity will come, and everything that is excellent will come when this sleeping soul is roused to self-conscious activity. Ay, if there is anything in the Gita that I like, it is these two verses, coming out strong as the very gist, the very essence, of Krishna's teaching— "He who sees the Supreme Lord dwelling alike in all beings, the Imperishable in things that perish, he sees indeed. For seeing the Lord as the same, every-where present, he does not destroy the Self by the Self, and thus he goes to the highest goal.'

Thought and action

Positive thinking and goal setting are habits - personal habits considered most important soft skills, the super highway conditions.

I have presented some concepts from scriptures - the cultural legacy - separately. Here I want to elaborate on the word Shraddha:

> The word Shraddha does not have an exact equivalent in English; it is usually translated as faith but it is not faith in a creed or dogma but faith in oneself, faith in the infinite power lodged in every soul: it is also faith in the power of truth and goodness, a firm conviction of the ultimate meaningfulness of the universe. It is the totality of positive attitudes, astikya buddhi, as Sankara defines it.
>
> ***Swami Ranganathananda***

> 'What makes the difference between man and man is the difference in this Shraddha and nothing else. What makes one man great and another weak and low is this Shraddha...Therefore, this Shraddha is what I want, and what all of us here want, this faith in ourselves, and before you is the great task to get that faith. Give up the awful disease. Give that up. Be strong, and have this Shraddha, and everything else is bound to follow.'
>
> ***Swami Vivekananda***

Let us replace 'positive thinking' are Shraddha, our cultural legacy. Let us turn to 'Goal setting' habit. It is a pity we have to turn to the West, when it is our cultural legacy to embark on any action with Sankalpa. Ordinary translation is 'vow'. It is goal setting plus an oath to complete it as a sacred duty. Westerners want the goal setting to be on paper, writing down. Our legacy is manasa, vacha, and karmanaya – thought, speech, and action. Through utterances with mind in it, the pathway is established in the brain. 'Mantras are formule; divine algebra' (Sri Aurobindo). Then you have tradition of Muhurtabalam. It gives strength to the doer.

> Where the mind is without fear and the head is held high;
> Where knowledge is free;
> Where the world has not been broken up into fragments by narrow domestic walls;
> Where words come out from the depth of truth;
> Where tireless striving stretches its arms towards perfection;
> Where the clear stream of reason has not lost its way into the dreary desert sand of dead habit;
> Where the mind is led forward by thee into ever-widening thought and action–
> Into that heaven of freedom, my Father, let my country awake.
>
> ***Ravindranath Tagore***

Though the book is about soft skills, with topics placed in the context of Career path with relevant stories about it. Personality Development is the ultimate goal of any career.

The stories, most of them real, enable the student to identify the talents, interests and values, and also understand his/her own-motivation, talents, interests, and moorings etc to get inspired to set forth embark on his own exciting journey in full awareness and appreciation with positive thinking and goal setting.

Soft Skills Repertoire

Every musician knows what is a repertoire. It is a complete reservoire of skills, supply of devices, ingredients used in a particular field, occupation, or practice, the whole of the resources one can summon at once and at will to perform. Long years of practice is to build this. The students' aim should be to build his own repertoire or reservoire, an extra supply of it.

GROW to your potential

Goal setting

GROW is the means. *Goal setting* is a habit, ingrained in Sankalpa culture. It is in your genes. Like breathing. But alas we do it wrongly. We forget what is natural and easy till a yoga teacher comes along and corrects it and put you back on the natural and easy track. You feel refreshed. Daily morning a few minutes of breathing exercise, the right way, will make the breathing whole day rhythmic. Restore in the same way the rhythm of *'Sankalpa'* or goal setting with an oath – like determination, preparation to lay the superhighway. There is a famously used acronym – SMART[7] for goal setting. *Specific, measurable, achievable, relevant,* and *time bound goals.*

Resource building

To achieve smart goals – short leading to long term – you need to allocate resources: time, money, matching knowledge and information, and skills, both hard and soft.

[7] **SMART:** *Specific; measurable; achievable; relevant,* and *time bound goals*

For details on Time Management, the reader may refer to 'Personal and Emotional Competence,' the companion volume. As regards money management we have richer legacy in India than in the West. Recent recession, job cuts, etc have made the Americans learn a few lessons from us. Simple living and holding wealth as trust, the values we have cherished for long are being invoked. We have always been setting aside monetary resources for the rainy day. But globalization and westernization have caused damage to those who ignored Indian value system. There can be loss of jobs, change of job, need for hibernation, sabbaticals, time and money for honing up skills – when financial cushion becomes imperative. Money is necessary for resource building itself. R in GROW stands for resource building as a means to grow to your full potential. The case of VV illustrates it; when he wanted to set up independent practice money support is a chief input in the decision making.

Time and space, both are resources; pujaroom, study, are distinct and are separated from the rest of the house. A quiet place, same place, sacred place, space for loneliness, make it a habitual rendezvous... it signifies both place and time, also a meeting place, it is a meeting of people... a meeting of minds... or simply a meeting of mind and body–secluded, solitary, isolated.. same place, same time, same purpose... spiritual... Desk... Brainstorming, free–writing, free reading... Sojourn–temporary stay–a resort... on the journey–sojourn as an opportunity for rest, change of occupation–leisure–stock taking–Respite–to look back–control.

Opportunities Seeking

'We do owe something to parentage and patronage' Malcolm Gladwell.

Parentage is given, you have no choice. But you can capitalize on the advantage while being independent. You can 'network' with them.. listen to their views and express yours and strike a compromise. Parentage could be an opportunity – utilizing their experience and wisdom – or it can turn out to be a threat depending on the cultural legacy. Negotiating and navigating the parentage. Dr. Homi Bhabha was sent by his father to study Engineering. In the middle of the course he expressed to his father that he had no interest in engineering. A compromise was struck: Homi Bhabha should complete the engineering course and then join science course which he was interested in. Similar compromise was struck between junior Venkat and his father. (Refer to the case – Junior Venkat). But result was different. Junior Venkat pursued same pure science which his father wanted. At the same time he followed his interest in photography as a hobby throughout his scientific career. There are instances of making use of the popularity their late father enjoyed to get business from customers who admired the father. Reflected glory can help up to a point. The same is true of IQ. Here is a case of patronage based on parental legacy.

'The people who stand before kings may look like they did it all by themselves. But in fact they are invariably the beneficiaries of hidden advantages and extraordinary opportunities and cultural legacies that allow them to learn and work hard and made sense of the world in ways others cannot'.

Gladwell

There are people who have false notion that they should succeed all alone by their own grit and not depend on parentage or patronage. The initial advantage – the legacy and opportunity – has enormous effect provided the persons work hard, learn and prove their intrinsic worth. What about those who neither have parentage or patronage? They may have to collectively seek opportunities through public affirmative action.

However in all cases if the personal qualities – soft and hard skills learnt assiduously that will ensure the growth. The school, college, and university are the other opportunities for the individual to make the most of his potential. I have seen people introducing themselves as proud products of IIM(A) and IIT(M); students of reputed institutions have the initial advantage – only initial. Environment and economy and technological growth at a particular point of time have given more opportunities for the talented. India, after freedom, economic and technological growth has given a variety of career opportunities. In the early days of independence the migration (or brain drain) to America, the land of opportunity for Europeans in 19th century, had been the same to Indians in the 60s and 70s of 20th century. The opportunities were in research in pure science and higher education. Later Doctors, Engineers, Software professionals on one side and trade and business for others whose cultural legacy was trade.

> 'But what truly distinguishes their histories is not their extraordinary talent but their extraordinary opportunities',
>
> ***Gladwell.***

Gladwell, ironically, gives examples from America, not about other countries like India. You will find Indian examples of ordinary people who made most of their potential in the cases presented in this book. While studying their histories look for cultural legacy and opportunities presented by the environment of the period.

Will to grow

Finally, 'W' stands for will and drill.

The will to grow and drill to make it happen. Will lies in opening 'the wicket gate' (Read later) and set forth on the journey with 'shraddha and Sankalpa.

I CAST[8] before the reader *cases, acronyms, snippets and titbits,* because of my bias for reading for knowledge and information. Francis Bacon four centuries back, and Harold Bloom in the recent past have cast their spell on humanity by stressing on reading, the former with his slogan, Reading maketh a full man and the latter with this snippet....

> 'Only deep, constant reading fully establishes and augments an autonomous self.'
>
> ***Bloom***

Both Bacon and Bloom were emphasizing same thing in different language. 'Fullman' embraces 'autonomous' self. The purpose of CAST is to persuade the students and the lifelong students to enjoy reading to acquire knowledge, gain wisdom through information.

---

[8] **CAST:** cases; acronyms; snippets; titbits

SUCCESSFUL Life

'It is not wealth what one life asks for but enough to work unhampered and to be free, frank and independent'

Somerset Maughum

There is some confusion on the word success which must be cleared before we embark on the topic career success. Let us begin with the dictionary meaning. Webster's gives a number meanings. Let us take what is relevant to the student, a life-long student.

1. Result, outcome, 2. A favourable or satisfactory outcome, 3. Gaining of wealth, fame, rank etc, 4. Successful person or thing.

You will be a success if you gain wealth, fame, rank, prestige, power, possessions material gains, monetary gain.

Deeper Things

Some authors have delinked the careers from the word success because of the confusion in the eyes of the general public. John Rees asks, 'What makes some careers *come together*, instead of what makes a career a success? He has a definition for careers that *come together.*

Careers that come together

'When what we do for a living aligns with deeper things, we want to get out of our life.'

Simple but superb definition. The difficulty with definition is that, do we really know what we want to get out of our life? If that is known then we can set-forth our goals and set-forth on our journey, for career is a journey towards set goals. You become successful when you achieve what you wanted-the deeper things. The deeper things vary. We often quote Gandhi. A good starting point meant everything for Gandhi, that was the deeper things he cared for. He was clear in his mind what he wanted to get out of his life. He wanted others to ask themselves whether their aims made sense to them. They become significant, more relevant now than before. There is a debate going on all TV channels and in Newspapers and magazines. In Oct, 2008 a financial crisis gripped the whole world affecting the West more than India and China. Reforms and globalisatioin have softened the blow where India is concerned. But the virus is gradually spreading.

Gandhi wrote in 1930s.

> 'The ability to refuse will not descend upon us all of a sudden. The first thing is to cultivate the mental attitude that will not have possessions or facilities denied to millions; and next immediate thing is to rearrange our lives as fast as possible in accordance with that mentality.'

Let me reiterate that *attitudes* stem from values, beliefs and the deeper selves. What Gandhi wrote is very relevant to our times. The current attitude among the youth of India, vis a vis. Westernization, Americanization, and globalization, based on aping has to change.

Simple Living

What we are into is *Nakli America*. As a result success has come to be wealth, possessions, power, and prestige. This attitude has not stemmed from our deeper self. Hence, attitudes can be changed and have to. In this mad race to get rich quick, we have given the go-by to our traditional values and beliefs- Simple living and high thinking; wealth is incidental not a set goal in life.

Thoreau, 19th century naturalist (American) wrote that a man can work for nine weeks cultivating soya beans and spend the remaining 43 weeks in intellectual pursuits. He lived by Walden Pond and demonstrated this. Thoreau was influenced by the Ashram life of our Rishis. Gandhi got many of his ideas from Thoreau.

This is not to suggest that every one must live in a hermitage. When greed and avarice eventually result in stock market crashes, lost jobs, and economic slow down we have to rearrange our lives and change our goals and priorities and still satisfy ourselves.

Direction

This volume advocates setting goals with a positive mentality. While setting life goals which are achieved through careers, don't fail to examine your attitudes, values, beliefs, and deeper yearning and longings.

Even so, you cannot have a precise goal. You know some what, you have to find out; but you know the direction. When one *vanara* team set forth south bound in search of Sita they did not know where she was. On the way they kept on inquiring and were informed by strangers, others. As information about the whereabouts poured in they had greater clarity about the target place. The approach is called heuristic or let's find out approach. The same is true of career success.

Setting forth apart it is good to keep in mind the *career choices* are unique to the *individual.* It is *unique, career choice, controlled.* First two parts titled 'No where to some where' and 'Wherefore you know where'.

At every stage of your career journey you must have control over your journey-the direction and the speed. Another measure is the degree of joy the journey gives you. I would like to add enterprise and entrepreneurship. The word enterprise itself has many elements. Drive is one of the key words. You can make it an acronym, break it further into sub elements. *Desire, Responsibility, Innovation, Value based, and Energetic.*

Recent developments in the world of business enterprises, ethics are missing among the highly educated and so called successful people. But the profiles of those whom I have chosen to present in these pages are all based on ethics. I have discussed 'code of ethics' under the heading 'professioinal manager'. I have also included excerpts from Aldous Huxley's book, *Ends and Means* which includes discourse on ethics.

He wrote in 1934, 'a discussion of political, economic, or educational problems containing no reference to ethics is incomplete! Year 2008 has seen most shocking revelations of a highly popular and 'successful' entrepreneur who had charitable foundations. He seemed to have taken 'lessons' from the Western models of scamsters.

I have also included another article written earlier under the title Indian Entrepreneur where I argued that the Indian entrepreneur should follow Indian tradition of self sacrifice besides the Western model.

That brings us to the third part titled 'Where on – to weather not wither' which deals with mid career problems and overcoming of obstacles where crucial decisions are made keeping the hard skills development in tune with the changes or crises in the environment –political, economic, social, and technological. It is here you have to summon all your soft skills and managing social spaces, self, partner, all the family members, career, and extended families. May be you can think of direct service to society at a later date. I discuss this topic in this part. There are two Ss: Steering through and Swerving and Severing. Career changes and employer changes are taken up in this part.

As I have seen that may people live longer than before say, two or three decades after superannuation, I thought there is need to discuss under three more heads: Fitness, Utility and Leaving a legacy cursorily. That completes the acronym SUCCESSFUL.

This last part I named as 'From here to eternity' for we do not know how long the journey would last to the 'undiscovered country from whose bourne no traveller returns' (Hamlet, the Prince of Denmark) Eternity according to our ethos is life beyond our sojourn on earth.

- Set Forth The Journey.
- Unique path.
- Career of choice.
- Control career.
- Enterprise, entrepreneurship and ethics.
- Steering Through, Soaring High.
- Swerve and Sever.
- Fitness.
- Utility.
- Legacy.

These are the elements of SUCCESSFUL life/careers that you bear in mind with career choices, changes, facing setbacks during and after superannuation. The case histories included in the book have these elements of the successful in mind.

Structure of the Book

Part A Successful Career and Soft Skills

Section-1 From Nowhere To Somewhere

- Set forth the Journey.
- Unique path.

It is a journey, nay a pilgrimage; it is characterized by uncertainty and risk. You need *positive attitude and set goals.* The path is unique to the individual based on his inheritance – parentage etc. no two individuals are alike. Each individuals has to travel inward for the outward journey. Invent himself or herself.

Section-2 Wherefore you know where

(Having travelled inward, now you know what you want from life.)

- Choice of career.
- Control of career.
- Enterprise, Enterpreneurship and Ethics.

There are stages in the career progression. These are 'dales', 'bogs', 'robbers'. All planning invariably must have control to see through.

If Part I is to 'Arise and Awake' you; Part II is to exhort you to 'stop not till the goal is reached'.

Section-3 Where on – To weather, not wither

- Steering Through; Soaring High.
- Swerve and sever.

This is your mid career muddles. Successful men and women maneuver the obstacles successfully. The common soft skills are willingness and ability to learn, adapt, and be flexible, if necessary start from the scratch all over again.. Setforth, re-invent yourself, change, and so on. It is never too late.

Section-4 From Here To Eternity

- Fitness
- Utility
- Legacy
- Epilogue

Part B Business English (Y.Kameswari)

- Where does Indian English Stand?
- Communication-Written and Oral
- Conversations in Writing
- Report-writing

SECTION - I

FROM NOWHERE TO SOMEWHERE

1
Set Forth the Journey

Pilgrim's Progress

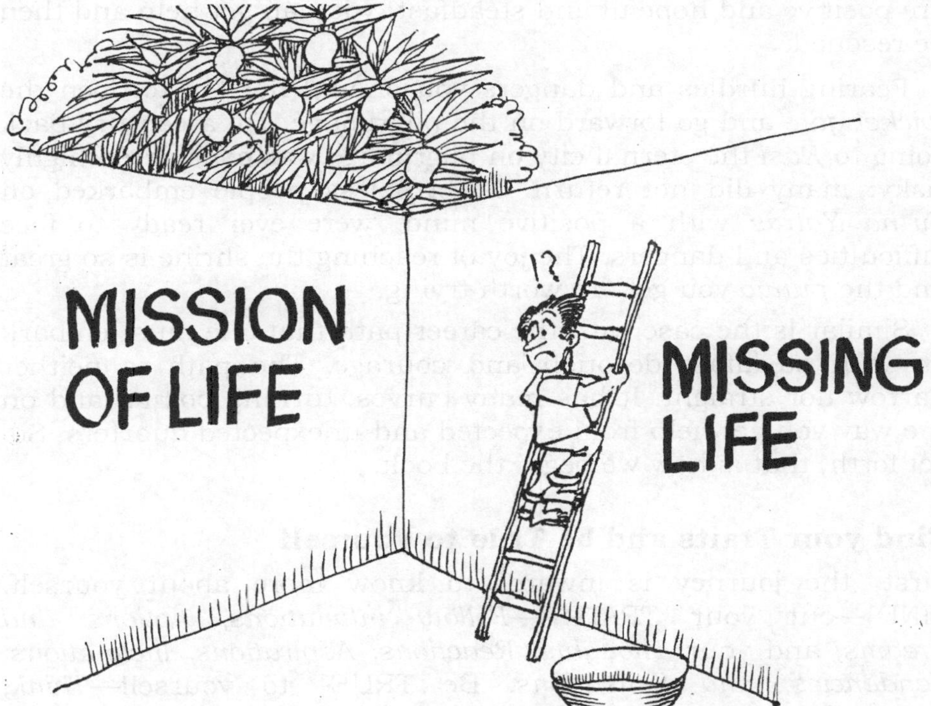

In John Bunyan's allegory, the Pilgrim's Progress, Mr. Christian sets out on a pilgrimage to the Celestial City, the heaven. After crossing hills and dales, and negotiating bogs and muddy roads, and after encounters with robbers, he comes to a wicket gate which opens to a straight, narrow path, which will lead him in the end to the Celestial City.

Christian opens the gate and sets forth on the journey towards heaven. He falls into a dreadful bog, slough of despond and is rescued by Mr. Help. Faithful, Hopeful, Prudence, Piety, Charity, The Great Heart, Old Honest, and Steadfast are his other companions on the path…

Are the companions metaphor for soft skills? We shall find out in due course.

Christian meets all kinds of difficulties before he arrives. An allegory is a story with a hidden meaning. Here is the story of a man who is trying to lead a good life and get to heaven in the end, in spite of sometimes giving up hope or being miserable. You realize that, when you are depressed and discouraged, it does feel like falling into a swamp from which you cannot escape. If you are positive and hopeful and steadfast, you can get help and then be rescued.

Fearing hurdles and dangers you should not fail to open the *wicket gate* and go forward on the pilgrimage. Till a century back going to *Kasi* the eternal city on pilgrimage was considered highly risky; many did not return. Nevertheless people embarked on *Tirtha Yatras* with a positive mind, were ever ready to face difficulties and dangers. The joy of reaching the shrine is so great and the *punya* you get are worth trying.

Similar is the case with the career path that one must embark on with steadfast devotion and courage. The path is neither narrow nor straight. It has many curves, turning points, and on the way you get help from expected and unexpected quarters. So, set forth, that is how we begin the book.

Find your Traits and be True to yourself

First, the journey is inward, to know more about yourself. FIND[1]—out your TRAITS[2]—*Follow intimations, notions and dreams;* and your *Thoughts, Reactions, Aspirations, Inclinations, Tendencies, and Sensations.* Be TRUE[3] to yourself—*Think, Research, Understand, and Express* yourself verbally and behaviorally.

---

[1] **FIND:** Follow; Intimations; Notions; Dreams.
[2] **TRAITS:** Thoughts; Reactions; Aspirations; Inclinations; Tendencies; Sensations.
[3] **TRUE:** Think; Research; Understand; Express.

As you discover yourself little by little, day by day, in your actions and thoughts you can do SWOT[4] analysis. *Strengths* and *Weaknesses* internally and weigh them against *Opportunities* and *Threats* externally, cultivate the habit so that it becomes automatic in day to day life.

Let me share my personal experience in this project. As I prepared to write for this book, I encountered difficulties and doubts. I followed intimations, notions, and dreams of making the project worthwhile. Strange things happened to me. After a night's rest I wake up with an idea or thought or just a word and I was not sure about its meaning. I make a bee-line to the dictionary to develop the word into a concept and commit it to writing before I lose it. If I don't put it on paper, then it might be lost for ever. These intimations and notions were not available to me before. Now they come rushing because I have a task on hand. That is like opening of the 'wicket gate' in the Bunyan allegory. That happens to Christian, you, me and or any one else who sets forth with *sankalpa,* a beautiful word in Sanskrit. That is the power of *Goal setting* and *positive thinking* and *setting forth.*

Open the wicket gate

In everybody's career there will be a situation, a setback, from which one is rescued by some outside help, hope or positive attitude, faith in Almighty, *steadfastness,* to restart the journey. You are rescued from the state of depression. As mentioned in the olden days when people go on pilgrimage to *Kasi*; there was no guarantee they would return, yet they would undertake the pilgrimage. Other pilgrims' help and show the path; no pilgrim shirks from seeking the help of others. In the same fashion you need to seek help from any one, even from the most unlikely quarters.

There is a childhood story told by grannies. A louse waged a war against the king. It took the help from its network of friends. It networked, so to say, with a scorpion, snake and a tiger. The strategy was similar to the well–planned terrorist attack on Mumbai in 2008. First the louse enters the king's beard and irritates him. He reaches for a comb, when the scorpion lounging in the place stings his hand. He cries out in pain and runs for a

---

[4] **SWOT:** Strengths; Weaknesses; Opportunities; Threats.

shoe to beat it when the snake chases him. He runs out in search of a stick to hit the snake; but alas the tiger waiting outside attacks him. That is how the louse takes revenge on the mighty monarch. The power of the louse lay in its **networking.** Your enemy is not something outside. It is your own despondency.

Never feel you are weak and helpless. Faith, Hope, Steadfastness, Honesty, are all honest serving 'men' who can help you out of the impasse.

GROW[5]

Goal setting, Resource building, Opportunity seeking, Will.

You should not stop with *goal setting.* You can't reach your goal unless you mobilize resources; so the next step is *resource building.* Resources include time, space, and family and cultural legacy. How you build and build on them is the moot point. But there you have to test the waters by using the resources whether they are adequate and right. Hence you must seek *opportunities* to test them for effectiveness and efficiency. *Opportunity seeking* is the third step. Finally you need will to grow. Acronym GROW epitomizes the steps involved thus far.

Exercise 1: Daily spend sometime in solitude. Solitude is not loneliness. You feel lonely when others keep away. In solitude you are not in the company of others but you are very much with yourself. That is the time when you're about to FIND out your self. Sages of yore retired to woods for solitude for enlightenment and emancipation of mankind. They never felt lonely. In the natural surroundings they could contemplate and made the inward journey. To experience solitude you need not retire to a hermitage. You need a quiet place and time.

Exercise 2: Write freely. Writing is *thinking on paper.* Organizing the thoughts on paper and correcting, editing, and re-writing till the expression becomes exact makes you an exact man. Bacon wrote, writing makes an exact man. Good writing in English has been identified as a soft skill.

---

[5] GROW: Goal setting; Resource building; Opportunity seeking; Will

Exercise 3: You and your friends can do the above exercises separately and join in writing or engage in group discussion both of which are soft skills too. These exercises are 'practicals' on soft skills without which the theory is barren. Only practice is groping in darkness.

STAGES of development

All the world is a stage, and all the men and women merely players. Shakespeare divided life into seven stages from infancy to old age. For our purpose I divided them into 6 stages from student life to old age. There was a longitudinal study made by some researchers, quite a long time ago, who studied the careers of men and women following them through from the college days to the retirement or 60th year to find out what were the promises they showed and what actually happened. They divided the stages of development in five stages. Inspired by what the study indicated I developed the following exposition. Putting the report of the study briefly, some who were not academically brilliant who did not promise much succeeded in their careers. Some others showed promise and succeeded. Yet others were failures inspite of promise in early life.

Striving Stage

This is the first stage when you complete school and college education. It is a period when you try hard to attain perfection in your studies. You concentrate on gathering knowledge. At the end of it, you are tested and certified.

Shakespeare has also given us another monumental piece—Polonius advice to his son, a student. The full text is given in my book, *communicative competence.*

He wrote, 'Be thou familiar but by no means vulgar'. Vulgarity refers to lack of culture, the personal habits and soft skills we might say—it shows in behaviour, language, decorum and diction,honesty, etiquette, morals etc.

'Knowing what to say to whom, knowing when to say it for maximum effect' it is a set of skills that have to be learned, if your upbringing has not made you learn at home. If you have not been fortunate for the training at home, at least make it up with friendship.

'Friends thou hast, and their adoption tried/grapple them to thy soul with hoops of steel; But do not dull the palm with entertainment/ of each new-hatched, unfledg'd comrade'.

Shakespeare

Friendship leads to fraternity, camaraderie and popularity. You have a chance to display or learn organizing and leadership skills. If you can't be good leader in the first instance learn to be a good follower. Leadership—followership is one—both leaders and followers display same qualities. One Harvard Business Review article mentions 4 Cs both for leader and the follower; Competence, Control, Commitment and Courage—all are soft skills. If you display the 4 Cs, then one day the leadership will be thrust on you.

Skilled behaviour is taught or learned by reinforcement and punishment. Friends are ideal in this regard more than parents. Losing friends is the result of poor soft skills. Correction is needed at the student stage. One of the things to be strived for Sharpening your decorum, diction, dignity and dresscode.

'Costly thy habit as they purse can buy,

But not expressed in fancy, rich, not gaudy;

For the apparel oft proclaims the man;

- Shakespeare

Many companies stipulate dress code to promote camaraderie. Learn to do at this stage itself even if the college does not insist. Decorum, propriety, is the key to it. In short, interpersonal skills/relationships are cultivated at this stage. If you had missed it in the family, then the school and college and extended families where correction can be made by choice.

Trying Stage

This stage begins with your practical experience, entry into the world of work. We will be discussing career choice, job selection, campus interview, preparation and process separately. The transition from college life to company life–the transition process has to be understood and appreciated.

You lose some of your freedom and carefree life you might have had. You had friends and time at your disposal. Now you have to adjust your life to somebody (organization) else's-work schedule. Much time is spent in commuting from home to the place of work. You have to be regular, punctual, synchronise your time with others' time. You have competed and shown individualistic orientation in school and college. Most of you with a job are members of a team. If you developed team skills in the striving stage, it would be easier for you to adjust to the life in this stage. Trying period is largely a period of adjustment.

You encounter beauracracy. The rules, regulations, and controls may suffocate you initially. If you are a creative person you may wonder at the statusquo. You may see them as meaningless and wasteful exercises. If you are a man of trust you find that people in the organization don't value honesty and trust. Then you find that when things go wrong people start blaming each other instead of sorting out the problems. I can go on and on. But it is enough if you accept that it is a struggle that you have to go through and overcome. If your value system is sound it pays to stick to your values and make others fall in line. You can change the rut.

There is a movie case in this monograph of a doctor who handled the trying period admirably and brought a turnaround in the management of the hospital. [Refer to Chapter 2 of this section.]

During the trying period of adjustment some special qualities are required. You may be recruited and selected for a particular job. Some companies give training and expose people to induction programmes. They brief you adequately. The Japanese are known for their induction programmes. The new comer is made fully comfortable. All companies or job situations are the same. Your learning on the job in the company of colleagues is significant. Learning by doing, experimenting, social networking are important modes (Discussed later). You have to be patient and be prepared to learn from staff placed below you in the hierarchy. If you are more qualified than the job requirements, then you may be a source of ridicule. If your inter-personal skills are good and you are a humble and modest person you can win over people and people will respond positively. Throughout you have to maintain your positive attitude. Discuss your problem with parents and friends. If you encounter difficulties, sharing can help you. Initial sharing troubles with others can help. If you are honest and trustworthy, it will help you tide over this trying period quickly. But it will take time during which time you must show steadfastness.

Aspiration Stage

Having adjusted to the organizational life and learnt a few lessons about yourself, now you move to the next stage with greater self confidence. You have still a long career ahead. You start aspiring for power, positions and promotion on the organizational ladder ready to shoulder greater responsibilities and demand and control larger and diverse resources. Your designations change giving prestige and pride. Your personality undergoes change. You become upwardly mobile. Things like a separate chamber, big chair, perks and attendants, attention of customers boost your ego. You may acquire some more qualifications-technical and managerial. You are still young in energy and spirit. You start looking ahead and may even dream of many things. A good employer will reward you suitably. Compensation package may go up. You need to be clever, display skills as a negotiator, a special kind of communication skills most useful of them all. You will face competition from your colleagues. If you are not vigilant, you may have to suffer disappointments, conflicts and frustration. As long as you are positive in your thinking you will tide over these difficulties and keep moving upwards.

The most important element of this stage of struggle and satisfaction is learning. Keep learning acquiring new knowledge, skills, and re-examine values. Many people do not allow this stage for long.

Getting Along Stage

They rush into the ***getting along* stage** by cultivating *chaltahai* mentality. You let opportunities go to others. You want to spend time more with the family and devote time for your interests, make use of leave and leave fare concessions, avoid additional responsibilities little knowing that you're missing life. You forget your mission. You lean your ladder on to the wrong wall. In this stage you do your 'duty' well, to your satisfaction as well as that of your boss. If you are self-employed you open your 'shop' late and close early. You are content with what you earn and not imagine that future will not be yours. We are living in a dynamic, interconnected, complex world, which is rapidly changing.

Easy Going Stage

Whether you're self-employed or employed, you slip into the next stage the ***easy going* stage**, when you are looking for retirement and begin counting days, months, and years. We discussed that the purpose of life, career and work is to realize your full potential. The easy going stage is going easy on this objective.

Senility Stage

When your body and mind takes respite, the last stage ***senility stage*** may advance ahead of real old age... sans faculties...'sans ears, sans eyes, sans everything' - (Shakespeare).

Wise people, people who are determined to strike their own longer will remain at the *aspiring stage*, keep pushing senility far into ripe old age. The dictionary meaning of senility is 'the condition of old age, weak-infirmity of mind and body', when other people avoid them, or even ignore. For a few senility does not come even at 90. There are people who are writing and publishing their works. D.N.Dhameja, an I.F.S., wrote, 'A quest for the Eternal' and published it at 88! Rajaji spent his twilight years writing the Ramayana and Mahabharat. For some senility may come at 40! Their productive lives are lost to themselves and to the society. Read what our tradition says in the section on 'Some Concepts from Scriptures'.

During this period of painful adjustment it is worth reflecting on the following thoughts:

> '**Work** is the kind of effort made when people try to solve a problem, make judgements and decisions, produce some useful objects, or try to cope with a situation that has meaning for them and involves them emotionally.
>
> **Labour** is exerted when people perform a task for reasons external to themselves according to procedures laid down by others for reasons not related to the people performing the task. The labourer is not psychologically involved in the task at hand......'
>
> **Hanna Arendt (1958)**
> ***The Human Condition***

Problem-solving, judging and decision making, coping with situations, emotional involvement, whole thing makes meaning to the worker. The meaning is personality development. Contrast to work is labour when we work for external reasons according to 'another man's rules'. The labourer is not emotionally involved in the thing he is doing–a mechanical routine.

Consider the job as work not as labour, choice is yours. You are not the horse, Black Beauty, to labour and get lost. (Read the story that follows)

Good Work

In 1970s, another great thinker, economist and author of *Small is Beautiful* E.F.Schumacher emphasized the three purposes of 'Good work'.

1. To provide necessary and useful goods and services for himself and others; (He produces useful objects for the others to use and earns for providing the same for himself)
2. To perfect his god given gifts through work;
3. To do so, in cooperation with others, so as to liberate himself from the in-born ego-centricity.

Man has certain inherited gifts, talents, aptitudes, knack, and genius. It is through work that he discovers and sharpens them. This purpose of work should not be lost sight of particularly during the *trying stage.* If *talent* is native ability, a *gift* is *special ability* that it is bestowed upon us by nature, but not acquired. *Aptitude* implies a natural inclination for a particular work. All these are inherited qualities. You must look for work environment in which these things thrive and develop giving you supreme satisfaction. Genius, ? also in-born, but mental endowment. But *knack*, doing things cleverly and skillfully is an acquired faculty.

What is inherited and what is acquired, both can be discovered by yourself on the job during this period, converting the trying period into active learning phase. During this learning phase you can identify what are your strengths and weaknesses so that you can strengthen your strengths and unlearn the weaknesses.

SPACES

There is another way of looking at life–as space for several things: 'as highly socialized beings our sense of self exists in the context of a few social spaces'. SPACES are our identities.

First is (a) Self–the individuality (b) Partnership with spouse (c) All family members (d) Career (e) Extended spaces (f) Society at large.

Space means here as 'opportunity to assert or experience one's identity or needs freely'; an opportunity for privacy or time to oneself; one's partner; all family members including parents and children and grand children; career–workspace; and extended spaces are, relatives, friends; and network and finally the society and ecology. The concepts can be depicted as under:

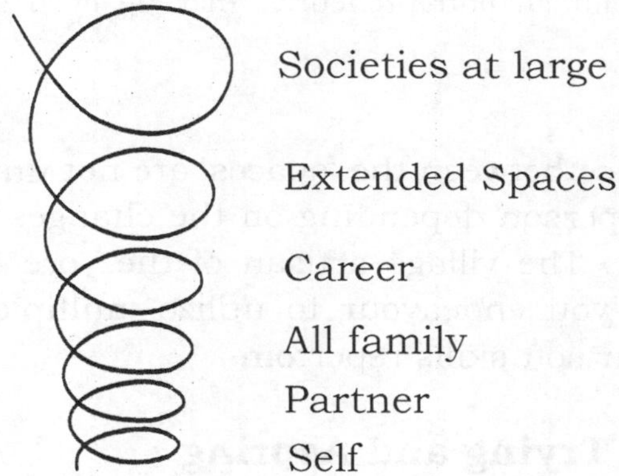

Spiral Space

The spiral is one but appears as several layers. The man is one, his identities are several. He plays several roles; he must balance all the roles to derive satisfaction, which is what we want from life.

When there is dissatisfaction one might reinvent himself without waiting for crisis to develop. Reexamine your investment-spread on all the SPACES. Am I too self–centric? Am I not spending enough time and space with family? Am I too much occupied with my career? Have I become workaholic? Do I care for friends and relatives and my community? What is my contribution to the society? What kind of redistribution is called for? Redistribution or readjustment periodically is what the author, the well known psychiatrist and author of 'the 24x7 Marriage' writes. We have seen something about workaholism. Here is reiteration of the same warning:

'Unfortunately today, since many urban Indians invest the bulk of their emotions in the work space, (wedded to work) they tend to periodically reinvent themselves only in this space, which I suppose is better than not reinventing themselves at all.

While making the career change you must take into account the other spaces–family and self.

'Who knows, a software professional could become an environmental activists, an accountant an entrepreneur... may be even a psychiatrist a novelist;

Author

Difference between the 'spaces' are not universal. It varies from person to person depending on the changes in other relationship or role–set. The village artisan of the yore combines all spaces. The more you endeavour to utilize multiple SPACES the better will be your soft skills repertoire.

Striving Trying and Aspring

The Story of an Extraordinary Bird

Jonathan Livingston Seagull, a story by Richard Bach is the story of an extraordinary bird.

'Many might have read to simply escape into a delightful adventure about freedom and flight'. A few 'people who make their own rules when they know they're right....... People who get a special pleasure out of doing something well (even if only for themselves). People who know there is more to this whole living thing than meets the eye; they will be with Jonathan Seagull all the way'. This inspiring story was dedicated 'to the real Jonathan Seagull who lives within us all'.

Blurb of JLS

> 'Life, that gorgeous quality of life, is not accomplished by following another man's rules....... Lay down your own day, follow it to its noon, your own noon, or you will sit in outer hall listening to the chimes but never reaching high enough to strike your own'.
>
> ***A Beautiful Mind***

That's a beautiful passage from the book, 'A Beautiful Mind', biography of John Nash, a Nobel Laureate. Books, good books, biographies, fiction, poetry etc can provide the necessary inspiration in youth to set one's goals, make one's own rules, think positively and act with commitment.

In my youth one of the books that set my thinking was, 'A hundred great-lives'. Another one was 'Gitanjali' by Rabindranath Tagore, whose life itself was inspiring. His line in one of the poems in it, quoted before.

> 'Where tireless striving stretches its arms towards perfection, into that Heaven of freedom, my Father, let my country awake'.

Country means people in it.

Coming back to Jonathan Livingston Seagull let us ask, 'What is extraordinary about it? The story begins with:

> 'It was morning and the new sun sparkled gold across the ripples of a gentle sea. A mile from shore a fishing boat chummed the water and the word for Breakfast Flock flashed through the air, till a crowd of a thousand seagulls came to dodge and fight for bits of food. It was another busy day beginning.

It goes on again and again for most birds who need only skills 'to dodge and fight' and fly a few feet high from the ground to reach the boat for dead fish. That's all their life seems to be.

> But way off alone out by himself beyond the boat and shore, Jonathan Livingston Seagull was practicing. Practicing what? 'A hundred feet in the sky he lowered his webbed feet, lifted his beak, and strained to hold painful hard twisting curve through his wings'.. fly slowly… 'He narrowed his eyes in fierce concentration, held his breath, forced one single.. more.. inch..of.. curve.. Then his feathers suffered, he stalled and fell…' Ordinary birds 'never falter, never stall. To stall in the air for them disgrace and it is dishonour'.

The rules of the flock. But Jonathan has his own rules! His mother was upset with Jonathan!:

'Why, Jon, Why? Why is it hard to be like rest of flock, Jon? Why can't you leave low flying to the pelicans, the albatross? Why don't you eat Jon, you're bone and feathers!'

The Extraordinary Jon replied emphatically :

'I don't mind being bone and feathers, mum. I just want to know what I can do in the air and what I can't, that's all. I just want to know.

You must know what you can do and what you can't, that's it. To cut the story short Jonathan goes to another world where every one excelled, learned many things, developed multiple skills and returned to the flock to inspire younger birds and teach them to learn to excel. Many join his classes.

'The hardest thing in the world is to convince a bird that he is free, and that he can prove it for himself if he would just spend a little time practicing. Why should that be so hard?,' 'You need to keep finding yourself, a little more each day, that real unlimited Seagull'

Keep finding yours a little more each day! That is the core message, thinking positively, setting goals for you.

'Don't believe what your eyes are telling you. All they show is limitation. Look with your understanding, find out what you already know, and you will see the way to fly.'

Excel

The book is full of the thought provoking sentences that can inspire every young person.

Reading such books early in life can make a difference. Parents encouragement and family background have made a difference for many. We hear of many success stories about people, whose family background was not so favourble and yet made their journey to the top, blossomed fully. Jonathan came back to the flock to inspire others and teach them. Here is another snippet.

> 'Every hour Jonathan was there at the side of his students demonstrating, suggesting, pressurizing, guiding. He flew with them, through night and cloud and storm, for the sport of it.'

This is for guides, teachers and trainers to reflect; you must learn, teach, for the sport of it.

Stop and Reflect: (Titbit)

Read what Greg Chappell wrote about Tendulkar.

> 'What is it that makes Tendulkar so good? He has exceptional physical talent. He has outstanding balance. He is very competitive and is strong. He has exceptional speed. He has great presence and an excellent temperament. He has huge desire to be best and he has extraordinary mental ability.' 'Batting at the highest levels of the game is as much about mental skills as it is about physical talents.' (Both soft and hard). 'Bradman seldom felt the pressured of batting that mere mortals feel. This allowed him to concentrate for long period'.... The most important part of batman's development happens in the early stages of learning the game. The instinctive skills are learnt rather than taught. A good coach will create the environment in which the young players will train these instincts. The early environment in which Sachin learnt his skills must have been excellent. His instincts are outstanding."

What is true of cricketing skills is true of soft skills, mental and physical. Skills become instinctive through practice, and practice. This is true of soft skills which are a must to shine in jobs and make a career in any field one chooses. You might pass over the above passage without stopping and reflecting.

There are many Ekalavya's, the self taught without a formal guru. Today the majority of the aspiring young men and women must have Ekalavya as their role-model.

I have reflected on books, articles and stories and even poetry. 'Reading maketh a fullman', wrote Francis Bacon, four centuries ago. Harold Bloom wrote, How to read and why'. Why read? Bloom answers. (Recall) '...only deep, constant reading fully establishes and augments an autonomous self. Until you become yourself, what benefit can you be to others?'

Read to educate yourself and educate others. That is the way to become a full man, complete man.

Autonomous self. You must become yourself. Be in touch with your true self. Then you can explore jobs and careers that enhance that true self. Sometimes books may not modify your behaviour unless you make an effort to change. Cognition is not enough. Behaviour modification requires training and self effort. There are self improvement books. You may read them without impact on you.

Positive thinking and goal setting

'To begin with you have got to understand that Seagull is an unlimited idea of freedom of the Great Gull, and your whole body from wingtip to wingtip, is nothing more than your thought itself'.

Yet another passage from Jonathan Livingston Seagull. Think freely and positively. Think you have enormous potential in you, although you do not know what it is now. You will discover little by little as you act according to your rules. It is progressive self culture-refining, improving, developing and endeavouring to perfects your talents. The more you know about yourself the better equipped you will be to make a meaningful and satisfying career decisions, now and in the future.

You have to set goals and priorities that shift with each stage of life.

Souring high in career is the story of a bird, an extraordinary seagull whose goal in life has been to excel and help others in the flock to excel.

Black Beauty

Hear is another story, *Black Beauty,* The autobiography of a horse written by a human being. We have in our ancient lore the *panchtantra, a niti sastra* written with animals and birds as characters.

Summary by a student

Black Beauty is the heart-warming autobiography of a horse that has seen a lot of life. He has seen many forms of human behaviour, the good, the bad, the snobbish and the wicked. He was born as a pure bred horse in a farm run by a kind master. This master introduced him to his training or breaking in (see a separate note Breaking in-excerpts from the book, Black Beauty), in a soft and mild manner.

He then moved to Squire Gordon's place. He had seen the death of the squire's son on a hunting expedition while chasing a hare. Here he met another mare known as Ginger who had in her all the bad qualities that Beauty's mother had warned him not to cultivate. He also had many other horses for company. His association with Ginger introduced him to the wicked side of humans. The shoddy treatment of Ginger by her previous owners explained her bad behaviour.

Soon Beauty settled down as a carriage pulling horse with a few hours of freedom once in a while. But this happy life was filled with Beauty's heroics and also a close shave with death and did not last. Their mistress was a weak lady and a change of climate was required, so… they moved. The horses had to be sold. The Beauty was traded to the snobbish rich man of England. After another accident, he and Ginger were separated. Finally, Beauty reached the city and was in the hands of a well-meaning owner. When his master was ill and could not drive a cab anymore, Beauty was sold again. This time he landed with load pullers and cab rentals and such like. Finally a worn out Beauty who had seen the lifeless body of Ginger being carried away during his stay in the city, was auctioned again. This time he attracted the attention of a small boy who persuaded his grandfather to make the purchase. As Beauty was reviving in a country atmosphere, he met people from his past, his happy past. He finally spends the last years of his life in the place he had spent his first after being trained, the Squire Gordon's

I have selected one chapter from this wonderful work written more than a century ago which impacted the Americans to treat the horses and dogs as if they were human beings with feelings.

The chapter title is *My Breaking in.* Read the excerpts keeping in mind the *trying stage* discussed in this chapter.

'Every one may not know what breaking in is, therefore I will *describe it.*

It means to *teach* a horse to wear a saddle and a bridle and carry on his back a man, woman, or child; to go just the way they *wish* to go *quietly.*

Besides this he has to *learn* to wear a collar a crupper and breaching and to stand still whilst they are put on; then to have a cart or a chaise fixed behind him, so that he cannot walk or trot without dragging it after him; and he must go fast or slow, just as the *driver* wishes.

He must not start at what he sees or talk to other horses, nor bite, no kick, nor have any *will* of his own, but always to do his master's bidding even though he may be tired or hungry; but worst of all is when his *harness* once on, he may neither *jump with joy* nor lie down with weariness. So you see this breaking in is a great thing.

Worse is still to come.

Bit in the mouth. Those who have neither had a bit into the mouth cannot think how bad it feels; a great piece of cold hard steel as thick as a man's finger to be pushed into one's mouth between one's teeth and over the tongue, with ends coming out at the corner of the mouth, held fast these by straps over your head, under your throat, round your nose and under your chin; so that in no way in the world can you get rid of the nasty hard thing, it is very bad.'….

'What with nice oats and what with my master's pats, kind words, and gentle ways I got to wear my bit and bridle…

Patting, talking to me all the time; then I had a few oats, then leading to look for the oats and saddle…. Proud to carry my master, as he continued to ride me a little each day, I soon became accustomed to it….

The blacksmith took… cut away some of the hoof…. Took a piece of iron the shape of my foot and clapped on and drove nails through the shoe quite into my hoof so that the shoe was firmly on my feet very stiff and heavy…. So in time I got used to everything, and could do my work well….

> There was training and experience in the neighbouring meadows too. The better I behaved the better I was treated and it was wisest to do the best always to please my master. But there are great many kinds of men, there are good thoughtful men like my master that any horse may be proud to serve; but there are bad cruel men who never ought to have a horse or a dog to call their own.
>
> Besides there are a great many foolish men, vain, ignorant and careless who never trouble themselves to think, these spoil more horses than all, just for want of sense; but they do it all that....
>
> It is all a chance for us, but I still say you do your best whatever it is and keep up your good name.....

The trying stage matches with 'breaking in'.

Humans no doubt are not birds and animals. But there is message for all living things. But there is more poignant message for self-aware, self-conscious human species as well. Man imitates birds and horses. Bird represents soaring higher and higher. Birds are a community. They fly together, in tandem and in formation. They help each other. Horse has horse-sense, horse-power. They die along with the master in the battlefield. Horse represents energy; harnessing energies. Horses are tamed, 'breaking in' and well trained. Well treated they obey the master's commands.

The difference between Ginger and Black Beauty is the up bringing and early childhood experiences which made one bad and rude, the other good. *Black Beauty's good nature is because of good nurture not because of birth.* They too have feelings, they know their masters, the only weakness is that they cannot communicate verbally, but they can react, respond, cooperate, be fearless, and so on. So, there is enough message for us if only we can infer intelligently and interpret and learn using horse-sense.

Bio-Social Model

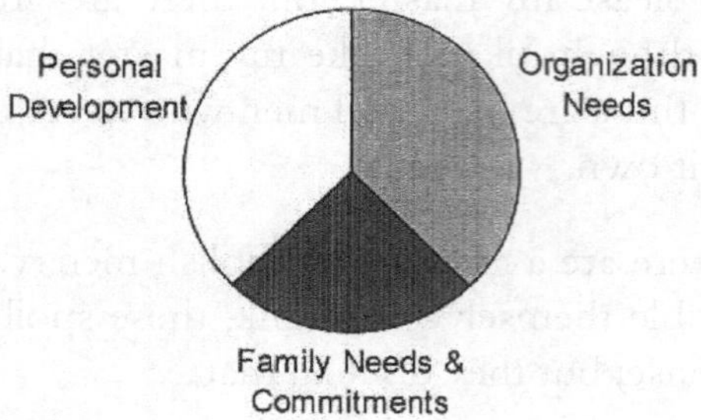

A pictorial presentation of the "Bio-Social Model' is a pie. It is divided into three segments. Each segment represents one aspect of a person's life. Every individual's life / career have the three components, personal development, the organisational demands and the family commitments. While it could be argued that there are other Maslowian needs as well, it is possible that these needs could be fitted into one of the three.

Personal development

From birth onwards the individual is directly or indirectly focused on the 'person' or himself. Getting educated, becoming a good sportsperson, socialising, leadership, growth in the organisation, all these are person-centric. They occupy a prominent position in one's priorities.

Family commitments

Again from childhood one gets ingrained in the process of **taking** on responsibility, which could be termed as a 'psychological' contract with the family. Many eyebrows could be raised doubting this aspect of one's life in the context of the present cyber world. Cultural variations might have changed the preciseness of the expression, but the context and essential meaning remain.

Organisational Demands

The employer always seeks his 'pound of flesh'. Rightly so! While human face of the organisation is an influencing factor in organisational behaviour and performance, no organisation could afford to forsake performance in favour of person. The employee is bound to fulfil his responsibilities to the employer to the fullest extent.

The model emphasises the need to recognise the existence of these three important, singly identifiable components of one's life- the pie. If an individual lays undue emphasis on any one aspect of it, it can only be at the cost of the other. To balance the three it requires the awareness of their existence, setting priorities and a review and revision of one's A,B,C – the attitude, the behaviour and the communication competence.

A Professional Manager

A profession is a *calling* requiring specialized knowledge and often long and intensive academic preparation. The word *calling* has a special significance. It is a strong inner impulse towards a particular course of action. Especially when accompanied by conviction or divine influence; and also the vocation or profession in which one customarily engages. If career becomes a calling, then the path becomes rewarding and fulfilling to the individual.

Doctors, Lawyers, Engineers, Accountants, Scientists, etc. exercise career options when they choose their profession. Are managers and managements professions? More and more occupations are trying to acquire professional status because of the prestige they command in society.

There is a concept called the professional ladder. Each vocation has to climb the ladder to reach the peak, before becoming a fully professional. That means there are some vocations that are at the lower rung of the ladder and others at higher. Similarly the individual vocational occupants are at different levels of professional status according his behaviour and values.

Here are a few characteristics of a profession.

Professional Status includes :

- Code of ethics
- Membership & Policing
- Client relationship
- *Community interest*
- *Higher order values*
- Commitment
- Competence
- Courage

- Standards of performance & Self-control
- Communicative competence
- Contribution to the growth of the profession
- Specialized knowledge & qualification
- Updating of knowledge

A professional's goals go beyond personal goals. Community interest is primary orientation than individual interest. While following the profession's code of ethics he has to keep in mind higher order societal values while arriving at decisions. Beginning with client's interest the professional must see to society's interest. If client's interests are in conflict with society's then he should prefer the latter. While choosing, a professional must weigh all these points and then decide whether he can display the courage of conviction and do justice to himself, the profession of his choosing, and the community.

All these elements apply to a manager who calls himself a professional. It is a calling he should remember, in the true sense. Competence, courage, conviction, and control are keys to success in any profession.

A systematic cultivation of all these requirements - a high degree of self-control of behaviour in the process of work socialization is needed.

Competence in the specialized technical field apart, the professional's general behaviour - social behaviour should be exemplary. His personal values and discipline are important. The client and the general public with whom the professional comes in contact expect more than ordinary social behaviour from the individual.

Social Skills Model

Social behaviour is defined as:

It is organized hierarchically in that there are small behavioural elements carried out more or less automatically, automatic, involuntary, and they are efficient and effective.

The automatic reflexes are developed after long years of practice. A professional's daily practice has this aspect. A professional with long practice has this advantage. But the practice itself must be systematic and preferably, under guidance, coaching, be he a doctor or manger or lawyer.

The social behaviour becomes skillful behaviour:

A skill is capacity to respond *flexibly* to circumstances in order to achieve a goal (strategically determined goal or 'game plan') with maximum efficiency. Skill is an efficient action, and effective in the outcome.

Social skill

> 'The *complex ability* both to emit behaviours which are *positively* or *negatively* reinforced and not to emit behaviours that are punished and extinguished by others'.

It demands explanation. Positive reinforcement means rewarding, acknowledging, complimenting, confirming, encouraging, praising etc; there is a positive response from others to your behaviour. Negative reinforcement has connection to the past. In the past your particular behaviour is not reinforced by others but you were punished for it. The particular other stops punishing for the same behaviour now. Then it is called negative reinforcement. Positive reinforcement is reward and negative reinforcement is withdrawal of punishment. Both are welcome gestures in response to your behaviour. In other words the skill hinges on being able to *influence* others,

(a) to do things that we value positively and also

(b) to stop doing things that we value negatively and also

(c) to refrain from alternative actions that bring about either negative outcomes or no worthwhile outcomes at all.

These definitions are meant to help research work into social behaviours; for developing social skill is to experiment with different behaviours and see how others are going to respond. It is learning by experimenting.

A professional manager who has to manage people through his or her behaviour to respond to his/her direction, instructions, or lead people must have this complex ability and practice to make them perfect like a tennis champion.

The behaviour is both verbal and non verbal. Listening skill for any manager is vital. When the subordinate or colleague or client talks to you face to face he or she must have eye contact or look at the eyes of speaker not in a threatening manner but actively and willingly. You must acknowledge verbally or non-verbally or through para-language. You can even repeat the words or phrases to confirm that you have heard properly. If there is reason to compliment or praise them, it should be done liberally and honestly. I have seen for many these things come naturally, others have to cultivate them. That's a learning process. Suppose you don't agree with what is being said by the others, you must be honest enough to say so, not in a hostile manner but politely. What normally happens is to turn away or betray disagreement facially.

Sometimes the clients or subordinates cannot or do not articulate clearly or coherently because they do not have the communication skill. The professional still should maintain positive reinforcement by reframing the sentences and seek confirmation. It is called *paraphrasing,* that is, putting the same point clearly and coherently in your own words. At times when the person, being non-professional is unable to articulate because of emotional disturbances, it is the duty of the professional to help the other person. It may become time consuming. Then the superior can negotiate to discuss at a later time when the professional is free from pressure, and the subordinate is free from emotional disturbance.

There is also a need to listen not only to the words but gauge emotions. At the same time the professional must have ability to make other person listen to him.

Speaking is the other side of the coin. There is lot of literature on oral communication from variety of disciplines from engineering, psychology, sociology, linguistics and media studies. It is beyond this text book to discuss exhaustively on it. The student is referred to 'Communicative Competence' by this author. Suffice to say here that you should remember that effective communication is always two-way. The most effective communications is two-way, face to face, authentic, candid between two honest people. Our scriptures always insisted on truthfulness.-*Satyamvada.* We added *Priyam* (loving) and non-hurting the other. If truth is harsh, it need not be told unless it is in the interest of the other person. Even so the *Priyam* principle should be kept in mind. Although brevity is a virtue, when truth is hurting a little more words, repetition, and extra effort and time may be required to reach the mind and heart of the client, subordinate, or any other. *Who, what, why,* will determine the *how* of communication. Where and when of the context become significant to the whole speaking.

SPEAKING, an acronym, says it all. First go through all the element of speaking in a work place. Reflect on them and then go through the explanation.

Situation	(setting and scene)
Participants	(Roles and Relationships)
Ends	(gains to the individual, to the group and to the organization)
Acts	(speech acts; form, function)
Key	(manner, tone or force)
Instrumentality	(Channels)
Norms	(of interactions e.g. turn-taking; interpretation)
Genre	(kind)

No two ***situations*** are alike in any place; it is true of work place in spite of the routine and rule book. It could be any where inside or outside the organization; in the manager's cabin or outside.

Participants vary, their roles and relationship vary, customers, employees, or any other depending on the context. Among employees it could be peers or subordinates or superiors. The mode of speaking and body language vary in each case.

There is always purpose which is organizational purpose.

End A gain to the other individual in terms of moral support, information input, instruction, clarity. It could be tangible and emotional support to subordinates in particular.

Acts Linguistics have identified what they call speech acts: instruction, warning, caution, pep up, with form and function. It is designed for the purpose according to organizational practice.

Key The key is an aspect of form of speech acts. Manner of uttering, tone and tenor or voice and force with which the words are uttered. Raised voice and aggressive manner may not produce best results. It may not serve the purpose.

Instrumentality stands for means or channels of communication, face to face or telephonic messages or messages through messengers.

Norms are mainly turn taking conversational style. Interpretation of the words by both parties are important. A professional manager must take pains to see no misinterpretation takes place.

Genre or the kind of speech is mostly conversational. If addressed to a group they are briefing, directing, merely telling or group discussion if strategic planning is involved in it.

Telephone, teleconferences, interviews with media, interviews for selection and recruitment are other genre. Whatever may be the genre a professional manager must be an adept in speaking.

Presentation

By far the most important of all kinds (genre) is presentation of facts, opinions, and information etc. The participants may be customers, colleagues or superior. The more successful presentations you make you become more visible asset and not a disposable asset to the company. (Refer to *Communicative Competence* for detailed discussion)

You might have got the job because of first impressions. What makes employers continue to notice you with interest is through effective presentations you make. It has been now found that first impressions do not last long. Snap judgements based on first impressions are proving costly in businesses. Your performance determines whether they retain you or not. One of the key performance parameters is skillful presentation.

So far we discussed about some of the human skills, there are two other categories of skills of a manager who is climbing the organizational ladder should have. These are *technical skills* which differ from profession to profession as also discipline to discipline and, *conceptual skills*. The term conceptual skill demands explanation. As a manager he needs more of technical skills at the lower or entry level when it is his technical knowledge and knowhow that are brought to bear on his management job. When he comes to middle level, when he organizes and controls a large number of employees, he needs to demonstrate more and more of *human skills* which include leadership skills. His face to face, group discussions, written or all manner of oral communication should be exemplary.

When the manager reaches the top there must be transformation, in his conceptual skills which will be explained in a minute. The diagram, at the end of this section summarises the concept. They are like the three sides of an equilateral triangle with conceptual skills forming the base.

My experience tells me, that conceptual skills are not restricted to the top only. Every manager at every level in the organization must cultivate and perfect all the three types of skills. They are in fact inseparable and are integral to decision making and solving problems.

Interview with CMD of a PSU

In reply to the question by a TV anchor, he says. 'People are the biggest resource of any company and my employees and their welfare comes before anything else. The company has 35,000 employees'. The media present are ever ready to corner the guest. The anchor reminds that the previous regime advocated high handed approach towards employees. A less competent person would have blamed the previous managements. Mark his reply, 'some people tried that approach Did it work?'. The word 'approach' is significant. There could be different approaches. Some approaches work for sometime, not at all times. No blame is apportioned to the previous CMD. He concludes with a question, 'How can you ever think of harming the soul of the company?'

The present CMD who was with the company for 20 years was known to be very tough when there is a need, but he would not reprimand any one in front of others. Respect and dignity of the individual, human skill is still demonstrated. He was a Cost and Works Accountant in an Engineering organization. He still uses his Accounts skill or technical skills but appreciates the large number of engineers and their problems.

Technical and human skills are vital for internal management, managing the whole organization. That is not enough. He has to manage the environment in relation to the internal organization. He was incharge of strife–ridden Assam early in his career. This was early training in managing the environment. As CMD he has been introducing new business plan diffusing tensions between the company and its key stake holders- the government, vendors, and contractors. He forged strategic alliances with other countries.

Now, for the definition of conceptual skill. It is the management of the internal milieu and external environment and the integration of the two.

Skill Complex

On Oct, 15th and 16th 2008, the media, both electronic and print covered sensational news about Jet Airways. First there was alliance between Jet Airways and Kingfisher airways to overcome the slowdown that hit the aviation sector. Next, Jet Airways sacked 1900 probationers and temporary staffers who demonstrated and protested as a reaction. They even sought the help of one political party who threatened the management of Jet Airways. There was nationwide debate, an excellent meat for controversy hungry electronic media. All political parties expressed solidarity with the sacked employees all of whom were young boys and girls of 20 years of age. The cameras showed many of them in tears for having lost lucrative jobs within 10 months of their employment, all 12th class passed. They even paid huge advances for rental accommodation to the tune of more than a lakh of rupees. It was a shock for them and their parents. All of them thought they were on to a wonderful career and the whole thing collapsed like a pack of cards. Next day was more dramatic. The chairman Jet Airways told the press that all the sacked employees would be taken back. He said a few things and refused to answer further questioning by the press and TV reporters.

It is an interesting case study for the three skills of top managers. First see what Mr. Naresh Goyal, the chairman, Jet Airways is reported to have said:

'The management has decided on the sacking of 1900 employees and when I read about it , I saw tears in their eyes. I decided on my own to call them back. There is no internal or external pressure... *as a family we will* decide how to fly and keep the airline afloat'.....It does not matter what anybody says. I have not even asked my wife. My daughter is 19 years old... I have gone through this... I cannot see their trauma and agony...'

Later the union Avation Minister claimed that he had asked Goyal to take back all the employees. The political parties competed with each other to take credit for the reinstatement.

Now for the management student to ask is what was the skill, technical, human or conceptual skill which the Chairman applied while deciding to take back the sacked employees.

We defined human skill is about dealing with and leading people. It is a people skill. He says, 'as a family we will decide' how to fly and make the Jet Airways afloat, viable. It is an internal management affair.

'The company has been incurring a loss of Rs. 10 crore daily', he was quoted as saying. How is he going to manage the internal milieu and external environment together, government, vendors, customers. He has to manage the government by asking them to do something to help them get out of the fix, if not bailout.

All this is due to the larger external environment-the whole world was facing financial crisis and suffering effects of recession. We referred to PEST control-political economic, social, and technological complexity. Managing the media is not outside the turbulent environment. Media is an aspect of social environment. Some of them started saying it was all drama. The sides of the triangle cannot be separated. Environment being dynamic, interconnected and multi-level reality it is a challenge for the top managers of any organization.

This is written in Oct, 2008. What will be the fate of Jet Airways, its employees, and Aviation industry when this monograph goes for print is anybody's guess.

Conceptual skill

Coming back to the first CMD-People would give their best under bosses like the new CMD. Careers are shaped by those at the top and what the culture of the organization is in which you are working.

Let us look at the CMD's career.

The new CMD began his career as a banker in a public sector bank and stayed there for almost a decade before joining another PSU and posted to Baghdad. He joined the present organization in 1988 as a Jt. Director of Finance in Assam, a strife-torn region in the North East of India.

He was a cost accountant heading finance. As one of his subordinates puts it the HR and finance people seem to be preferred over engineers in this monolithic giant. He worked in Assam between 1991 and 1994 when this gentleman was Head of Finance in Assam. In 1998 the gentleman became Director of Finance, a functional head. As a fellow member of the Institute of Cost and Works Accountant of India, he has received many awards and recognitions for his performance. He brought about changes in the systems and accounts.

CMD admits that his main achievement consists in improving employer-employee relations and morale along with introducing new business strategy to defuse tensions between the company and its key stake-holders–government, vendors, and contractors. He forged strategic alliances with other countries to attract quality collaborators. The CMD is concerned about number of engineers of different expertise some of whom have left the company for better-paid jobs.

The CMD is a man of high order of conceptual skill. Whether he is from finance or HR or engineering discipline, once he is appointed as CMD he must display, conceptual skills. It is holistic perspective and total approach.

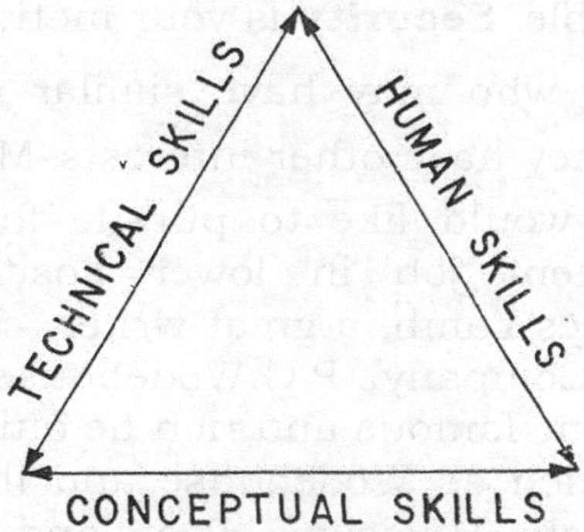

Work Preference – Motivation

Below are given certain reasons which people usually attribute for choosing a vocation.

Read them carefully and rank them in the order of importance to you in choosing it.

It provides	Description	Rank
R	Retirement benefits	
E	Enough leisure	
J	Just and stable income	
O	Opportunities to learn	
I	Independence & Freedom to work	
C	Challenging work	
E	Enjoyment of prestige in society	

REJOICE[6]

Rejoice in your Choice (Rejoice in your Motivation)

Your ranking in the above exercise reveals your motivation.

If *Retirement Benefits* is your first rank, the close second could be *just and stable income.* You may even love to *enjoy leisure* so that you can spend more time with your family. You may feel very happy and comfortable. **Security** is your motivation.

There are others who may have similar orientation but for different reasons. They have other interests–Music, Art, Poetry or Sports which they would like to pursue for which they may choose a Government job in lower position with minimal responsibility. Charles Lamb, a great writer, chose a clerical post in The East India Company, P.G.Wodehouse was a clerk in a Bank. After he became famous and rich he quit the job. All people cannot become as rich as Wodehouse and ill-afford to quit the job. Now-a-days Artists, Musicians, Poets and Sportsmen are able to make lucrative careers. For all these, interest and gifts will enable them to carry on with the parallel career with no senility setting in. Sportsmen can become writers and commentators.

For most people who would like to make a career, this book helps. For them, to make a successful career they need to look for *Challenging job,* loving *independence and freedom* and *opportunities for learning* and *growth.* Automatically they will have *prestige* in society.

There are a few who chose their interests or hobbies in Music and Art like photography and struggled or succeeded late in life. Those who rank challenging work, independence and freedom and opportunity to learn have high **achievement motivation**. These people set their own goals which are reasonably difficult, but not impossible to achieve. They monitor their own progress and take corrective action when necessary. Such people become self-employed entrepreneurs.

---

[6]**REJOICE:** Retirement benefits: Enough leisure; Just and stable income; Opportunities to learn; Independence & Freedom to work; Challenging work; Enjoyment of prestige in society

'The achievement motivated person is a hard working person who seeks personal responsibility, who sets realistic but challenging goals and who seeks feedback about the effects of his efforts. As such, he tends to do particularly well in those situations which allow for personal control and innovation, particularly entrepreneurial business situations. They choose self–employment. They take risks and give employment to many. They have unique personalities with a combination of qualities that facilitate their success in life. More on it in the subsequent chapters.

Motivation

Motivation is an important concept the beginner to the world of work must appreciate, become aware and be convinced. It helps in the self-discovery, we have been discussing about. There are several theories, Maslow's is the chief. He treated the subject as need fulfillment theory and presented it as hierarchy of needs, wants and motivations. At the lowest level or base level man seems to say, 'I want to live today'. 'I need food, shelter, and clothes to maintain the warmth'. It gives rise to what Maslow calls as physiological needs. When you seek a job for *just income* you are seeking the satisfaction of basic needs. When you want stable income you are talking of next level need termed security needs. You are, in other words, saying 'I want to live tomorrow'. When you extend the time frame, your concern is *Retirement benefits.* When these things are guaranteed then the man begins to look for social needs. 'I want to be loved'. Man is a social animal and he wants to live in human environment. He does not like to be alone, even if it is for a short period. Longer periods of isolation are unbearable. Solitary confinement in a penitentiary is a punishment. There can be voluntary *withdrawal* or self imposed loneliness. Ancient sages practised penance punished themselves at one level, absence of social environment, for gaining something higher and richer in body and mind. Gandhiji practiced *mounavratam and fasting,* foregoing something, the lower order needs satisfying the higher order mental purification. From the withdrawal state, man changes to rituals, simple activities, past-times, and even dishonest or honest encounters with people around to satisfy his social needs.

The next higher order need in Maslow's hierarchy of needs is *esteem.* Here man says, 'I want to be respected'. 'I want to be loved' is different from 'I want to be respected'. He moves from social *contact* to *recognition* and respect from others. That is why when a man is psychologically hurt it is more painful than physical injury. It lingers longer.

Self-respect and self-esteem are same. It is because of self-esteem that one gets hurt when some one treats him with disrespect. Understanding the dynamics helps you in your interpersonal relationship and skills besides understanding your own motivation. Motivation, a force that prompts one to do a thing or abstain from it. It is the power behind all actions.

The most important contribution Maslow made is the highest need–*self actualization.* Man at this level says, 'I want to achieve!' when pure challenge and sense of achievement come into play. Before we go into self-actualization or realizing one's full potential of Maslow, we note here, Maslow was a changed man in his later years when he abandoned his earlier theory of motivation and became a humanist and accepted Gita's tenets. He wrote a book on *'Religious values and experience'.* He was deeply convinced that 'ought' is derived from the 'is', meaning that man 'ought' to do according to the purpose of his life and not merely be a passive living thing. He quoted John Mac Murray thus :

> 'Now is the point in history at which it becomes possible for man to *adopt consciously* as his own purpose, the purpose which is already in his nature'.

Between 1943 and 1976 he was a changed man. 'Man knows not his purpose on the surface, not visible to casual glance'. He has to 'use his power of thought' to discover his nature and read from it his purpose. Gita (ch.6) tells man to lift himself to his higher self from the lower self. Maslow was convinced that it is possible.

Another motivation theorist is David C.McClelland. According to him there are three kinds of motivations: Achievement motivation, Affiliation motivation and Security motivation.

What leads to Self-Actualization

Some of the behaviours that are likely to lead to self-actualization state include the following.

Altruistic & Absorbing : Unselfish acts for the benefit of others. Selfless service to community is paid back to the individual in the long run. In fact most work that we do for eking our livelihood is somehow for the benefit and welfare of others. If we keep this in our focus while discharging our duties, not focusing on rights, then that action becomes altruistic action. There is a beautiful word *yajna* which is translated as altruistic action by many commentators of Gita. Yajna is performed for the welfare of all; It is selfless or desire less service.

That very action if done with absorption, then you are in the direction of self-actualization state. Cultivate it a little more each day.

Creative work: This aspect has already been discussed. Absorbing and creative work done for the welfare of others; with this feeling perform your work.

Taking responsibility for events

In many discussions on the subject of personality development we come across the responsibility as a concept that creeps in. You must be a responsible person. You must behave always responsibly to yourself and to others. Self-actualization process involves taking responsibility for events and consequences or results. There is a tendency to blame others every where at home and in public places; politicians are seen to be doing it all the time. 'You are wrong, I am right' is what we hear from them all the time. You may also have the habit of blaming others when something goes wrong. It is a habit because it comes automatically. We must all unlearn this habit by developing problem–solving skills and positive thinking.

Unpopular at times

When you look at the problem and not look for a scapegoat then you are likely to become unpopular because you are reduced to a minority. There is a famous story of 7 princes who went for fishing. They brought back 7 fish and dried them on the lawn.

One of the fish did not dry up. Why? Because grass blades obstructed it. Why? Because the cow did not graze. Why? Because the shepherd boy did not take the cow for grazing. Why? He was not served food by the old woman. Why? She was attending to the small child crying the whole day. Why? The little child was bitten by an ant. Why? The innocent child put the finger in an anthole. Why? Innocence! Why did the ant bite? That's its nature!

'Causes Cause Causes to Cause Causes'

Causes all the way.. That's profound moral for all those who do not have holistic approach. The only way to avoid this is to make sure the grass is cut before placing the fish on the lawn. Planning & Preparation. The unpopularity is due to your not towing everybody's line.

Authenticity and non-defensive

Honest and genuine responses to things, ideas, and people. Others do not have exactly the same views that you have. Don't defend yourself without examining the views of others. Listen to others.

Listens to own feelings

Self-actualized persons are not robots. They too have feelings. They don't react. They listen to their own feeling, count ten before responding to others.

Spontaneous

They still respond naturally and spontaneously without external agency, well controlled and without fear.

ACTUALS[7] – altruistic; creative work; taking responsibility for events; unpopular at times; authenticity and non–defensive; listens to own feeling; spontaneous. You need these concepts to discover yourself- your motives, and behaviour.

[7] **ACTUALS:** Altruistic; Creative work; Taking responsibility for events; Unpopular at times; Authenticity and non–defensive; Listens to own feeling; Spontaneous;

Characteristics of A self-actualized man

We have seen the behaviour that lead to self-actualization. This is a behaviourist's model in which by changing the behaviour we can change personality. They advocate this model because they think it is easier to modify behaviour than modifying characteristics.

Here are a few characteristics of a self-actualized man. How does he perceive the reality? Accurately and accepts it readily. He responds to it naturally and spontaneously. He is not stereotyped. He is capable of appreciating things, events, and people in a non-defensive manner. He resists pressures to conform and ready (as already mentioned) to be unpopular. He holds strong values and does not confuse means with ends. He is able to transcend dichotomies, reconciling the opposites.

His relationship with others is significant. He is humane and experiences shared social bonds. He has deep relationships with a few of many friends he may have. He is democratic and believes in equality and human rights.

His focus is on the problem rather than on self. Self-sufficient and independent, needing privacy. **He has peak experiences, spiritual or ecstatic on occasions.** Because of them he is creative and able to see things in new ways. He may not be an intellectual or an academician.

India the World Leader (A titbit)

'India will be world leader in next 28 years: Saibaba'.

Whether you are a devotee of Saibaba or not the remark made by Bhagwan Satya Saibaba to devotees may not be lucid. It may be taken as a prediction that will come true coming from their God incarnate.

For an objective reader, rational economics students, or philosopher or a historian, linguist, or careerist it can appeal and make a different sense. The exact words are:

> "The world will *shrink* further in terms of separate entities from the *point of view* of races and religions and would come under one canopy. India would be in a position to provide assistance to many countries in the next three decades."

His audience were students at the 27th convocation of Sri Satya Sai University held in Saikulwant Hall in Puttaparthi on Saturday 22nd evening of November, 2008.

Indian society has every quality including *CULTURE* and knowledge to make the country world leader in every respect. The student, at the striving stage, listening to a trusted speaker, will develop totally positive attributes *shraddha* necessary for acquiring *vidya*, competence, and conviction and commitment–all of which form the culture – loosely called soft skills.

It is one thing to believe the living God for some, another thing altogether to the rational and the objective man or woman. They need 'Upanishad', the third requirement for excellence as described elsewhere in the book.

Discuss, debate, dialogue – let there be discourse ensuring the flow of thoughts that are behind such a poignant point…a soft skills practicals.

The world is shrinking–literally not but figuratively people have become migrating birds.

'Where the world is not broken up into fragments into narrow domestic walls'.

The Berlin wall is literally broken – to enable people to have free access – free movement – flow of people means flow of ideas, meanings and thoughts.

The narrow boundaries are artificially created by people – races, religions, creeds, castes, nationalities, separate entities must become one–complete coherent organic whole–common, natural, interdependent.

'The culture coupled with knowledge of the society would take the country beyond all powers that be in the years to come', he noted.

What more do you need to enthuse the youth to prepare and contribute to the goal envisaged? *Positive thinking is set in motion.*

He highlighted what is present – not a precept – but an actuality – recognition – facts made visible. He said;

> 'It is the mothers in this country who bring up their children in Righteousness, Love, Peace and Non-violence, Truth'. (Soft skills)

There is no mention of negative aspects. Every thing is positive – speak no evil, see no evil, and hear no evil. In the days when media, electronic media produces venom, these words come as soothing diversion to the youth who must be exposed to more spirituality.

He cautioned the elders who are polluting the entire society in addition to environmental pollution – which is creeping into human lives in every aspect. This is entropic – what Bhagawan is doing is anti-entropic. He is trying to clean the mess created by the elders - like a 'mahout' controlling a wild elephant. Taming the wild horse.

Experienced Learning

Gestalt Cycle

Follow your Inner promptings, Notions and Drives. All of us daydream experience fantasies when we are alone. If you sit quietly in a secluded place and meditate and allow your thoughts to flow you may be able to get in touch with your inner conscience and promptings coming from some where, don't brush them aside. Take note of them for later use.

Sensations come out of depths of conscience like the waves in the sea. Some of them do not rise enough to form tides. A few rise sufficiently, ride on as you go sea surfing, like a sport. Allow the sensations and act according to the promptings to reach the peak. At the end there is fulfillment, sense of completion and achievement. Musicians and artists experience this very often. At the end of it they look back and relax. This is a cycle. Each cycle is consummate action, skilled and perfect. When you a have goal and positive orientation, even small, little actions can give you this feeling, also called gestalt experience or total experience starting from sensation, awareness built up energy, peak performance and withdrawal for relaxation and reflection. The matter in the box contains a narrative as an illustration.

The Episode

I left college in the year 1952. I never took part in college debates. After 11 years of service in 1963 I was pushed into it. Although I had my dreams and fantasies about becoming a great speaker, I needed the push which came my way in September 1963. I was undergoing a 13 week training in the Bank's Staff College as a Junior Officer. The principal, who was dedicated to the development of human potential, had regular debates as part of the course.

I could not escape his attention beyond 10 weeks. During the 11th week he called me to his cabin and gave me the ultimatum. I must speak that week end on the topic, 'Should Capital Punishment be abolished?'. I could have 'fallen sick' and escaped it. My conscience told me to do otherwise: 'Try', it said, 'you will succeed'. My fantasies came back. I visualized the audience applauding - giving me standing ovation. I had the skill of fantasising and visualizing, which I believe everyone has these soft skills. If anyone is lacking I recommend they should acquire through practice.

I had two room mates in the lodge where I was staying. They had been through the ordeal and told me about it. I asked them for details and I listened to them intensely. I bought a book on Public Speaking from a pavement vendor. Luckily I could lay my hands on a book of English Essays which contained an essay by William Hazlit on Death Penalty. I browsed through it quickly and went to my lodge with the book on Public Speaking which I needed to read reflectively. Next two days I read, took down points, and discussed with my friends who were very eager to help me. They liked me. At the instance of my mentors I wrote down my speech. It took several drafts. Hesitantly I showed it to my room mates as they insisted on seeing it. They gave me feedback and needed corrections were made.

I memorized the text which would have taken five minutes to deliver at normal speed. I was the seventh speaker. To my dismay I was given only three minutes. I didn't know how to deal with the new situation. The only thing I could do was to speed up delivery.

Once I began, the show went on involuntarily. I was looking at a mass of audience and not faces. After finishing I made a bee line for my seat and then 'woken up' to thunderous applause. A few close friends walked up to me and shook me by the hand.

That was the 'Gestalt' experience about which I read only in the year 1996.

'Try it, you will succeed' is the prompting from within; sensation like the wave from the depth of ocean surfaced. I became aware. It was energy. That energy comes from the fantasizing and visualizing the future event-the result of positive thinking.

I began talking of it with others who gave the necessary external motivation. This exercise can be done before appearing for a selection interview. Imagine positive result. Anticipating of negative outcomes could be disastrous. Think positive for Gestalt experience.

The responses from room-mates are part of the larger design. Believe in it. How is it I could get the books I needed but not exactly looking for? Luck? Providence? Power of positive thinking? Or just a coincidence? I could have simply prayed for success and do nothing. Then it would be superstition. There was lot of effort. I thought of nothing else except about the outcome.

How did I cope with the time factor? I spoke rapidly, forgetting everything else. Nothing else existed for me.

It was like a trance. It can happen to any one who is absorbed in the work on hand.

2

UNIQUE PATH

Each individual is different and distinct from others. Personality is defined as totality of traits. The integration of all the qualities, modes of reaction etc which set off an individual as distinct from all others. From this premise let us proceed further.

Personality and Development

Behaviour is a function of 3 Es

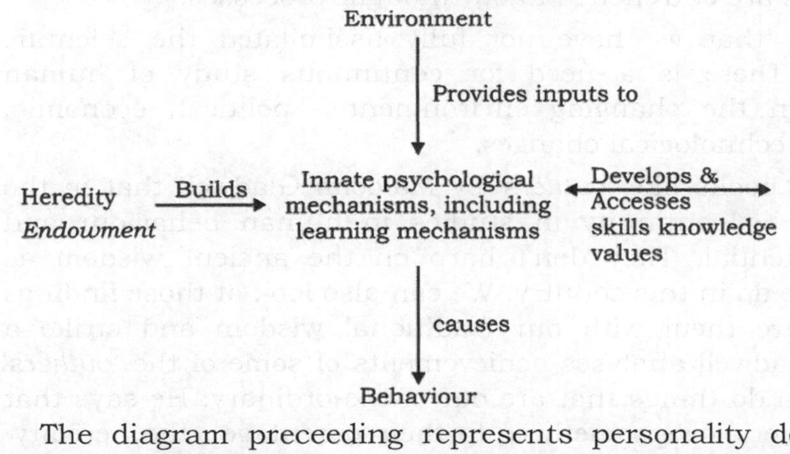

The diagram preceeding represents personality development process. As personality means totality of characteristics of an individual which distinguish him from others, each individual is distinct and separate.

First of all there is something that comes with heredity. The innate psychological mechanisms which include learning mechanisms. The individual interacts with the *environment.* We may use the word *endowment* for what is inherited, the interaction between the two causes his behaviour.

Endowment and Environment

What we inherit is in our genes. It is cultural legacy, what tradition has handed over to us. Over a time we get exposed to alien cultures through interaction with foreign cultures. India because of rich culture and being a land of plenty centuries back attracted other races to invade or migrate with the result the natives lost sight of their original culture in the inter-mingling.

Today we are in the twilight zone of that cultural milieu a mixture of the West and the East in respect of cultural legacy. The educated youth look more to West and less to East. Science from the West, traditional values from the East is a gain for us, if we integrate the two. English education and the promotion of scientific temper made us have a relook at our own scriptures. I present below some of the traditional concepts relating to behaviour and personality development vis-à-vis the Western ideas which are entrenched in our thought processes.

I believe that we have not fully assimilated the scientific approach. There is a need for continuous study of human condition in the changing environment – political, economic, social and technological changes.

I find in books like '*outliers*' by Malcolm Gladwell that in the West there is continuity in studies in human behaviour and human potential. They don't harp on the ancient wisdom as much as we do in this country. We can also look at those findings and compare them with our traditional wisdom and strike a balance. Gladwell analyses achievements of some of the '*outliers*' – those who do things that are out of the ordinary. He says that these 'out-liers' owe something to their parentage.. the heredity. He also adds that these great people owe something to their patronage – the cultural legacy. In fact his book is divided into two parts – opportunity and legacy. Both factors make significant contribution to the successful lives of outliers. He draws information from a variety of studies made in the West in support of his arguments. Similar support of studies,–the scientific temper is missing in our country. An attempt is made in the following pages to integrate both.

Endowment – Legacy – Soft skills are in our genes

> 'Cultural legacies are a powerful force. They have deep roots and long lives. They persist generation after generation, virtually intact, even as the economic and social and demographic conditions that spawned them have vanished, and they play such a role in directing *attitudes* and *behaviour* that we can not make sense of our world without them'.
>
> ***Malcolm Gladwell***

This is a significant point: rural India has the 'cultural legacies' in tact. That explains – honour killings, faction fights, and other forms violences, public punishments, mob killings and so on. Many may argue that this is not the true culture of India. Non-violence, spirit of forgiveness, respect for law, were the ancient values that got eroded in medieval age. Cultural legacy is a force in the genes, violence is not in our genes. Training and development is a long term process for desired cultural re-charge. Generations of change has brought us to this stage. Indian tradition of truth, non-violence, simple living has to be sustained through our education system – the soft skills culture is in our tradition – thousands of year's effort – a legacy we are losing. It should be put back on the track after being freed from the greed, avarice, cut throat competition, selfishness and violence.

There are some corrections to be made in the legacy with an open mind. Caste and religious prejudices pervade every walk of life. Hierarchical arrangement of the society of our forefathers may be doing harm to our own fundamental values. For revaluation and adaptation – soft skills are called for. I discuss later on the benefit of the castes in the economic sense.

> 'Plane crashes are much more likely to be the result of an accumulation of minor difficulties and seemingly trivial malfunctions,...'The typical accident involved seven consecutive human errors – rarely problems of flying skills or knowledge... the kinds of errors that cause plane crashes are invariably errors of teamwork and communication (soft skills)'

'Cultural Consequence'

PDI (Power Distance Index) of Hofstede is concerned with attitudes towards hierarchy, specifically with how much a particular culture values and respects authority.

Malcolm Gladwell

PDI is low among Americans, high in France and in Asian countries.

There is cultural difference among countries. Similarly there are cultural differences among companies within the countries; professions have their own cultures. Dutch psychologist Greet Hofstede had identified certain dimensions, the ways in which cultures differ from one another.

Here are a few dimensions:

- Individualistic – collective
- Uncertainty avoidance
- Power distance index

'Each of us have our our distinct personality. But over laid on top of that are 'tendencies and assumptions and reflexes handed down to us by the history of the community we grew up in, and those differences are extraordinarily specific.'

Greet Hofstede

This has implications for our discussion. Every careerist must understand the culture of the organization particularly power dimensions. In most Indian organizations established in pre-independence period, the power hierarchy plays major role. Respect for elders and authority is ingrained in the culture. [yet there were, some like *Pothana* and *Thyagaraja* for whom only almighty mattered and they did not dedicate their work to worldy authority].

'High-power distance communication works when the receiver is highly competent to interpret and pay attention to the instruction and is ready to explain in case he is made accountable. Where the company or authority is not ready to take the risk, there are dynamic grass–roots managers who took personal risks to achieve what they are expected to achieve in terms of responsibilities and discretion they are entrusted with. Such men make their way up on the hierarchy much faster than others. They make use of opportunities presented by the environment. In 2000 Korean Air brought David Greenberg to remedy the high-power distance index of South Korean pilots.

> 'He evaluated the English language skills of airline flight crew.' 'He set up a program to assist and improve the proficiency of aviation English'. 'The rationale for English is that the language of the aviation world was English, the check lists were in English… when they talked to ATC any where in the world, those conversations would be in English'.

Language is the medium of communication. Business communication in the globalised world is in English. Hence, its inclusion in non-hard skills, the soft skills. There cannot be any room for mis-communication in businesses. In Aviation, it is dangerous... second the *cultural legacy* – (The authority of superiors must be respected). Now there is a need both in Aviation and businesses to step outside the cultural legacy – the power distance high index. Once the pilot sits in the cockpit – or a manager is made responsible for results, they must be free from the ethnic or company 'culture traps'. There is no place for sharply defined gradients of the cultural hierarchy. A different legacy of culture and language is needed.

The purpose both in Korean case or any other business enterprise is not usurping of the traditional culture. They can respect it and, follow it at other places than in work place where a different culture is more appropriate for effectiveness. The soft skill adaptability is sacrosanct. (More on adaptability later).

'We took them out of their culture' Greenberg explained, 'and re-normed them'. When people understand the need to adopt the orientation that will help the individuals' professional success, then it is truly liberating from the frustration the individual suffers and the organization losing the market. For effectiveness and efficiency, the flexibility, a soft skill, will help the individual and the company he serves. He can make successful careers without hassles created by the differences in cultures.

There is another story from *Outliers:*

'In 1889 Louis and Regina Borgenicht boarded an ocean liner in Hamburg bound for America,' the land of *opportunity.* ...Like so many other immigrants to America in those years, theirs was a leap of faith! They needed something to make both ends meet. After trying selling many things, they pitched on clothes. Louis noticed that in America even poor people going into a store and walking out with what they needed instead of making their own clothes.

'There was a field to go into, a field to thrill to' they bought a sewing machine and started making children's aprons. They were seasoned dress makers. They needed something more than the hard skills of tailoring. They needed entrepreneurial abilities, a soft skill par excellence.

'What he was getting in his 18 hour a day work was a lesson in modern economy. He was learning market research, manufacturing; he was learning *how to negotiate* with imperious yankees. He was learning how to plug himself into popular culture in order to understand new fashion trends'.

'Willing to learn', itself a soft skills; he was learning conceptual and marketing skills too, thanks to relocating. Gujarat has been a land of entrepreneurs. They migrated to other countries. Progressive farmers from Andhra Pradesh migrated to other states wherever major irrigation projects came up.

Compare what these Jews did with what 'Italian and Irish immigrants who came to New York in the same period. They didn't have a skill, specific to the urban economy.

'They went to work as day labourers, domestic and construction workers... for thirty years and never learned market research... how to navigate the popular culture and how to negotiate with the Yankees, who ran the world'

– The difference is the gap in soft skills!

One was that he was his own boss. He was responsible for his own decisions and direction. His work was complex: it engaged his mind and imagination. And in his work, there was relationship between effort and reward' – The other immigrants laboured; did not 'work'. (Recall the difference between work and labour quoted before).

Education vis-à-vis Endowment

We have a problem – a debate on reservation – for and against, without any study... Read the following passage from 'Outliers',

> 'We see that white students do better than the minority black students'. 'In fact, an attack on the University of Michigan's affirmative action program recently went all the way to the US Supreme Court. For many people it is troubling that elite educational institution lets in students who are less qualified than their peers'...
>
> 'The university decided to look closely at how the law school' minority students had fared after they graduated. How much money did they make? How far up in the profession did they go? How satisfied were they with their careers? What kind of social and community contribution did they make? What kind of honours had they won?
>
> Richard Lempert, one of the authors of the Michigan study said, "I think our expectation was that we would find a half or two–thirds – full glass, that they had not done as well as the white students... *But we were completely surprised.* We found that they were doing every bit as well. There was no place we saw any serious discrepancy'.
>
> ***Malcolm Gladwell***

It is not my intention to join the controversy raging in the country on reservation and neglect of merit etc. What I liked in Gladwell's argument is that all those students who pass out of such institutions are equally good enough to make successful careers irrespective of caste, creed, and religion.

There are other qualities which are important to the student. There is something called *practical intelligence* that seems to contribute to the success in the market which has nothing to do with endowment.

> 'Knowing what to say who to whom, knowing when to say it, and knowing how to say it for maximum effect'. It is procedural: it is knowing *how* to do something without necessarily knowing why you know it or being able to explain it. It is practical in nature: not knowledge for not knowledge sake.
>
> **Malcolm Gladwell**

They are skills in the realm of soft skills.

The examinations, even if they are conducted throughout the year right through all the years in the college, cannot test or predict them. There are any number of tests for analytical skill; they cannot test practical intelligence which can be done by the senior on the job. It is internship that reveals.

'Where does this practical intelligence come from? "Analytical skills, partly come from your genes'. Practical intelligence is acquired from the upbringing and environment. To answer this question Gladwell refers us to another study by the sociologist Annette Lareau.

'She picked up children from 12 families, black and white, wealthy and poor. She found that the wealthier family parents raised their kids one way, and the poorer parents raised their kids in another way.

Cultural advantage – concerted cultivation

What are the 'philosophies' as she called the two kinds of raising children? That is important to us.

'The wealthier parents, (black or white), were heavily involved in their children's free time, shuttling them from one activity to the next, quizzing them about their teachers, coaches, and team mates. Child gets the message of encouragement when father or mother drops him or her at the tennis court, swimming pool, or piano lessons, any of the extra curricular activities'.

These things are true in the case of middle class India.

'That kind of *intensive scheduling* is almost entirely absent from the lives of the poor children'.

There was no *concerted cultivation* – the poor children playing cricket in the streets is common sight in India. Concerted cultivation is a beautiful expression. It tells of mutually agreed on harmoniously, performed by parents and children, regimen. The street cricket of the poor children is separate from the parent's concern. The children grow haphazardly; it lacks synergy one sees in the concerted cultivation. There is synthesis of energies. There is cultivation of synergistic habits beneficial in the career in adult life. These are the findings of an American study on the differences and family advantage of individuals grown in wealthier middle class and disadvantage of poorer working class several years back. But in India parents of working class are raising the first generation literate for white collar jobs. There is *concerted cultivation* of hard skills and technical knowledge. But what is lacking both in the parents and the children is concerned cultivation of soft skills.

The wealthier boys and girls have the advantage in the cultivation of soft skills. This is proving a big gap. This absence is mistaken for lack of IQ for no one takes IQ tests here. Nor any studies like this one are taking place. There are TV reality shows which has eye on TRP rating than identifying and promoting talent. The parents interest is lukewarm; even those parents who want to develop their wards' talent do not have wherewithal to do any concerted cultivation.

> The middle class parents talked things with their children, reasoning them. The poorer parents just issued commands. The rich children 'talked back to negotiate, to question adults in *position of authority*.

This habit of questioning the authority helps them in asking questions and negotiating with the hirers later in the job interview. Again the poor student is at an advantage and settle for lesser salary, lesser post. Further in the career they miss their promotion because they avoid confrontation and conflict, they don't have bargaining power. Lareau explains the term concerted cultivation:

> It is an attempt to actively foster and assess child's talents, opinion and skills.

Let me give an example from richer middle class. Hony, a third year engineering student is neglecting her studies according to the parents. She wanted to go to Madurai to compete in an all India elocution contest. She argues and bargains with parents who yield to her request. She comes back with a consolation prize! Now there is reassessment of girls' *talents, opinions and skills* and priorities. The experiment succeeded. In another of equally talented from poorer class would not have been experimented simply because they had no money. What was more interesting, Hony not only brought a prize back but she was reimbursed with all the travel and stay expenses!

Poor children have their own advantages. By contrast they were raised with the philosophy of 'accomplishment of natural growth'. Parents let their children grow and develop on their own. These children could be more creative and self-reliant. 'Put in practical terms, concerted cultivation has enormous advantages', the child 'learns teamwork and how to cope up in a highly structured setting.' They participate in company meeting and catch the eye of superiors. 'She is taught how to interact comfortably with adults, and to speak up when she needs to'. They tend to become assertive. The working class employee may become submissive or aggressive both behaviours are dysfunctional. Lareau gives us some more jargon:

> 'By contrast, the working class and poor children were characterized by *an emerging sense of distance,* distrust, and constraint.. they didn't know… how to *customize*. Whatever environment they were in, for their best purposes'.

'The adapting flexibly to the circumstances without any fear or doubt confronting the position of authority for their best purposes' – the customization is not generic, not an endowment but an acquired trait through training at home. It has nothing to do with caste, creed, or reservation. It is a cultural advantage which everyone is entitled to. It is here affirmative action from the democratic government becomes significant. In short all those who did not have 'concerted cultivation' or cultural advantage must be trained to remedy the situation and put on the development path. In the bank I served we conducted special coaching classes on written examination and facing interviews for the promotion exercise for certain identified class of candidates.

In spite of the short duration courses, only those who had favourable background and training did well in the interviews. Whether it was through concerted cultivation or a cultural advantage of hailing from the 'creamy layer', one cannot say.

What they miss in their upbringing has to be remedied through affirmative action of a different kind, *training in soft skills* which is time consuming requiring commitment from the trainer.

> 'Western communication has what linguists call a *transmitter orientation* – that is, it is considered the responsibility of the speaker (transmitter) to communicate ideas clearly and unambiguously!'

Added to lack of this legacy, Indian culture does not entitle the subordinate to seek clarification, but bosses could talk only once, not always unambiguously.

I have seen Banks issuing circulars on RBI instructions perfunctorily. For example RBI does not want Banks to do any window-dressing to boost the balance sheets, before the year end. The time gap between the date of issue is usually 15 days.. The managers know the intention and indulge in window dressing. The studies revealed that the Asian countries share what is 'Receiver Orientation'. The responsibility and therefore the accountability fall on the receiver, the subordinate.

There is a continuity and link between endowment, what you inherit, what is in your genes and what comes from the environment. The thing that serves as bridge between them is 'upbringing'. An individual, whether his IQ is high or low, has relative advantage if he is born into a family rich in possessions and rich in culture. We in India have not made many studies in these matters and generally rely on the findings of researchers from the West. At least the news titbits should make us open our eyes and examine our prejudices or predilections in forming our opinions.

Malcolm Gladwell relied on several studies made since 1921 to this date in support of his arguments reminding us of what, Newton said, 'I soared to heights because I stood on the shoulders of giants'. There is continuity to our achievements. For every success we have to acknowledge that it was predecessors who contributed to our success. That explains the role of environment — past and present and prediction of the future environment.

I read it from end to end because of its flow of arguments. I asked myself whether it is true of any country like India.

'It hinges on the culture they grow up in and the way they spend their time'.

When I turned the pages randomly I found a sentence 'Achievement is talent plus preparation.' But the latent talent emerges with preparation. Another sentence 'the emerging picture from such studies is that ten thousand hours of practice is required to achieve the level of mastery associated with being a world class expert—in any thing'

This is equally true of a Mozart or a Sarkar.

Mozart, a prodigy, 'famously started writing music at six.' But he produced his 'master work (No 9, K.271) composed not until he was twenty one: by that time Mozart had already been composing concerts for ten years' writes Michael Howe in his book, *Genius Explained.*

There is no dearth of such examples in India; but there appears to be no such studies in our country.

Reading biographies makes a huge difference to the talented to work hard—10000 hours of practice. How do we get ten thousand hours from to spare for practice for those whose family background does not permit? It is an enormous amount of time. 'You have to have parents, who encourage and support you. (they) can't be poor and free from family responsibilities.' Eking a livelihood takes major part of time. Elsewhere I wrote about Havell's cables ad. If that kid in the ad had talent for music, he would never be in the limelight.

In the case, the Holistic Doctor quoted the little master Sachin Tendulkar who could practice and play thousands of hours—17 years now—because he had not to bother about his family. Preparation and family support go together.

We are not concerned about geniuses or celebrities who have media support but ordinary people who can make successful careers through planning and preparation. Part of the preparation is to overcome the disadvantages, result of lack of family support.

'Outliers' challenges you to make most of your own potential. You must come to grips-GRIPS[1]-with your life—*Goal direction, Responsibility* for self, *Initiating actions, Perspective of reality, and Self confidence.*

Gladwell discussed at length a 1921 study by Lewis Terman, just after the World War I. Terman's speciality was Intelligence

[1] **GRIPS:** Goal direction; Responsibility; Initiating actions; Perspective of reality; Self confidence.

Testing (IQ). He tested Henry Cowell, who sneaked away from his job to play school piano.

> He was 'raised in poverty and chaos'. Terman found Cowell's IQ was above 140, the measure of IQ, near genius level. Einstein's was 150. He found another girl reading Dickens and Shakespeare at 4. So, Terman embarked on a study. He called the young geniuses he discovered as *Termites* who's IQs averaged over 140 and ranged as high as 200! He follows their lives like 'a mother hen'. They were 'tracked tested and analysed'.
>
> He concluded, that 'there is nothing about an individual as important as his I.Q, except possibly his morals. Terman's ideas prevailed on the American society for a long time. The story of 'outliers'—the stories-proved Terman was wrong. 'The relationship between success and IQ works only up to a point, once someone has reached an IQ of somewhere around 120, having additional IQ points doesn't seem to translate into any measurable real world advantage'.

Here is an analogy from the book.

Height is like IQ in basketball. Beyond 6'2" height does not matter. Up to a point, IQ matters, 115 or 120; in basket ball beyond which what matters is other things: 'speed, court sense, agility, ball handling skills and shooting touch'. (all acquired skills both soft and hard skills).

Gladwell quotes the family sources,

> 'Chris Langan (a genius whose IQ was 195!) was always bored to actually sit there and listen to his teachers. If someone had recognized his intelligence and if he was from a family where there was some kind of value on *education*, they would have made sure he was not bored.'
>
> 'Today, Chris Langan lives in a rural Missouri or a horse farm… he seemed content… he had been working now on a project of enormous sophistication… 'He conceded', writes Gladwell, 'that he could not find an agent to get a good publisher… 'I am not interested now.'

It was an admission of defeat... frustration. He could not negotiate, navigate, steer his life which others with less endowed minds could master easily. Hard skills he had, but not soft skills.

The others had network who had helped along the way to become outliers which Chris Langan never had.

'He had to make his way alone, and no one—rock stars, not professionals athletes, not software billionaires and not even geniuses—ever make it alone'.

You must be lucky enough to be at the right place, at the right time, doing the right job. In 1947 India became free. Many knew that independence was imminent. It was not only politicians who were looking for an *opportunity* to enter politics and the Government. Nehru became the Prime Minister. He was looking for people in every field; many caught his eye and became his advisors. That was an opportunity confined to the chosen few.

Government began nationalizing the industries in the Banking, Insurance, and key manufacturing sectors. It established scientific institutions. SBI, LIC, ONGC, Atomic Energy, were established. Many top jobs were available. Then media was growing. Those who were entering careers with high academic qualifications seized the opportunity with both hands. Those who joined as probationary officers eventually automatically reached the top and their children who had good IQ score flourished. Others lagged behind.

Many top rung managers in British companies of those days, handed over the enterprises to their trusted Indian subordinates by installing them as chairmen of their companies leaving India for good.

Who were these trusted lieutenants? They neither had high academic qualification not family connections. They were loyal to the company, hardworking, with business acumen, above all excellent soft skills. I know a steno and registered accountant who studied and became a registered accountant (RA) eventually became chairman of a group 16 companies. Another, a non-matriculate became the chairman of a tea company. A third became heir to another big British company having served the company for several decades by then.

They might not have had that fortune but for the fact India became independent. External factors more than other things was responsible for their meteoric rise, sudden in that. They probably never anticipated, that the British would leave India so suddenly.

The Jumble of Personality

When the umbilical cord is cut and the new-born is separated from the mother, the organism becomes viable–capable of independent existence in a specified and supportive environment. It is capable, but does not display independence. It is dependent on parents for its needs both physiological and psychological. As the child grows, the needs increase–contact or touch, recognition, approval etc. all these needs are met by parents and the family and is dependent on this environment.

The growing child gradually tries to exercise independence, resisting the parental moves to have control. If the controls are stringent then the individual may develop a habit of dependency. One of the obstacles to the growth in some individuals is this *Parental* controls and programming. The *Internal* and *External aspirations* form the small part of the individual. The pie diagram sums up the situation.

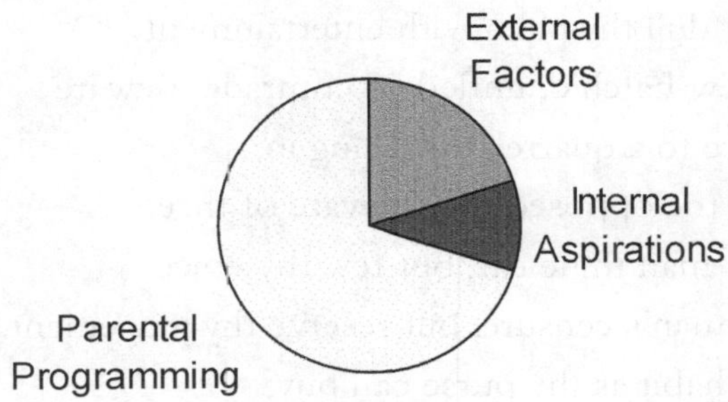

If the parents allow the children to express and enjoy the autonomy, then the unfolding of personality could be rapid. Whatever might have been the background, you can decide to become more autonomous and strike your own, hence forth. Break the circuit.

Start believing in yourself and start investigating into yourself. That brings us to the third factor education. The external factors school, college, work can educate you provided you make use of innate learning mechanism to the full. Personality development is the result of interaction between the three Es–Endowment, Environment and Education. Education is more than what you learn in school and college.

Examples of Parental Programming are given in the boxes below.

A Father to his Son Polonius Advice to His Son.

(Hamlet, the prince of the Denmark)

Polonius. Yet here, Laertes ! aboard, aboard, for shame!
The wind sits in the shoulder of your sail,
And you are stay'd for. There; my blessing with thee!
And these few precepts in thy memory
See thou character
Give thy thoughts no tongue,
Nor any unproportion'd thought his act,
Be thou familiar, but by no means vulgar;
The friends thou hast, and their adoption tried,
Grapple them to thy soul with hoops of steel;
But do not dull thy palm with entertainment
Of each new-hatch'd, unfledg'd comrade. Beware
Of entrance to a quarrel, but being in,
Bear't that the opposed may beware of thee.
Give every man thine ear, but few thy voice;
Take each man's censure, but reserve thy judgement.
Costly thy habit as thy purse can buy,
But not express'd in fancy; rich, not gaudy;
For the apparel oft proclaims the man,
And they in France of the best rank and station
Are most select and generous, chief in that.
Neither a borrower nor a lender be;
For loan oft loses both itself and friend,
And borrowing dulls the edge of husbandry.
This above all : to thine own self be true,
And it must follow, as the night the day,
Thou canst not then be false to any man.
Farewell; my blessing season this in thee!

A Father to His Son's Teacher

Abraham Lincoln's Appeal to the Teacher of his Son

Dear Mr. Teacher

My Son. He will have to learn, I know, that all men are not just, all men are not true. But teach him also that for every scoundrel, there is a hero, that for every selfish politician, there is a dedicated leader. Teach him that for every enemy, there is a friend. It will take time, I know, but teach him, if you can, that a dollar earned is of far more value than five found. Teach him to learn to lose and also to enjoy winning. Steer him away from envy. If you can, teach him the secret of quiet laughter. Let him learn early that the bullies are the easiest to lick. Teach him, if you can, the wonder of books, but also give him quiet time to ponder the eternal mystery of birds in the sky, bees in the sun and flowers on the green hillside.

In school, teach him it is far more honourable to fall than to cheat. Teach him to have faith in his own ideas even if everyone tells him they are wrong. Teach him to be gentle with gentle people, and tough with the tough. Try to give my son the strength not to follow the crowd when everyone is getting on the bandwagon. Teach him to listen to all men, but teach him also to filter all he hears on a secret of truth, and take only the good that comes through.

Teach him how to laugh when he is sad. Teach him there is not shame in tears. Teach him to scoff at cynics and beware of too much sweetness. Teach him to sell his brain to the highest bidders, but never to put a price tag on his heart and soul. Teach him to close his ears to a howling mob, and to stand and fight if he thinks he's right.

Teach him gently, but do not cuddle him, because only the test of fire makes fine steel. Let him have the courage to be patient. Let him have patience to be brave. Teach him to always have sublime faith in mankind.

This is a big order, but see what you can do. He is such a fine little fellow, my son.

-Abraham Lincoln

Education

Teaching-learning

The education in school and college is based on teaching, mediation of the teacher. Ancient Guru-Sisya relationship is more intimate and it is in question-answer mode, more questions from the student than the teacher. It is largely based on experience based teaching. The modern class-room instruction is deficient. Modern educators emphasise on learning. With the changes and development of technology, there are more opportunities to learn. It is beyond class-room. Some believe that the class-room will disappear. But the class-room has certain advantages if the methodology undergoes change towards more participative methods.

Three hundred years ago Alexander Pope wrote.

Men must be taught as if you taught them not;
And things proposed as things forgot;

Pope was advocating modesty in the teacher. Teacher instead of sharing of his or her knowledge may focus in collective learning in the class-room in which the teacher also becomes beneficiary.

Phases of learning

According to D. Kolb (1984) there are 4 phases of experiential learning: Concrete experience, Reflective observation, Abstract conceptualization and Active experimentation. I call them 4Es: Experience, Examination, Explanation, Experimentation.

Concrete experience does not automatically result in learning. One might keep repeating the same behaviour. It is said 20 years of experience is just one year experience multiplied by 20 unless it is followed by the second phase, reflective observation after or during concrete experience of an event or episode; one must reflect on it. Most people are mechanical, absent minded, and random in their day to day behaviour with the result there is no learning whatsoever.

But to retain in memory what has been learnt through Reflective Observation of Concrete Experience, one must be able to conceptualize abstractly. It is becoming aware of the principles extracted out of the experience so that the knowledge gained is transferred to several but, similar situations. Many people are unable to do this abstract conceptualization. The knowledge remains tacit. With the result he or she is unable to pass on this tacit knowledge to others.

Yet another phase, the fourth, is Active Experimentation in which one acts as a scientist. You are experimenting creating necessary and sufficient conditions to look for results. You learn both from successful experiments and the failures. This is superior to the first phase Concrete Experience. Some are practical using only the first two phases. Others who start from Abstract Conceptualization, theoretical inputs gained through explicit knowledge (Books and class-room instruction) and proceed with Active Experimentation with theories.

For balanced learning we need to summon all the 4 phases of experiential learning.

Kolb's Model – Four Phases of Learning from Experiences

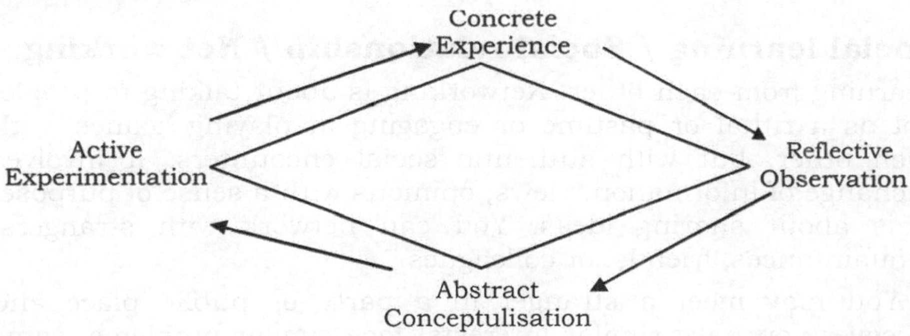

Looked from a different stand point, there are several MODES[2] of learning; *Media & Mediated, Observation, Direct experience, Experimentation, and social learning or socialization.* (Networking)

Reading books magazines etc. using computers and internet is media learning. One may do it all alone. He may become a loner developing individualistic or competitive orientation. Such a person is a misfit in a cooperative situation. Mediated learning is

---

[2] **MODES:** Media & Mediated; Observation; Direct experience, Experimentation, Social learning

a class-room learning when group learning or cooperative orientation is called for. As stated before some say the class-room may disappear or it will become too costly. Observation and imitation has been the principal mode of learning which we all used when young. It does continue when we have role-models whom we observe and imitate. When we do this involuntarily there is a danger of indiscriminate copying. We can extend this ability to observe by watching and viewing. Watching is observing with a specific intention. Viewing is more critical and evaluatory. Unfortunately for most people T.V. viewing is none of these. They are called passive viewers, simply bombarded with stimuli from outside. If you can become an active viewer you can learn a great deal. Active viewing involves watching the program with a specific objective in mind.

Direct experience and Experimentation are the two phases of Kolb's model referred to above. Together with media, mediated, observation and imitation` the 4 phases complete the balanced learning. Socialization, learning interacting with others brings out the great potential.

Social learning / Social relationship / Net working

Learning from each other. Networking is about talking to people, not as a ritual or pastime or engaging in playing 'games' with each other, but with authentic social encounters. It involves exchange of information, views, opinions with a sense of purpose. It is about sharing ideas. You can network with strangers, acquaintances, friends, or colleagues.

You may meet a stranger in a party or public place and discover you have similar interests, face similar problems, same anxieties, fears, doubts. Don't you mentally note or exchange visiting cards for future use? Next time you may ring up and talk to the person concerned. The exchanges increase. Now you have a member in the network of contacts. You may suggest his name to another friend who might need some information which you don't have.

The mystery of networking is not so much about information exchange or service trying to help each other but we are not quite sure how it helps in career planning and personality development. It helps in many unexpected ways not contemplated before hand.

These things happen but we don't recognize the chance happenings that lead to definite goal. I was searching for some information about our family history. I could not do it and left that part hanging and completed compilation. I met a stranger a year later on the train and soon we engaged ourselves in earnest conversation. I even explained my difficulty to him without expecting any help from him. He had the vital information which I had been looking for. He shared it with me. My joy knew no bounds. He did not understand why I was so excited.

Instead of leaving things to chance we can keep adding to our network of friends and acquaintances deliberately. It is an important mode of learning in our lifelong learning process.

You have already made your journey. If you are not like the seven fools then you must have known your motives, beliefs, and values.

Recall one of your childhood experiences which you remember and which episode keeps coming to your mind time and again. It might be a very pleasant one or a painful memory. Have you learnt anything from It.? Experience, they say, is the best teacher. It is, provided you learn from it. You may be one of those who do not learn from past mistakes. That is a weakness. You must recognize that and correct it.

Homi Bhabha's PIE

We have discussed about PIE[3] of personality. *Parental programming, Internal aspiration, and External factors.* Read the following legend.

'Homi Bhabha's parents sent him to study engineering in Cambridge University, UK. He could not say no to his parents even though he had burning desire to study physics-theoretical physics. In 1928 he wrote to his father about his lack of interest in engineering and passion for physics.

His father asked him to complete the course of engineering and promised to support him for further studies in physics. He

---

[3] **PIE:** Parental Programming; Internal aspiration; External factors.

completed engineering in 1932. Bhabha continued his research in physics in the UK. His first paper appeared in 1934 based on the theoretical explanation of shower production in Cosmic rays.

At the age of 31 he was elected a fellow of Royal Society, London (Recall M.Faraday's association in 18th century) where he enjoyed the company of physicists like Bohr and others who became Nobel Laureate.

Something happened in 1939 when he came back to India for vacation and could not return to London because of World War II. He then joined Indian Institute of Science, Bangalore and worked under Sir C.V. Raman.

Raman introduced Bhabha to the audience at the Nagpur Indian Academy meeting in 1941 thus:

> Bhabha is a great lover of music, a gifted artist, a brilliant engineer, and an outstanding scientist.. a modern equivalent of Leonardo da Vinci.

That he was a visionary can be gauged from his letter to the Tata Trust seeking support for setting up a centre for research work in nuclear science, in 1944 itself, which could play a crucial role in the development of nuclear energy.

The reader might recall and remember the controversy of 123 agreement with the US. It was in 1942 just two years before Bhabha wrote his letter that first nuclear reactor was built in the US and our country was still under the British Rule!

He converted his misfortune of not going back to UK because of World War II into an *opportunity* to promote education, scientific research, and human resources developments for the growth of the country. He combined both vision and action. The last stanza of Gita says where Krishna, the visionary and Arjuna, the mighty bowman (the man of action) are there, there is wealth, victory, stability.

Bhabha's closeness to Nehru provided synergy in the country. He never accepted mediocrity, never compromised on excellence... This legend died in 1965 in a plane crash. Had he lived for a few more years!? The scientific pursuit in India would have been different. He was a pursuit manager par excellence, a multi-faceted, multi-skilled personality.

The personality of Homi Bhabha was such an example that integrated in him the three aspects, the PIE. He respected his parent's wish which made him a mechanical engineer. He communicated his conflict to his parent politely but firmly without mincing words. The father responded with a condition to which the son relented even though his passion for research in pure science – physics was driving. Patient reconciliation and postponement of goals in the short run – the qualities helped him in serving the country. It was Nehru who became his patriarch in the matters of patriotism – concrete steps – programmes for the country's future self-reliance in the nuclear field. (Recall the concept, conceptual skills). The vision of Bhabha and the vision of Nehru resulted in many a concrete action.

Sir C.V.Raman's PIE

Parentage & Cultural Legacy

His father was a lecturer in Mrs. A.V.N. College of Visakhapatnam. Family is from orthodox South Indian family known for discipline and spiritualities and high moral values. No greed whatever; IQ is high, concerted cultivation, a prodigy; he published his first paper on his experiment at the age of 16.

Opportunity (External Factors)

He chose like all bright students F.C.S. He could have chosen I.C.S. but for his inhibition to going abroad. F.C.S. – financial civil service was more for livelihood – may be his parents' choice. But his passion was always science from childhood.

He lived in Kolkata near to the place where the Indian Association for Cultivation of Science was situated. He spent all his leisure time, 'which meant the evenings and very late into night conducting experiments in acoustics and optics in the Association' which had 'considerable space and laboratory facilities for the aspirants' like Raman to pursue.

Soft skills

His English language skills both in writing papers and giving lectures on latest researches were highly appreciated. His speeches were captivating.

His observation was powerful. 'During a voyage, he examined the color of the sea from the ship using simple equipment eliminating the sky light reflection.. blue of the sea persisted much richer than the blue sky.'

Values

In spite of laurels and awards he remained simple and humane man, similar to Michael Faraday. When he was awarded Bharat Ratna in 1954, he could not spare time to be present at the ceremony because he was finalizing thesis of one of his students!

That was the true Indian tradition and legacy – self-less service and humility and commitment.

Case of two Scientists

I know a couple of scientists, veterans into their 70s. Talking to them I got some interesting points to illustrate PIE–parental programming, internal aspirations, external factors.

Dr. Rao's interest was Telugu literature. His father felt there was little scope for growth for his son in it because of changing environment. Rao obliged his father by studying science and developed an interest in chemistry proving a point that interests change with exposure–you may have hands on experience before you determine your interests are fixed. New interests crop up at any stage of life.

Rao's aspirations rose high enough to yearn to learn under the supervision of Sri Venkatraman, Pune. Responding to his request Mr. Venkatraman directed Rao to the Indian Institute of Science, Bangalore, where he was to be made its Director.

Although Mr.Venkatraman did not become Director of the Institute Dr. Rao landed in it. He reconciled to chance happenings. To cut a long story short, Dr. Rao got his Ph.D, went abroad did post doctoral research, available in the West and finally returned home for two reasons: ailing father at home, love for one's own motherland. Father and Motherland had driven him back home. After giving his life for R&D in Private sector he retired and settled down in Hyderabad. As gradually R&D getting importance in the pharmaceutical companies, he had opportunity to pursue his interest. But alas he did not find the profit maximising corporations congenial for they do not want real R&D that a scientist desires.

To give concrete shape to his passion, chemistry, he began writing a book, his first attempt in his late 60s; It was an outstanding success in the international market, with the result the demand for his services gradually increased, boosting his monetary returns. His book project is on at the point of writing. He is planning to write his second book.

Or like in another case of pure science pursuit, you may land up as lecturer in a university not known for academic excellence. Yet you get an opportunity to go abroad and make a mark only to return home because of parental pressures. Earlier you shunned lucrative careers in a public sector giant, where your colleagues made a mark. Never mind they had their goals, he has his. There is an opportunity coming in the form of becoming vice-chancellor, you shun it because that is not your passion. Is it lack of aspiration or ambition or is it because your anchors are different. You are content with the regard you command in the profession as an outstanding teacher and man of values and ethics. You may like to call yourself as a *'solitary scientist'* which is true and accepted as true by the colleagues in the profession.

Tip of the Ice-Berg

Tip of the ice-berg is a phrase used to denote what we know or what we see is a small portion of the whole. Ice-berg is a mountain of ice, a great mass of ice broken off from a glacier and floating in the sea. From the distance the navigator of a ship can see only one tenth of the whole mass, ninetenth part of it lies underneath the water. So, what you know about yourself, your (TIP[4]) *talents, interests, and personality traits* is only a fraction of the whole. You have to look deep into yourself to know more and more of it, that too with a conscious effort.

There are many personality tests which you can take and learn something about yourself. That's diving beneath the surface a bit. But not enough. These tests are not intended to restrict your being. They are guidelines for further probe by reviewing your

[4] **TIP:** Talents; Interests; Personality

personal history so far. You can brainstorm with your friends and compare notes. Your parents and other family members who are, all the while sizing you up can help in identifying your personality traits. Above all, keep questioning yourself. The vital answers come from within. You need intra-personal skills to explore yourself.

You can sit at the table and unburden all about yourself on paper, without caring for grammer, articles, or punctuation. The idea of free writing is to generate ideas without restraint. You will be surprised at what you have written on the topic 'Who am I'. That which is hidden so far comes out. You can show the unedited written work to a trusted friend and ask him or her to give honest feedback. This will lead to questions that you had not asked yourself.

Read books on the subject using yourself as the subject. More of it in the section "tools for self-discovery". Coming back to the tests, based on John Holland's study I present six types of vocational personalities and their respective attributes.

Vocational personalities are not clearly demarcated. There are a combination of characteristics and degree of differences depending on your background, interests, education, life, experiences and so on.

The aptitude tests help you in obtaining information about your personality traits that can help you choose a career path. But use them only as guidelines, not a presentation for what you should do. They give ideas about discovering your unique personality.

These tests are not intended to restrict you from being your true self. You can examine by investigating yourself into what you truly are. Other means of doing this are reviewing your personal history, brainstorming with your friends, discussing with your parents or other members of the family and listing your strengths and weaknesses (improvements) based on your own observations. What you have to look for is your evolving, the ever-evolving picture of yourself like an artist who applies a stroke with the brush on the canvas which gives him the feedback, before attempting the next stroke. Gradually, the picture that emerges is more often a different one than what has been contemplated.

Gita tells that man cannot be inactive, he has to work, that is his nature. It exhorts man to perform work as yajna (selfless service). What he is asked to sacrifice is self interest and attachment to the results. Even Lord has taken upon himself the task of creation. Even if the ignorant work with attachment, let them work. It is through work that you realize who you are, what are your interests, talents and what truly is your personality.

Holland's study identified six different categories of personalities based on different interests. Remember the acronym CREAMS[5]: *Conventional, Realistic, Enterprising, Artistic, Meticulous, Social.* The *artistic* and *social* personalities overlap with many common traits. Similarly the *conventional* and the *realistic* personalities have a lot in common. But the *meticulous* and *enterprising* have few attributes in common.

CREAMS of personalities based on different interests

The Conventional an organized, dependable, efficient, conscientious

The Realistic are frank, practical, down-to-earth, and self-reliant

The Enterprising are ambitious, driving, energetic, competitive

The Artistic are expressive, imaginative, idealistic and original

The Meticulous or *investigative* are careful, independent, analytical, and precise

The Social are helpful, friendly, understanding, tactful.

There are many other attributes in each category not listed here.

Ask yourself what attributes fit you more than the other attributes. A combination is possible. The *Social, enterprising,* and *artistic* can be grouped together. Such people can become self employed entrepreneurs. There is a concept less known is *intrapreneurs* who are employed with companies who allow entrepreneurial qualities to flourish to reap organization goals /results.

---

[5] **CREAMS:** Conventional; Realistic; Enterprising; Artistic; Meticulous; Social.

CRISP talents

'Talent is 'latent'. In both words the alphabets are same. If you rearrange the alphabets in 'latent' you get talent. You need talent to make the latent, real.

Creativity is latent; as you use it, it grows. *Reasoning* ability may be native but it can be cultivated. *I.T. skills* is literally child's play. *Soft skills* are not as easy as hard skills to develop. Hard skills are easy to learn because there is no un-learning involved as in soft skills learning. It is because the behaviour is ingrained and to make it skillful, there is need for correction, un-learning. All learned behaviour is not skilled behaviour. *Professional* or hard skills, are the skills of the trade.

All skills have something common, they become habits–efficient economical and effective if learned systematically.

Interest CAMPS

Interest CAMPS[6] and career opportunities. Broadly there are a few interests that people develop early in life. They are *Commercial, Art, Music, Poetry and literature, Science and sports camps.*

For many music, art, poetry, and sports may not form career options but are merely hobbies. They may pursue them as parallel avocations or they become major interests with jobs merely for livelihood purpose. These hobbies if pursued in a professional manner, they earn enough to quit the 'pedestrian' jobs. It may happen sooner or later. There are a few, whose number is increasing, whose passion for these interests drive them to make them career options.

Even the commercial world makes use of their talents for ads and publicity. The corporate sector uses them and pays them fabulously to retain them as their brand embassadors. Business world is competing for them and are out to grab them. Many companies appoint sportsmen who rarely work for the company till they retire from the sport and use the soft skills they

---

[6] **CAMPS:** Commercial; Art; Music; Poetry; Science.

developed in the sport to progress in them. There are commercial artists, R & D scientists, in the corporate enterprises.

This takes place in a specified environment, happy, enjoying freedom and friendship with little or no responsibility for living. Parents and teachers devote their time and energy to help you in studies. The modes of learning are mainly confined to mediation and media learning although you have opportunity to learn observing others around you.

Career Anchors[7]

What type of managerial position do you aspire?

Rank the following in the order of your preference *Autonomy* (where you have freedom and discretion) *Novelty* (Creative work) *Challenge, Holistic Management, Offset Manager* (Balance between personal life & official life) *Rigour of Technical competence* (where you are technically competent) *Service / Stability*

ANCHORS

An anchor is a support or mainstay. To cast anchor means to become fixed, fixated, some what unchangeable. Each manager has his preferences. Form the list above find out. what are your anchors or life supports as a manager? If your preferences are as under,

Autonomy

You prefer self-control. Control of all the resources. You need to take responsibility for results, to harness and put to best use of all the resources, human, material, etc. you become accountable. You set your own goals, monitor them and achieve them. Otherwise you do not deserve autonomy. You will soon lose it.

Novelty

You are creative and want newness, novelty. Elsewhere I have defined with the help of acronym CREATIVE[8] – *Challenge status*

---

[7] **ANCHORS:** Autonomy; Novelty; Challenge; Holistic Management; Offset Manager; Rigour of Technical competence; Service or Stability.

[8] **CREATIVE:** Challenge status quo; Reconcile the opposites; Evaluate; Adopt the old; Tolerance for ambiguities; Intuitive; Validate; Energetic.

quo; reconcile the opposites; evaluate; adopt the old; tolerance for ambiguities; intuitive; validate; energetic. Each anchor compels you to carry with you the associated traits or you must team up with others who have them.

Challenge

You might have rated this in an earlier exercise: REJOICE – Those who rank *challenging work* high, are in trouble if they don't understand the meaning and significance of the word. It is used for disability, presented with difficulties, an invitation to compete. Once challenging goals are set, you have to strive and stretch to accomplish them. Both motivation and support from within and without are called for. You need both hard skills and soft skills combined to meet the challenges. A sure way towards personality development.

Holistic management

You need to be anchored with big picture. Overall supervision. You must develop helicopter view or birds-eye view without getting involved in the nitty gritty of the daily routine. You are truly General Manager in the middle. You can be blamed by the 'top' and challenged by the 'bottom'. You have to be firm without being rude. You have to be fair and firm.

Offset Manager

For these people work and career is not everything. They balance personal life with work life. They prefer a stable and steady job. It is a decision. You may not be able to compete with workaholics and colleagues who are upwardly mobile.

Rigour of technical competence

Your strength lies in technical competence and knowledge. Your domain knowledge is your strength. You will have referral power, you become problem-solver and trouble shooter in any technical matter. You do not compromise on the rigour and research. You keep updating in the knowledge escalating age. You can be an offset manager balancing your life's priorities.

Service to Society or Superordinate role

This seems to come naturally to some people. They enjoy serving larger sections of society; particularly weaker sections. With this your anchor you don't hanker after positions and power.

Through your anchors you can know your interests and your personality TRAITS – (*tendencies, reactions, aspirations, inclinations, thoughts, and sensations*).

What is important for you to note is your talents must aligns with your anchors. If they are not among your god given gifts, then you have to work hard to develop them. Only then you will succeed and your success will ensure your development. You will have opportunities to grow.

A Doctor's Journey (Self-Discovery)

There is an old English Movie, *Awakenings* which I had seen several times. It is based on the biography of a young doctor, who transformed a hospital in New York which was in a bad shape, into a vibrant one.

The doctor, having completed his studies applied for a research project in a hospital. He chose this project to make a career as a professional in the medical field, based on his 'self-assessment'. He concluded, on the basis of his experience in a research project, that his interests and talents lie there. He knew he had the right aptitude and attitude for research work where he thought he did not have to deal with people. He was a loner, with few friends; he spent most of his time studying books. He could work long hours, late into night; did not care for company.

Thus his talents, interests and personal traits pointed to the position of a researcher in medicine. He made this choice. The New York hospital called him for a face-to-face interview for which he was well prepared. In those days that was the only the means of getting a job. There were no agencies for jobs, nor were there campus interviews or career counseling on how to prepare for interviews.

But our doctor knew what he wanted and his experience of a research project and recognition and appreciation he got for the work done. Armed with relevant documents, he appeared before the panel. After he made self-disclosure with confidence projecting a favourable image of himself before the selectors, he waited for their response.

To his surprise the interviewers dropped a bomb-shell: “we have no research position in our hospital. We have no money for research. But we very much need a regular doctor to admit and attend to the patients who have been suffering from brain-disorders for years. Many of them are not even visited by friends and relatives for a long time.”

Disappointed, the applicant started leaving the conference room when the panelists stopped him, pleaded and persuaded him to accept their offer. He thought of the salary he needed most. What we call today compensation package and place of posting made him accept the offer albeit reluctantly.

Soon the doctor’s attitude to work and hard work earned him good name from the staff of the hospital, who had been indifferent to the patients and neglected the routine. There is no motivation or morale in the work place. Soon the doctor’s talent for investigation and analysis started paying dividends. His thoroughness and dedication and working late hours, pouring into the history files of patients, all earned him respect. Though his peers were jealous of the new man who was setting new, inconvenient standards of performance and commitment, which they lacked. Gradually they too gave up the skepticism and began following the discipline of the professional new entrant. Gradually people began listening to him. He became a leader because others followed him. Teams emerged in the hospital, targets set, projects undertaken, all for the good of the patients and the hospital’s reputation. What the doctor saw in himself and others saw in him have been different. He thought he was no good dealing with people. Others saw him a dedicated leader and achiever.

The film has many dramatic moments. There are many points for human relationship – inter-personal and intra–personal relationship, job search, self-assessment, interviews, preparation and so on, all that you find in books now a days. At that time such books were hard to come by. There were only biographies of great men.

This is a true story of yesteryears. Today's world and job market have undergone a sea-change. Today's youth have no life – planning. There is competition, pressure from parents and friends. Aspirations and expectations run ahead of capacities to fulfil their desires.

This doctor certainly enjoyed his work. He was not in a hurry to get rich. He took time to discover himself, his true talents, interests; he proved that inward looking people could become outgoing. What he probably never articulated for himself or for others his professional outlook, values or service to the society and such other laudable things. There is an inner urge to serve society at large that had been working with the man and his observed behaviour.

He is not a self-oriented, egoistic individual but truly other-directed. These are lasting values, the biography reveals.

We need to try our hands at many things before we discover the latent talents, interests, and realize our true potential.

Recalling CREAMS: *Conventional, Realistic, Enterprising, Artist, Meticulous, Social* he belongs to *realistic* and *meticulous* combination. He led the staff and peers from the front, by exemplary behaviour. Above all his values helped him lead the followers. As regards his ANCHORS: *Autonomy, Novelty, Challenge, Holistic management, Offset-manager, Rigour of Technical Competence, Service and Stability*, he was *autonomous*, self-directed, pure *challenge, rigueur of technical competence* were his anchors. Above all it was spirit of *service* unknown to self, probably that was key anchor to him.

He thought he had more hard skills the research rigour demanded but infact the research involves primary data collection which is 'talking and getting' data from the people. He had no difficulty in acquiring the necessary soft skills on the job.

Errand Boy to Earnest Student

Life of Michael Faraday. Source:- Children's Britannica

SIR HUMPHRY DAVY, the great chemist, was almost at the end of his days.... when he said, of his Chela "the greatest of all my discoveries was the discovery of Michael Faraday."... That was in 1829, Michael made his path-breaking discovery in 1831 regarding the principles of the electric motor and the dynamo.

Michael Faraday was born at Newington, Surrey, on September 22, 1791. His father, James Faraday, was a poor village blacksmith.... the young Michael experienced the hardships of poverty throughout his childhood. (Refer to the box on the description of blacksmith and his line of work). Michael's other achievements include the discovery of new organic compounds, including Benzene, he was the first to liquefy a "Permanent" gas.

A Note on Blacksmith

There is nothing romantic about the old village blacksmith; it *meant hard work, long hours, and skills.* Shoeing horses and sharpening of farmers tools and implements... burning and hammering and moulding iron into different shapes; it called for an understanding of horses, their strengths, weaknesses... It demanded patience, gentleness, firmness... rare skills... At times he is called upon to fix iron rings around cart wheels... an out-door work and teamwork and deft handling. Because of the comforting fire, his work place attract villagers – and becomes rendezvous, a favourite gathering place.

It was in such an environment that young Michael Faraday grew up till his 10th year. (A place and vocation demanding both hard skills and soft skills)

.... His education, he said years later, was of

"The most ordinary description, consisting of little more than the rudiments of reading, writing and arithmetic at a common day school....."

At the age of thirteen, Michael Faraday had to leave school and go out to earn his living in London. There he became an errand boy for a neighbouring book-seller, named Riebau. Faraday's job consisted mainly of carrying and delivering newspapers. In the words of Professor Tyndall, Faraday's friend and successor,

"He slid along the London pavements, a bright-eyed errand boy, with a load of brown curls upon his head and a packet of newspapers under his arm."

His trial year as an errand boy was so satisfactory that, in October, 1805, Faraday was apprenticed, without premium, by Riebau to learn the trade of bookbinder and stationer..... Riebau, who was a considerate master, allowed him occasional leisure to attend Shilling Lectures on natural philosophy. Faraday made friends at the lectures and learned quickly from the books and papers: his interests turned particularly to science and chemistry.... He grew from an errand boy to an earnest student of science! On these occasions he took copious notes from the lectures.

Faraday's own words

"During my apprenticeship I had the good fortune, through the kindness of Mr. Dance, who was a customer of my master's shop, and also a member of the Royal Institution; to hear four of the last lectures of Sir H. Davy in that locality. . . . The desire to be engaged in scientific occupation, even though of the lowest kind, induced me, whilst an apprentice, to write, in my ignorance of the world and simplicity of my mind, to Sir Joseph Banks, then President of the Royal Society. . . . (But there was no reply).

Faraday then sent the notes of Davy's lectures, which he had absorbed with interest and delight, to Sir Humphry himself, and asked to be allowed to quite trade, which he thought.... to devote himself to science.. .....Davy's servant handed Faraday a note, as a result of which he called next morning at the Royal Institution,... as a laboratory assistant... That was a turning point in the life of Michael Faraday!

In the autumn of 1813 Sir Humphry Davy and his wife went abroad, and Faraday accompanied them, partly as secretary and assistant, partly as valet. Davy, who was Faraday's life-long friend, treated his assistant with every consideration, but Lady Davy used him as a menial, and almost drove him to return home. ... He had to struggle to overcome the temptation to leave the master and mentor Davy.

Faraday was away two years with Davy. He kept an interesting journal of their tour. ... His affectionate letters to his mother at this period are typical of the man.... "a hale, elderly man, bearing the red ribbon, and very free in conversation." The physical scientist was a social scientist of modern age.

The travellers returned to London in 1815 and Faraday was re-engaged at the Royal Institution. He now settled down to a life of research and discovery:... his life was a time of steady intellectual growth, spent in chemical research,...

In 1823 Faraday was elected a Fellow of the Royal Society, and two years later was made director of the laboratory at the Royal Institution. In 1833 he was appointed Fullerian Professor of Chemistry in the Royal Institution for life, without the obligation to give lectures. (But he had to learn English composition to give lectures to repay in the same coin to the society).

In November, 1831, Faraday announced his epoch-making discovery to the Royal Society :

He showed that an electro-motive force is set up in a conducting wire when it is moved at right angles to a magnetic field. If the wire is part of a close circuit, its motion results in an "induced" current.

In 1841 Faraday had a breakdown in health.... At Interlaken, on August 2, 1841, he wrote: ... ('I love smith's shop and anything relating to smithery. My father was a smith.") His mind wandered back into his early childhood at the time of failing health. Poor health makes us nostalgic. Poor financial health too can make us long for home. Or some vague feeling of alienation makes one return home and find 'love in the native rock' like the shepherd in Virgil.

... when sitting for his bust to Noble, he was agitated when the sculptor made a clattering noise with his chisel. Noble apologized.... "No, my dear Mr.Noble,".... Faraday answered, "but the noise reminded me of my father's anvil and took me back to my boyhood."

Despite several honours, Faraday remained a simple and modest man; he never bothered about the money he might have made from his inventions, and several times refused offers of employment from manufactures. He declined a Knighthood.

.... His affection for his parents and for his wife was strong and lasting.... His intimate friend wrote about him:

> *"Nature, not education, made Faraday strong and refined. A favourite experiment of his own was representative of himself. He loved to show that water, in crystallizing, excluded all foreign ingredients, however intimately they might be mixed with it. Out of acids, alkalis, or saline solutions, the crystal came sweet and pure. By some such natural process in the formation of this man, beauty and nobleness coalesced, to the exclusion of everything vulgar and low."*

Like in water the vulgar and the low are mixed up in every one of us. We have to 'crystallize' to exclude all foreign ingredients

What were the MODES of learning and STAGES of development? Discuss in small groups and identify the soft skills; opportunity he sought; resources built and the will with which he grew, in Faraday.

Environment in which Faraday grew

We have already discussed the interaction of 3Es–endowment, environment and education. Let us apply the formula to Faraday's life.

Faraday's early life had been spent in a village in the home of a blacksmith. What were his innate psychological and learning mechanisms ? Obedience? Helpful? Interacting with people? Sociable? Yes, most probably yes. He picked up the, 3Rs–Reading, Arithmetic and Writing, the RAW material.

In those days in Britain ordinary people got the minimal education. Even in contemporary America that the case. We've the example of Abraham Lincoln who had one year schooling when he learned 3Rs. They struggled on their own, one became a great scientist, the other a great lawyer and President of the United States of America. In the case of Faraday the environment in Britain promoted science. Children like those of the village blacksmith dreamt of becoming scientists; was however, not the dream of the parents but that of the children. There came about a change in environment, which was to the good. Faraday's father moved to London, closer to the Royal Institute of Science. The young Faraday had another opportunity to become a book-binder of scientific books and consequently came in contact with the people of the Royal Institute.

Environment in India is changing for better now as can be seen from the newspaper reports

'We are witnessing a growing tendency among talented students to pursue studies in areas other than mathematics and basic sciences. To realize our vision of India as a knowledge society, it is essential to build a strong foundation in basic sciences by attracting a larger number of talented students to this stream. This foundation in science is needed to create the next generation of leaders and competent scientific talent and teachers.

..Sam Pitroda, Chairman, National Knowledge Commission (NKC).

There is a need to provide self-learning aids in local languages to attract rural students retaining technical and scientific terms in English. It will make it easier to migrate to English medium at higher levels.

This was not a problem for Faraday. Our students from vernacular background have additional problems.

'Special teaching aids need to be developed for tribal children and children from the rural background to attract them'……..

NKC adds, that

'Existing careers in sciences, namely teaching and research should be made more attractive by increasing the salaries of teachers and researchers. There is a myth that science bachelors are less employable than other graduates from other streams. This myth has to be dispelled by quality institutes. They should collaborate with professionals to pursue and create more opportunities. They must give publicity to career opportunities'…...

'Science popularization programmes should be launched throughout the country. A large chain of science talent cells should be created and each school should be funded to open a science club. Mobile labs in reaching the rural will be very effective'…..

'Industry must participate in promoting sciences at all levels as more and more companies will need employees qualified in basic sciences, for the research based industries are flourishing in India. They should sponsor students for Master's and Ph.D in sciences and also *internships of longer duration*… under graduates should be exposed to various applications of science in industry through seminars and lectures by industry leaders.

'Novel funding mechanisms by academicians and industry to explore other possible modes of industry participation'.

Close on the heels of NKC report comes Lead India 2020 programme report.

> 'The programme organized by the Lead India 2020 Foundation in Hyderabad on 15th Oct 2008, brought out the latent talent among school children from rural background studying in Government schools. They underwent a five day training programme; they expressed their views. The way they articulated their ideas showed the high degree of self-confidence in expressing their views on making India a global leader on the 77th birthday of APJ Kalam. The youngsters surprised everyone with their fluent speech and clarity of practical ideas to uplift the country.

It is interesting to read another news item in the very column:

> India is an English speaking country and there is no need to check English language proficiency among Indian students? [No TOFEL, GRE, GMAT, SAT score! The waiver comes from a US University!]

Values

Coming back to the Faraday story, he already developed social skills or soft-skills by meeting and talking to people both at village smithy and as errand or delivery boy in London.

What were his values, skills, and knowledge? He was not educated in values. Whichever values he might have developed were from home and working in London. They where inherited as well as acquired through observation of the people around. Keen observation, imitation, and social networking apart from experience have been his principal modes of learning. What did people say about him as a growing boy, assistant and a scientist.

Does the biography inspire you to discover your own values, and skills, the personality type, and find out your own modes of learning both innate and acquired.

A list of value words are given below. Identify the values Faraday might have cherished from the biographical sketch.

Also attempt to find out your own value system. You may check and confirm with your parents, family members, and some close friends

Adventurous	Ambitious	Brave
Calm	Cooperative	Committed
Decisive	Enthusiastic	Earnest
Honest	Humane	Independent
Industrious	Joyful	Kind
Loyal	Loving	Mature
Neat	Organized	Peaceful
Positive	Powerful	Prompt
Serious	Trustworthy	

A job where these personal values are required, if one gets it, then the person job integration takes place when the work produced is mutually satisfying to both the employer and the employee. You become employable and promotable. Your career choices should be a reflection of what you value in your life, not the other way round.

Values stem from beliefs, often unidentified but ever present. Values, what we believe in, give us a framework from which to make some of the most important decisions in our lives. The more strongly we hold on to a belief, the more motivated we are to make it a part of our lives.

Values Made Visible

If I want to value honesty/fair, then I must believe in it. All children are generally honest. They learn dis-honesty from parents, teachers, and other elders. At first they face conflict and are confused.

The little boy in the Havels ad who helped his mother with an improvised handle made of the company's cable to roast the rotis, has displayed a number of beliefs and values. He was reading a book–education is the value. Helping mother is another value. To be creative is next. Promptness, cooperation, loving, strong will all can be discerned in that one act. After helping mother he goes back to his book carrying on studies which shows adaptability, flexibility, calmness. A single act can point towards several values.

This young fellow is fit for many jobs, careers and vocations where these values are imperative. He needs hard skills, that is easy.

There is no dearth for Faradays in India

A poor coconut vendor's son becomes a nuclear scientist who participated in the CERN'S 'Big Bang' experiment, a replica of Faraday of 18th century in India.

> A graduate in Maths, Chemistry, and Physics from Sir CRR College in Eluru, a town in Andhra Pradesh, Master's in the University of Hyderabad and a Ph.D from IIT Kanpur launched himself into nuclear research at BARC, Mumbai.

He had his career under his control right through. He has this to say.

> 'I reached this stage by completing my studies with scholarships from different donor agencies as my family could not afford to provide me education.'

There is a need for creative brains to get into the field of science. He exhorts the students to shun rote learning. The student must have a strong foundation in the fundamentals.

For the students to follow his advise the time is ripe.

Tools for Self-discovery

Tool 1 – Reading (Read Appendix III)

Read books on the subject. You can buy them from the local book store. Do you have a habit of buying books? 'I can't afford'. You might say. They are available at the rate of cinema tickets for one, two, or three shows. It will cost you less than what you have to pay when you take friends to a restaurant. You need not sacrifice any of your pleasures; just allocate money and time for books.

To buy a book and read it you need to find two resources money and time. Time management, goal setting, allocating resources are elements of planning.

You can't afford to buy every book that's useful. You can visit a library at least once in a way. You may save money that way but you spend more hours. The hours spent on going to a library, searching, picking and reading have alternate uses. You have to fix your priorities. So, time management is managing minutes, hours, days, weeks, months and so on, your planning horizon changing from immediate, short-term to long-term.

All these are not independent: one goal merges in to other goals till you reach your mission, purpose itself. There is a proverb, '*take care of pence*; the *pounds will take care of themselves*'. Begin with immediate goals, short-term goals and the long-term goals will take care of themselves.

If you cultivate the reading habit by doing it with a purpose or whatever interests you, then you can pick and choose what you read.

What should a student pick? The biographies of great men. They tell you stories of men who rose from humble beginnings to great heights. You might have heard of their names, say, Abraham Lincoln, Ambedkar. Mahatma Gandhi's story should be read for his humility and never-say-die spirit, etc. Their lives give the reader great insights into the process of growth and development. These books are worth reading a second time or third time like you see good movies again and again once alone, another time with friends, yet another time with family members. Then you internalize some of the important events, incidents, values, hardships etc. You notice in the story some turning points, some key decisions, world events, many environmental factors that influenced the hero of the story. There may be key personalities who influenced them or some books they read had a bearing, or childhood events might have brought about a change in the thinking of these men.

Scan and skim, are two skills of reading efficiency. I have been quoting copiously from M.Gladwell's book. Let me share the process of my reading of it.

As I embarked on writing this book I have been reading the daily news paper with an intent to get the latest information–the titbits on the subject I discuss. I saw a book review on Malcolm Gladwell's 'Outliers'-about men and women who do things that are out of the ordinary. As usual I read the back cover, the blurb as a part of scanning, the first step. It is appended in the box for your ready reference.

Why do some people achieve so much more than others?

Can they lie so far outside the ordinary?

What is the secret of their success?

"In this provocative and inspiring book, Malcolm Gladwell examines everyone from business giants to scientific geniuses, sports stars to musicians, and reveals what they have in common. He looks behind the spectacular results, the myths and the legends to show what really explains exceptionally successful people.

Gladwell argues that, when we try to understand success, we normally start with the wrong question. We ask 'what is this person like?' when we should really be asking 'where are they from?' The real secret of success turns out to be surprisingly simple, and it hinges on a few crucial twists in people's life stories - on the culture they grow up in and the way they spend their time.

What does Bill Gates have in common with the Beatles? How does your IQ relate to your salary? What can a linguist tell us about airline safety? How does the way your child speaks to an adult affect his success in life? What do rice paddies have to do with maths results? And how can you predict a maths star without even making him take a test? Malcolm Cladwell has the answers.

This book really will change the way you think about your life. And it will challenge you to make the most of your own potential."

That is enough to make you curious enough to read the book, buy or borrow from a library. I bought it.

On turning the pages-skimming-I find the book is in story telling style drawing meaning from each story. It is divided into two parts–opportunity and legacy. They form endowment (legacy) and environment (opportunity).

Education is also an opportunity depending on the culture (legacy) 'they grew up in', the way they spend time (culture-endowment) fostered and nurtured by parents (endowment). My thoughts ran in this fashion. I read the book for facts, assumptions, and opinions of the author who acknowledges the people who inspired, and those who helped with critiques, from whom he learned what including parents, proving *networking* is imperative for any successful completion of a job on hand. It reinforces my stress on networking in the book.

Find time and money for learning from books. Some of the biographies have been made into movies. You can watch them and then read the book or quickly read the book and see the movie. They will have a profound influence on your thinking and behaviour. We hero–worship the actors. We should learn to admire the characters.

Tool 2 - Writing

Write; put your thoughts on paper freely. Writing is thinking on paper. You can write about an experience. Putting down your experiences on paper has many future benefits. One topic on which you can write is 'Who am I?' What do I want? What are my talents, interests, and what are my personality traits? Francis Bacon wrote, 'Writing makes an exact man'. Writing and revising and editing are skills that make you employable in many jobs. Any way you are required to write your resume. If you have practised writing all through, then resume writing will post no problem.

One of the reasons why you are not able to put on paper your ideas is lack of language proficiency, lack of vocabulary, lack of exposure to good writing. Cultivating reading and writing habits will, to a large extent, mitigate the problems. Interest is either in-born or acquired. It is acquired with exposure to good books, well written books. Writing is picked up gradually. It required patient practice and concentration and is matter of time management. Time management is life management. You must get your priorities right. Cultivate the habit of setting goals and carrying them out.

There are obstacles for every effort we put in. You must overcome the obstacles. It is your value system that is affecting you here. You must be able to say 'no' to disturbances. Once you plan something with a goal you must be determined to ward off diversions. That's management.

Tool 3 - Seminars

Attend classes and discourses on self-development, self-improvement. Attend training programmes. Again time and money are involved. Attend seminars, conferences in your college or outside. They are opportunities to learn. Whether it is in class or outside, go to conference with a pad and pencil to note salient points. The aim is to enhance your knowledge or gain new knowledge, the presentation techniques, logic, reasoning, the paper presentation etc. Look at the speaker, content, language, and his skills in presentation.

Never attend them without the purpose of learning in mind, learning about yourself and the world outside. Invariably share with some one else about what you have learned from the discourse. The tendency for most people is to appreciate the speaker and his knowledge and leave the learning part. The emphasis should be on self discovery, what are your values and notions and action plan on the basis of the learning.

Tool 4 - Observation

You can observe people and their nature. You must learn to become a keen observer. When you go to the beach and look at the ocean, what do you see? Have you tried to see the ocean as a whole, as an indivisible whole? Then shift to the waves. Waves are separate from the vast sea. Are they? If you are a student of science do you use your knowledge of science? Poets use metaphors. They may liken the ocean with universal consciousness and treat a wave as an individual identity and start reflecting on the metaphor while people around in the beach, children playing in the sand and some others observing the tides and waves hitting the shore wetting their feet... and enjoying. They are right in their own way and wonder at you watching alone lost in your own world. Your personality and preference are different from others on the beach.

There is yet another deeper student, who sees them that there is no ultimate separation of wave from the ocean. He has spiritual orientation, lost in deeper thought. He may go further. He turns around and notices waves breaking on rocks and spraying droplets of water into the air, which are separated for a fleeting movement and merges into the ocean. The tide that hits the shore sometimes leaves a small pool of water on the beach. The pool is reclaimed by the next bigger tide. From fleeting momentary separate existence the pool has longer separate existence before it returns to the source.

Extending the metaphor to vapourization, formation of clouds and rain takes more time to return to the original source. He may write a beautiful poem on the whole process which may be sold to any one for money. What is important is that you have imaginative skills, skills in poetic representation. You can nourish your talents. Every artist has the power of observation and translating it into a piece of art, music or poetry. If there is an artist in you, he needs to be brought out.

Sri Aurobindo wrote

> 'It is not necessary that every man should be an artist. It is necessary that every man should have his artistic faculty developed, his taste trained, his sense of beauty and insight into form and colour and that which is expressed in form and colour, made *habitually* active, correct, and sensitive'.

The talent and interest must be made *habitually active, correct and sensitive.*

Many poets may be introverts and would not share their thoughts before the poem is out. If the idea is shared with another like-minded person he will probably ask, how about snow-flakes. Ice is also water. Both of them reflect to extend the metaphor to suggest highly structured, highly individualistic egoist; he needs sophisticated knowledge about water to recognize that snowflake is the ocean and ocean is the snowflake. Like the individual snowflake gives up its structure and individuality, the human individual has to destroy his ego.

The foregoing is an adaptation from Fritjof Capra's writing. Capra was a nuclear scientist with a holistic vision. He brings science and religion closer. You can observe the behaviour of others learn to imitate or avoid aping.

There are certain behaviours which will make you less effective. Observing them in your self and in others is a good way to learn. Observation, the power of observation is part of human endowment and as children, we used it. As we grow, we seem to become less and less observant.

Tool 5 - Direct Experience

Learning by doing. All people have likes and dislikes, some tasks we like and others we don't. Are you aware of your dislikes and likes? If you ask the question why? For most the answer is 'I don't know, why? You have to probe and understand. If you ask others you'll most probably get wrong answers.

The best way is to have hands on experience and see whether the work is interesting or not; whether you are able to use your talents or not or whether it gives you joy or not. Or you find the work simply boring. Therefore you must volunteer to do whatever comes your way, simply, to test it.

A friend of mine used to sell Parry's sweets during summer vacation for pocket money. He was able to earn good commission; that encouraged him to do more often. After completing Intermediate he had to go to his elder brother's place, Bombay. His brother was working in Glaxo Pharmaceutical company. My friend discontinued studies and opted for a salesman's job on a regular basis. After some experience his brother got him a job as a Medical Representative in a multinational company in which he became eventually top executive and retired. The company, in recognition of his past service gave him distribution rights for their products in Andhra Pradesh. He never bothered to change his career or seek further education. Thanks to the summer occupation, he could decide and pursue the career of his choice and was successful. This is the advantage of experiential learning to discover what interests you and what talents and personality traits you have.

In another case in this volume there is a case of one who disliked selling and changed his career. He had to lose precious number of years in the process.

If you are not sure of your orientation, you may experiment to test your aptitude, that is what it is called. Aptitude implies a natural inclination for a particular work with probability of success. Or you can take aptitude tests to find out your inclinations.

Tool 6 - Net working

Social networking can help you learn about yourself. You can discuss each other's interests, talents, and inclinations. In small groups of three or four persons you can share keeping aside your inhibitions and fears. The feedback you receive and what you give to each other increases your insights into talents and interests.

The disagreements from others on what you claim stem from their observations and their past experience with you. On the other hand they may give positive feedback on your merits which you did not recognize. Like the doctor in the movie '*Awakenings*' story you might have thought that you are no good at dealing with people. What the doctor realized only after working with people in the story, he could have got from feedback from others. Unfortunately he did not have friends. Socializing and social networking can help in quicker self-discovery provided you are open to feedback, sensitive to others and ready to make self-disclosure.

Through all these means you are not only learning about self but also developing social skills or soft skills.

Build your network

Almost all are agreed that you need to have *moral, information, tangible,* and *emotional* (MITE[9]) support from the environment. Supportive environment is universal requirement for any viable system, including all human beings. Network is the modern name given to the supportive human environment. For some it is parents, enlisted senior and influential figures who can champion their case. Having friends, family and colleagues who are prepared to listen are also important, particularly if they are the kind of people who believe in you.

Self-directed Behavioural Change

There is sufficient evidence to show that an individual can modify his behaviour without the help of change agents from outside in many cases. This can be accomplished through awareness,

---

[9] **MITE:** Moral; Information; Tangible; Emotional.

attention, intention and commitment. There is bias for action in commitment.

No professional help is needed except in rare cases. In fact, what the therapist does is to facilitate self-inquiry. Among the innate mechanisms and psychological mechanisms, hereditary endowments, problem-solving and creativity are present. The individual can use these in-born faculties for self-directed change. We have seen learning mechanism is an in-born talent in every one.

The change in behaviour is to correct the direction and speed of our journey towards our goals. The goal is realizing our potential. If we want to grow or progress, we must set goals, develop resources, look for opportunities. With will or determination, we must first identify obstacles to our growth and development, the forces that prevent change. That is where 'will' plays a part.

If man is taught to understand psychological laws which govern his behaviour, his capacity for self-directed change enhances. The individual often is found to blame the environment for his current behaviour and hence sees obstacles to his growth.

There is an ABC theory of behavior A-antecedents, B-behaviour, C-consequences. The consequences become antecedents and the vicious circle continues. If I some how change my behaviour with awareness and appreciation of psychological concepts like motivation, the role of environment, education etc. then I can overcome the hurdles. That is where will or positive thinking plays a part. The vicious circle becomes virtuous one.

The antecedents of Michael Faraday were not at all favourable. But he was determined to become a scientist. As man becomes self-determined, even the environment could be bent to his will. He took up whatever job that came along with intense desire for scientific occupation at the back of his mind.

Inter-Personal Skills

To interact with others is a human need – want. Discussing motivation and need hierarchy we said that social, esteem needs, and need for self-actualization are higher order needs.

To satisfy our social and psychological needs we interact with others. We have seen we need to reinforce positively or negatively. When we say 'hello' to some one known to you; you feel bad if the other person does not respond. But if the man responds with 'hello' and moves on you feel ok. But if you are both not in a hurry you may both stop and exchange niceties. That gives greater satisfaction. You may not have deep relationship with the other person but both are satisfied with the interaction. Inter-personal relationship can become skillful. Several authorities studied the inter-personal skills. Most of them come from West. There was one study made in India which is more useful for us. From the study of large number of interactions, Prof. Udai Pareekh identified 12 dimensions or 12 kinds of interpersonal needs.

Given below are 12 statements. How true these statements are in your case?

1. I join groups when I get an opportunity. (Inclusion expressed)
2. I like to be made a member of committees (Inclusion wanted)
3. I try to develop personal relations with others (Affection expressed)
4. I like people to be close to me (Affection wanted)
5. I tend to help people to resolve their conflicts (Extension expressed)
6. I like people to empathise with me (try to feel as I do) (Extension wanted)
7. I appreciate other people's accomplishments (Recognition expressed)
8. I like people to appreciate my work (Recognition wanted)
9. I tend to dominate the group I work with (Control expressed)
10. I dislike taking independent decisions (Control wanted)
11. I try to maintain my reputation in a group (Influence expressed)
12. I enjoy trying out something after reading about it. (Influence wanted)

If you are able to identify the statements that apply to you, then you can practise studying other peoples' orientation. That will help in interactions.

Let us look at each of the 12 statements. The first statement denotes, if it is true in your case, *inclusion expressed* (1). Second denotes *inclusion wanted* (2). You may want inclusion but when an opportunity comes to join you may hesitate. Your expression is not forthcoming. You are an introvert. In which case you may not express affection (3). *Affection Expressed* will be also low. Reading from your behaviour others may not come close to you which you really want. *Affection wanted* (4) you become loner and suffer from lack of intimate relationships.

Next two statements (5) (6) are *Extension Expressed* and *Extension wanted.* You don't extend a helping hand but expect people to care for you. Empathy is a beautiful word in the English language which psychologists brought into the vocabulary–dictionary. It means experiencing the feelings of the other. You 'step into the other's shoes'. You place yourself in the position of the others and experience objectively. It increases the understanding of the other. If a person wants to help others, he must first fully step into the other's world and understand the help he or she needs. There are times you express extension to some one who does not want any help from you. Inter-personal skill lies where you are able to size the other before you offer help.

7 & 8 is about *recognition expressed* and *recognition wanted.* You want other people to appreciate your achievements but you forget to appreciate the accomplishments of others. One way. It should be always two-way.

Next two (9) & (10) is about control. You may like to control others. *Control expressed* but would not like to be controlled. *Control (not) wanted.* Or the other way round.

The last two statements (11) (12) relate to *influence expressed* and *wanted*. I influence people and also get influenced by others.

Vocational Personalities (Creams) and Opportunities and Soft Skills Mix

All services–civil services through banking, insurance, audit and other public services domain have undergone metamorphosis. In a democratic set up where government of the people, for the people, and by the people is the norm, there is growing recognition that soft skills coupled with meta-values or societal values are a must. They help all the six types of vocational personalities to make successful careers.

Though the above mentioned services attracted the *conventional*, the *realistic*, and the *meticulous* (investigative) types of vocational personalities in the past, with governments' stress on 'inclusiveness' of all sections of society's participation, the other three types, the *social*, the *enterprising*, and the artistic types are also attracted. Some of them whose aim and motivation was *just and stable income* and *retirement benefits* and *enjoying enough leisure* also could make successful careers because of a particular set of soft skills–excellent relations, going out and meeting people. They were the ones who were even going out of the way to reach out to people. For them people alone mattered. Their decisions and problem solving revolved round people's problems not the rules. Their interpersonal skills and empathy helped them in helping people.

Recalling the 12 dimensions of IPR orientation, wanting and expressed diads, extention expressed is predominant in them. They play superordinate or *expanded role* (Refer to the book *Personal and Emotional Competence* for detailed discussion), also superordinate role.

It is this orientation, practiced throughout their careers and developed as autonomous selves, that comes in goodstead in the later life and they are remembered long after their retirement, leaving a legacy. They become legends in their own spheres of activity.

Pattabhi's Case

As one whose score is high on most of the dimensions.. 3,4,6,7,8, his nature more than communication skills helped him develop business.

At school level Pattabhi, an adept in making friends, followed Polononius advice, 'the friends thou hast, and their adoption tried, grapple'd them...' But the friends he had were not bright in studies, but smart in sports. He developed camaraderie that sportsmen develop and control, competence, both in hard and soft skills, they develop. There are sportsmen who even excelled in their studies, a rare combination, which Pattabhi lacked. He took up the first job that came along a railway clerk in a large cement manufacturing company. The job involved booking wagons for dispatching stocks. It demands interpersonal skills to deal with the railway officials at the lower level. The company had their yard allotted by the railways. Pattabhi's work involved less of paperwork more of relations. He had to handle cash which he was losing because of some bad elements found in these jobs. He was made to quit the job by his father and take up a job of open loan representative–OLR-in a bank.

Here is an example of student poor academically, joined as an 'open loan representative' of a bank. OLR as the position is called is representative of a bank, not in the musters of the organization, whose salary is recovered from the credit client of the bank. OLR supervised the movement of goods, security to bank, and reports the stock position to the bank periodically to enable the bank to arrive at the drawing power of the client. He got the job with the help of his father. He not only got the job but he inherited his father's personality traits which earned a good name both with the bank and the bank's clients. Earlier his job as a 'Railway Clerk' of a cement factory where he worked as a go between the company and railways set forth his typical career journey.

It is in these two jobs that his talents, interests, and personalities surfaced. Being not a studious or academic in his approach he would not recognize them in himself. It was more mechanical than reflective experience. Had he knew his strengths, he would have made a resume pitching his post and made a career choice better. But soon the bank appointed him as a cashier and took him into permanent service. He invoked his father's name, who was no more, to secure the permanent job to just eke out a livelihood. The cashiers job is far from his cup of tea, while working as a cashier, he was losing money. He neither had the talent, traits, or liking for the job. But it gave him an *opportunity*. With his helping nature and soft skills—interpersonal skills—he was interacting with the customers at the counter, particularly senior and influential citizens among customers.

He began delivering the pass books and deposit receipts in their homes. It served two purposes. Contacts for future business of the bank and own personal satisfaction. These contacts made by a lowly employee gave the bank huge business in the form deposit mobilization.

Recognizing the talent, the managers relieved him from the duties of cashier and made him customers relations man; no such post ever existed in banks in those days, not even now.

Yet the man could not make any progress in his career because he was "not qualified" in the academic sense. If after 15 years of seniority he was at last made a junior officer and transferred to a place, an industrial hub. He retired a contended man. Long after his retirement people in service recall his qualities and not the absence of qualification.

Some Concepts from Scriptures

(The Indian Culture)

Before I conclude the chapter 'Unique Path', let me draw some poignant ideas from our own tradition.

Gita exhorts man not to live 'Yantrarudhasya' - mounted on a machine, living a mechanical, absent minded routine devoid of goals and purpose. Instead it appeals to man to live 'Yogarudhasya', mounted on yoga. The term yoga means the union of the body and mind. Life should be mind-centred, instead of mechanical, the presence of mind is paramount. Elsewhere in GITA there is a comment *'Yoga is skill in action'*; 'perform work with yoga'. Perform skilfully with mind steadfast in yoga.

In Chandogya Upanisad there is a beautiful verse :

Yadeva Vidyaya Karoti
Sraddhaya, upanisada,
Tadeva Viryavattaram bhavati-

Whatever is done with Vidya
Sraddha, and upanisad, that
Alone becomes supremely efficient (Excellencee)

Vidya (competence), *Shraddha,* (commitment) and *upanisada,* (calm contemplation) are the three elements of excellence in work (3 Cs- Competence, Commitments and Contemplation)

As already discussed, *Shraddha* ordinarily means faith, faith in one self and faith in the work contemplated, and faith in supernatural power. Upanisad literally means 'sitting close to destroy ignorance'. Sitting close to the Guru or in a group. It is intimate effort to destroy ignorance. Before starting any work there must be clear goal and understanding of the process and consensus among the team-mates.

How would you acquire Vidya, Shraddha, and upanisada in the modern context ?

Through education and culture.

Progressive self culture-A better alternative to Soft Skills-Development

The phrase was coined by Sri Aurobindo. Man attains the highest through systematic progressive self culture.

The meaning of the word, as given by the Webster's Dictionary will make it clearer.

'It has many meanings (1) The cultivation of soil (a preparation for larger thing, harvesting a crop); (2) Raising, improving, or development of some plant, animal, or product (humans not excluded); (3) The growth of bacteria or other micro organisms in a specially prepared nourishing substance, as agar. (Applied to human beings makes profound sense); (4) Improvements, refinement or development by study (including self-study); training etc; (6) The training and refining of mind, emotions, manners, tasks, etc (all personality characteristics); (7) The result of this; refinement of thought, emotion, manners, tasks, etc. (8) the concepts, habits, skills, etc instruments, institutions etc of a given people in a given period; civilization.'

When I looked up this elaborate explanation in the dictionary I felt thrilled at the meaning of the word. The thrill was due to my learning of a number of things. 'Progressive self-culture'... Each word is meaningful and significant and relevant to our subject matter. Personality development takes place progressively. It does not happen overnight without effort. Self is in control.

Gita says lift your self by your own self. Self is your friend and foe. You can lift yourself or harm yourself. Means: Culture, *Refine, Improve, Develop, Empower.* Have a RIDE[10]!

KAIZEN[11] is a Japanese word meaning a change for the better. It has become a popular management jargon, representing continuous improvement with small changes involving everyone. I have made its an acronym:

Keep Always Improving with Zeal, Enthusiasm and *No Respite.*

That is what the tortoise did in the famous story, 'Slow and Steady Wins The Race'. The hare's attention was on the competitor, had no strategy, got tired and lost the race. For tortoise it was not a race in the first place. If it were so it would not have participated because it was a race between two unequals. It took it as a journey towards a destination. It moved at *its own pace,* in the right direction, without respite unmindful of the other and accomplished its goal.

Our progressive self-culture has all these dimensions – destination, direction and determination. That's what Kaizen, change for better is significant for. We have our own word in our culture: *Sankranti* – A good revolution / change. There should always be a *Sankranti* in our lives.

The whole *Gita* of 700 verses is about self-knowledge. The learner *Arjuna* begins with many doubts. He never hesitated to seek clarifications. Ask questions and get answers. *Gita* can guide you in your journey into the deeper self. (Chapters 14/18 of Gita)

Nature has made us into three aspects of personality, *Triguna.* All the three are binding us. *Tamasic,* the passivity, *Rajasic,* the active and the dynamic, and finally the balanced *Satvic* nature.

---

[10] **RIDE:** Refine; Improve; Develop; Empower.

[11] **KAIZEN:** Keep; Always; Improving with; Zeal; Enthusiasm; No Respite.

There is nature with capital 'N' and the nature in us with small 'n'. Small 'n' has come from the larger 'N'. When you are indolent, lazy and negligent it is *tamasic* nature which is dominant. *Gita* says *know* this. You can't do anything about it. At that level/plane that is what it is.

When you are dynamic, passionate, and action-oriented, then it is Rajasic nature dominating your self. *Know* this too. Be aware and beware.

When you are happy and fulfilled, know this is *Sattvic* nature that is ruling you. The difference between *Sattvic* and the *Tamasic* both of which appear similar, know former is with full knowledge and the other is with ignorance. One is wise and the other is a fool. One is wisdom and the other foolishness. *Tamasic* nature is characterized by lack of effort and delusion. Rajasic nature gradually leads to greed, ceaseless activity, restlessness and self-centred, egoistic.

The growth and development of economy, politics, power, corruption, dishonesty and all the excesses are the result of Rajasic nature, primarily, in the world. You must temper the *Rajasic* nature with morals, values, and ethics. 'Thus far, no further' principle is the moral value that should be brought in here. Drinking alcohol serves as an example. When you begin taking the drink, the pleasure is noticed. This is positive feed back which is escalatory. As you drink more, a little more, till the negative signals start coming when your vision blurs. Things get out of control. For success in life and career you need *Rajasic* nature. When it exceeds the limit, you need to have checks and balances. To control the *Rajasic* you need the help from the *Satvic,* not the *tamasic*. You should not go into passive and inactive state and pray. You need to act to control the situation.

The seeker of happiness, the *satvic* and the dynamic nature of the *rajasic* must work together to restore order in both personal life and in the community. Action orientation of the *Rajasic* must be enhanced by the conscious choice and curb the greed and avarice of the *rajasic* nature.

Gita's ultimate message is to transcend all the three *gunas* which are binding us.

> 'Without steady pursuit of self-knowledge man tries to actualize pseudoself, false self, leading to reversal of values.'
>
> ***Lvimay***

Another psychologist Koren Horney classified that the real self as

> 'That central force, common to all human beings and yet unique in each, which is the deep source of growth. The way towards this goal is an increasing awareness and understanding ourselves.'
>
> 'Self knowledge then, is not an aim in itself but a means of liberating the forces of spontaneous growth'. 'The work at ourselves is both a moral privilege and moral obligation.'

In the 18th chapter we come across verses 36, 37, 38 which are worth reflecting.

> "Hear from Me now about the three kinds of pleasures, O the greatest of the Bharata clan! That pleasure is said to be of the nature of *Sattva* which is gained by long practice of disciplines, which puts an end to all sorrows that man is heir to, which is like poison in the beginning but nectar-like at the end, and which springs from the serenity arising from the consciousness of the Atman.
>
> That pleasure is declared to be of the nature of *Rajas*, which is born of the union of the senses with their objects, which appears nectar-like in the beginning but turns out to be poison in the end.
>
> That pleasure is of the nature of Tamas, which springs from sleepiness, sloth and heedlessness, and which is delusive in its effect on the spirit from beginning to end.

These profound truths are worth reflecting upon in times of the current financial crises–greed leading to depression both in the psychological and economic sense.

Vibhuti Yoga

> 'The message of the Gita is the Gospel of Divinity in man, who by force of an increasing union *unfolds himself* out of the veil of the lower nature, reveals to the human soul his cosmic spirit, reveals himself in man and in all beings'.

.... Is our liberation from the limited ego and our elevation to the higher nature of a divine humanity...

Arjuna or the modern man needs the knowledge given through the Vibhuti-yoga to grasp the full meaning of life of action.

'He who knows in truth the splendour and action of Mine, is united with me by unfaltering yoga'... (7/10).

'What so ever... universe' (41 & 42/10)*

'O Arjuna! I am the self, abiding in the hearts of all beings.....'

'I am the splendour of the splendit' 'I am goodness in good'.

It means wherever there is splendour and vigour in action there is Divinity. You can take it as by grace of God or the God in you shining and excelling – you embrace God Head.

In other words you align yourself with the God's design (Nature – endowment – latent talents etc) then you will realize, your potential. The striving man makes most of his potential, by the grace of God. A striving man is never denied the grace of the Divine for the divinity is in his nature in the form of seed. That is the equal opportunity, a birth right.

'There is a relation between grace and human initiative' when you initiate action upon inner promptings then you are aligning yourself with the benign design – God's or Nature's. I have narrated Gestalt Experience elsewhere. It is about peak experience when God is with you. One scholar talking about 'Vibhuti Yoga' used the metaphor of waves and ocean. Waves are the individual *atma* and ocean as *paramatma.* Waves are not separate from the ocean. When waves rise to become high tides, you have the individual excelling, experiencing and displaying Vibhuti yoga by the grace of the ocean, not other wise. The brilliant and the best – the outliers – must acknowledge this with humility. This is where Western culture as it is imbibed by some of the successful people have failed. They think their success was entirely because of their own effort.

There is a movie titled, 'Bucket List' about two terminally ill cancer patients preperating the 'things to do' list before they kick the bucket. I discuss the story in greater detail in the chapter 'Leaving Legacy'.

---

* 'Whatsoever there is, endowed with splendor, grace and vigour, know that to have, sprung from fragment of my splendour'...

Section - II

Wherefore you Know Where

1

CHOICE OF CAREER

Many believe that life must be allowed to run its course 'like water to flow, towards a goal'. Like DSM's case (16) By Gods grace. DSM believed all that happened to him was due to divine intervention. Others who were equally successful might attribute it to sheer luck. Yet others think that they were at the right time at right place with right backing. As Gladwell stressed that great people were great because of legacy and opportunities from outside the individual outliers.

Learning, earning, and yearning

Given the philosophical discourse let us examine the reality–here and now. There is a pattern after the striving stage in the young-adult's life. Learning and earning. All education is aimed at earning. Opportunity means earning opportunity. Careers are for earning. Learning on the career is also aimed at for more earning. This pattern is part of parental programming.

Internally there is secret longing and sacred yearning to realize the potential. Sooner or later the individual comes out of shackles of parental programming and asserts internal aspirations. Then external factors, the influencing factors exert themselves in the form of chance happenings.

Learning yearning earning – pattern – parents choice.

All learning is for earning a livelihood.

So goes a Telugu proverb. Aspirations rising in the society, many an illiterate mother dreams of her son becoming–District

Collector or a high official in the Government. First generation graduates are growing day by day. Their aspirations are not mere earning a livelihood. This is how environment and education, two wings of the bird are lifting the body, the endowment.

Wings to fly like Jonathan Livingston Seagull. Yearning for position, prestige, and power and in many cases power and influence to pay back to the poor, the society in which they grew.

Although 'realizing the full potential' 'lifting the body' (endowment), is not set as a goal, it is a 'secret mission', secret even to himself or herself. It is like a 'growing crystal'. Steadfast patience is called for. You cannot hurry the process.

Entry into the world of work

At the end of striving stage–formal student life – and having appreciated the concepts of positive thinking, goal setting, etc and understanding your uniqueness some what, now open the gateway to the world of work...

Now–a–days the university education offers practicals, projects, opportunities for extracurricular activities. There are avenues or opportunities to test the waters of latent talents and develop interests that suit your inherited–endowment–gifts, legacies. These are spaces where soft skills, particularly team playing and leadership, interpersonal skills can be developed.

As I write this I came across an article titled 'Pride in Prejudice' by Vijay Nagaswami. Absence of dysfunctional pride and deep rooted prejudices can be reckoned as soft skill. He writes:

> Many of our prejudices will have roots in our adolescent and young–adult years when our personal experiences started becoming more substantial.

He also stated:

Some of our prejudices may only be based on what our parents taught us from the way they lived their lives.

These absorbed prejudices can be got rid of because we spend our lives more in spaces other than parental environment.

The extracurricular activities in mini societies in NSS, Scouts, with friends, and strangers in team activities, can help us get rid of unwelcome prejudices which colour our thinking and forming of opinions in a democratic life.

The writer asks the question:

Do we hang on to them, do we let them go or do we wear them on the sleeve with pride?

He answers:

Frankly I have found that letting them go is the most mentally healthy option. Also this gives us an opportunity to experience a greater sense of inner peace... Happily, it is possible to stop doing so (deriving pride in our prejudices) in the interest of our personal growth and development.

Exposure to extra-curricular activities and developing healthy 'prejudices' or 'predilections' in the young–adult life should be part of striving stage.

Here is what a young–adult narrates:

My Tryst with Service

(Extra-Curricular Activity)

I am an Engineering student studying in 3rd year. I was in 1st year when President of Rotary Club of the city and a very close acquaintance had come over to my college to discuss the setting up of a Rotaract club in our college (Rotaract is the youth wing of Rotary). Since I was the only one he knew, it was inevitable that I had to be a part of the club. Before I start off with the Rotaract chapter let me tell you a little about myself.

That I always been oriented towards service is wrong to say, but at heart whenever I saw an underprivileged, a downtrodden or just about anybody who was in trouble there would be an urge within me to help. But I didn't have an avenue to channelise those feelings, they just stayed within me. I made donations to orphanages and such other establishments from my pocket money on birthdays and other such occasions. I didn't do much apart from giving donations. Service activities at college were however, different. With Rotaract I was part of those activities, providing food at an old age home, conducting a blood donation camp in college, conducting games for the deaf and dumb were some of the activities we had undertaken through Rotaract and a lot of planning and co-ordination between members was necessary for this. I got my first feeling of how a board functions. Weekly meetings and activity once a month, giving farewell parties or just meeting like minded people was what anybody wants.

And thus Rotaract turned out to be a new experience for me; people called me for old–age home and orphanages. They associated me with service! About a year later two graduates from my college approached me for help on similar lines. They had ideas and were looking for ways to implement them. Mr. Patnaik and Patro, one is a mechanical engineer with the distinction of being known as the topper who is presently pursuing an MS in the UK and wants to some day build cars. The other worked for Satyam for a couple of months, quit and came back to prepare for his MBA entrance exam. He works with 'TIME' simultaneously.

They and their group of about 7-6 members wanted to give back something to the city they grew up in which had taught them so much. And so came about Young Guns of India (YGOI). We are an NGO registered as Generation Jagruthi who are in the process of making Brand India. Through YGOI we visit a government school for boys every Sunday to instill an urge to study in them and discuss other worldy matters. We've started a career-employment module that aims at 9th, 10th, 11th, 12th, classes and bachelors 1st, 2nd years. We'd like to give them an insight into all the various careers available to them at their level.

This way new avenues and opportunities came knocking at my door. They've been enriching experiences and I did what I enjoy doing! Today it has influenced my career and I get to guide my juniors with similar interests in such activities.

A Student

Internship (Titbit)

Four young women from the West headed for Kancheepuram town in TamilNadu for their management internship programme. They were volunteers working on the projects with NGO(HIH) Hand in Hand in Kancheepuram.

What made them opt for such a project far away from home? *Novelty* (A NC H ORS) It is also *Challenge*; the anchors are combined. One of them said,

'I work for a consultant in Sweden which did some development projects for UN; my interest and curiosity in micro-finance led me here.

Curiosity is the characteristic of *investigator* or *meticulous* type of personality (CREA(M)S). Out of TIP the I & P are in place. What about Talent? Internship will bring them out.

> The second, a student at Stanford University had a different reason for opting for the internship travelling around the world and exploring the area of developmental work. She is *enterprising* and adventurous by nature. She worked with an industrial management firm for four years before starting a school. She strongly believes in field work which helps her in her later life.

It is again curiosity and positivity. (CRE (AM) S).

For yet another woman, it was her sheer desire to set up her own microfinance company, and the fourth woman was inspired by an ex-CEO of ABB.

For three women it was inner urge or motivation from within and it was external motivation, inspiration given by a mentor for the fourth. She was fortunate that an eminent person was in her network.

> During the first week of the four week internship, the students underwent a training programme on micro-finance to familiarize themselves with concepts and nuances of working in India.

After the training one of them said, 'all our preconceived notions about micro-finance have been turned upside down.' Such is the value of class-room training before taking up a project.

What a beginning for field work!

> Two students with American accents, the other two with Swedish accents and interpreters with Tamil accent, it was a terrible experience—a veritable Babel of tongues!. Soon things began to settle down, they shared.
>
> The programme opened a new world for all of them. They learnt that most people out there are self-driven and have an amazing entrepreneurial zest in them.

Birds of the same feather flock together. One girl particularly, said, that 'development happens through empowerment and not through dependence'. That's what their brief experience taught them.

Practical experience with the knowledge of abstract concepts provide them new insights. They see things in a particular light as if they are wearing a new pair of glasses. Mere class-room instruction without project work does not give insights.

They left the place after the programme with a firm belief that micro-finance actually works.

How many MBA students undertake project work or internship for insight to internalize the abstract ideas into concrete experience? When field work is taken up with zeal, it becomes easy to write the resumes and impress interviewers? The resumes become meaningful.

Let us turn to internship with a difference- an extended internship next.

Parents' Choice (Titbit)

'Free exemption scheme fills engineering seats- BC, minority parents use the opportunity to the hilt'

So run the headlines.

It is a good subject for group discussion for MBA students.

> 'Except senior government employees, majority of them managed to get income certificate to avail fee exemptions.'....Nearly 70 percent of open category seats are cornered by BC candidates.

How many will complete the course?

How many of these students will remain on the campus and face campus interview and obtain lucrative and attractive jobs? Is financing the main criterion for entry into engineering.

Some are bound to drop out because of hard work and rigorous discipline that engineering requires. Some may drop out for sheer lack of interest and aptitude.

'Politicians hold JNTU to Ransom' (Titbit)

- It is mandatory for every student to have 75% attendance.
- Of late, peoples representatives, MLAs and MPs, calling up officials to grant required attendance for their candidates... warned of dharnas if it is not done.. the representatives are themselves under pressure..
- 'The officials attribute this absenteeism to non-serious students joining engineering courses given the ample availability. It is these students who seek help from their student unions and politicians of the respective parties.'
- 'If the attendance issue is not viewed seriously it will encourage, even the good candidates to bunk'

There are black sheep in every walk of life creating hurdles to genuine students and even career makers later in life.

I asked a mechanical engineer, whose case history is included in this book about engineering study in REC with 5 years duration. He has this to say:

> 'The Regional Engineering college where I did my BSc Engineering Mechanical was a five year degree course. Mechanical engineering is a very vast subject. Some subjects which are optional in some engineering colleges are taught as compulsory subject at REC, Rourkela. Subjects such as Automobile engineering, refrigeration and air conditioning were compulsory subjects in 6th /7th semester. We were the last batch of the 5-year course.
>
> Ragging used to be dreaded but integral part of our baptism into the professional course. Ragging was very brutal, vulgar and rough. Many students ran away to their houses and had to be convinced to come back to resume studies. So much so that they climbed down the water pipe from the window of their 3rd floor of their hostels and ran through a cemetry which was behind the first year hostel, climbed a hill to take a short cut to the railway station and travelled without ticket to reach their homes.
>
> Those who survived ragging had to survive the food, weather (extremes from 4 to 50 degrees). The college has a plaque in the building which reads "the highest temperature recorded ever was 51 degrees in the year 1971". Generally students who come from the cosy confines of the family are generally very pampered. The induction into professional life is very harsh by way ragging particularly in the Eastern sector.

All this prepares the student for mental toughness for the factory or field jobs. Those days the branches taught were mechanical, electrical, metallurgical, civil and chemical, only very few of the students ended up with cosy jobs like those with call centers, control rooms, etc.

Practical Experience

As a part of our curriculum we had to undergo two months training, (after third and fourth year) one month each in any industry and come up with a report and give a presentation on certain aspect of the training. Also since the REC was located in a steel city the course was planned in such a way that we had frequent visits to steel plant from 3rd year onwards and also to mines, cement factory, etc which prepared us for the jobs ahead.

We had good interaction with the IIT at Kharagpur as many senior professors used to come for viva voce to our college from 4th year onwards The professors of the college were very senior people. Our principal was a Ph.D from Massachusetts Institute of Technology. We were generally thorough in metallurgy and his class used to be very well attended. He was a very highly respected professor.

The college ragging* helped me to withstand the rigours of field job, the indiscipline, union problems, general disorder as most our work is in remote open fields, the work goes on round the clock and the temptation to leave and run away is always there.

> Do the parents who rushed to put their wards in the engineering stream know all this? Are the entrants to engineering college aware of this ?
>
> Definitely a few, very few, might weather all the hardship and come out with flying colours and do justice to their careers and serve society. They may even take up the cause of uplifting the downtrodden by providing career counseling. Others will, whither, or while away. A set back to personality development early in life.

* Ragging is banned in India for good reasons. There must be other avenues than ragging to develop toughness in young adults.

'It's temporary phenomenon' (Titbit)

- Here is another News item from Education plus a supplement designed exclusively to the students and job seekers, an excellent search engine for career and jobs.

> 'The financial crisis, however, is bound to change things in the IT industry. Greater focus will be on quality,' say senior IT professionals.

A valuable information vital for those who make career choices.

Bloom is over. Gloom sets in

> Uncertain times, retrenchment and recession. The campus recruitment glooming.

What does this scenario mean to a student aspiring for a career in the IT industry?....

> In the long run.. it is very positive… customers of IT expect more which means, employees must perform better.
>
> The recruitment norms will become more stringent… those who can make a difference, those who come out with innovative solutions developed at low cost….. provide the customer more value.

Does the present education system produce creative people with innovation, experience while they are on the campus?

'When the ship is sinking, there is no place for rats.' The companies will weed out the rodents – the inefficient. It is not enough you get a job of your choice. You have to hold onto it.

Weeding is a two pronged process. The inefficient are weeded out while the efficient, effective, productive and innovative are retained. We talked of *Trying* and *striving* stages of development. Learning on the job during the former stage and keep learning both on the job and preparing for the newly emerging technologies. Sharpening skills on a continuous basis for improving the current performance are imperative. The seminars found that there is general *apathy* or *inability* to learn and update knowledge and upgrade skills. They lament the new crop of employees are not proactive; they do not take interest in their growth. These expressions will tell what type of people employer are looking for. A valuable information for preparation for tests and interviews. You can list the type of questions the interviewers ask for and probe to make sure that they are not wasting time and money by recruiting the wrong ones.

Small is beautiful

Here is a gem of an advice.

'Not getting a job in a big company is definitely not the end of the road. You can join a smaller firm. But make sure the company has enough revenue to sustain down turn'.

This is what our IIT–IIM did before he took up organic farming. (Refer to the case No. 10 of K.P.S....). He served a small software firm, as if he was the owner for nine long years taking up a variety of responsibilities gaining confidence to start on his own which is not a software enterprise!

Small is beautiful. 'In a small firm you get a lot of freedom. If you do well to inspire the proprietor with confidence in you, you can bargain for higher salary which is not easy in a company with a bureaucratic outlook. If you are passionate enough to win over the superiors, customers, vendors, employees and there will be synergy in learning. To work with passion you have got to ensure that your choice of career coincides with the area of your interest. Talents, interests, personality, anchors all become one. Winning over people who matter with performance is a mixture of hard and soft skills.

Influencing Factors (Lamb and Robert Clive case)

Books, particularly, biographies, can influence our thinking and goal setting in life. We have seen the life of Michael Faraday and his journey to realize his ambition. We have drawn a few lessons about modes of learning, stages of development, help from social environment and so on. He could anchor a career in the Royal Institute where he found the 'wall' to lean his scientific career 'ladder'.

But in the same 18th century we have two examples, one is that of Charles Lamb and the other is Robert Clive.

'Clive was despair of his teachers for he used to go on perilous adventures instead of attending to books.' But he became a statesman! 'At 18 he joined East India Company and went to Madras (now Chennai) as a clerk where he hoped to make his fortune'. The goal of all adventures is to make a fortune. That was then as it is now. Ambitious risk takers gamble with their lives as it happened in the case of Robert Clive. 'The French attacked the British and captured Madras; Clive escaped'. 'The resilient Clive became a soldier – a clerk transformed into a fighter. He discovered and so the British that he has a talent, may be gift, or 'genius for organizing for fighting.'

'Eventually he became a statesman who founded the British Empire in India'. Poor fellow 'had to defend himself in Parliament, against the charges of corruption'. He 'pleaded that he was being treated more like sheep-stealer than a founder of an empire'.

His life ended in tragedy–'he took his own life.'

Clive's ignoble end is a pointer to the greedy. We witness this now in the globalized world.

Charles Lamb worked as an accountant for his living in the East India Company in the city of London, whereas, at 18 Robert Clive went to India as clerk became founder of British Empire.

'When he was 21 a terrible tragedy struck Charles Lamb but for which he would not have worked in the East India Company.'

He had to take care of his sister, Mary, all her life, as she was a mental patient. He had to earn enough to look after his sister by 'writing books for children, the best being *Tales from Shakespeare.*'

'He wrote busily in spare time and became known for his poems and essays. He had many friends, many of them famous literary men. He was a *good talker* and also *very good at getting other people to talk*'.

These qualities epitomise the communicative competence-conversations. 'Any one who reads his delightful essays to-day comes away with the feeling of actually coming face to face with the author!'

SEARCHING FOR A JOB

Goal Setting–Getting Started

You are ready with your portfolio of talents, interests and personality perceptions to enter the arena, vast...

Regardless of whether or not you have a specific or general idea of career interest-CREAMS, ANCHORS, TIPS, CRISP, etc- you need to begin to set some goals and make a plan to carry them out. The path or the map is before you. Career success means you must be serious about securing a series of job successes and eliminating an 'I need some job and can think of career later' attitude.

Venkat in the case No. 3, 'passion impels...' wanted a career in the cinema industry as a photographer. But he accepted laboratory assistant's post for an opening. Sai after engineering, joined a tool room. The three months internship was memorable experience which he remembers for a long time.

Even if you want to eliminate the attitude of getting into any job, it becomes imperative because of the pressures for earning in middle-class families. Another, joined a multi-national company as salesman which was not to his liking just because of the attraction of salary and commission. But the period cannot be considered a waste of time. He did learn some transferable skills which he could transfer on to other jobs in banking career: Customer orientation and interpersonal skills and personal qualities like punctuality and hard work and regular timely visits to the customers. Much later in the banking career some of the abilities came to be used in the banking career, though late joining in the bank had made rising in the hierarchy difficult.

There are many ex-service men who join corporate world after retirement with special reservation. Their experience in military is thus not wasted. A captain who joins the bank at lower level may go up faster upwards by sheer performance and excellence. However, he may not have the same scope as the one who joins early as a probationary officer.

Goal setting, thus, is not a one-time affair. At each change in career you have to reset the goals, short or medium. The captain comes with transferable skills kit, and add some new set of skills which a Bank Manager needs. Quick learning helps in quick adjustment and excellence in the job.

His goals include developing new skills. The best way is to set small, manageable goals that can be achieved. Learning is cumulative and the speed of learning increases in rapid strides. Venkat learned laboratory skills and grasped in no time what went wrong on the shooting sets of the cinematic world. By watching the 'rushes' and sitting with sound recording, editing, and other functions, he developed a holistic picture of cinematography. His dreams became clear.

SCAN THE ENVIRONMENT

Job Search and Research

Scan the environment for career choice and industry choice. Don't limit your search to companies that put an ad in the paper, or referred by your college placement office, or in the recruiter's data base, or of those who are interested in you. You are making the choice for which you need more information before you short list as the companies do in the case of applicants to jobs.

You need to collect information about the company from the published data or through networking. Always keep your eyes and ears open to data from primary (people) sources.

Now that you have a fair idea about yourself and what you want to do in life, apart from earning a livelihood. After all 'what one wants is not wealth, but just enough to work unhampered and to be free, frank and independent'. You must lead 'a good life and also a life that is good' I have given an acronym SUCCESSFUL for defining success. Set forth, Unique, Career choice, Controlled, Enterprising enjoyable and ethical. Steer, Swerve, Fringe working, Utility, Leave a legacy. Selfishness is part of our nature, but it is not the best of our nature. It can be subordinated to a nobler ideal. The nobler ideal is realization of our true potential. Careers are the means to that end. Keep serving the society and leave a legacy.

Seminars, Fairs, Expos etc

Now go out and look out. Newspaper, the print media, has supplements and special features. They report events that go on a regular basis. Here is a heading that must interest young people who want to take up medicine for a professional career.

Live workshop at MNJ hospital. (A live workshop show-casing techniques to take up complicated cancer surgeries related to stomach, thyroid, oesophagus, breast and rectum was organized by MNJ Cancer hospital on Sunday)

Such workshops, if attended by you, stimulates your interest or enhance already existing interest in Medicine. You start dreaming to become a great surgeon and you can decide it for a career. There are many who have such dreams but fail to make it for want of preparation at entrance exam level or subsequent stages. You may have interest, dream, or passion without the diligence and hard work. There are several steps to attain your wish. You must convert your dream into a mission, vision, long term goals, broken into smaller goals each collapsing into the next.

Scan your newspaper regularly for vital information. You must appreciate the power of information. It is said information is that which changes us. You must scan with a particular mind set viz. for career decisions. From seminars, job fairs, and career expos information gathered becomes your resource. You must allocate time and money for such occasions. You may have umpteen excuses for not attending to them, but remember you are the loser. All planning involves setting goals and allocating resources *including time,* making sure your path is working for you. Some times we get starry-eyed about what we believe will be our perfect career without *exploring* whether the day-to-day work involved in that career will be interesting to us...We may choose a banking career and join a bank as a clerk or godown keeper or counter clerk or cashier. Each job involves different day-to-day activities. It may be that our strengths do not match the job you are asked to do. Some people study further and join as a probationary officer whose job requirements match with their interests and talents. You may have to investigate through reading or networking or job descriptions in the ads.

Don't sell yourself short. The job descriptions given in the ads specify matching skills, knowledge and attitudes called for. You demonstrate that you have them first in the resume and later in the interview. So read ads carefully and between the lines.

I have come across news article in a vernacular paper on 'Temping' organizations. They give press notes, ads, and conduct job fairs to promote their services. They are called Temping groups because of the work they do. They provide workers to the needy companies from out of their pool purely on *temporary basis.* It is a new service providing picking up in India. Students, home-makers, retired persons, etc can register themselves with temping companies. If those registered need any training the Temping company will arrange to upgrade their skills, training in Computers, English language, etc in whatever areas the job seekers want improvement.

Although they are sent as temporary workers the companies hiring them may absorb them on a permanent basis.

The virtue of practical or hands-on experience is such that the candidate is putting to the test his latent talents. This is a discovery channel for a beginner. One can find what work interests and what does not interest one. It serves as apprenticeship or internship. You may do well, but it may not interest you; or you may find something more interesting a little later.

> 'At present banking, insurance, finance, agriculture, retail and manufacturing companies are availing themselves of the facility from temping companies mostly for lower level jobs. FMCG (Fast Moving Consumer Goods) , IT, Health care, Pharmaceuticals, Automobile and Aviation companies are among them.'

> A few hirers ask for team leaders, project managers, marketing officers etc-the next higher level employees.

Companies which cannot afford full-fledged HR departments or who do not want such departments as a matter of policy prefer using temping companies. The temping companies in turn seek help of trainers to train their registered candidates. There is outsourcing for each of the HR functions. As mentioned before,

'Material enters the factory and comes out up graded; but men go into it and come out down graded and corrupted'.

Temping companies solve this problem by upgrading human resources before they are sent to companies by reorienting the new entrants into corporate world. Elsewhere I discussed trying stage-the painful adjustment period after joining the workforce. The arrangements mitigates the age old problem/paradox.

Temporary staff is nothing new. Banks and others large scale organizations were taking employees as temporary workers. The temporary workers are exploited by the managers as well as the existing permanent employees. They were made to work long hours and take up left over work.

Many good things are happening. You must be aware of them. Be informed and vigilant.

There is another news item that is relevant to you. It's called 'employability' fair by TMI. It is similar to temping in its work except that it is not for temporary posts. The similarity is for the kind of service they are doing for bridging the gap between employers and employees or job seekers. The venue was Institute of Public Enterprises which runs a PG Diploma in Business Management, signifying that the institutes and colleges show interest in such fairs to attract students and to serve them beyond syllabi.

In these job fairs some candidates are selected for employment and others rejected because they are not 'employable'. The novelty of this fair was that the organizers enroll the rejected candidates into a course where a job is guaranteed after completion of the course or give information about *employability coaching programmes.* Moreover the rejected candidates are put through *seminars* which will train them in:

- Preparing effective resume
- Preparing them for interviews

Seminars, job fairs, career expos, etc. are sources of information more than opportunities to make an entry into the job world or career choice. Before you make a decision to choose a career and a job, you need to do research. That's what everyone who is in the field of career counseling tells you. You attend any seminar, conference, fairs, or expose, they are all meant to help you in your research.

'The new age recruitment in the private sector is a different affair', different from public sector and government where the recruitment takes painfully long drawn process. Half a century ago, majority of job seekers were looking for stable and permanent employment and the government happened to be the biggest employer. Even the large organizations in the private sector many of which eventually became public sector thanks to nationalization of vital industries, the story is same.

The difference in to-day's private sector is that there are more jobs created in the I.T and I.Tes and related sectors. The private sector employer is on the look out for good workers. They are hunting for job-hunters. The hirers go out to meet prospective employees. Instead of the candidates, it is the companies which are rushing to job fairs where the 'buyers' and 'sellers' of jobs meet and exchange information. To-day's candidate for jobs can be choosy.

Imagine your application for a job results in a interview on a particular date. The anxiety, anticipation, and preparation is enormous. Your success or failure to get selected has enormous effect on your confidence. But you go to fair with no such anxiety. Any failure is not devastating. If it is not in one booth you go to another booth. If you don't succeed, you have more *information* about jobs, skills, opportunities etc, for your research purpose. Going to a job fair is fun where lot of information sharing goes on between candidates, candidates and company executives. You become sensitized to the environment not only as of now but you get a peep into the future.

Fairs are fair enough

The Director, Institute for Electronic Governance who conducted a fair on 17th Nov, 2008 at the PG College, Secunderabad where in top MNCs in I.Tes, Media, Retail, Sales and Marketing, Logistics, Services, and Education participated. The report said that fresh graduates from science and arts streams would be recruited. Some of the top participants were Satyam BPO, Wipro BPO, Southerland, Sitel, 24/7 customer, Tata Business support, TMI Networks and scores of others. All these data was available through daily news papers, a vital primary source, so to say, the supplement of views, and opinions. They contain what the candidate should do before the fair, during, and after the fair. Fairs are fair enough training grounds.

You can search and research for more companies all at one place. You can find what kind of companies and what type of jobs, interest you. It depends on your soft skills how the job fair will turn out to be. You can put questions to company representative to know more about of what type of talents, soft skills included, interests and personality traits they are looking, for what positions you are interested in? etc.

Apart from information gathering, the fresh candidates can go through the 'preparation exercise' for resume writing and facing interview. We have dealt with the topic of resume preparation elsewhere. You need to make several trials in building up an ideal resumes—different resumes for different jobs. The preparation exercise includes dressing and address etc to make the best impressions. There is lot of fun; you go with your friends and enjoy asking questions to companies, putting them at the receiving end. You have time to bother about immediate appointment.

With the experience of job fair you lose some of the stage fear you encounter in the formal interviews conducted where you are most of the time at the receiving end with lot of anxiety. In a fair you can face the interview with confidence. You do all the homework that you are required to do to attend a formal interview as if it is one such interview. To complete the exercise you can do some follow up work and experience contacting the company on your chances. Experts agree that *follow up* is an important part of attending job fair. If you have picked up a business card of the company representative, send a 'thank you' letter by which you are not just being polite but showing your earnestness and seriousness about the job. You say you are the right person for the company and hence hopeful of selection. Your communication skills in verbal and written, the most vital soft skills, you display once again.

College placement cells

Needless to say that every student must make best use of this support system. They also arrange seminars, guest lectures, fairs etc to give opportunities to expose the students to information, campus interviews, summer placements. These are well known activities and opportunities.

Ads and Ad columns in news papers

Companies advertise for jobs with job description. These are mandatory and sometimes obligatory or a formality. The jobs are already filled! Let the candidate accept them as genuine. Before we come to job description part and what the candidate should look for, ad columns are useful for a different reason. The job descriptions throw light into jobs and their description you have not thought of.

May be you have relevant skills and responsibilities which you can handle; a creative way of self-assessment and seeking job opportunities. Know this that your career explorations are limited only by your imagination and time. There are advertisement features in newspapers and business magazines which give you more information than meets the eye. In fact the avowed purpose of advertisement is to inform the consumers of products/services and the totality of all the features. It is upto the consumer of the information, to use the information, that which changes us, enables us to take decisions on career and job choices. Check for in-house publications of corporations who may have monthly newsletters.

For reviewing the publicity material the underlying assumption is that you are good at reading–rapid, reflective, and receptive reading. Reading habit is not merely a hobby as most people make out to be, but it is necessary condition for survival in the world where knowledge is escalating continuously. Knowledge is information assimilated.

What do you make out of this news? How does it impact you?

Recruitment drive for BPO

The Institute of Electronic Governance has conducted a recruitment drive for Wipro BPO from 9 a.m on October 30 at the Rishi UBR Degree College in Kukatpally. An orientation on career opportunities with Wipro BPO was also to be held at the same venue. Graduate, under-graduates and post-graduates were eligible. Candidates working with domestic BPOs can also attend. Interested candidates had to carry a copy of their resume, one passport size photograph, photocopies of identity proof, address proof and their academic and professional certificates.

Net and Networking

Be your own job/career hunter online

- Log on to know the latest
- Feel free to write to us. Also feel free to share with your networking friends.

"When was the last time you knew of a great opportunity–only too late?" asks Nitin Rao, founder of the portal, *Let Me Know* (www.LetMeKnow.in).

A number of students in Indian universities miss out on opportunities simply because they never hear of them. Organizers of events or even recruiters, in turn, miss the opportunity to reach a broader talent pool. *Let Me Know* seeks to share information with the Indian youth and overcome gaps in information.

Rao's tips for getting the best out of the site are simple. "Keep a close track of updates on opportunities of your interest through our personalized alerts. Use our advanced search to drill down to what you are looking for. And if there's something specific you are still looking for, *feel free to write to our team.*"

Strategies for Success in Job Hunting

- Do a good job in the pre-interview activities to insure a successful interview.
- Interview with a variety of organizations. Don't focus all your attention on the top companies. Remember, the largest growth in the job market will be with small to medium size companies.
- Prepare for any and all contingencies. This means that you should consider all possibilities. Don't reject an employer or a position because you think you know something about the industry/job. Talk to the employer. Explore the opportunity. Remember, you are under no obligation to accept an offer if one comes your way.
- Look throughout the region, and to the extent possible, look at opportunities across the country. Flexibility will be key to any successful job search.
- Interview with any and all organizations, using all resources available to you. Take on-campus interviews, develop your own leads, follow up newspaper ads and develop your own network.
- Most importantly, keep at it!

Job Hunting Online

- The first step to a good hunt, as you might be aware, is to make a nice, easy to read, but compact resume of yours.
- Then log in (create a user-id & Password) on Job sites like www.naukri.com, www.monsterindia.com, www.firstnaukri.com, etc.
- Make sure that you make your profile, on these websites. It is quite easy to do, as the website itself will guide you in this process. Do not go for the default options like selecting the text in the help menu, or in choosing a font. Especially important is the heading that appears after your name in the jobseekers' list.
- Do not forget to attach your resume', as a part of your profile.
- Apart from your mobile No. give one landline no. as an alternative. This will help the company wanting to talk to you get a message across, in case you are out of calling area, or your mobile is switched off for some reason or other. And inform the person/s, who normally takes the call on the landline, about the possibility of the call from companies.
- While selecting the job categories, tick all those, which you feel that you would like to be a part of.
- There is an option for salary range; it is better to select the lowest ones. Better still, if there is an option of being flexible on the salary front, select the same. You can discuss this, once you go for the Interview.
- As far as the geographical locations of your job posting is concerned, select a reasonable one like for example, South India, or cities like Hyderabad, Chennai, Bangalore, Pune, Vishakhapatnam, etc. Don't restrict yourself to the city of your stay or of your origin.
- It is important to visit these sites, at least on alternate days, and do a minor modification to your profile, so that the Search engine will always throw your Name and Summary on page 1, if anybody's search criteria matches your profile.
    - ❖ Once, this is done; as you are a fresher looking for a first job; you need to visit these sites on a daily basis.

- ❖ Do an intelligent job search; from the postings put in by the companies. Even if the company mentions at least one year experience, you can still apply for the same. Maybe, you can highlight the project work you have done, as an experience.
- ❖ Collect the e-mail id of the company, and after clicking on the SUBMIT button; make sure you send a personal e-mail from your e-mail id. In this, make sure that you mention "Your job posting on ------- site for ---------- position" in the subject line of your message. Also, never send a blank message, with just your resume' attached. It will be treated as junk mail. So, take a few minutes to type out a few lines stating the purpose of the message and that you are eagerly looking forward to meeting them, at the earliest.
- ❖ At least 5 or 6 such e-mails everyday will increase the probability of your success in getting that elusive interview call.

- Apart from these job websites, many major recruitment consultancies have their own websites, where you can fill in your profile. Follow the same suggestions as above.
- Also, make a list of target companies that you would like to work for. Then visit their company websites and click on a link "Careers" or "Jobs", and then send your profile to them. Take a chance. You never know, do you?

'Online search is cheaper/inexpensive for the array of information. It can be done 24/7. Your college library offers free access to the internet. "Many companies, professional bodies, colleges, and government agencies have pages where you can find news about job opportunities, upcoming events, useful documents to obtain and so on.' The more you learn about the internet, the more useful it is to you.

You need computer skills for collection of information cheaply and easily. Every search, investigation is based on curiosity, patience, creativity, and computer, reading skills. You are skillful when you enjoy doing a thing

A word of caution, you may get addicted to it and strain yourself. It has become cause of many ailments. Time management principles apply-when to start when to stop.

Here is a news item that must interest freshers.

> Exclusive job site for freshers' www.access2campus.com launched by International school of information technology. Hirers seeking freshers find it difficult to get fresher through job sites. To help them this website is launched. It is exclusive website dedicated to freshers and students. However, students preferring to upload their resumes have to pay for the service. This gives favourable deal for freshers', the school chairman says. The HR teams cannot directly use the resumes free of cost.
>
> The companies can ask the website for candidates that suit their job requirements. The school does the job for companies. The resumes have to be certified by the principals of their colleges.
>
> The data is removed after one year. The web site has a quite a few salient features such as video resume, applying for the jobs on behalf of candidates, informing events, and arranging interviews with the companies among others.

The job seekers get so much of news/information and services from print and electronic media. You reap the benefits if you can cultivate the habit of browsing and searching. Keep it in mind always information means that there is a change in you, your understanding that will enable you to take right decisions.

SCAN demands a variety of soft skills. Recall what Michael Faraday did when he attended the four shilling lectures of Sir Humphry. 'He took copious notes from the lectures'.

Listening and taking notes shows commitment to learning; *taking notes* and *listening* is one process.

Changing Horizon of the World of Work

Most people prefer now to opt for permanent jobs even though sizeable number of people in some industries like IT, are changing jobs.

A few generations before people looked aged at 55 and were glad to retire. They had pension to fall back and their children look after them. With the average life span increasing, we notice that many people are living up 90 and beyond, thanks to the medical progress. Aged parents have become a reason for many generation career conscious people for not opting for transfer from the place of posting. Some defied this difficulty and left the parents to take care of themselves. Recently Indian Government passed a bill making it obligatory for children to take care of their aged parents. There is also a trend for most people to seek re-employment after retirement, competing for jobs with younger people.

In cities spending more time on transport with less time with their parents and children – with more spouses getting employment for extra income and some of them making a career of them, normal family life gets disturbed. There is more stress on all family members. Yet another change is the life styles are changing for better. Luxuries become necessities. Borrowing for buying house, articles, clothes etc. More and more people are turning aesthetic. Naturally they have to change jobs for better salary. Children's education and their demands takes away big share of salaries. Credit cards, ATMs, Consumer Loans, Hire-purchase make money management a formidable tasks. This comes in the way of making decisions of quitting job for a change difficult.

When wife and husband live in different places, extra time & money is spent in travel at the week end to be together. Two establishments is not a only financial problem but effects family support system when the one has to spend in isolation of each other. This has all kinds of economic and psychological problems. When a man returns to residence late after hard work away from parents and wife and children, it will affect the performance at work place.

All these factors affect the career decisions. For example the banks promote officers with transfer. If they don't want transfer they have to forego promotion. Many people lost their careers and remained stagnant. The children of these people believe that their parents' generation paid too high a price for career success in terms of health and family relationship.

Today's generation learn from the previous generation and make strong decisions regarding their careers. I know a case of a person who became Chairman of a leading bank put his daughter in boarding school to enable himself free to move from place to place in the younger days. There was a time when he suggested to his daughter to put her child in a boarding school so that she could pursue her career. Pat came the reply: I suffered and missed living with my parents; but I don't want my child to live away from me. The gentleman was hurt and broke down, saying, 'I never knew that you did not like the arrangement for you. Had you opposed I would have done something different', said shocked man who shared this in a group.

There is thus world of change. Everyone wants to make their own career choice weighing all the pros and cons vis-à-vis family.

Balancing work-life and family life is choice of man. There are people who resigned after a long service in an organization because of transfer to another place. They could do it because they are financially independent and confident they could earn through other means-*freelance, consultancy* etc. The company which knew their value even cancelled the transfer.

That is the advantage of personality development-development of knowledge and multiple skills when you can dictate terms to the employers and keep your values intact. There are many fringe workers today who care for their independence and freedom opt for free-lance work, part-time jobs while pursuing something that interests them most. There are interim managers who work for a month or two on a project enjoying autonomy with competence as their forte. You find such jobs mainly technical in the film field and TV and radio media. They are engaged, paid for their expertise and competence. They don't look for permanent jobs. But they manage their finances well. Sometimes they may work 18 hours day or for days together they are out of work. Their success depends on their technical competence and self-reliance and self management.

What Hirers Say

"I recruit people for niche skill and approach the institutes that train the graduates in these skills. The skill, which I am talking about, pertain to Software testing. Recently, we took the decision to hire science graduates, as trainees.

There were three levels for them to cross. One was the test, the next was the group discussion and finally the Technical interview. The test is straight forward - one has to pass the cut-off stage to go to the next round. The tests can be multiple choice or long answers, and depends upon how the company chooses to formulate it.

Group discussion was evaluated by the HR. Topics addressed are popular issues and topics. We saw to it that the topics chosen gave everyone a fair chance to speak. For instance we did not consider a topic such a "Nuclear Deal - Is it good or bad for India". Certainly, this would require a lot of knowledge on Current Affairs. So we chose a more popular topic such as "Is 20-20 tournament good for cricket". Also the duration was neither too long nor too short-just enough. Normally, the HR takes a call on this.

There will always be someone to start the discussion. That has its plus points. There will be someone who will take control and summarise and arbitrate. All these were being closely watched. There will be some who will have something to say and will say it very succinctly. Those who fail to participate have no chance of making it to the next round. Also, the content of discussion was mostly observed to see if they are talking sense. We select anyone whose contribution made sense. It was HR's sole discretion as to who would make it to the next round.

Technical interviewers bore in mind that the candidates would be trained over a period of time and all the candidates would need to understand the concepts and basics well. Knowing this and expressing this clearly using the right technical terms (and correctly so) would take the candidate a long way. This would express his grasp of basics well.

Interviewing experienced candidates is entirely a different ball game. One of the things I notice is that, they know what they have mentioned in the resume. It is very important that the resume honestly reflects the skills. This is because the employee's selection for other projects much after the selection will be based on the resume. A well written resume also becomes a good starting point for selection. It impresses the HR and enables you to get shortlisted for the next level of interview. Also, be very careful in declaring your skills in the resume. Declare all the qualifications and certifications. Declare all your international travel, if your new job demands it. Declare if you have any valid visas. These things add value to your resume. Also, if you are leading a team, state the size of your team.

Good Communication skills for any level of experience matter. As you climb higher in the hierarchical ladder it becomes a necessity to communicate well with your subordinates, peers, and particularly, the clients. Sometimes in body-shopping firms, and in key roles, the client would like to interview the candidate before bringing him onboard to the project. In such a case strong relevant technical and communication skills become important. Some clients do a video conferencing and presentation skills become important.

In some companies HR will have a say in the recruitment and can decide on high salary for deserving candidates. They can even override decision of the technical team!

While searching for a job in Hyderabad, I met a friend in a leading company. He forwarded my resume to HR. A technical interview was conducted for senior position in the company. The interview result turned out to be negative. However, the HR interview went in favor of me and HR was convinced I was a good candidate for the job. My friend also had a discussion on my selection with HR. HR had a discussion with the Technical Interviewer. Finally, the organization decided to take me in, provided I would accept a position much lower than what I was interviewed for. *Since I needed a break in a good company, I relented. Since then, there was no turning back.* I quote this example to say that HR can be powerful enough in some organizations to influence decisions of selection. They can gauge the person and decide on their salaries a candidate deserves. They also have the power to provide "joining bonus". Sometimes they can pay for the notice period to the relieving company and get the candidate immediately."

A Software Professional in Mid Career

Comment

A good candidate with soft skills can get a chance to sharpen his or her hard skills. The sentence in italics is significant.

Preparation

Preparation for interview is similar to preparation for the examinations in the schools and colleges you were engaged in. There are students and students. Some who make last minute preparations. Some study systematically throughout the year participating in the classroom, weekly, monthly, or half-yearly examinations. Each school has its own regimen.

Rishi valley school of Madanapally wanted to dispense with examinations completely because the founder, the late Sri Krishnamurthy, did not believe in the system of examination. But the school had to fall in line with the Government rules and regulations. But they kept it to a minimum.

In those days there were no tutorial institutes or guides. But students were going through previous year's question papers for the type of questions or standard questions. Some questions are repeated. Problems are repeated. Some questions appear in a different form. There are guides which provide standard answers, alternatives.

These practices are extended to job selections too. Internet provides information and guidance. All this is preparation for the content, language, context and process of interviewing to both the parties. There are other aspects—the soft skills testing.

Even in the written examination system, the presentation of answers varies from student to student. There are those who reproduce standard answers verbatim learned by rote. A clever examiner knows it at a glance. There are others who give BOLD answers—Brief, Own, Lucid, and Direct to the point. They impress the awarder of marks who see the difference readily. The pity is that in these days of mass valuations and the money involved and the labour, the unpleasant nature of the work, are making awarding of marks not uniform or equitable.

These and many other factors make selection through interview least effective although a routine affair, not a right instrument to select candidates for employment and engagement for a long tenure or career.

However you have to go through the ritual; go through it well enough not be rejected.

Your preparation for the interview is part of your preparation for the job and career. It is continuous process of self assessment and presentation of self. Self expression. The key is management. You have to manage the internal milieu (self) and manage the external environment (employers) and the relationship between the two.

The ideas about interviews are changing for better. The panel members who visit campuses are trained. They do lot of preparation work. Look at their problem. When selected candidates are given to the departments or projects, one hears that the project managers who are not involved in the process of selection complain and reject the candidate after a few days and blame the recruiters. The recruiters on the other hand, blame the project managers for lack of leadership skills or ability to manage talent. On your side it is not enough if you impress people the 'wicket gate' keepers, to gain entry; but you keep impressing the people who matter in the organization. If you adopt the impression management continuously, you will spend life with anxiety and with no focus on the purpose of the job and career, managing impressions. What is important is quality of your personality, your values, knowledge, skills, soft skills in particular over and above the required hard skills. The most important thing is learning skill. Interviewers have learnt to ask questions like, what are your strengths, and what are your weaknesses? The guides pitch on these questions and give you best answers and next best answers.

Second important thing is to find out what the employer is looking for. Behind every question there is this need of the employer hidden or expressed. Most interviewers don't put all their cards on the table. For both the hirer and the hunter of jobs it is a process, a journey, inquiry, information, reduction of uncertainty, simply knowing each as well as possible in the short time of say, 30 minutes.

What both need is *authentic encounters*. Honest transactions without any hidden agenda to trap the other.

I came across a guide titled 'How to answer 64 tough questions'. Browsing the list I found more 'clever questions' to trap the candidates. The authors suggest the means to avoid the trap. Instead authentic transactions benefit both the parties.

Preparation is the key soft skill. The idea of Planning, Preparation, and Practice must be firmly established in our minds. You need 10000 hours of practice to make you perfect in any art. It is said that Sir C.P.Ramaswamy Iyer took up his first case after 10 years of internship and study and graduation. His first case was a sensational adoption case of Jiddu Krishnamurthy's father Vs Anne Besant which Sir C.P. won. You must add to 3ps a fourth P–patience. There is no exception to this rule even in the case of geniuses and prodigies. Thomas Alwa Edison, the great inventor himself has said, that genius is 1% inspiration and 99% perspiration. Perspiration is yet another P–that needs to be added.

Recall what we discussed under *Vibhuti yoga... Splendour of the splendid.* Keep practicing like Jonathan Livingston Seagul, invoking the divine residing in your heart, *you will grow and glow!* Remember Mozart was a prodigy, who composed music at 6. He mastered it only at 21!

'US Defence Secretary Colin Powel made a critical presentation to the United Nations in Feb 2003 – not only did he rehearse, write, and research his speech painstakingly, he delivered it several times in advance to colleagues. At one stage he had a room set up to replicate exactly the room where he would be speaking. There is no such thing as too much preparation.

No amount of preparation is too much. Abraham Lincoln once told a club President that he needed 5 days' preparation to give a speech of 5 minutes; if it is one hour speech, he would need a day for preparation. If there is no time limit, then he said he was ready. Similarly shorter the interview longer is the preparation.

RESUME[1]. An Exposition

Resume is a Realistic Exposition of Self Underscoring Major Exploits –

Reaslistic: It is real not imaginary. What you are, what you can do, and what you will do if an opportunity is given. It is down-to-earth and practical.

Exposition: A setting forth *in writing* a proposition, something difficult to explain to the reader who can make sense at a glance for first impression so that it is one among the short listed resumes. It demands exactitude, the written communication is all about. You need to develop proficiency in written (English) language. That itself is an indication of your soft skills... It should be – BOLD; brief, own, lucid, and direct – *brief* unlike most expositions. Hence it becomes doubly difficult to set forth on paper. It has to be own, not a copy which is what the lazy do. lucid (or clarity, logical, stimulating) and direct to the point. A good resume will emerge only after several attempts. It is iterative, re-writing, correcting, and rewriting and so on till something worthwhile emerges.

Self : It is all about self. Self expression in writing, a rewarding and reinforcing exercise. It rejuvenates, energises, a motivating force. Temper it, to make it realistic. The process leads to self

---

[1] **RESUME**: Reaslistic; Exposition; Self; Underscoring; Major; Exploits

discovery – a little deeper with each draft revised. An excellent way to probe into self. Remember 3Es of personality development discussed before. What are your endowments, the contribution from the environment, and the gains from education and experience. A good resume is an outcome of self discovery as nearly true as possible to the self and others.

Underscoring: It does not contain everything. Only salient features of true self that have utility value. Therefore you need to be selective, keeping the norm, realistic appraisal about self. Dictionary meaning of *underscore:*

To draw a line under, to make *evident, emphasise, stress;* to provide (action on film) with accompanying music;

For us emphasis and stress are suitable meanings; make evident can be more significant. The resume, in writing, makes your 'self' evident to the judge who picks it up out of a large pile. It must standout. That is the objective of underscoring used as a metaphor, the last cited meaning of the dictionary—*to provide music to the action* in a film.

When you underscore you are providing 'music', melody, rhythm, tone, tune, texture; fine tune the exposition without ignoring the realistic aspect. The underscoring or the background music, as it is called here, should be appropriate to the mood and sentiment. The audience is enthralled when audio is mixed with visuals. Musical scoring or under scoring is done on paper from which the reader can play. The reader of your resume must respond to the underscoring with the same excitement to call you for the next stage of selection.

Major: Brevity makes it imperative for you to focus only on the major accomplishments, evidences; what is major or minor depends on the situation. It involves sifting and sieving. A difficult exercise. A rummy player who finds it difficult to discard ends up with unwanted cards, leaving others to take the booty.

It depends on the job, career, industry you are applying for. The employer may not nearly think of the job you have applied for. He thinks of your utility in the long run. They have their succession plans. He may not simply rely on your present resume but your future resumes—your true potential. To day's employers are looking for soft skills set more than the hard or job–specific skills. It depends on the research you made on the company and tasks involved and their expectations.

Let me give an illustration:

When I began my career in a bank as branch level employee, there were no resumes, only references. The banks wanted honest, loyal, pen-pushers to man their counters and back office operations. Because they were lending for short-term or working capital to traders, they wanted some shroffs from the business community to assess the borrower's solvency and business acumen.

Soon banks diversified into industrial finance, both working capital and later for long-term capital formation. They further diversified, in keeping with government policies, into small scale industries, financing of entrepreneurs and self-employed; this made banks recruit specialists, as directly recruited officers, like chartered accountants, cost accountants, engineers, and even MBAs.

After nationalization of 14 major banks, they began recruiting agricultural scientists first at the apex level and later at the grass-roots level. All this put banks into manpower planning, succession planning, compensation packaging, requiring the appointment of yet another specialized category HR managers.

All these changes are significant for discussion on resumes. First bank's reliance on resumes for calling candidates making them go through the process of selection and recruitment. Those who joined the bank in the earlier period have also been aspiring and competing with the specialists who eventually became generalists. If they had the opportunity to present their resumes-realistic exposition of self underscoring, major exploits-achievements and there would have been realistic appraisal of these resumes. They would have had better chance to come up. There was no such a concept of resume preparation. It epitomizes ones' progression in career, in the unfolding of personalities. Each failure will become a cause for re-examination and re-education and renewal.

Exploits: One's feats, heroic deeds, outstanding achievements. They stem from exploitation of talents, hidden or actual, interests, personality traits—tendencies, reactions aptitudes, innerurges, temperament, specialization.

Exploit them to your fullest

The employers' interest in your past exploits is limited to their future utility. It is TRAITS that must be evident in the exploits—tendency gives rise to reactions; the in-born aptitudes give rise to inner urges, your temperament is seen in your speciality-uniqueness

A unique combination of *transferable* skills with *flexibility*.... They are apart from job specific technical skills which may be classified under hard skills. Therefore hard skills are more than skills in operating machinery....There are certain skills beyond these hard skills, universally sought by employers—call them soft skills.

Most job seekers do possess a few of them to some extent. But all employees whatever may be the extent or lack of it, can be *trained*. These are trainable skills. That is the good news. Through training, professional development, coaching, mentoring they can be acquired, refined, improved, developed, enhanced; if there is will there is the way.

There is process, a systematic way; I call it ADEPT programme—Appreciation, Demonstration, Experimentation, Practice, and Transfer to real situations. The list of skills is too long. But if you know in advance what a particular employer seeks, then you can match or tailor your job search.

You can show case what you possess through resume, covering letter, and face-to-face interview. For all this you need to be clear about your own strengths and weaknesses; be sensitive to what you have gained through various projects and work experience, etc. It is quite possible that you do not know your own strengths leave alone your weaknesses.

There is a more appropriate name given–*employability skills*. To know the verbiage-the words that are understood by every employer is useful so that you can use them in your written communication and oral presentations.

Jargon

Numerous studies which identified them and developed jargon on employability elements, which a job seeker must know.

Jargon, a somewhat derogatory term, is specialized vocabulary and idiom of those in the same work, way of life, etc. Each profession has its own jargon, if used in the correct sense it makes for efficient way of communication between the professionals. Soft skills is a phrase that creeps into the jargon of social science, management, and HR professions. It is now used widely and everybody uses it without meaning anything to the job seeker or hirer, the two who should know what they actually represent in terms of the observable behaviour and the result these behaviours produce. But jargon is necessary for precise communication between the sender and receiver – effective communication with no communication gap, another jargon.

What are they, the jargon? Most often mentioned skill by the employers is communication skills, oral and written, both verbal. This is where most troubles in business arise. So they insist on these skills. The reader may refer to my earlier book titled 'Communicative Competence' published in 2006.

Use of Radar[2]

Radar is a device that emits radio waves and processes their reflections for detecting and locating objects or surface features...

Echolocation is what a bat, the creature does... physiological process for locating distant or invisible objects by sound waves reflected back to the emitter.

RADAR is a device used for echolocation. That is what an interviewer for job selection does. His questions are echolocations. The reflections are of RADAR questions are used to detect your employability.

- Reason (why)
- Aspirations (what level) (your expectation)

---

[2] **RADAR:** Reason; Aspirations; Duration; Asset value; Reliability.

- Duration (how long)
- Asset value (how useful are you in the long term)
- Reliability (can you work without supervision)
  - Why are you leaving your current employer?
  - Why have you chosen our company?
  - How long did you serve the present employer?
  - We can only offer you a temporary job
  - Asset value – long term value. How quickly can you become one of us?
  - Reliability – can you set your own goals.

Ravi Varanasi shares his experience in Resume writing and Interviewing

My Experience

During my final year at Engineering, I had received an offer from Siemens Engineering (Circuit Boards) for a pre-sales engineer. Unfortunately, Siemens had a pretty bad quarter and froze all the existing offers. The first important lesson that I learned was not to take things for granted. After a brief stint as an intern at Square-D software of India, I decided to pursue higher studies in Binghamton, NY. In my final semester, I started interviewing with several companies. Thanks to the good economy, I had received offers from Goldman Sachs, American Management Systems, Thought works and Trilogy. Thought Works is a global IT consultancy company. The interview process involved an aptitude test along with a coding exercise. As a fresh graduate, I wanted to pick a company that would provide me the best chance to learn and Thought works provided that, (even though it wasn't the best paying). The work involved traveling to customer sites and implementing projects for them. The world of consulting provides a different environment and problem set at different clients. The flip side to the consulting world is the travel that is involved and the need to establish your work at every client place. The move to Dallas forced me to change companies. The consulting rigours made me feel at ease in the subsequent interviews. The subsequent change of jobs originated from contacts from my previous jobs.

The best way to prepare for an interview is to get information about the position from an ex-colleague or a friend who is already working in the company. It helps one to understand the situation from an insider and also know what kind of skills the position entails.

The more interviews I had attended the more it became a fun and challenging exercise. A failed interview provided me good feedback on self-evaluation. The important takeaway from it might be reading a new book to enhance my skills in a certain area.

My current position's interview process was one of the different interviews. The company had a set of interviews and also made me go through a coding exercise that would mimic a normal working day. The interview made me evaluate the company in a normal working day mode.

As an interviewer

When I interview a candidate, these are the following things I look for -

1. Technical competence for the position.
2. Role as a good team player.
3. Ability to answer questions in a direct and succinct manner.
4. Ability to communicate one's experience in a succinct way.
5. Is he compatible with the company's culture.?
6. Does he have passion and enthusiasm?
7. Do books/blogs and other things interest him outside his work?
8. Has he done anything related to work in his spare time?

As an interviewee

Here are a few of things I look for in a company and seek answers to the following questions—

1. Does company subscribe to the same set of beliefs/culture shared by me?
2. Does company provide an environment that fosters independent thinking?
3. Does it treat developers as another entity?
4. Does it expect me to strike a good balance between life and work?
5. Does the interviewers create in me a feeling they enjoy working for the company?
6. Does the company invest in me to improve my skills?

Advice for fresh graduates

1. Have interest in the position you are applying for. Once you take the job, you will spend a good amount of time working in that area. So if you don't have interest in that area, you are better off finding what interests you.

2. Use the internet to read blogs/articles to keep up with the latest in the field.
3. Show enthusiasm to learn. Learning is the best investment.
4. Do not worry too much about compensation.
5. Read lots of books and tap into your intellectual curiosity.
6. Be professional – talk in ENGLISH at work place. Professional behaviour is more important than just dressing in a professional manner. That is not be all, end all. It is always dress plus. That plus is behaviour which stems from professionalism. (Ravi appears to be a regular reader as (2) suggests).
7. Avoid grammatical errors in resume
8. Provide your intent in your objective/summary in a clear and simple manner.
9. Attach a covering letter for the positions of special interest to you. Explain to them why you are suited to the position.
10. Have patience and keep a smiling face.
11. Expand your contacts using online forums, user group meetings or intern positions.
12. Have confidence in your position.

Aspirations of an NRI

For the past 10 years I have been working in the Information Technology domain. Starting out as a programmer, I have grown to become a Business Intelligence Technical Architect. I am currently an Asst Vice-President in their Enterprise Technology Group at Marsh, World leader in Risk and Insurance Services Industry. At Marsh, I lead major work streams of various Business Intelligence projects. This responsibility as work stream lead provides me an opportunity to take up project management tasks and also managing a 5 to 6–member development team along with the primary responsibility of providing solutions in the Technology domain. Part of the Application development is outsourced to India and managing and solving the challenges that arise as part of outsourcing have been a major component of the work streams that I lead. During the last few years, I got substantial exposure to managerial context at Marsh.

I plan to enhance these on–job learnt management skills by augmenting them with formal education in management. Together these will provide me right skills to reach my short-term goal of succeeding at a higher level managerial role in the Technology domain. The managerial role I aspire for will deal with all aspects of management, including project planning, budgeting and resource management, and will involve larger teams.

Later, the experience gained in a managerial role along with my technical expertise and experience of handling outsourced projects should help me reach my long-term goal of setting up an India–based Software Development company initially focusing on the Business Intelligence domain. Changes in macro-economic policies over the last 15 years in India had resulted in its Software Industry achieving tremendous growth rates. NASSCOM-Mckinsey Report 2005 on Indian Software Industry estimates that Software Industry in India is likely to achieve 25 per cent growth rate year-on-year for the next few years. I plan to utilize this business opportunity through my company to achieve good growth rates.

I have looked at Part-time MBA program offered by NYU very closely and am sure that it will provide me with the right tools to help me accomplish my short-term goal of succeeding in a higher level managerial role as well as prepare me better for pursuing my long-term goal of establishing my own business through its 'Entrepreneurship & Innovation' curriculum.

9 Reasons for Rejecting of Candidates

1. *Vague statements* 2. *Abstract words* 3. *Incomplete data* 4. *Not showing enthusiasm in writing* 5. *Giving no concrete examples* 6. *Long, and showy language* 7. *Over reaching (trying to hoodwink)* 8. *Rushed through applications* 9. *Yawning gaps in information*

- Vague statements in the resume, covering letter, or in the interview.
- Abstract words instead of action verbs.
- Incomplete data in the applications
- Not showing enthusiasm in written and oral communication and body language.

  Add to them vain attempts to impress the hirer's among others characteristics.
- Giving no concrete examples—this is very important. This is particularly true of the project work, internship, any work experience prior to seeking employment. You can not leave things to the hirers imagination, inference, interpretation, or assumptions.
- Language not being BOLD—brief, own, lucid and direct. Showy language shows shallowness of the speaker or writer.
- Overreaching (trying to hoodwink)
- Rushed through applications—you will fill so many applications you hardly spend time it deserves. No doubt filling in details in a printed form is a boring task. Yet it should not show you are slipshod.
- Yawning gaps in the information supplied. There must be some orderly presentation—chronological or logical.

Studies over a time have revealed some of the reasons for rejection of candidate at different stages of the selection process. The above sums up: VAINGLORY[3]–Vain though in vain.

---

[3] **VAINGLORY:** Vague statements; Abstract words; Incomplete data; Not showing enthusiasm in writing; Giving no concrete examples; Long, and showy language; Over reaching; Rushed through applications; Yawning gaps in information.

2

CONTROL OF CAREERS

Control is a management function. As managers of your own careers you need to know that control is simply looking back, whereas planning is looking ahead. One management writer gave us rather an inelegant acronym PLORDICOCO: Planning, organizing, directing, coordinating, and controlling as management functions. Between planning and control, three more functions are inserted. In fact all the functions are continuous without hiatus. Organizing, directing, and coordinating applies to resources.. Resource building, and using them – allocating – against the opportunities with will, goal setting being part of planning.

You can only control what you have planned. No planning, no control. What MARS[1] people's lives are *Mechanical, Absent minded, Random, Shuffled*. It is like shuffling a pack of playing cards. The original order of the cards becomes disorderly. Shuffling is done mechanically, absent mindedly and randomly.

To put them back into order, you have to sort out. Sorting involves strategy, openness, rigour and is time consuming. Controlling is similar to sorting. The three Ds: Desire, design, and determined effort.

Michael Faraday had a desire, a dream, but no design up to 13. Nor his father had any except eking out a livelihood. Nothing deeper than that. His life was MARS like. But he had his 'endowment' right; sincere, hardworking, learning. A dropout from school did not stop learning on the job. One year internship – the errand boy who impressed his master who probably got

[1] **MARS:** Mechanical; Absent minded; Random; Shuffled.

feed-back from his customers. An errand boy's work involves loyalty, punctuality, saying 'hello' to customers, etc. In terms of interpersonal skills, he must have helping nature – extension expressed. Later his 'extension wanted' orientation was visible when he sought help of Sir Humphry Davy for a job in the Royal Institution. These things came to him naturally as part of his inheritance.

We discussed the environment in which he grew. He capitalized on it. It is an aspect of control? May be it is destiny. Then he had a change of job, apprenticeship in book binding section; when a completely different orientation and skills were required. He quickly adjusted – adaptability and flexibility two of the most important soft skills; he was willingness to learn, and learning by direct experience under the guidance of a mentor are always in Faraday throughout his career as a scientist.

To control career one must be always on the learning mode which we can appreciate in Faraday. He had to learn English language skills (soft skill) at an advanced age – after becoming director of Royal Institution to give lectures.

What was he doing while binding books? He was reading! Reading and writing skills he learnt before dropping out from school for no fault of his. All of us have these skills, that is what literate means. Yet, how much of them do we use for our progress? Faraday made full use of them. The very fact that he found time to read and take notes from some of the books he bound and yet his master allowed him 'occasional leisure' to attend shilling lectures' speaks that he was efficient in book binding too. Here is a lesson for you. During the course of your career you may have to perform certain tasks which do not form part of your agenda for career success. Yet you have to perform well whether it interests you or not. Each job can be seen as an opportunity, relevant or irrelevant to one's design. It is an important soft skill to produce quality work bearing your brand.

When he attended the lectures, again he took notes. Listening to lectures and seminars or class room lectures is an important learning skill which Faraday had in abundance. Poor listening is attributed to day-dreaming, detouring, and debating and private planning while speaker goes on, missing important sequence of presentation. Physically present, mentally absent with zero benefit. Combining active listening and note taking is mutually reinforcing. But note taking itself is a skill one should develop. There are books on the subject. You start doing, it you can learn the art and even teach others.

His entry into the Royal Institution was not easy. I reproduce what you might not have read with intent before.

> "During my apprenticeship I had the good fortune, through the kindness of Mr. Dance, who was a customer of my master's shop, and also a member of the Royal Institution; to hear four of the last lectures of Sir H. Davy in that locality. . . . The desire to be engaged in scientific occupation, even though of the lowest kind, induced me, whilst an apprentice, to write, in my ignorance of the world and simplicity of my mind, to Sir Joseph Banks, then President of the Royal Society. . . . (But there was no reply).

This is a first person account. We can read into it 'networking', 'resume writing', 'his desire, design, determination'. The design proved faulty. He was quick to learn and take alternate route. 'He sent the notes to Sir Humphry Davy, the speaker, right person who has the time and inclination to examine the notes. It worked. Davy was delighted and absorbed with interest because the notes represented exactly his own lectures. He was delighted because, probably, he took credit for such lucidity that a 13 year old school drop-out could understand it. Faraday was patient. He 'stooped to conquer!' He bore the ill-treatment of Davy's wife to conquer Davy.

3D Approach

Destination, Direction, and Determination was the tortoise's strategy in the old fable 'slow and steady wins the race'. You don't waste your time looking at others and what their designs are. You have your own plan and carry it through. Background and birth do not come in the way of progress if we are determined to advance.

Subba Reddy, a poor farmer's son had to attend school as well as work at home. At home he had to help his poor parents in their farm as a labourer and shepherd boy. He could not compete with other boys who could entirely concentrate on studies. They were naturally ahead of him in studies. With these difficulties he managed to pass the 10th class with just 51% marks.

He completed intermediate and acquired a degree in the same way. During this period he started giving tuitions to students and earned a name for himself. Teaching, he knew, is the best form of learning. Giving tuitions has been a different kind of work experience compared to farming or tending cattle.

What next? Yes, he was having a long term goal but his focus was always on the *next step*. There is Distance Education module available to people who are employed or self employed. Through it he added one more feather to his academic cap B.Ed. It will enhance his teaching opportunities.

Now he has become a better student, striving hard. He obtained PG degree from the university in Chemistry- with 74%. His confidence levels have gone up. He began doing odd jobs. He gave enough importance to practical experience and earning money.

He is not satisfied. What next? He sat for a number of competitive examinations. But success was eluding him. He wrote DSc examination and got the 9th rank and joined as a teacher. Next year he made a determined effort and obtained a chemistry lecturer's post.

Still something was bothering him. He discovered that he would be satisfied if his service is useful to the society in which he had grown – the rural poor. Service was his anchor. His personality was a *mixture of the conventional, realistic, and social.* He says that many of his friends helped by way of information, moral support and emotional involvement. He can never forget their help. He had his own network of friends and well wishers.

He constantly kept in mind his mothers desire-occupy a big position. Prestige was her wish. He looked around for a career which will fulfill his mother's wish and his own wish. He applied for a Deputy Education Officer's post. His was one among 50,000 applications. Believe it, he stood first in the selection examination. He can enable many poor rural youth in realizing their potential, by raising himself by the boot straps.

What lessons can you learn from the saga of Subba Reddy?

There are a thousand Subba Reddys, unknown warriors, who fought their way up, who have been striving and struggling and winning and serving. They say they are repaying a debt to the society that has nurtured them, altruistic *Karmayogis*. Two things are common themes of the book, positive thinking and setting goals. Here is an example that you can savour.

Presently pursing his Ph.D in Pharmacy, Rajesh, another from the poorer class was brought up by grand father and mother and it was his teacher who gave tangible (financial) support. He had moral support and emotional support to lay his career path. His work on drugs for diabetics won him the scholarship. He got an offer from a university in the United States.

Desire, Design and Deliberate Effort

There must be a *desire* to know about yourself-self awareness; the desire itself could be accidental or by choice or cultivation or exposure to the ideas. Now if you're desirous of knowing yourself which was wanting before you read this book, then the purpose is served. Now you must have *design*, a game plan, the means to an end – deeper knowledge of the self which is a means to another larger end. It is end-means chain.

The advocates of career planning suggest that you must choose a career that interests you. That is, what you do for a living must align with what you want to accomplish in your life – *the deeper things*.

There are many who separate the two: livelihood and living with a purpose. If you divide a day of 24 hours into three parts of 8 hours each, one part for eking a livelihood, the other part for sleep and rest; still there are 8 hours left for the pursuit of deeper things. That is where the career anchors and vocational personality come in. Once the second pursuit–Right livelihood–itself is income generating occupation, then both merge giving superior satisfaction. In the beginning of earning and living for earning you may compartmentalize your life, gradually as quickly as possible merge the compartments into our larger free moving space. Let us come to the last D-*Deliberate effort*. In fact the design is itself defined as 'conscious effort to impose meaningful order' Deliberate, planned, and sustained effort is what is advocated.

Keeping Record of your own Accomplishments

Positive thoughts and setting goals yearly—a personal record for review and revision can keep your career under control and on the right course. *Steering* is an extension of *control* to which we come later. Direction and speed are important in mid career. In a bureaucratic, large-scale organization you may be silently working with dedication with no one to speak for you.

In the beginning of my career in the bank my manager took me off from the current job and gave me an assignment with a deadline. Inspectors landed from head office which is always a surprise visit. There was long pending work in collections department where the books had not been balanced for six months. I was asked to balance them within 10 days—six months backlog to be competed in 10 days! I had no idea of how difficult the task would be because I was new to the bank. The manager was not given to listening to clarification or doubts. That much I knew, about the man. I nodded and accepted meekly. By nature I don't keep my doubts to myself. I started talking to others in the bank. Some encouraged, others sympathized with me. One senior offered help. He explained to me the process which was laborious, but it was the right procedure. He advised me to do it systematically and not bother about the deadline. If you are sure of what you have accomplished in these 10 days and what is left to be done and seek additional hand or ask for extra time. The boss who knows the procedure and the time it would take, will definitely appreciate the work. I listened as a keen learner. This was a very encouraging advice. I followed the procedure scrupulously, seeking no further help.

I completed the task well in time with the help of a few other colleagues.

Armed with the achievements I went to the manager who was happy with my work. The secret of my success and saved labour was 'networking', a modern equivalent for old, socialization. It pays dividends. Sincere and hard working people can take a lesson from this.

The modern career counsellors advise us to keep a track and record for future use. As you move up the ladder, these episodes are the ones that you need to keep record.

When we assume responsibility at higher level the critical incidents differ in their significance and relevance. Many of the senior citizens who shared their thoughts, never recorded them, but now they do state them. The progressive organizations have long introduced self appraisal system which is a sort of resume to the own employer. If you had kept a file of your monthly achievements up to date in your self-appraisal dossier, it can be used to steer or alternately prepare resume for a prospective employer when you decide to sever links with your old organization.

Case presentation

The next two chapters are packed with cases. A case is usually a chunk of reality brought into the class room for detailed discussion.

Case method of learning was first introduced in the Harvard Law School in 1871 in the US. Now they are widely used in Business Schools and Schools of Medicine. Law schools use for precedents, medical schools for diagnosis and prescription, business schools for analysis and decision making.

The cases, most of them, are first person accounts, and therefore are case–histories, past events.

Stefan Zweig in his Foreword to *'The tide of fortune'*, writes:

> Like Nature itself, history, which is the spiritual mirror of Nature, assumes infinitely diversified and incalculable forms. It laughs at method, and contemptuously disregards laws. Now like water, it seems to flow towards a goal; at another time it pursues chance happenings that are sport of the wind. Often times it builds up epochs with steadfast patience of a growing crystal – till a dramatic instant comes when crowded spheres are generated in a flash.

Careful reading of several cases presented will reveal some thing similar to the above observation.

'Life must be allowed to run its natural course'... knowing that course or discovering one's talents, interests and personalities helps in allowing the course to run smoothly.

Nature and history of individuals can 'laugh at method, and disregard laws. Like water does flow towards a goal in some cases. They dream, develop interests, choose a career and carry it through. It is far from being smooth. Never mind, they never deviate from the course.

There are those for whom 'chance happenings' direct the careers. Others build up their careers as 'epochs' with steadfast patience of a growing crystal. Faraday built his 'epoch' once he found entry into the Royal Institution. He had to wait till a dramatic instant came in the form of Mr. Dance's invitation of the Institution.

Cases that follow

- Prabhakar, versatile musician, who is pursuing his chosen career which is progressing according to plan.
- Prasad reached the top as a scientist in the currently hot subject Global Warming and is a member of IPCC - Intergovernmental Panel on Climate Change which got the Nobel Prize in 2008.
- Venkat and Narayana had checkered careers. Venkat's journey in photography and cinematography had been exciting in spite of hard struggle. His wide range of experience stood him in good stead. He however lacked the support such people need to enable them to achieve their ambitions. Narayana had to change several jobs and institutions before he could find his footing. Having located in the US where his daughters grew up, he could leave a legacy to them; continue to stay in the US where one of them has became NASA scientist.
- There are several other cases where determined people could take control of their careers after listening to their deeper yearnings.

Cases 1

A Versatile Musician
Garikipati Venkata Prabhakar
Professional Singer and Music Director B.com, M.A.Music Director, S.S. Music Academy, Hyderabad. Is a Renowned Musician and Composer

Music is catching up with times. In to-day's society music is becoming daily routine thanks to Radio and TV in the lives of all classes of people. With the result as in other occupations, music as a profession is becoming common. As in the West it acquired professional status [All the attributes of a professional like qualification, Association, peer pressure, support, standards, competence, client relationship, service to society, code of ethic etc are applicable to the musicians as well]

Let us hear his story in his own words—

I am fortunate to have been into the family of music lovers and musicians who have limited their interest to hobby and leisure activity. My father, a lawyer by profession played veena with competence. He also promoted the arts by starting a 'Saraswati Samithi'. The Samithi was inviting eminent artists, classical Karnataka singers. It was established in 1950 eight years before I was born. I got inspiration by my elder brother who sang beautifully cinema songs in classical mode. I was entrusted to a renowned music teacher in Machlipatnam at the age 7. At 13 I gave a concert for three hours. When I went to Hubli for a programme, I met Padma Lalitha, who became my life partner. How did I go to Hubli? I joined NSM public school where the principal gave excellent support to me. We started light music academy and organized programmes with students throughout A.P. we extended our activities to Bangalore and Hubli.

It was here I learnt organizing and conducting programmes with students. I enjoyed teaching and presenting my students' performances to audience. This is my discovery. There is no point in pursuing one's own path of development. There is greater satisfaction when you enhance the talents of innumerable young boys and girls and when their collective and individual performances are applauded. You unleash the society's talents of so many musicians who would have otherwise been languishing in occupations that don't interest them. In my endeavour to serve the society my wife Padma Lalitha is manifestation of the adage 'behind every great man there is a woman who made the greatness possible'.

Besides being a diploma holder in music and accomplished singer who specialized in 'Krishna Tarangalu' of Narayana Thirtha, she has been able in running the S.S.Academy we started after migrating to Hyderabad.

We have set up a library of recordings at the academy. We also do research work and innovations. Our joint mission is to upgrade society in the area of music.

I have been invited to the US, Canada and other countries where we received encomiums and awards and rewards.

The S.S.Music Academy, named after my father, Subbaraya Sastri, must grow, should become a force in the state and the country, that is my ambition. I have the support of my family, and many well-wishers, parents who entrust their children to the academy and every one with whom I have come in contact.

In 1979 I stood first in the state in the competition conducted by YMCA in Eluru A.P.

In the meantime, my formal education at school and college proceeded smoothly. Finally I got my B.Com degree. My father who wanted me to study law and practice with him, died suddenly in 1977. He collapsed in the court arguing a workman's case on 'Vaikuntha Ekadasi' day.

I never thought of law again and concentrated on music my deeper interest, and passion.

I served for some time for a living in private companies, applying for leave frequently for music endeavors. Finally, I got a job in NSM public school, Vijayawada as music teacher, and from then onwards I never looked back.

I along with a few other started 'Gitanjali' light music academy. It was the first of its kind in Vijayawada. We conducted innumerable programmes under banner of 'Gitanjali' in Krishna and Nellore districts and at Hubli and Bangalore and received appreciation.

I have acquired the talent of composing music which won the laurels both from the cultivated and the illiterate. I learnt to change the style and rendering to suit the audience, both in number and quality of audience. I worked for one year in AIR, Chennai, where attending the recordings by eminent music directors like Rajeswara Rao and Master Venu.

My effort in this regard is 'Jayadeva' lyrics, Astapadis which are meant for dance drama, I could transform into sound extragavanza after tremendous effort. I rendered to a enthralled audiences for $2^{1/2}$ hours, which is considered as no small matter by me and all. I presented 'Dasavatharas', 7 songs in 'Ragamalica', and several other ragas. It gave me immense satisfaction not because of audience applause but because I became aware of my creative talent and perseverance and tenacity to achieve my set goals. A moment's reflection reveals to me that not a day passes in my life without some objective and effort to achieve it.

One innovation I have done and developed is to tune for lyrics written extempore extolling the virtues of departed souls – outstanding figures who made sacrifices for a worthy cause without self interest. I am grateful to Mr.Stanly who composed a poem on famous rationalist GORA on his death anniversary. After everybody gave their eulogies to the great man, Stanly asked me to recite his poem written as his eulogy. Within minutes I composed the tune without changing a single word or emotional tenor of the expression, I sang with equal emotion which moved the audience. It was a fitting climax, a tribute from me and Stanly together.

In 2006, my grand uncle, the late Venkatachalam's birth centenary was celebrated. After making all the arrangements I stayed behind the scene of 2 hour long celebration. In the fag-end I was asked to sing.

I was ready with a patriotic song written by Toleti and sung beautifully by Ghantasala. It is nothing but a long list of freedom fighters from 1857 to 1947. Without disturbing tune or tone I repeated in Ghatasala's tone and tenor, but added at one place the name of 'Venkatachalam'. As soon as the audience comprising of friends and relatives of over 200 spontaneously applauded when my grand uncle's name was heard.

Presence of mind has always been my strength. *'Samayai'* is a talent which any good musician has automatic development.

"In our family history there is a place given to me as, 'combining the two qualities of his father (lover of music and humane lawyer)".

Prabhakar is rendering yeoman's services by spotting talent, developing and nurturing it. Hundreds of his students had made a mark in the world of music. Every year he encourages his students to give public performances which are appreciated by music lovers and scholars. His students include adults, and even retired people. His wife Lalitha gave him all the help in his enterprise.

"I am grateful to my uncle who made research traced back for several centuries to find music in the blood from my mother's side.

Truly this driving force is the spirit of service from my late father. I know by what means and tribulation I have come up in this field. I want to pay back offering same path to others who have similar interest by holding into the successful careers in music itself without stagnating in conventional livelihoods.

Our mission is not individualistic but it is collective growth of music. Society must develop as a whole in the field of music with more and more people opting for it as a career.

Everybody loves and enjoys music, particularly light music or pop music. We must cater to that need of the society. That's our mission".

Prabhakar's Resume

Career Prabhakar started singing at the age of 13 and has been performing before on Radio and TV audiences since 1980 beside he has more than 1,000 public concerts all over India to his credit.

He was invited by TANA (Telugu Association of North America) in 1991 and 2001, presented 25 programmes in classical and light music in the USA.

Later, he received the Music Excellence Award in 2004 by **Silicon Andhra, Sanhose, California.** After the US trip he visited U.A.E. in April 2002 and presented classical, semi classical concerts at Dubai, Abu Dhabi, Sharja etc.

Received the blessings of his holiness *Bhagawan Sri Sathya Sai Baba* by rendering his Bhajans at Puttaparthi on his 75th Birthday Celebrations -2000 November.

Awards Pandit Ravi Shankar Award by Tirumala Tirupati Devasthanam.

Best Carnatic & Light Music Singer award **Madhura Gayaka** title given by the **Telegu Cultural and Socio club Chennai.**

Strengths Prabhakar specialised in singing Annamacharya *Keerthanas* and also *Asthapadis*, Narayana Teertha's *Tarangams*, Ramada's *Kirthis* apart from his regular classical music concerts.

Honorary Positions

- Official Music Director for – Ramakrishna Mission and Vivekananda Institute of Human Excellence-Hyderabad. Also, Ananda Buddha Vihara Trust (Buddha Trust), Secunderabad, A.P.
- Blessed by his holiness **Sri Ganapati Sachidananda Swami** as an **"Adhikara Gayaka"** and **"Sangeetha Darshaka"** for composing and singing his Bhajans.

Commercial Achievements

- Arogya Sudha – A selected composition of Sanskrit slokas with the blessing of his holiness **Sri Kanchi Kama Koti Sankaracharya.**
- Board Member and Examination Panel Member of **Gandharva University of Music and Dance, Miraj, Maharashtra.**
- **Dharma Padam** – Paali slokas of Buddha prepared by Ananda Buddha Vihara Trust, Manasa Veena and Ee Prasantha Velalo (Bhava Geetalu), Vemana Padyalu, Tyagarajam Bhajeham – audio cassette and Cds.

Background – Part of Resume

Resume says 'Prabhakar started singing at the age 13 and has been giving concerts in Radio and TV since 1980 and performed more than thousand public concerts all over India.

Parental Programming – Parentage

His father the late Subbaraya Sastry was a leading lawyer who espoused in the cause of workers and was a trade union leader who could have become a politician had he so chosen by accepting the offer of one of the Left parties.

He played *veena* as a hobby on the *veena* which was his maternal grandmother's. She was wife of a District and Sessions judge in Tanjavuru where she had her music lessons! That is all the music tradition in the family.

Young Prabhakar watched his father playing veena with interest. His elder brother was singing film songs with great fervour. But he chose a different stream because he was good in maths and became engineer. Both father and brother's talent and interest crystallized young Prabhakar's ardent interest, passion for music.

There is growing appreciation of music/dance in our society. These arts have become part of daily life in many families. Most people attend concerts and few encourage their children learn music and dance under good teachers. With the result there is growing demand for teachers in these arts and hence many are opting for a career in music and dance.

For some it became supplementary income for others a profession. As Sri Aurobindo said every child whose interests and talents are in these art forms must be encouraged to develop and realize their full potential.

Case 2

Global Warming Scientist – (NRI)

Prasad studied Mathematical Physics at Andhra University, then he went to the Indian Institute of Science to study Aerodynamics. Prof. Dhavan was his teacher there. He took a D.Sc. and then proceeded to the U.S. At one time he was offered a job at H.A.L. Bangalore. He did not take it up at that time because H.A.L. did not have the advanced type of wind tunnel which was necessary for his research. At Waltair he was the student of Prof.Meenakshi Sundaram, the Mathematical genius. Once before, an Andhra made good in the U.S. That was the redoubtable Yellapragada Subba Rao, of Lederle Laboratories. Now-a-days every third Andhra goes to the U.S., but when Prasad left our native shores things were not that easy. Like Subba Rao, Prasad was not born with a silver spoon in his mouth. He came up no doubt because of his brilliance. He had another qualification, he had the bull-dog tenacity of his forefathers.

Profile of Scientist – (NRI) Prasad Varanasi

First UCSD Engineering Graduate is a leader in Global Warming Research. [He is member of I.P.C.C. which won the Nobel Prize]

For nearly three and half decades, he has been one of world's leading researchers in the area of global warming and the measurement of the infrared spectra of greenhouse gases. The data from his laboratory are widely used in long term climatic change predictions. And it all began when Prasad Varanasi was a graduate in mid sixtees, a time he recalls fondly after more than 34 years Long Island, Nywinters.

'I have always felt home sick for La Jola' says Varanasi, a professor at the State University of New York at Stony Brook since 1967.

'Looking back, I almost wish I had spent 12 years instead of two and a half at UCSD and forced them to drag me out of Urcy Hall fact first.

Varanasi occupies a unique niche in the history of Jacobs School of Engineering. In 1967 he was the first student to be awarded Ph.D in an engineering discipline at UCSD.

'I was the only graduate that year wearing an orange hood representing engineering' recalls Varanasi, 'I remember an elderly woman who came up and congratulated me for standing out in the crowd'.

Varanasi got to La Jolla only a week after his mentor (and now Professor Emeritus) Sol Penner arrived in 1964 to set up what was then the Aerospace and Mechanical Engineering Sciences department.

'Even before graduating from USCD, Varanasi's reputation was solidified with his co-discovery with Penner of the 'water vapour continuum'. 'The absorption by water vapour of the outgoing long-wave radiation or heat escaping, from the earth creates a double whammy,' says Varanasi.

'The continuum absorption by water vapour, which increases as the square of the density of water vapour in the atmosphere (unlike the absorption due to any other constituent of the atmosphere) creates a situation whereby small and seemingly insignificant changes in the temperature of the planet can produce whopping effects in the global warming phenomenon.

His research interests range from atmosphere spectroscopy and remote sensing to global warming and solar system exploration.

Prof. Penner notes, 'Prasad had an outstanding career in research, education, and as an editor and international statesman of science in a highly charged political area of research and environmental planning'.

But he also finds time to indulge in his private passions, from singing and compering classical Indian music to painting in India ink and water color, to cooking traditional Indian fare. He writes poems in Telugu and publishes them even to this day.

At 70 plus away from his kith and kin he finds solace in composing and singing his own lyrics. Recently his name was heard as a significant contributor to I.P.C.C.–Intergovernmental Panel On Climatic Change which won 2007 Nobel Prize. But Prasad enjoys music, art, and poetry and pursues other interests as some of the scientists of 20th century seem to enjoy.

The two cases presented are examples of well chosen and well controlled careers.

Recall 3Es and the role of environment in the development of personality. It is pertinent to refer to a snippet from Darwin's Autobiography.

Rational Man's Grief

"Up to the age of thirty, or beyond it, poetry of many kinds... gave me great pleasure, and even as a school boy I took **intense delight** in Shakespeare, especially in the historical plays. I have also said that formerly pictures gave me considerable, and music very great, **delight.** But now for many years I cannot endure to read a line of poetry: I have tried lately to read Shakespeare, and found it so intolerably dull that it nauseated me. I have also lost almost any taste for picture or music.... My mind seems to have become a kind of machine for grinding general laws out of large collections of fact, but why this should have caused the atrophy of that part of brain alone, on which the higher tastes depend, and may possibly be injurious to the intellect, and more probably to the moral character, by enfeebling the emotional part of nature."

Modern scientists like Prasad seem to enjoy music, art, and poetry an like scientists of earlier scientists.

Case 3
CHECKERED CAREERS

When Passion impels a Career

"Venkat, the first child was a self-made man. Venkat had little interest in studies. He did not complete graduation. He joined the Vijaya Studios in 1949 as a laboratory assistant.

He had the unique distinction of being the first cinematographer in the family. He was interested in still photography. His tryst with the camera began right from his school days when he pestered his mother into buying him a box camera. There was a gramophone in the house in which Venkat had shown a lot of interest. His interest in music, photography and dramatics stood him in good stead when he chose a career in films. He was a voracious reader of fiction. He was also fond of Shakespeare's dramas.

Once he got the job in Vijaya's labs, he gave up his studies and earnestly learnt various facets of filmmaking. His reading habits were very purposeful. He would read novels, biographies and Shakespeare's dramas before the release of films made in Hollywood and Britain. This coupled with watching the films gave him valuable insights into the intricacies of filmmaking.

He used to work hard late into night in labs and return home in the early hours of the morning. He often used to share his progress in his newfound interests with family members. He used to read lot of literature on films and photography. He would reel out the names of great producers, directors, cameramen, musicians, script writers, etc. He was a self-made man.

Soon, he became assistant to Marcus Bartley, Vauhini's ace cameraman. Later on he got interested in sound recording and editing as well. He used to acquire much talent in all these fields. It was because of such masters that he was able to hone his skills in the early years. He had an eye for recognizing talent and hold on to such people. Because of his trusting nature, he often became a victim of injustice, but he never mentioned it. He had a happy break when the famous Bhanumati took him as an operating cameraman in her Bharani Studios. He was director of photography for Bharani's classic 'Batasari'. Even to this day the hero of the film Sri Akkineni Nageswara Rao considers 'Batasari' as an outstanding film. Venkat was always hard pressed for money and was a poor manger of finances.

The turning point came in his career when a T.V. center was established in India, in New Delhi and Sri S.N. Murthy, a distant relative of his became its first director. He offered him a job. Sri Murthy helped several people and was Director of AIR Madras, Bombay and Delhi.

Venkat was interviewed by a German Adviser to the TV center over a cup of coffee in a Five Star Hotel. He instantly selected him for his wide knowledge in film making. He even remarked to him that a person like him in Germany, with 18 years of experience, would not join Government service. Thus, Venkat became the first TV cameraman in India, a proud moment for the family. He had the opportunity to show his originality. As there were no precendents he had to improvise. His assistants continued to remember him long after his death. He gave jobs to many who later rose in position and importance in Doordarshan.

There was one Perumal who came to him as a man-servant, became light boy and eventually became the chief cameraman. Qualified people did not dominate the scene in those initial days. Mr. Reddy owner of a Studio, Hyderabad, recalls how Venkat sent him a telegram to Madras offering a job in T.V. Center, New Delhi. He shared that Venkat was a very intelligent cameraman, who drafted proposals to the directors in very good English. He said that it was difficult to believe that Venkat was a non-graduate. He added that he was very friendly with his staff and often invited them to parties at his house. Venkat was voracious reader of English literature; that was his strength in communicating in English, apart from a wealth of ideas.

He now got himself *interested* more in documentaries. He produced a film on the Twin Cities of Hyderabad and Secunderabad for children in Japan.

He shot the film without help carrying the heavy movie camera on his shoulder the whole day. There were no video cameras. He would acknowledge a good turn spontaneously. This trait in him endeared him to many.

One remarkable thing about Venkat was his holistic approach, the entire range of cinematography, not merely the viewfinder. The surroundings– physical, psychological, social, cultural and ecological – formed part of his total vision. He used to appreciate camera, music, settings, acting, background music, and above all he used to place editing on the high pedestal.

He accompanied the then Prime Minister Indira Gandhi on her tours to Algeria, Jamaica and other places. He used to speak about Indira Gandhi's style, tastes, the meticulous care she took before posing for a camera. He would specially mention her choice of sarees, complete with their border, colours, her hairstyle, etc. He would not stop there. He would describe her shrewdness, her communication skills with the press and others, the respect she commanded in the world. He was absolutely objective like the camera he handled!

He always spoke good things about many dignitaries whom he accompanied, his superiors at TV center or later in DD. He was least bothered about scandals. He always parried any question that touched the seamy side of life.

Venkat had covered the Bangladesh surrender after war. It was the first and last experience of its kind. It remained in his mind for ever not merely as a camera assignment but as a political experience that testified to the shrewdness of Indira Gandhi. He always felt sorry for the merciless killings in the streets of Dhaka after the city had fallen.

He did not view the world from his view finder. He would see what was not visible to the naked eye. He saw everything with his mind's eye. All these things he used to share with anyone who cared to listen. Venkat cannot be viewed through a narrow lens. We need wide angle lens to understand this self-taught cinematographer. He accepted what ever he got out of the world like his camera. He cranked camera for the first ever English film from South India produced by the son of President of India Sri V.V. Giri. Jayalalitha, later Chief Minister of Tamil Nadu, was the young heroine in that film.

During the last phase Venkat moved to Bombay when DD was established and he became its first chief cameraman. He knew Bombay was a world of excitement and opportunities. He was getting suffocated within the four walls where the Directors became dictators. The freedom he enjoyed in Delhi was missing. He began breaking the rules. He produced full length film with a team of friends in *Kannada* . That was a Raghavendra Swamy of Mantralayam. From Indira Gandhi's politics he moved to spiritualism. He would talk for hours of siddhas and spirit power. Whatever may be the theme he was fully involved in it. He admired giants like Shyam Benegal, Govind Nihalani, Basu Chatterjee. But he admitted that he could never reach their level. He was aware of his limitations.

He had to quit Government job because of his misadventure and became a freelancer. Though Bombay gave plenty of opportunities he did not make money because of exploitation and cutthroat competition.

He was the only cameraman from T.V. center to be sent to BBC London to be trained in News telecast in the early days.

He got an interesting break when he worked as a stringer for P.T.I. He shot interviews with many dignitaries like Governor of R.B.I and other prominent people. There was great diversity from politicians to men of letters. Because of his holistic vision the otherwise tiresome and time consuming job, gave him satisfaction. He had influence with them because he satisfied their ego by taking shots to please them, although they were not acceptable. He had to work with editors and accommodate their viewpoint which was not always technically sound.

The last act

Venkat mooted the idea of a mega serial on Bombay beginning with the Dharawi slum.

After about two years DD gave clearance for his proposal. These two years he struggled. It was a surprise and he was excited. He called a team of technicians, actors, script writers to house to discuss and inaugurate the venture. Discussions went till midnight. After all the guests had left he retired for the night a happy and contended man. Once completed he would have no reason to live for he would have achieved his goal and realized his potential.

It was not to be. The next morning the servant found him dead. He died in sleep. He appeared smiling. Alone, at home, his wife having passed away a year before.

Venkat's Struggle-(A Checkered Career)

Here is a case of clear goals and positive orientation of a man who did not have second thoughts on his career objectives.

He selected the film industry and chose his career according to his interest and hobby. It turned out that his interest was actually a passion. It is true that you are likely to succeed when you make such a choice. He was happy and developed talent along the same lines. He was an extrovert, quick and action oriented; he was quick to realize that the film industry in India held bright prospects for the creative and enterprising. To what extent intuition played part in his career choice is difficult to assess from the case history.

Being an extrovert he was less analytical in his decision making. He did not take into account the financial security. Though he did not have permanent and stable employment he was never out of job. He was the feeling type, than the thinking type. He was perceptive, starting more than one project at a time and not a discerning judge of things. These are some of the personality attributes that we assume about Venkat. He was holistic and heuristic in his approach. He had the big picture and looked ahead with anticipation, but seemed to have neglected the ground realities. He was heuristic in the sense he had direction but no precise goal. Above all, he did not have the luck the adventurers needed.

His interests were many but they were related to industry he chose. His basic skills, reading, observation, and interpersonal skills had earned him many supporters. His networking helped him a lot. His habit of seeing only good in others must have endeared him to many. The description of Faraday by his friend aptly fits Venkat's personality:

> Water free from acids, alkalis, or saline solutions becomes crystal, sweet and pure. "By some such natural process in the formation of this man, beauty and nobleness coalesced, to the exclusion of everything vulgar and low."

No wonder death came to him in sleep and peaceful at that.

What were venkat's career anchors ? (ANCHORS)

Check Match

- Autonomy (where you have freedom and discretion)
- Novelty (Creative work)
- Challenge
- Holistic Mangement
- Offset Manager (Balance between personal life & official life)
- Rigour and Technical competence (where you are technically competent)
- Service and Stability

Exercise:

1. The above are some of the principal supports (anchors) which researchers of careers have found. Apply them to the case-history of Venkat. What are his basic skills, thinking skills, communication and leadership skills, enterprising skills that you attribute ?
2. What about own anchors ? identify them.
3. Think of your own passions?
4. What soft skills did Venkat did not possess which restricted his success?

Case 4

The Late Narayana S Varanasi – A Profile

Narayana S Varanasi started his career in 1950 at the Andhra Scientific Company Machilipatnam as an apprentice in the Optics Division.

He persisted all his life in the field of Optics, Spectroscopy and Laser Optics and lasers, etc.

Narayana was a graduate in Physics from Andhra University and took some special courses in Optics and Optical Instruments at Optical Sciences Center, Arizona State University, Arizona, USA.

He worked for five years (1959-64) as a research Assistant at Central Glass and Ceramic Institute under Council of Scientific and Industrial Research, Government of India. He assisted in the manufacture of Optical Glass in India *for the first time.*

When CGCRI started supplying Optical Glass to industries in India he came in contact with Mr. Vinod Bhargava, owner of Harvin Optical and Scientific Engineering House at Hyderabad. He moved to Hyderabad when Harvin Industries offered him, a Senior Executive position.. He developed the manufacturing methods for camera optics at this industry and supplied optics to AGFA (a German company located at Baroda).

In 1965 he moved to Department of Physics, Spectroscopy and lasers Division at the Indian Institute of Technology, Kanpur, as a Technical Scientist to work on a Naval Air force Project of the USA. When he was at IIT Kanpur, he, with the help of his colleagues and students, developed the He-Ne Gas laser for the first time in India. Students used this laser as a light source for spectroscopy work.

In the year 1974 he was offered a research scholarship at the Institute Of Optics, Puebla, Mexico by Prof Noble to work under renowned scientist Prof Malacara. There he worked on laser Interferometer techniques. The laser interferometer techniques were used for testing the astronomical telescope mirrors at the Optical work shop of the institute of Optics at Mexico.

In the year 1976 he joined Higher Technological Institute (CISESE) at Ensenada, Mexico.

In 1980 he joined as a manufacturing Engineer at II-VI Inc. Saxon burgh PA USA a high power CO_2 laser materials and components manufacturing industry. He was entrusted with the task of developing laser components testing laboratories. He developed "long Distance Radius measuring laser interferometer" which is used as a tool to measure radius of curvature and focal length of long radius optics in many optics industries in the USA.

The Common Wealth of Pennsylvania Ben Franklin seed grant was awarded to him for his project on CdS wave plates.

He became a US citizen in the year 1986.

After retiring from II-VI Inc. in 1993 he worked for one year as a volunteer Manager at Sri Venkateswara temple at Pittsburgh PA.

He moved to India in 1995 to work as a consultant for II-VI Inc in India. He was helping the CO_2 laser users in India in trouble shooting and selection of laser optics.

His worthy daughter

Narayana's daughter, Padmaja, did her Electrical Engineering and Computer Sciences from University of California at Santiago. She is presently working at the Jet Propulsion Laboratory as a NASA scientist. She is now on deputation to ISRO and participated as one among the group of scientists manning the monitoring consoles on October 25, 2008 at the Indian Deep Space Network Control Centre of Byalalu Village near Benguluru where a huge bowl-shaped antennae have been set up to track and communicate with Chandrayan I.

On September 24, 2002 Padmaja, got a NASA exceptional service medal in recognition of her outstanding service in developing the operational capability of the Multi-angle imaging spectrometer, and for overseeing its integration into Terra Mission System and its deployment in Earth orbit.

Exceptional service medal is awarded for significant, sustained performance characterized by *unusual initiative* or *creative ability* that clearly demonstrates substantial improvements or contributions in engineering aeronautics, space flight, administration support, or space-related endeavours that contribute to the NASA missions. ISRO signed an agreement with JPL in 2005 for JPL instrument M3 (Moon Minerology Mapped) to launch on India's satellite Chandrayaan I built by ISRO. Padmaja is leading this mission operations effort for JPL instruments M3.

She has reason to be proud of India's Moon Mission-a big success-as an NRI.

Comment

Daughter's case where all the three factors, that make up for personality viz. PIE – Parental Programming, Internal Aspirations, and External factors combine. Moreover opportunities in the US and the legacy of the family of hard working people. Initiative and creativity and a score of other soft skills can be identified gleaning through the details. Narayana had his contacts working in IIT, Kanpur as a technical scientist with a mere graduation in science. A family hailing from a middle class ordinary family with no monetary support could make because of values and skills.

P.P.P: Public – Private Participation

In the context of emergence of P.P.P. I felt like adding the following comment.

Bhargava's offer was an opportunity. The industry is always on the look out for talented young men, 'languishing' in Government organizations where bureaucracy is stifling. You might say PPP – what is in vogue in 2008 – Public Private Participation, indirect then, direct now. The politicians must understand the synergies in PPP, not wrangle, quarrel, and stifle the good effects. I have seen some bright young officers from banks lured away by private enterprises. It can be both ways. The talented in private can move to public organizations. Though Narayana had not gone for higher studies, (had he done so, he would have become another Prasad among the Varanasis) and remained a technician but took special courses in mid-career in the US when he got opportunity to go abroad.

Yet another opportunity in 1965; he quickly moved to IIT Kanpur, as a technical assistant, where his talent was nurtured and his contribution reaped. From Kanpur he moved to Mexico, not the US; Mexico to US was a short route and easy to move. He changed companies but not career. He had complete control on the direction, he made his journey slowly but steadily like, the tortoise in the story.

Both the cases cited above are histories of those who did not deviate from their chosen careers and had a good grip over themselves.

Case 5

NRI Couple

There is another case history of pair who landed in the US and pursuing successful careers. It is different from the first case. Sobhashree studied in Bangalore (now Benguluru) earned her B.E. in electrical engineering from Bangalore University in 1987. She married a cousin who also did engineering in Bangalore and obtained a doctorate in the US. Following the marriage in the same year Shobashree moved to the US and got an MS in Electronics in 1990. She is currently a Senior Research Assistant in a reputed company. Ashok, her husband worked for reputed companies in the US for two decades as engineer and then as researcher. Since a couple of years he has become an entrepreneur having experienced discrimination to ethnic Indians who are found not inferior to native Americans, particularly in the area of research.

The couple lives in New Jersey, USA happy and contended. They are extremely busy couple with tours, attending conferences and seminars, and meeting clients, where their soft skills make an impact.

They have changed jobs successfully with full control over the careers without sacrificing attention on children, or social life. The SUCCESS[2] apply to them-*set forth, unique* to each other and yet managing together, *controlled chosen careers, enjoyable*, and *enterprising, stable* and *satisfying.* Their relations with their parents and cousins are excellent. Applying the test of vocational personality, together they have all the six types in them. Conventional, realistic, enterprising, artistic, meticulous, and social. They are made for each other. At the beginning of the education choices, or marriage choice did they expect or plan all this to happen? Do you think they would have had mentors or role models? Their parents could have tried to influence them. Being obedient children of their parents, they might have listened to them. But what ultimately happens is their assertive choices and decision making.

[2] **SUCCESS:** Setforth; unique; Chose; Controlled; Enjoyable; Stable; Satisfying

Case 6

Junior Venkat

We have seen passion for career not financially successful one– Venkat's. His nephew, a junior Venkat had equal passion for photography. When he was studying M.Sc in Botany in Chennai his uncle, the senior Venkat tried to influence him not to waste his time in studying something for which he has no passion. He advised him to study something related to photography. The junior was attracted to the idea and wrote a long letter to his father. His father wrote an equally long letter explaining his view point. He explained to him that he was not at all against his interest in photography. He asked him to continue with studies and complete his M.Sc without wavering and promised to send money for his hobby. He need not account for the expenditure.

Junior Venkat acknowledges today and is ever grateful to his late father for he has now become a scientist and naturalized American citizen. His love for photography, which he learned from uncle Venkat as a school boy continued with the same passion. He is even grateful to his uncle.

His career as scientist is also a journey with milestones. Junior completed his Ph.d in Bangalore in 1987 and in 1988 relocated to the US to pursue post doctoral research. Then in 1990 he moved to Germany also for research after being awarded a fellowship from Alexander Von Humboldt Stiftung (Foundation). In 1992 he returned to the US to pursue research. Under pressure from mother he joined a commercial organization but in a research department. He remained unmarried because of uncertainty about career changes in future. He is very assertive and independent in his decision making. He finds solace in his hobby– photography.

'He invests huge sums on the photography equipment-even the professional photographer do not invest', that was the comment of a professional.

Homi Bhabha's father's advice and junior Venkat's father's advice are identical. One can choose more than one career. That can be a norm for SUCCESSFUL life.

A Stepping Stone (Titbit)

1. Workers of Indian BPO Industry see their work in call centres as temporary and are constantly on the look out for more fulfilling work.
2. They are neither satisfied with the so-called *comfortable* jobs which allow them to escape the perils of joblessness or work; nor do they want the sub contracting trend to end despite their recognition of the many negative professional, social and physical effects of the jobs'.

Mohan Thite and Bob Russel, in the Introduction to *The Next Available operator: Managing Human Resources in Indian Business* say:

> Research on call centres indicates that where cost minimization is a dominant business approach, the work environment is generally fast-paced, routine, monotonous, tightly controlled and contains *little scope for employee's discretion.*

Recall the distinction made in the chapter **'Introduction'** between labour and work. Discretion and autonomy that distinguish work from labour in which the labourer is not emotionally involved.

I was impressed with Deepthi, a degree student who expressed her anguish that her friends were being lured into the BPO industry instead of choosing a career. She refused to attend campus interviews. But she had family support which may not be available to such people the above titbit makes sense.

3

Enterprise, Entrepreneurship and Ethics

Entrepreneurship

The urge to start something on my own,
The desire to make a mark;
To get a smile replace that frown,
And make a difference and not for a lark.

The journey begins with high hopes,
A lot of enthusiasm and loads of passion,
The initial days; whiz by, learning the ropes,
Slowly, unknowingly, seeps in the frustration.

As one realizes that it is no bed of roses,
Rather one with many a thorn,
The cash burn happens in small doses,
And others begin to look at your in scorn!

But self-belief, you do not lose,
Patience becomes your friend,
New schemes, you start to propose,
And taste success, in the end.

The keys to this success,
Is determination & dedication;
Never do anything in excess,
And serve the society & the nation!

Vinay

We have seen the six vocational personalities. CR Ⓔ AMS: E stands for enterprising personality. Some of the attributes Holland identified are ambition, drive, energy, and competitive spirit. Other studies revealed they are essentially business risk-takers. David Maclelland (1961) studied the causal relationship between achievement motivation and entrepreneurial behaviour. Maclelland and his co-workers chose from a variety of theories – learning theory, education, mass media research, theories of attitude change, motivation theory, and psychotherapy.

Achievement Motivation Training

If we can train people to increase achievement motivation, which is needed for achievement in an individual, has been found that, 'even a moderate increase in the strength of achievement motivation would lead to better performance; it will enhance entrepreneurial behaviour.

The first achievement motivation training course was conducted for executives of a major American Corporation more than half-a-century ago. It was like selling ice-boxes to Eskimos because the target audience were already successful middle-level managers. Two years later two groups, one without training, the other with training, were compared. There was a marked increase in the trained group and negative change in the other.

The researchers chose developing countries like India where they could expect marked increase in performance because of existing low achievement motivation in general. 'The Indian training courses were given as a part of a research design which allowed a scientific assessments of the impact of the training in entrepreneurial behaviour and economic indices (McClelland & Winter, 1969). The experiments carried out in Kakinada in AP and Vellore in TamilNadu were revealing regarding promotions, increases in salary, starting a new business and/or expanding business. 'In all cases, the trained business group showed a substantial and significant increase in entrepreneurial activity in two years after training...' At the least, it brings out latent potential for entrepreneurial activity. The training, like all trainings, acted as a catalyst.

Elements of Training

Goal setting depends on the possibility and desirability of change. Two things are important: Confidence and commitment.

Motives Thoughts and actions that lead to the goal. Swami Vivekananda's words, 'Arise, Awake, stop not till the goal is reached', fell on deaf ears as if the listener lacked confidence in himself.

Recall what Swamiji had said about Western motivation.

> "An English boy will tell you, I am an English man, and I can do any thing'. 'The American boy will tell you the same thing, and so will any European boy. Can our boys say the same thing here? No, not even the boys' fathers. We have lost faith in ourselves".

The achievement motivation is consistent with the dominant cultural values. Much water has flowed since 1897 when Swamiji delivered this stirring speech. Today there is greater self confidence and commitment to succeed. They need support from the family, society and the Government.

Together with soft skills, like decision making, problem solving, and interpersonal and professional competence, will have synergetic and cumulative effect.

> 'Entrepreneurial training is apparently effective in generating a common concern among trainees for community betterment as a criterion for exploring or initiating a new venture'.

The fruits of 1960s training, the cascading effect is visible in India over years after those efforts of Mr.McClelland and others. There have been many role models for the next generation with latent talent to copy and flourish in an achieving society that is emerging in the country ever since.

Let me sum up the concepts as usual with two acronyms, besides those which were presented already in earlier chapters:

DRIVE[1] – *Desire* is strong; *Responsibility* for own actions; *Initiative*; behaviour based on *Values*; and *Energy* to work long hours, hard work. We might add **S** for *soft skills* repertoire making it DRIVE**S**. **S** also stands for service to the community.

---

[1] **DRIVES:** Desire; Responsibility; Initiative; Values; Energy; Soft skills.

The student may go through the appendix V, *A new model for Indian Entrepreneurship.*

They are a CASTE[2] unto themselves. Craft based castes flourished in India. We need entrepreneurial creed: *Concern for the community; Achievement motivation; Self-control; Taking calculated risks* and hedging against them*; Energy, Earnestness,* etc; the new caste with a new CREED[3]: *Commitment; Resourcefulness; Ethics; Earnestness; Devoid of greed,* where GREED[4] is *Getting; Rich; Easily; Eagerly; Devoid of ethics.* Complete absence of greed is the need of for this country with so much of poverty, poor health, and illiteracy.

Some of our boys and girls who are being exposed to the Western dominant cultural values are showing entrepreneurial behaviour, the Western concept of entrepreneurship discussed above.

Before we embark on cases of identified entrepreneurship, let us search for entrepreneurial behaviour in the cases already discussed in the previous chapter.

Where interest becomes passions, how does the career proceed? Here are some cases: We classified 'interests' under CAMPS: Commercial; art; music; poetry and literature; science & sports.

Case 1 : Venkat's (Cinematography) (Case 3)

Case 2 : Junior Venkat (Scientist, NRI) (Case 6)

Case 3 : Prabhakar's vocal music (Music) (Case 1)

- From early school days he dreamt he should become Movie Cameraman. He chose his career at the first opportunity, discontinuing studies in graduation. Careful study of Venkat's case reveals his entrepreneurial spirit: he attempted to produce films, tried his hand in TV serials, the most important of them, the very last would have given real break though late in life but for the fact that his heart failed him.

---

[2] **CASTE:** Concern for the community; Achievement motivation; Self-control; Taking calculated risks; Energy & Earnestness.

[3] **CREED:** Commitment; Resourcefulness; Ethics; Earnestness; Devoid of Greed.

[4] **GREED:** Getting; Rich; Easily; Eagerly; Devoid of ethics.

- Junior Venkat had Venkat as his role-model. Under parental influence he pursued pure science retaining photography as hobby life long.
- Prabhakar's father wanted him to become a lawyer. After his father's demise, he made music full time career.
- None of them had any commercial interest. Two of them, senior and junior Venkat's were members of an organization, the other set up his own organization, Prabhakar is showing entrepreneurial behaviour. There is the effect of globalization in every field. Music, Art and dance have no national boundaries. Commerce is globalised but with regulation and restriction.

TIPS-CAMPS

> "The British Council music entrepreneur award. "British Council will present *Young Music Entrepreneur Award* for entrepreneurs in the age group of 25 and 35 working in the field of music directly or its related wings… their work as an *artiste* should be secondary to their focus as an entrepreneur in the promotion of music. The candidates will be judged on the basis of their entrepreneurial abilities in *music business*".

What CAMPS do they belong? Commerce or Music? C or M? It is the business of Music. Music has already become business where more of soft skills than hard music skills are called for.

What personality CREAMS does such an award winner belong? It is a combination–Enterprising, Artist, not artiste of performing art. His performance is judged in promoting music. He must have DRIVE–desire, responsibility, initiative, values, and energy–He must have achievement motivation, creativity, risk taking ability, self-reliance and self monitoring after setting challenging but achievable goals.

In the previous chapter we have seen Prabhakar's mission, to spread music among all sections of the society which was confined to a small sections with music tradition. Like artisans of village economy singing was confined to communities. So also instrumental music. Folk music is again a community affair. Theatre troops, *jangam* and so on. 'Promotion of music', that is what Prabhakar has been doing, not Music business.

Entrepreneur is used with reference to business... marketing skills are called for. A professional becomes a businessman with a mission. There are others who remain professionals. After their attainment and receiving award, they may divert their attention to larger society–teachers, heads of music institutions, networking, seminars, workshops, expos, and so on.

Alternative Careers – Right Livelihood

In this book I have included some rare careers whose number is on the increase. Or is it because these careers are gaining more and more attention? I have culled these cases from newspapers.

1. Ms S.S. who wanted to become a doctor but landed in social service with a post graduate qualification in social work.
2. J.K.Rowling's rags-to-riches story by persisting with her interest and talent for writing fiction. She developed Harry Potter's world as a means of escape.
3. The Hollywood hero, Paul Newman had many side careers. Newman's food products with his name and photo on the labels earned huge profits which he used for philanthropy. He left a charitable legacy after death.
4. Gandhi is remembered but not scores of his followers who silently do the service which he had propagated. They are rarely noticed. Tamil Nadu's couple among 'Alternative Noble Winners'. Their organization LAFTI won an award of about Rs.1.34 crores.
5. Three more women, a journalist from America, a Swiss-born doctor, and an activist from Somalia were named winners of the Right Livelihood Award, also known as the 'Alternative Nobel'. A brief account is given to make the students stop and think of laudable careers of self-motivated persons.
6. Journey to unlock 'out-of-body' mysteries. Dr.Penny Sartori began a research, which is the largest clinical study to date, in 1997 and completed data collection in 2003. The project was written up and results analysed in 2005 and awarded Ph.D. It was a research on Near Death Experiences-NDE!. Talent and interest and rare personality characteristics combined in a career of this nature.

7. Four young women from west headed to Kancheepuram in Tamil Nadu to study the power of micro finance. They discovered that 'development happens through empowerment and not through dependence.' A first hand knowledge.

These cases, if studied with focus on own dreams, values, and interest will give insights into one's own self.

Right Livelihood Career

- Dr. Hauser and her colleagues have helped more than 70,000 traumatized women and girls in war and post-war areas. A Swiss born with Italian passport and living in Germany does all this work. Such people are free people. They have no boundaries. They remind us of what Sri Rabindranath Tagore wrote, 'Where the world is not broken up into fragments by narrow domestic walls... into that heaven of *freedom* my Lord, let my country awake.'
- Asha Hagi, Somali lawmaker promotes peace in her homeland continuing to lead at *great personal risk* the female participation in the peace and reconciliation process. She helps women get involved in politics.
- Amy Goodman founder and host of the syndicated radio and television programme Democracy Now! She was 'truly independent political journalist whose Democracy Now! brings to millions of people the alternative *voices* that are often excluded by main stream media'.
- Krishnammal and Jagannathan, the Sarvodaya couple, have devoted their long lives for putting into practise Gandhian principles. Gandhi is known all over the world. There are may silent Gandhians work life long to realize in practice the Gandhian vision of social justice and sustainable human development. They are referred as India's Soul.

All these are self-actualized persons, living gods who do not clamour for limelight.

A Swedish-German philanthropist Jakob Von Uexkull founded 'alternative Nobel' prize or Right Livelihood Award in 1980 to recognize the work he felt was being ignored by the Nobel prizes.

All the four above mentioned women were awarded the alternative Nobels this year. They did not work for awards but the awards are a recognition to them, an encouragement to others to do same.

A story of a Striving Woman who made News– An entrepreneur with a difference

Ms. SS wanted to become a doctor. But her parents would not let her to go to a boys' college. She ended up with a post-graduate degree in social work. Social work, became a passion with her. She learned through her PG course how to help people. She corrects herself 'helping' is the wrong word 'You must render service, and realize you are actually empowering not helping'. Articulation is a must soft skill; one should express emphatically, with clarity.

Marriage brought her to Mumbai where she did doctoral programme in Sociology from Bombay University. The Ph.D has given more knowledge and additional impact to her resolve to continue with the career. She participated in debates on Marxism and feminism. 'Those five years', she believes, 'developed her character, her thought processes and her analytical skills'.

She refined, improved and developed her communication skills in all branches/genre. She feels that social work and sociology are a wonderful combination to serve people.

She worked with a leading publisher picking up the important commercial nuances in the of publishing trade. (MO Ⓓ ES – Direct Experience)

Entrepreneur with a difference – Big Deal – Dignity for the aged.

Craving for creative expression she joined the Tata Institute of Social Services. (TISS) hoping to introduce the concept of 'University Press' there without success. Frustrated she started her own magazine 'Dignity Dialogue'. In three months the magazine touched a circulation of 4000 copies. 'Serve the aged in such a way that they cherish and retain their dignity.' That's the slogan she developed for her guidance.

She found Dignity Foundation. She became an entrepreneur. The achievement motivation is very much in evidence. If she is asked to rank the REJOICE questionnaire, her automatic choice would be *challenging work, independence and freedom and opportunities to learn.* She was taking risks, tenacity was her forte. An entrepreneur with a difference. She is also an institution builder.

The Dignity Foundation was formed in 1998 and this grew into the most comprehensive service and care provider for elders. The scope of its activities include helpline, job counseling service, teaching programme, a vigilance project, a network of protection for elders, a loneliness mitigation project, a dementia care services and even a senior citizens' ID card.

Their most recent and ambitious project is Dignity Lifestyle, a sprawling complex spread over 25 acres near Matheran, which positions itself as a 'hassle-free' retirement township, not an old age home. Such a gigantic task needs money. What are her fund-raising skills? Mother Teresa is known to be mega fund raiser. Otherwise all the service she is rendering is not feasible. 'Somehow money comes from some where.' (Power of positive thinking).

'It is not enough if you are social worker. You have to market your cause. You have to brand it in marketing language. She has to be a brand ambassador herself.' She says.

'India is not yet in the mode of the corporate NGO' she continues, *yet NGO field is a huge career opportunity'.* Entrepreneurial Behaviour is called for. It is a calling.

Money is important but you feel you are contributing to something tangible and the joy is immense.... The contribution is visible and gives important gratification.

'The joy of making sunset years of thousands of elders most meaningful and happy is most fulfilling.' Helping people advanced in age advance to leave a legacy of their own.

Case 7

Travails of an Entrepreneur

I am a Mechanical Engineer by chance and not by choice. However, I always wanted to be either an independent professional or an entrepreneur.

My academic career kept on taking turns from my early childhood. First I shifted from ICSE syllabus to Matriculation by choice because I had no interest in Geography, History and Civics for the sake of examinations. It is not that I hated History or Civics. I later went on to read a lot of books written by Romila Thapar and DD Kosombi on Indian History and participated in debates on positive and negative aspects of Democracy and Communism. I am the only person in my house who watches National Geographic channel on TV.

The shift from ICSE to Matriculation was in 8th class. While joining the Pre-Matriculation I chose Biology and Physics as my main subjects, this was done on the advice of my elders as I felt that I would be able to pursue my ambition of being an independent professional. However, I could not get through the Medical Entrance exam after my intermediate.

After that, I did not want to continue with Biology stream because I did not see any future as an independent professional in it if I were not to become a Doctor. Even though I got myself admitted into B.Com class I was not very keen on continuing because I was not sure that I would be able to be independently work with my father and brother who are also in the same field.

Since my father was a committee member in one of the Engineering colleges I wanted to try switching over to engineering stream and get a seat on the management quota. I took up mathematics in 1982 after a gap of four years, because my matriculation syllabus had only arithmetic and I was not familiar with subjects like trigonometry. I had to struggle a bit to be on par with the regular intermediate students with maths background. I continued my efforts sincerely and even though donation and management quotas had been abolished by NT Rama Rao during his first year as chief minister. I could get through the engineering entrance exam and secured an engineering seat on merit in 1983.

I was not a very meritorious student throughout my academic career and the percentage of marks I got in any subject depended on the interest I had in the subject. I never studied with examination in mind. I was an active student who participated in debates with teachers in the class! However, when it came to studies I would spend relatively less time but always tried to thoroughly understand what I was studying. Wanting to understand but not ready to spare enough time always affected my examination results. However, I was confident that I had a command on whatever I had learnt.

I was a student during the times when the student community was actively involved in the political thinking process. It was the time when there were Police camps in RECs. I was very much attracted towards Marxist theories during my student days. People might find this a bit contradictory on one trying to be an independent professional / entrepreneur and being a believer in Marxism. I would like to clarify the point that the interest in Marxism had only made me feel more independent and made me able to think beyond the traditional lines like God, luck, destiny etc. and made me believe that only we ourselves should be blamed and god and destiny should not be held responsible for whatever happens to us.

Search of a Job

Immediately after my engineering, even before I could get my degree certificate, I was off to Hyderabad in search of a Job. I took up the first opportunity that came by way and joined as a Production Supervisor in a Tool Room. The owner of the Tool Room offered me a job only because I told him that I came to Hyderabad just because some one had told me that the Tool Room was looking for some fresh Engineers. He was surprised at my initiative. Even though I worked there for only few months, I gathered rich experience in the manufacturing process in Mechanical engineering.

I tried a brief stint as a publisher after my first job. I got into publishing only because my brother was funding the business and my friend was promising to run it. In my enthusiasm to run an enterprise, I had not looked into what is required to be a successful publisher. The venture failed within 6 months. This failure has taught me that I should not get into running an enterprise until I was confident enough of handling it by myself.

I wavered for some time in deciding whether I should pursue further studies or to take up a job. The only time I again tried for a Job was in 1990 and I could clear the interview because I could confidently answer the questions in the field of manufacturing processes in Mechanical Engineering. My ability to grasp things fast and my involvement in my earlier job (Even though it was few months) made me answer the questions like some one who has had two years experience. I got into ITW India Limited, a US multinational and continued to work till 1994. ITW is a packaging Machines Manufacturing Company and I worked as a Product Development Engineer in its R&D Division. During my four and a half years stint in ITW I was mainly into production of machines and conveyors. However; I got involved in the design and development of various machines and conveyors and gained rich experience in the same.

Immediately after joining ITW I got married to Ratna Kumari. Since I was always very clear on being an independent professional / entrepreneur I chose to marry an independent woman who would be able to take the responsibility of running the house in case I were to take some chances in trying to be independent. I think this decision helped me a lot because I did not have to face much of a resistance during my initial days of adventure as an entrepreneur. As we knew each other since our college Days (1985) she was very much aware of my attitude and ambitions and hence my decision to start on enterprise did not come as a surprise to her. She was ready to face the difficulties associated with starting an enterprise and was aware that we might have to go without much income from the enterprise in the initial stage.

During my stay in Hyderabad I renewed contacts with many of my college class mates, especially spent more time with Srinivas Garimella and we spent a lot of time in discussing the possibilities of starting different enterprises. Garimella was working for an IT Company at that time. Most of my class mates had rich experience in Marketing and did well in their respective careers. We deliberated different options in IT, HR and Manufacturing. Since I was more comfortable in manufacturing and Garimella's Marketing experience can be utilized in any field, we chose to get into the manufacturing sector.

We started a manufacturing company – Vega, with an initial investment of around Rs.60,000 for the next four years, we pumped in an additional five lakhs by borrowing from our family members. Over and above the borrowings, another indirect source of funding was our working without drawing any remuneration. We could manage our personnel finances for four years without getting paid. My colleague had to undergo a lot of difficulties due to lack of finance. Even though my wife was working, I had the responsibility of bringing up two children by the time I became an entrepreneur and my colleague had to postpone getting married due to lack of financial support.

Initially Vega was a product company, i.e. we manufactured a product as per an initial design and sold it to customers who were in need of it. The product we dealt with is called the Carton Sealing Machine—which is a machine used in secondary packaging. A product company requires a distribution network, economies of scale, capability to develop a cost effective, esthetic product. Over a period of time we felt that we need to change the type of business we were into because we felt that our core strength lay in our ability to understand the customer's requirements and finding a solution to it. We got into the field of Conveying and automation because the knowledge required to develop packaging machines can be applied to designing conveyors. Since conveyors are generic products which are required in any industry we could go to different industries to discuss about their requirements. During the initial stage of business itself my colleague's strength of marketing helped us in getting orders from reputed companies like SKF Bearings, Ashok Leyland, etc. This helped us in establishing a good foundation and the experience in understanding the requirements.

Initially we did not have any track record to prove our capabilities to our customers. Hence they used to make demands of us which their regular vendors were not willing to give. This made us to undertake complicated projects and execute them. Even though not all of our solutions were successful, customers never doubted out sincerity in trying to give a workable solution. The sincere efforts helped us to build a good customer base and we are proud to say that 60% of the customers in any given year are our old customers.

Sai Srinivas

Case of Sai Srinivas - Entrepreneurship

Engineering was not his choice. But he became a successful self-employed engineer. It was not as if he does not make choice. He skipped school career to jump to matriculation. Did it make any difference? Of the MODES of learning (Media & Mediation) he avoided mediation and emphasized on media-print medium as his learning mode of history books-original authors-not text books. He participated in debates, thereby sharpened his political and sociology subjects. His interest appears to be in humanities not sciences. He seems to give value to elders' advice. He chose biology and physics subjects! He wanted to be an *independent* professional. He could not get through the entrance examination. Had he, he would have become a doctor and set up independent practice as per his *desire.*

Again studying B.Com could have been due to pressure from family members. He was afraid he would lose his *independence* had he graduated in commerce, for he would have to serve in his father's firm. He hoped he could get into engineering through the back door. Once the back door was closed by the Government (managements quota was abolished), he worked hard and got a seat in Engineering on merit which shows that the fellow has *determination* and can put in hard work. These qualities get well with the freedom and independence he desired so much. He could take up challenging work. It appears he does not like learning by rote. But he was debating with his teachers. Questioning assumptions and facts, seeking clarification, debating and discussing, he might have earned the wrath of the teachers whose only concern was to complete the course!

Modern teaching methods like participatory methods, he would have loved. He retained whatever he learned and understood. It has long term implications to the enterprising and the independent. There is no place for words like 'luck', 'destiny' in his dictionary.

Practical experience. Armed with the 'abstract concepts', be joined a tool room for practical experience as a production supervisor. Sai admits it was rich experience even though short.

(Read Appendix V for Indian entrepreneurship).

Practical experience gives a very high degree of confidence. It is true in his case. Whether he consciously set goals for the learning during internship, or not, the way he went about first experience, we must believe that he did. One thing that is apparent was he did not have a course in career planning, goal setting, etc. One thing is certain that he had positive thinking which was his strength.

He had a negative learning, learning through failure when he published a magazine. Why did he take up the venture? He answered that he wants to gain experience of independent enterprise. The failure would have affected his confidence level, but for his attitude towards success and failure. That is the only explanation we can give because he went on to gain many success experiences.

The short experience in the tool room has boosted his confidence which enabled him to present and impress the ITW(India) officials.

From production supervisor in a tool room to product development engineer was a jump to Sai. That was in R & D division. It is here his creative talent came to light. As in the case of *Awakening* movie hero, the doctor, who discovered his talent for inter-personal skills by working as a regular duty doctor in a hospital, Sai discovered his talent for designing machines. This is the key difference between *direct* practical experience and *mediated* or *media* (print or electronic) learning. In R & D department there is more scope for learning by experimentation at the cost of the company. It was this experience that made him quit the job and declare independence that paved the way for entrepreneur to 'awake and arise' and he has not stopped or looked back till he reached his goal, to borrow Swami Vivekananda's call: *'Awake, arise, and stop not till the goal is reached.'*

His choice of life's partner and choice of business partner too are well designed products.

Elsewhere in this book I presented a questionnaire-REJOICE your motivation. The spirit of independence and freedom predominant in Sai, a value made visible.

I have come across a beautiful definition of design; 'values made visible.'

What are other values of Sai visible to you?

Opportunities to learn. He is a learner who sees opportunities to learn for future use. There is a pithy saying that '*an optimist is one who sees opportunity in every calamity; the pessimist sees calamity in every opportunity.* Sai, the positive thinker is an optimist. Every decision he took from school days onwards point to this optimism and positive thinking. That's his power. That should be yours, too.

ITW is a packaging machines manufacturing company. The knowledge he applied to designing conveyers which has mass market in industrial sector. Before actually starting the designing conveyers he and his friend, a marketing man, began market research, a new skill altogether for Sai, but his friend has this knowledge and skills. Together they have larger portfolio of skills.

At this stage we have to digress and discuss multiplicity of talents to be recognised: CRISS[5] Talents - *creativity, reasoning ability, information processing, speed and spatial relations,* and *a portfolio of skills*, euphemistically called by a variety of names– social skills, human skills, soft skills. life skills, etc, remained 'soft-skills' in keeping with the IT boom and hype. More and more skills are being brought under its umbrella-Business English to leadership skills. Under *portfolio* of skills I venture to include reading and writing. We can add *precision movement, manual dexterity* as engineering or hard-skills. Just as you cannot design software products without the necessary hardware, the soft skills need appropriate hard skills or technical skills.

I have discussed triangle of skills of a professional manager elsewhere which includes conceptual skills. I referred to this skill–viewing the enterprise as a viable system in a specified environment. Do Sai and his partner have conceptual skills? Marketing people develop this skill which is a manner of seeing than doing. But the skill leads to appropriate *decision making* (skill) and *problem-solving* (skill) both of which are integral to the

---

[5] CRISS: Creativity; Reasoning ability; Information processing; Speed & Spatial relations; portfolio of skills

portfolio of skills they combine. To *collaborate* and build *consensus,* they need the ability in *information processing* like *data collection, analysis,* etc. each one is a skill or talent that one acquires more on the job than in the mediated class-room, or reading books.

Direct experience, also called experiential learning is the most potent of all learning modes as can be seen in the case of Sai's career progress.

Data collection for market research

'Initially Vega (the name of the company) was a product company'. They merely sell what they have. Thanks to guidance of people with marketing and market orientation it turned into a marketing company-identifying the requirements of the customers and satisfying them by giving *what they need and want.* This means collection of primary data. Go to the customers company and talk to the them, listen to them, and understand their needs and wants. Between what they need and what they want, there should not be any gap. Sai says, 'own core strength lies in our ability to understand the customer's requirement.' Sai is not an MBA. His partner supplied this knowledge and value which Sai learned and imbibed. This is the reason why MBA (Marketing) has additional value to all other professionals-better understanding of the environment and managing it, (conceptual skill)

The conventional and the realistic wife can caution enterprising husband. She can present another scenario necessary for decision making and goal setting. We used the phrase 'come together' to define the successful career; 'What we do for a living must align with what we want from life-the deeper things.' Both family life and work life have to 'come together'.

Success, we have considered as, Set forth (planning), Unique to individual and the family as a unit of life, Career choices, Controlled, Enjoyable and Enterprising too, steady, stable, and satisfying. We may have to take the family as a unit, not stop with the individual in focus.

As one poet put it, 'if husband is the aerial, wife should be earth,' only then the Radio reception is clear.

She can be a CREDIBLE[6] supporter: (*Collaborate, Re-Appraise, Evaluate, Diagnose, Inform; Build* (financial resources), *Leaven* (influence) *Encourage,* in normal times, in times of changes, challenges and crises.

Cultural Legacy

The old CASTE system must go. A new CASTE[7] system should come. Community, Artisan, *Self*-reliant, Traditional, *employment/*economic system

India, centuries back, flourished and prospered only to invite invasions and plundering leading to impoverishment of our masses.

'But politically caste has become a scourge. The solution does not lie in its abolishing, but in its modernity. In the economic senses'.

Small is Beautiful applies to caste as a segment of employment. Alvin Tofler coined the phrase 'electronic cottage' akin to village craftsman's cottage, in which self, partner, all the family, career or work, extended family life (community or caste) and finally village society merge. Where all the 'spaces' needs are met to lead a happy and contended life of interdependence.

New village artisan family will produce not what the local customer needs but goes beyond, with the help of community–caste which ensures loyalty. He can now produce to the global market. The same thing was done by the East India Company but not for the growth and development of the Indian artisan but for his impoverishment. Gandhi's solution was localizing, not globalizing. If Gandhi were living today, probably he would have redefined it. Although he said, 'local production is meant for local markets'; he also said,

---

[6] **CREDIBLE:** Collaborate; Re-Appraise, Evaluate; Diagnose; Inform; Build, Leaven; Encourage

[7] **CASTE:** Community; Artisans; Self-reliant; Traditional; Economic activity.

'I am not interested in mass production but I am interested in production by the masses.' His concern at that point of time was unemployment because of factory system which crippled the artisans.

Production by the masses marketed mass scale through community and country initiatives.

Case 8

Careers in Contrast, Two Career Paths But One Goal

After graduating from the Regional Engineering College, Rourkela, in August 1983, I joined one of the public sector Navaratnas. I wrote several competitive exams and was very hopeful of getting a job with the premier organization. Since the recruitment formalities and process was very slow I got my job offer sometime in March 1984 and joined the company on 26th April 1984.

Meanwhile, I took up a job as an Apprentice Engineer on a salary Rs.600 in 1983 in Ambica Steel Tubes a pipe manufacturing company where I took up a job while I was waiting for my job. That was when I used my Engineering knowledge as I was asked to design and order a double spring for the cutting machine. I went through my mechanical design books and ordered the spring costing about a thousand rupees from a private factory. I left the job in two months time when I got my offer from a Navaratna Public sector organization.

Ours is a HR centric organization where the growth up the ladder is very fast for disciplines like HR and to some extent, finance. After joining in Western sector at Mehsana, I underwent a training for four months on various aspects. After a brief posting at Mehsana, I worked in Baroda where I was deputed to Import Purchases department on a fast track multi million dollar World Bank funded project and I won a Director's award there.

Fearing that I would lose my promotions in my parent discipline due to lack of experience I opted out and joined field duty at Ahmedabad. I supervised work in Ahmedabad. Meanwhile, I got my promotion to the next grade and was working as Executive Engineer by 1989.

I learnt by then that promotions upto the fourth rank from joining were time bound, except in very rare cases when they are denied due to compelling reasons. I was lucky to be posted at Ahmedabad just after my marriage, where my in laws and my parents stayed. Though the field job was extremely tough as a young man I took everything in my stride.

I was posted to Assam in 1991 where I went with my wife and the first kid. The moment we landed there it was chaos as ULFA was very active and kidnappings for ransom were the order of the day. My superior officer was shot dead and there was a general strike-like situation for months. Eventually we settled down. By then I had my second kid and was also getting used to my field job. North east tenure is a must for promotions and my discipline is the only discipline where it is strictly enforced. I left Assam in 1994 and after working in Rajahmundry I was sent on deputation to Internal Audit. I was reporting to finance head and it was a very powerful post. By then the company became the only public sector to have an ISO certification for its Internal Audit department and audit manual was rewritten. I won Regional Director's group award in 2001 when I was in charge of data base for southern region. I got a chance to work on Unix server and data base was in oracle. I also got a certificate as Data Base Administrator in Oracle-8i.

Meanwhile, I was transferred once to Karaikal for two years as head of planning and technology division where I stayed alone and used to commute on week ends. I was called back to Chennai Internal audit from Karaikal and could stay with my family for three years till getting a Transfer to Assam in 2007. While in Audit I got a good exposure to SAP as I was trained in 10 modules (front end) of SAP.

Now I could not take my family to Assam as my elder daughter was in second year of Engineering at Manipal and younger daughter was in class X. I was given charge of Area Manager for working on a budget of about Rs.75 crore per annum.

I did well in the first year. I am presently working in the personal cell as adviser to Group General Manager-Head of my specialization,. I got a lot of job satisfaction unlike my colleagues most of whom have left for fat pay packages, mostly in the Middle East. Due to my job rotation and exposure to various departments, places and nature of jobs I never got a chance to get bored. By the time I settled down in any new assignment I had a transfer within the same sector for a different assignment or out of the sector. Very few people in my company have had as many transfers (a few I had by choice) as me. I had eight transfers in 24 years. This is my 25th year.

I am working as Chief Engineer and expect to get a promotion as Dy GM in August 2009. My only regret is that I could not take my family everywhere after my first tenure in Assam as my children started their schooling at Chennai at one of the best schools and both of them will complete the basic education there itself.

The company is one of the few public sector giants that allows you to retain your family in any city and pays for all allowances and vehicle allowance and extra facilities while staying alone. The company has paid about Rs.15 lakh for an expensive cancer treatment which saved the life of my father. There are two extreme views about my company, which people normally entertain.

1. People are not cared for, overlooked often during promotions, Field people are the worst neglected lot. Only appeasing the boss works here. Transfers are quite frequent and second tenure in Assam is done mostly for specialists engineers like me.
2. The company is the best PSU, a Navaratna, which cares for its people. There is a lot of job security.

It became a Public Limited Company in 1994. Each employee was given 650 shares. By now they have grown to more than 1,000 shares worth Rs.1000 each. The allowances and perks are very handsome.

So far, I am satisfied with my career progress and I have no regrets with decisions I had to take from time to time regarding my wife, children and also aged parents.

R.S.

Compare and contrast with the Sai Srinivas's a mechanical engineer turned an entrepreneur. Identify their distinct soft skills.

One studied in high profile institution, the other in ambitious new college. Their personalities vary; their career anchors are different. One became an intrapreneur a member of an organization as employee showing characteristics of an entrepreneur and the other entrepreneur. Both have same zeal, enthusiasm and commitment. Both made sacrifices. One enjoyed freedom and independence and the other had to content with bureaucratic shackles.

Both believe in the philosophy-

'What one asks for is not wealth, but enough to work unhampered, to be free, frank, and independent'

Somerset Mougham

Case 9

A journey to engineer information

Ambitions take different turns in one's life. Some people achieve what they aim at, though at different stages in their lives. However, for some, the aims change and the achievements become a relative term. During my school-going days, when I was asked what I would become, my response was shaped by my affinity to science. Becoming a scientist was my first choice. Today, I am an information engineer, working for a software company. This journey has been a roller-coaster ride. It would be interesting for me to remember the track of the ride.

The visit to moon by the Indian astronaut, Rakesh Sharma, left a deep impression on me. At the age of 14, when I passed my tenth, I was closely watching the developments in the field of science and technology. Ancient Indian science fascinated me. Considering my background, I was deeply inclined towards philosophical topics. Without being aware of the working of my mind, a fusion of science and philosophy was taking place in my mind.

Like in any middle-class family, my parents wanted me to become an engineer or a doctor. However, thair's were based on what the world thought about these professions and not on my interests. There is a phase when a child is confused and is torn between instincts and the desire to satisfy parent's ambitions. But as I grew up I figured out that the dream of becoming an engineer was not realizable. Keeping in view the career options, I went for a B.Sc course in Maths, Physics and Chemistry.

In the early 90s, I went on to finish a Postgraduate Diploma course in Management Information Systems with Computer Applications. At this stage, I was looking for an opening in a software company. This was only to keep my ambition of becoming a scientist alive. My first interview was a disaster. I did not match the expectations of the panel that interviewed me. I was candid enough to tell them that I was interested in this job to fulfil my dream in space science. And that was the end of it.

With the social interaction I had with my friends, my interest switched to civil services. The next opportunity that came my way was looking after a computer lab in a management institute. I thought this job would give me enough time to prepare for the competitive exams. Though I could successfully discharge the duties at the institute, my preparation for the competitive exams was inadequate. I could not hold on to this job for a long time because of my *wavering ambitions.*

At the same time, I came under the influence of the teachings of Jiddu Krishnamurti. It was a liberating experience for a young man in search of social security. I realized that the security blanket that we would like to create did not really exist.

With introduction to teaching and drama, I found myself teaching at a school for a short time. I am always interested in teaching, but I can never think of it as a source of livelihood.

Then came an interesting turn in my life. I got introduced to people at a publishing house. That triggered my passion in the universe of book editing. I was trained and employed as a Production Editor at a reputed publisher. The 2-year stint at this place taught me a lot of interesting things. The mind took a detour from science to language. This was another great twist. I could never imagine that the day would come when I would seriously think of language. Due to a layoff in the company, I had to quit this job. However, I did not quit the profession. I continued with freelance editing during this time. I got a job in another startup publishing house as an editor in medical literature. I was also working with charitable trusts to edit and typeset their journals.

The BPOs were making an entry into India. Language played an important role for people working in BPOs. Medical Transcription caught my attention. Six months into it, I became a medical transcriptionist. The fact that medical transcription is a specialized skill is undeniable. However, the nature of job frustrated me. The mechanical aspect of the profession such as listening to the same dictations, working in night shifts, and leading a sedentary lifestyle, put me down. I resigned without any job on hand. There was just one thing that I could fall back on, and that was teaching. I pursued MA English during this time and was exploring opportunities to teach. I had uploaded my resumes in various job portals. One day I received a call from a research institute for an opening in their communications department. They considered me for the post of editor because of my language skills and not because I had the domain knowledge.

The interesting part in this journey to becoming an editor is the realization that my resume morphed into a form where the employer could consider it. Resumes play a vital role in clinching a call for the interview. The presentation, layout, and grammar should proclaim what you are. I must confess that it took me eight years to understand the significance of resume writing and interview calls.

Coming back to my profession at the research institute as an editor, I was happy with it as long as I learnt new things about writing. This job gave me an opportunity to pursue other educational interests. At that time, I became interested in media studies. There were institutes offering courses in Communications and Journalism. I completed a course in the media studies. This helped me leverage my position as an editor to writer. I noticed the difference between the two. Editing somebody's content is a language issue. However, writing gives one immense satisfaction.

I continued exploring opportunities in the areas of writing. Technical Writing was becoming the most sought-after profession in the software industry. To strengthen my language skills, I trained myself in Instructional Design. My resume was forwarded to software companies.

Finally I got a call from a data storage firm. As a writer in a software firm, you need many roles rolled into one. You are the typesetter, writer, editor, interviewer, and planner. Today, I am happy to be a writer. You cannot ask for more if you are working with a multinational company that is among top 20 best places to work. I joined this company a year and 9 months ago, and the job satisfaction index shot up exponentially. Working for such a company not only provided me an opportunity to understand new technologies. It also helped me understand the work-life balance. For a person to be productive at office, the family life is as important as the professional life. Financially, I am better off with a good pay package.

In fact, the term technical writer is an old-fashioned term. This term is slowly losing its sheen and is being replaced with a new term called "Information Engineer." Though my parents will not agree that I am an engineer, my heart tells me that I became one in my own way. From here, I intend to become an Information Architect. If engineering information is supporting a software product with user-centric content, then information architecture is the underlying structure that regulates information engineering.

- *Ashwathama*

Comment

Look at the way our information engineer changed his jobs and careers. On the way he gathered more qualifications PGDMIS, M.A.(English), course on media studies, trained himself in Instructions Design. One day he may become an Information Architect!

He found happiness in being a writer—a technical writer, euphemistically called information engineer, which his parents refuse to accept. Their dream remained a dream. Will he become a scientist to fulfill his own dream?

What about his soft skills? He was candid enough to admit, 'my wavering ambitions'. 'wandering mind'. He says, 'that teaching is not a source of livelihood'?! Had he not been layed off from the reputed publishing house? He lost the job not the career; from editor he graduated to writer—career is same.

What do you make out of his being influenced by the exposure to the late Jiddu Krishnamurthy. There are others who were influenced by the novels of Ayn Rand. All of them were steadfast in their beliefs and therefore their behaviours. To say they have exemplary soft skills is to say the least. They take control of their own careers whatever they are.

Case 10

A career In the Living Laboratory

I studied computer engineering, and did my MBA majoring in finance and minoring in marketing, strategy, etc. Finally, I ended up in a software company as the boom was picking up then. I was interested in getting exposed to multiple areas, technology, marketing, people interaction, etc. for nine years. I was with a small software company managing software teams that developed small and large products. I conceptualized products/features based on R&D and feedback, lead implementation and customization projects, did business development and marketing for these right up to billing products. Simultaneously, I was involved in project costing, recruitment, appraisals, and people issues. Thus I was involved in everything except what I majored in, finance, and I enjoyed , nonetheless.

Though I studied finance, internally I think I am not cut out for it and my natural, internal inclination for technology, people, variety asserted itself during my career. It certainly helped that for these inclinations I had corresponding training (software, MBA), which was also needed for the job. Thus since I was not keen in switching jobs, I rose in position as the company grew. Over time, whether I liked the job or not I stayed with the company and tried to feel and understand its deeper problems and its uses; help to do whatever it took, to address these what they call 'taking full responsibility', an attitude which is an important skill

How do we recruiters judge these skills and aptitude for assuring responsibility in the course of a 30-minute, three-hour or three-day interview? I think it takes at least a year to know if you have chosen the right candidate.

It is important also to understand what one's inner inclinations are and do work that matches these besides addressing social needs. My own inclination had not been for a corporate career. I liked nature and wanted to live in a village as I found city life artificial in many ways. I was not too clear on what I would do in the midst of natural setting in a village, neither did I have any skills or experience in this. Luckily in my college days we had professors who encouraged those interests, introduced us to people who had done things in our areas and made us read more to develop deeper understanding. Slowly, I visited a few others who have done work and my path crystalised to owning land in a village, farming on it, restoring natural biodiversity and living sustainably in relation with it. I felt I needed time, say 5 years-to see if I can acquire skills and feel reassured that I am cut out for such a life. For the last three years I have been farming and staying in villages, and developed some contacts to pick up the requisite skills. I hope to be able to really live on more friendlier terms with nature and have greater biodiversity given some more time.

It has taken me many years to find out what I want and create a situation to try it out. It takes time and struggle to find our inclinations and courage to give up some of the comforts we have been used to. This is the price we have to pay during this *exploratory stage.* The savings I managed from the software career came in handy in pursuing my inclinations in a meaningful way.'

K.P.S

[He is an I.I.T. from Chennai and an MBA of IIM, Kolkota.]

The last para is significant: Exploratory stage backed by financial support. Self-discovery takes time, struggle, and courage.

'The savings I managed etc.' is a message to all; not to change the life style because of higher income which needs to be saved for the future experiments which are by very nature are risky. The entrepreneurial behaviour may ignore the fact that the risks have to be managed too. Financial independence comes handy for risky decisions. The achievement motivation has this in-built quality in that they set moderately difficult and challenging goals and do not gamble.

Money is not Everything

A brilliant student, graduated from IIT followed it up with post graduation for IIM, Calcutta worked in a software company with a fat salary. But he was not happy.

He took up organic farming in Mysore with two of his former classmates. The two friends left him.

Then he went back to his native district and started organic farming. Although struggling he is happy because he finds it challenging and is interested in doing something beneficial to farming and farmers who are at present spending huge sums on seeds, fertilizers and pesticides. His experimentation will bring rewards to him and to the agricultural economy...

Case 11

India Abroad

RR was three years old when her neighbour took her to their home and taught dance steps. That was the exposure of the tiny tot to dance; that was in Mumbai.

Later the family came to Bangalore. In those days the places were still Bombay and Bangalore.

She joined a mission school at 6. When she was 7 years old, the school started dance lessons for extra fees.

The child asked her mother for permission. She was in the maternity home, after the birth of her younger sister. Child was asked to wait a month when mother would go to school and pay the fees. Next month mother went to school. The Principal asked her to pay fees for two months! The Principal explained that her child joined classes the previous month itself promising that her mother would pay for both months. How did Principal permit child in the first place? Perseverance of the Child!

This is an innate quality. It remained faithful to her in her later life, when she had to face innumerable problems. Her parents encouraged her talent and interest and allowed her personality to unfold.

But her parents never wanted her to become a professional dancer. Her father encouraged her to study the literature on Bharta's Natya Sastra. He even began writing a book for beginners. He could not complete which RR feels bad about it. Had he lived for another year he would have completed.

While she did not make up her mind on becoming a full time professional she got married to Ramesh who was employed in Germany.

RR accompanied her husband, almost cutting her career plans in dancing. With her science degree in India she could get a job in American embassy as an assistant. In the meantime she learnt and became proficient in German language. With her proficiency in both English and German she had an advantage over others. Because Indian degree was not recognized in Germany and there were no career opportunities for growth, she quit the job and joined TWA an Air Lines organization.

As she was progressing well in the company her two children were growing and the couple had to take an important and hard decision. Either wife or her husband, one of them had to resign to take care of the children and their education. RR resigned.

After the children have sufficiently grown up and learnt to take care of themselves and selected their own education. In Germany you cannot choose any course you want. It is their aptitude that limit their choices. Daughter took social science and the son linguistics course. Both of them learned music and dance respectively.

Now the children are more or less settled. She started to look at dance, her passion. Result – The establishment of the R.R. Academy for performing Art and Dance Theatre Productions.

As a resident of Berlin since 1977 she has taken dance and music far beyond the borders of India. Starting at the age of 9 she had presented innumerable solo and ensemble performances at prestigious venues in India, Europe and USA, earning rare reviews from dance critics and audiences for her 'rare grace, refinement and flawless technique, deft artistry, in *abhinaya* and posturing' 'sense of joy', 'sublime expression', 'strong expressiveness', innovative abilities, 'dexterity in foot work and rhythm' etc. she became a talented dancer and teacher, all hard skills of a dancer are in place.

By 1980 she launched a special programme in Germany for students of non-Indian origin and has trained many accomplished dancers from various countries at her academy.

In her multi-national dance theatre productions, she has incorporated disciplines like spoken theatre, martial arts and dances Flamenco, Balanese, and Modern Dance with artists of many countries creating awareness for the universality of movement and expression.

Her latest work consists of guiding a comparative study of modern movement analysis and the ancient art of Bharatha Natyam and presence at international conferences on dance and theatre research during yoga teachers training courses all over Europe.

She has publications both in English and German to her credit. She is creating social, cultural, and spiritual understanding to innumerable foreign audiences the world over. A professional, an activist and entrepreneur rolled into one.

As a teacher of dance and yoga her workshops and seminars are known for their intense pedagogic content. She received recognition from the District Mayor of Berlin in 1994. She herself learns new items.

From the foregoing account you can easily list many skills, values, and personality characteristics. She has almost all the qualities and values of a true professional. Her commitment competencies, control and courage are evident from the narrative.

Creativity innovation and entrepreneurship visible and effective.

Not a day passes in her life without a clear goal and plan of action harnessing of resources, hers and others, to accomplish her goal and task on hand.

When did she plan all this? There is drive and direction and series of short term goals merging into a larger mission of her life. Yes. She chose her career after some wandering. When opportunity came she did not look back. She has kept on growing and developing and helping many others accomplish their goals in life.

She took control of her career completely. She has no cause to blame anyone else for anything. She dedicates all she does to her late father and ever grateful to him for the freedom and guidance he gave her.

She found resemblance to Indian worship of goddesses in some of the countries of erstwhile Russian countries where Prechristian Pagan culture is visible.

Recall CREAMS of 6 vocational personalities we have seen. She combined in her SEA- *Social, Enterprising,* and *Artistic personality.* As she grew in name and fame and a responsible teacher she learnt characteristics of *realistic* and *meticulous* personalities of being practical and careful.

Life long learning is feasible. She is a role model for others.

Every year she comes to India with her students to acclimatize them to Indian cultural milieu. Students give their performances and win applause from Indian audiences. During her visits to India she learnt developments in different forms of dance. She invariably visits Kuchipudi Village. She networks with dancers of many countries.

For the past few years RR has been toying with the idea of getting a doctorate. She is only a science graduate from an Indian university which is not recognized in Germany. More over, she has to do Master's first and then go in for doctoral studies. She shared her aspiration with several professors both in India and in Germany. One Indian professor advised her to do some Masters from any Indian university. With papers she had on the subject of Natyasastra it would not be difficult to get a Ph.d. About a year back her daughter entered a university in Germany for her Masters in Public Policy in Berlin.

She wrote in her recent e-mail to the group.com:

'I Completed my Integrated Movement Studies programme in the US and am now a Certified Movement Analyst. Also I am happy to inform you all that I have joined the University for a Masters Programme in Sociocultural Studies (MASS) in a town about an hour-and-half from Berlin on the German-Polish border, the Europe University Viadrina (where, her daughter just completed her Bachelors). I met a Professor last year who is doing research on gestures and we found each other's work mutually inspiring. I am working with her on a research paper to be published next year. Since she teaches at this University, I thought I could get a Masters degree and do my research more 'officially' rather than as an independent researcher, as we dancers working on papers finally tend to be called. I am excited about bringing in *my movement observation skills* I learnt during the course in the US and my many years of dance experience to combine Western theoretical and academic concepts with Eastern practical experiential knowledge. Since we students are encouraged to spend a term in a foreign University, I may land up in Hyderabad at the Central University next year. Who knows. I have to reduce my dance activities a bit for a while, but it is worthwhile I think.'

Her children's studies and careers

She has a daughter who chose sociology and also learnt dancing in pursuing with zeal her own career. RR who is independent and assertive allows her own children to do whatever they are passionate about. They found in Europe a congenial environment for pursuing and thriving in their own chosen careers and control.

RR's son is outstanding in Maths. His natural choice is engineering. But his love is music. He wanted to do Aeronautics but chose some course in Audio or sound engineering and moved to NewYork. Many of his well wishers and close relatives are cautioning him, counseling him to concentrate on engineering not anything to do with music. He promises that after one year in NewYork he would complete engineering course. Education, personality, interest are all inter-linked. There are many hard decisions to be taken. Their success is intimately tied with what they want deeper inside.

R.R's career path had its quota of ups and downs, hurdles, and was uphill. Once she got over the difficulties she has been steering it in the superhighway on top gear. She balanced family interest with her passion for dance. Her husband's support was always there.

I read in a weekend magazine another story of a dancer who is a medical doctor by profession. It was a smooth life all along. Her paths–dance career and doctor's career–run parallel. In between she has time for family. She says 'beyond careers family is everything... staying bonded is important'.

Medical career–'well thought out path with planned moves. She hails from a family of doctors.' Parental programming. Internal aspirations are twofold –pursue her interest in dance which started early at the age of three and a profession whose dynamics are well known to her. Her choice of the specialization is significant. She chose Public Health and Preventive Medicine and a job in a private super speciality hospital. It is not wealth she was aiming although she does not state it. Besides she gets the support of the hospital staff 'who draw up worksheets, make sure everything is scheduled'. With this arrangement she has time for dance and for the family. She enjoys dancing. 'Practice sessions are sometimes more fulfilling than performing before the audience'. Her public performances are deliberately kept to a minimum, not too many to rob her of her other two responsibilities which are also not onerous. 'No emergencies and late night calls.'

She makes her choices even in the public performances to suit her personality. 'A classical dance, her choice, is not like rock concert. The audience may not cheer and clap'. 'That's why I choose subjects that the audience can relate to'. There is deep satisfaction visible in their faces rather than in their applause. This is what I call steering your career and controlling. She has two vehicles, nay, three vehicles she is steering, dancer, doctor, and family woman.

Note the differences the former is an entrepreneur; the latter is not.

Home making as career/Family as a unit
Careers and Families

A home maker's career is an intimate part of the husband's career. Women in family businesses play important roles: decision-making and problem-solving, besides planning organizing and control of family matters –home-making. They are home and finance ministers rolled into one. What about in single-member earning families? Professionals and the employed. The home makers help, assist, support in the career progress of their husbands. The support could bring additional earnings or any other tangible support, besides moral and emotional support. They can help in information processing for decision making. Wife is involved more particularly in decision of changes of career, jobs, transfers, promotions, etc. Apart from providing support, they can counsel, caution, or even warn; by bringing a new perspective. They ask different kind of questions. Naturally, security conscious womenfolk remind the ambitious and avaricious men of down-to-earth realities. We have seen that there are six vocational personalities represented by the acronomonic—CREAMS. Woman's personality type can balance and offset husband's types.

Traditionally the village craftsmen, artisans, and cottage industries, all private enterprises are family careers—joint ventures and partnership. Modern youth can put the old wine in new bottles. Old is gold is true in career planning at the family unit level.

Let us look at the cases of spouses planning and controlling their life plans a part of which is career planning.

Career was never my priority

I never had any aim of choosing a career. In Intermediate I had taken up B.P.C because I was very poor in maths. I don't remember why I had not opted for arts subjects in which I was interested later. At degree level also I wanted to shift to literature, psychology and sociology but that combination was not there in the place we were staying. Of course I had applied for medical entrance. But I was not serious.

I was always interested in service activities. I was a member of Pradipti a Service organization during graduation days. Later at the Master's level I took up literature which I should have done earlier. I was always interested in teaching which provided me great satisfaction. So after marriage I have taken up teaching, not on a regular basis, due to family constraints; in between I was busy with the kids and their upbringing. But I never was a homebird. I became an active member of a service club, served as its president and then took up music as hobby and developed the art. Again I did not take up music as my career. So career was never my priority. At the same time I always had a wish to run some organization with service as its motto, for that also I wanted to do it with somebody to take main responsibility. So when my friend started the school for children in a rural area I grabbed the opportunity to join her in running the school. I am happy doing this. It keeps me active and gives me satisfaction of doing something worthwhile instead of whiling away my time. Of course it also helps me to grow and it's a great experience.

V.S

Learning and adapting

I am the youngest of the three siblings. Life was a cake walk and with no responsibilities as a youngest child grew up in a very protective environment. After graduating in commerce from Gujarat university I and a group of friends took a collective decision to do masters with management as we had nothing else to do. Of course, we thoroughly enjoyed our college life. After college I worked as asst. teacher in a private school for a couple of months and enjoyed the work.

After my marriage to one who is the eldest son in their family, my responsibilities grew. The initial days taught me new things and lots of adjustments as their family background was totally different from ours. My husband was a drilling engineer with Oil Company and had to work in shifts, which had odd timings. It was a new family setup, learning household chores. Being a housewife all this I managed quite easily under my mother-in-law's training. Moreover by nature I am a homely person with fewer ambitions and expectations. It was thus smooth sailing.

It was a joint family and my sister in law and in laws-were with us for about four years after which we got transferred to Assam. There was utter chaos as we landed in Assam as my husband's colleagues got kidnapped and few were shot by militants.

When normalcy returned it was two months from the time we landed there. We settled down at a new place with colleagues families for company and we spent three years in the North East after which I came to Chennai.

My husband got transferred to Chennai in 1994 when Anjana first child was in 1st std and Anupama second child was one and half yrs old. I was fully occupied in bringing up the children as he used to be away mostly on shift duties or transfers. My sister-in-law was with us working as Company Secretary and Finance Manager who was link for me with the outside world because I was at home managing the family. My husband could work without much worries. As the children grew up I started to take interest to inculcate hobbies for the sake of children, providing opportunities which they can develop later to achieve their goals . In the absence of my husband I learnt to do bank jobs, paying bills.

In spite of several transfers I managed to stay with the kids and in-laws at Chennai. On and off my husband got postings in Chennai and now he is back in Assam staying alone as I have to stay with my younger kid who is in her class XI. My eldest daughter finished her schooling at Chennai and Joined Manipal Institute of Technology for Electrical and Electronics Engineering.

Being a home maker one can do a lot of things channelising the earnings into proper investments and be support system to the spouse and ease their duties and responsibilities at home. It gives equal satisfaction as if on a job with job satisfaction and freedom.

R.S.S

- Read SPACE – devoting space for the partner, the home-maker who devotes more space to all the other members of the family. Family as a unit of an organization can apply the principle of 'division of labour' in creating space to extended families and society at large for total satisfaction.
- After all, the cybernetical principle – 'growth with stability' holds good for all living systems – individuals, families, extended family, ad infinitum.

Thanks to the financial crisis and recession, the Western societies have learnt a lesson or two from Eastern societies like the Indian. One lesson is regarding lifestyle. The other is family bondage. Here is a titbit to prove my point.

> 'Casual dating seemed to be a by-product of the go-go days of past years when the stock market was booming', said Rachel Greenwald, match maker and author of a new book called 'Why Didn't he Call You Back!'
>
> 'People had disposable money and they wanted disposable relationships now things have really shifted emotionally'.
>
> Another match maker says, 'some men simply have more time to focus on *relationships* because their businesses is on the hold, for example those in real estate or hedge funds',

Those wcfho were busy to Get Rich Earnestly, Efficiently, Devoid of ethics – GREED – that is what GREED stands for.

> 'Others are not in the mood for endless first dates with different women and want a partner who will deal with their ups and down! That's wisdom dawned!

(Titbit)

I am reminded of what the late justice ASP Iyer told us in 1950 when I was a student in Loyala College, Chennai. The then retired ICS officer turned a Jurist, justice Iyer was a popular speaker among students for his wit and witticisms. He narrated his encounter with a white-man (he was always citing anecdotes) he who criticized Indian culture of arranged marriages because there was no love and no dating in it. Pat came the reply from ICS officer from the South of India and an orthodox family:

Our 'love' begins where your 'love' ends!

A report

> 'Features tales of disgruntled women forced to give up pricey restaurant meals (spicy too), for example, for home cooking.'
>
> Women are preferring occupations, from where they select their partner, which are less risky than finance.

But the divorce lawyers say hard times also can destroy love. There had been a spike in divorces – 'a lot of mice want to leave the sinking ship'.

> Love or no love traditional Indian women would not abandon 'the sinking ship'; together they have the fortitude to sail safe to the shore together– acting in the 'living present trusting the future Heart within and God over head'.
>
> Please refer to appendix VI

Section - III

Where on – To weather, not wither

1

STEERING THROUGH, SOARING HIGH

Steering through changes that effect your current performance in any field. My experience and that of my junior colleagues in banking industry who grew up reveal certain problems.

Traditionally bankers were lenders to traders. After the resolution on industrialization and 5-year plans, there is an opportunity and threat from the political and economic environment. The banks had to adapt themselves to changes in order to finance industries both for working capital and long term capital requirements.

They needed specialists who could understand the financial requirements of industries. At the same time the existing employees were re-oriented to take care of the new products—loans, overdrafts, term loans, cash credits, expertise in the study of balance sheets, cash flows, project reports etc. Because of the speed with which managements had to change to the rapidly growing needs of the clients, to meet the new demands they recruited specialists like engineers, chartered accountants, management accountants at higher level which normally would have been occupied by the existing mangers, who were placed at a disadvantage.

Some of the old guard took it up as a challenge, quickly learned new areas of knowledge, attended training programmes reaping the benefits. Some of them reached the level of Deputy General Manager and General Manager level and retired with satisfaction.

They steered through admirably. Some of the profiles included in this chapter illustrate the point.

Then came the unexpected—Nationalization of major banks. For the banker whose policy was 'ostrich' like, burying the head in the sand and thought nothing of what was happening in the outside world. The nationalization and the consequent changes did not matter initially. When the Government forced banks to go into rural areas and finance to priority sectors, the changes began to be felt. But for those who had kept abreast of political and economic changes it was not unexpected. Just because you have landed a job or career you have been looking for, it would not mean the end of the matter. Your education and experience and the training on and off the job will continue But the important point is that you must be able to articulate to yourself and others the knowledge and skills you have developed out of direct experience—wide and varied. The very recognition of your talents, interests and personality traits—the strengths that are currently utilized by the organization you are serving, soft skills in particular, is the outcome of the changes, challenges, and responses.

This is particularly true when the performance appraisal system is taken away from the immediate superior and handed over to the HR function.

Training and Development

The exposure to training in the apex staff colleges or outside is very valuable. I have seen resistance to be trained, an aversion born out of the misinterpretation and misconception of training programmes. The continuing education for engineers, doctors, managers—takes many forms. Immediately after introduction of industrial finance, banks trained identified existing officers in their own training system or outside. They sent some privileged officers abroad for exposure to foreign banks. There is job rotation or functional rotation given as means of direct experience and training. Getting relieved to attend seminars, conferences, factory visits, etc. demands certain soft skills of negotiating with the relieving authorities. Pending work may come in the way and appear genuine reason for losing the opportunity. Tenacity and hard work to sit late and complete the pending work and influence the boss come under soft skills. There are some who get several opportunities more often for training and re-training because they make an impact on the trainers because of exemplary participation in the seminars and training programmes. Some big bosses whose eye you are able to catch in these places make you more wanted. Most of the cases where some one is not very good in operations may get a posting in another functional area nearer to the power centres or even training [K.K, in one of the case No. 15 was exemplary in his steering through his career in the bank].

You choose to continue to grow and be aware how important growth can be both for career progression and personality development. (Read case 18 of K.S)

> 'While this growth (hierarchy) gave me pride and ego satisfaction, it added to my responsibilities and a thorough revision of my inter-personal relationship. It was at this time that I opted to undergo a series of 'person'-oriented programmes. The ISISD, ISABS, IIM(A), ASCI, were some of the (outside) organization that took me under their fold and mentored me, as a trainer….this changed my entire outlook in life…'
>
> ***K.S***

This man retired as General Manager in public sector company. Many middle aged bankers at that time who did not strive to learn and steer their careers put an end to the career by not opting for movement or promotion and stagnated. Then banks had to weed out the people who were inflexible and extended to them the voluntary retirement facility (for some VRS came as boon to change careers).

As we discussed earlier they get into *'chalta hai'* mode–getting along stage-shows slipping into *easy going* stage leading to early senility. Same is the situation in Government service where the majority withdrew from active career control.

But those who took stock of the situation adjusted to the new situation and HONE UP—*Having positive altitude, Opportunity seeking, Networking, Enhancing* knowledge and skills and *Update knowledge, Proactive approach.*

HONEUP[1] for a change

Change of jobs is common now-a-days compared to 'good' olden days when there was life long secure employment. Employment was only considered as a means of livelihood rather than a means to realizing one's potential.

But change of career is not easy. There are many reasons for thinking of a change. Some feel they are just not happy. The career has lost its charm. You are bored with the repetitive work; there is no challenge, no growth professionally; there is a new boss, take over, merger; there is a cultural change. There is a discovery of talent, new interest, new revelation; change in technology. When computers came into organizational life, there were many who could not adjust themselves to the new demands because of their aversion to change in the workstyle. The job responsibilities are not matching with the skills. You have soft skills in abundance but you are utilizing only hard skills.

Whatever may be the reason you have to manage the change– plan, organize, and control the whole process. Lack of financial support could be a stumbling block, with the result you keep postponing change. You may have to sacrifice some of the luxuries and comforts. Several factors, children's education, spouses career, aged parents, become variables to be taken into account in managing the change.

There is the case No. 17 of 'V.V' included in this chapter. He has considerable experience and surplus talents, particularly soft skills. He feels he has been languishing in the manufacturing company. Age is another factor. Corporate sectors absorbs many professionals–engineers, scientists, chartered accountants, company secretaries, etc. They do rise in the organizational hierarchy to satisfactory levels and retire. Many of them fail when they set up private practice. They soon give up. There are lawyers in this category who put on the black coat after enrolment and are not able to have practice because of the stiff competition from the younger, more dynamic and energetic and from the well established seniors. They might have succeeded had they quit the corporate service and set up practice ideally 10 or 15 years before

[1] **HONEUP:** Have positive attitude; opportunity search; networking; enhance knowledge; update resume; proactive.

the superannuation, overlooking the lure of pension and terminal benefits.

Remember there is a gestation period for changed careers. During that time they need financial support. But that is not sufficient. There are other things: HONEUP.

- Have positive attitude. Negative thoughts that stem from fear can undo the planning.
- Opportunity search — This takes time, and energy; you need information. All the search mechanisms at the beginning of a career are applicable at this stage.
- Networking — The contacts during the present employment can come in handy. You'll have contacts only if you had soft skills. You may have contacts; but you may be too proud to use them.
- Enhance — Knowledge, qualifications, cultivate new values, habits; move from loyalty to the employer to self. Study entrepreneurs. Till now your boss has set goals for you. Now you have to do it yourself which demands conceptual skills. There is no boss to monitor your progress. You have to do it yourself.
- Update — Your resume is not for employment purpose but for self assessment! Updating of resume can be an annual affair. January 14 every year is Sankranti day–ideal for review and setting goals for the current year. Sankranti means change for better. Good change.
- Proactive — While you were employed, somebody else, top management or immediate boss would decide for you. You may have *reacted* to please the boss whether you like it or not. When you are on your own you have a chance to be *proactive.* But long years of reactive habits die hard. You have to wipe the old slate and start afresh. Everyday

you have to plan and prepare a schedule of activities–things to be done 'musts, shoulds and coulds'. You need to develop a new culture. Time management is critical. (Refer to Section on Time Management in the book *Personal and Emotional Competence*)

Exhaust all avenues available within the same organization. There may be a change of place, function, or immediate boss possible, without your initiative. Wait and see. But not too long. You must sever your links with least heart burn. Your name may not be in the muster roll; but you may keep the relationship. That's what V.V did. (Case Life Planning and career planning of couples) Case No 17.

Another selected a different course—he kept aloof from the rat race and chose a *sabbatical* and moved to an apex training institution of the same organization. Not to compete in the race can be seen as defeatist or running away. To keep your positive profile intact take it as *stayaway*—voluntary act not forced by others. But now set your new goals in the new assignment and never look back. Self-reliance, resilience, deciding under pressure, communication, all–soft skills are called for. From here and now, you are moving towards a 'new calling'; it is in fact a mid-career crisis. If you fail to take the risk and uncertainty factors in your stride, you may lapse into the easy going or '*Chalta hai'* mentality, making it more difficult to rejuvenate yourself. (Refer to a case of Changing careers – Life Long Learning) Case No 18.

When to change and where to go are two difficult considerations. If you have decided to go in for self-employment, then the situation should be under your control. If you are seeking employment in another company with a change of career, it is a challenge to convince the new employer to take the risk and hire you over some one from within the same fraternity. Interview will be tough. You have to SHARE[2]—*sincerely, honestly, apprise, with reason* and *emotion*. You are actually making an emotional appeal tempered by reason. Presenting yourself through resume, covering letter, and face to face interview has to

---

[2] **SHARE:** Sincere; honest; appraisal; reason; emotion.

be exemplary. Strenuous preparation is called for. Research, on the career, company, skills the immediate job, applied for, demands, is most important. Discussion in Section I and Section II, particularly the Chapter on choosing a career apply. Change of career is starting the exercise all over. But there is another case in the officer in public sector bank managed with soft skills to get into the training system—a change in career in the same company. He shared in the class room his experiments and experiences in rural areas and in the mass banking. The change was not easy because of age restriction. He attended a training programmes where the faculty and the principal of the college were so impressed with his language and communication skills that they asked him to take a session in the programme. The rest of the job of roping him for training system on promotion was done by the principal. He never returned to operations or sought normal promotion and retired as chief manager training. He too is a case of steering and swerving from the course in order to pave the way for post retirement career as an HR trainer and writer.

Hard and Soft choices

For some of the mid-life careers there is competition among colleagues, jealousies, disillusionment with the higher management and so on. Emotional disturbance, the result of conflicts, may make one make ineffective decisions ruining one's own career progression. It is at such time, calm contemplation and use of soft skills become imperative to steer, swerve, or sever one's connections with the organization which gave him many opportunities till then.

I have shown the way: ARMED[3]. *Awareness, Regulation, Motivation, Empathy, Deft handling. [Read Appendix II]*

The last two steps are the key skills. Empathy, I repeat, is 'stepping into the shoes of the other'. Listen to the other.

Intraprenerus – Skill Development

Some three decades ago I read a book which classified members of organizations into three: a few *upwardly mobiles* and a vast

[3] **ARMED:** Awareness; Regulations; Motivation; Empathy; Deft handling.

majority of *drifters*. The first category has little competition and they make their way upward to the top without much ado. The rest among them leave the organization to greener pastures. The researcher-author identified a third category, *theoreticians* whom he called the soul of the enterprise. The organization, the organism survives because of their forethought, foresight, and farsighted ideas. They have ideas but they cannot implement them unless they have the support of the *upwardly mobiles* who are called by another name – Intrapreneurs: (intra + entrepreneur), a corporate executives who develops new enterprise within the corporations. Utilizing the wisdom of the few *theoreticians* who do not aspire for positions or power and authority in organizations behave with entrepreneural zeal. They have the power to influence the men in authority. They are happy their ideas become innovations. These *'theoreticians'* in organizations have all the soft skills of communication and persuasive reasoning and ability to influence. One thing is true – they are generally averse to take personal risks. There are a few, I have seen, very few, who combine both, the *upwardly mobile* traits and *'theoreticians'* wisdom.

A few of my colleagues much junior to me at the time of my retirement in 1992, who have become CMDs and EDs in the beginning of 21st century of PSU banks have displayed this rare combination. In the first decade of their service they showed pretty little of the desire to move up the organizational ladder. Their career path after 1990s was meteoric. One of them still in service as CMD of a PSU bank waiting for further rise to be chosen as a Deputy Governor of RBI. (He has since completed that distinction also)

All of them have developed and displayed entrepreneurial behaviour through 'natural selection'. There is something internal to evolution, not purely adapting to the environment entirely, chance and necessity. Necessity is internal desire to achieve. To achieve you need power and authority. Therefore some people choose private enterprise. But thanks to organizations trying to survive through adaptation and internal drive–collective aspiration of the majority of members of the organization, there are members of organisation driven by entrepreneurial spirit pushed the entire organization on upward path. These are intrapreneurs who took personal risks in the process but were also lucky to be at the helm of affairs of the organization at the right time in right environment. I have not talked of the importance of the so called *drifters*. They are *drifters* because of their own choice; for they have limited space for careers in organizations, but have interests that suited their personalities. They may have plans for post retirement career when they have financial independence or children who might themselves had become upwardly mobiles and NRIs or entrepreneurs. The total SPACES are fully occupied deriving maximum satisfaction. None of them should regret so long as there is progress as defined by themselves.

What you want, What you get

In most of our careers there will be set-backs. What appears sudden are not really sudden. It is sudden because we neglect the forewarnings. When we arrive at career crisis it is necessary whether we shift the focus to solve our problems.

'Problem solving'. Arthur Koestler wrote, 'is bridging the gap between the initial situation and the target.' He also suggests a problem solving method:

"A good example is Duncker puzzle about two trains and the bird. Two goods trains, a hundred miles apart; start moving towards each other, each at a speed of twenty miles per hour. A silly bird, frightened at the starting hiss of one of the trains, flies away at thirty miles per hour in a straight line along the railway track until it meets the other train; it reverses its direction until it meets the first train again, and so forth. What distance will the bird cover in its flight to and fro until the two trains meet?

To compute sum of the series of flight-stretches is a rather complicated task. But if we think aside, forget about the distances covered by the bird, and compute the *time* until the two trains will meet–two and half hours–we see at once that the bird has also flown for two and half hours and hence covered a *total* of seventy five miles."

Using the analogy if we, instead of focusing on material possessions or simply money, shift our focus on a career(s) that 'comes together', we instantly see the solution and manage our financial problems and get the cushion to take control of our careers. All that you have to do is to obey our traditional values of plain living and high thinking in any career or careers.

Most of the case histories presented in this monograph are of this type of men and women from middle class and lower middle class of Indian society who did really move up economically and who took sufficient care of their security needs.

Whenever crucial decisions for change and challenge are taken, financial stability will hedge the risk in times of uncertainty in the environment. When you want to become independent and want to fully utilize your talents wasted in employment and underutilization.

Banks used to lend vast sums to self-employed against the personal property and personal insurance. During bad times the banks recall the loans and put property for sale jeopardizing family life. There is a notorious saying about bankers.

'He is one who gives you umbrella when sun shines and takes it away when it starts raining.

Self-reliance is the key to success in life.

Self-Attribution bias (SAB)

SAB refers to attribution of good outcomes to skill and bad outcomes to bad luck or outside factors. We should remember that the environment, society and organization, and the country and period contribute to our success. We would have successfully managed our lives when we feel success at the end of the day.

Steering through; Soaring high

'The Genetic Code: with ability to sequence genes and whole genomes has come new understanding about how evolution occurs at the most basic level. Individual 'letters' of genetic code can get changed; bits in DNA can be deleted, added, or transposed; genes can get duplicated and take on new functions or, when they are no longer needed, wither away. Yet natural selection preserves important genes and their associated cellular processes across extraordinary long periods of evolutionary changes'.

We can reflect on this as an analogy for evolutionary changes through natural selection at the individual and community level across shorter periods within one's life time. What we need is to appreciate the evolutionary process, a belief in change characterized by chance and necessity.

It is a natural process, why then some individuals and groups are unable to adjust to the changes in environment?

Subversive education at home and in the extended homes, is only reason that comes to mind; fear, negative emotions, lack of '*Shraddha*', faith in one self, result of generations of mis-conceptions and training: **Not allowing the life to run its natural course – not allow the natural selection mechanism run smoothly – re-educating is the solution.**

Besides educating yourself there is lot of opportunity available in the form of variety of service providers for life long learning. They are TRIBE[4] unto themselves.

Traditionalists – who pass on perennial knowledge; Re-educators (change agents) Inspirers – they inspire and prepare people for change Builders of Institutions – who train, retrain, continual education for the betterment of individuals and organization. Emancipators – whose attention is on educating the have-nots.

The change agents play Several roles; Collaborators; Re-educators; Evaluators; Diagnostician; Information specialist; Builder of teams; Leavener; Emanicipators. They are CREDIBLE[5] lot with multi-skills who form teams to multiply the combined resources; together become CREDIBLE TRIBE of men and women who found alternative careers. Professionals, Activists, Entrepreneurs, Intrapreneurs; lot of synergy is taking place in the globalized world.

Opportunity Seeking and Risk Taking

Opportunity seeking and Risk taking (GR(O)W), go together; vital for potential development of soft skills. It is certainly a personal habit and in that sense a soft skill. Then we have the other factor – Legacy. In fact the very knowledge about our legacy, heredity,

---

[4] **TRIBE:** Traditionalists; Re-educators; Inspirers; Builder of Institution; Emancipators.

[5] **CREDIBLE:** Collaborators; Re-educators; Evaluators; Diagnostician; Information specialist; Builder of teams; Leavener; Emanicipators.

family background, ancestral knowledge, tradition and other legacies to which the parents were exposed and changed for better. Understanding 'history and geography' of our lives and those of our ancestors can be reckoned as a soft skill – analytical and research skills.

I had compiled and written about our family tree going back to a few centuries. In the process of my search for information I gained good insights into our behaviours. We are all hard working, generally free from greed, but there have been entrepreneurial behaviour noticed when a few stepped out of the inheritance and moved on to places of opportunity and developed cosmopolitan outlook, a legacy we took in as our strength. A few case histories – career profiles included in this volume illustrate the point. Free from *Ostentation.*

Adaptability, flexibility, conflict resolution

We have been harping on the idea of adaptability etc as soft skills. Broadly adjustability is of two kinds: ends and means. If you adjust the 'means', it is adaptability; if you adjust the ends or revise the goals it is flexibility. Often conflicts arise on account of the rigidity of goals and maintenance of relationship. The whole thing can be brought under problem solving in which people, their wants and needs, their goals and aspiration, become areas of conflicts.

Resolution lies in mutuality. It is an aspect of communicative competence of the parties involved.

We talked of 'SPACES' problem. Intra-personal, inter-role, and interpersonal in nature.

Conflict Resolution

It demands a cluster of soft skills to negotiate. There are principally four ways of resolving conflicts that arise.. with joy. Conflicts arise around mistakes, opinions, objectives, priorities, necessities, and demand for resources apart from status or ego clashes. Different people have different styles of dealing with conflict resolution. Some avoid, others bully or force their views on others by exercising their power and authority; yet others compromise and are satisfied with lesser gains. Avoidance, bullying, compromise are all good for different situations.

Where goals and relationships with people in the situation are not important, it is good to 'avoid' conflict. Where relationships are of importance but the goals are less important it is good to settle for a compromise, if relationships are less important and goals are of great importance then one might bully or force, a resolution towards the accomplishment of goals.

Where both goals and relationships are of great importance, then you need to adopt a fourth style *viz.*, 'DIG' strategy. You go 'deep into gaps' in understanding the reality that confronts the parties.

As the myriad plants send down their roots deep into interrelated gaps in a bountiful forest, so also, as members of a team look into the gaps in the understanding, the discussion becomes 'dialogue' in which it does not matter any more who is right. The entire group begins to 'dance' together with joy.

I have discussed the concept of dialogue in my book *Communicative Competence.*

Case 12

Holistic Doctor

I became a doctor more by accident than by intent. Like many of my generation I aspired for an engineering career as that seemed to be a challenge. Doing well in mathematics was considered the best course to become an engineer in 1966. The only problem was seats were fewer compared to other professional courses. Honestly I wanted be in IIT. As a matter of fact, I did one year bachelor's in maths as I wasn't eligible for a seat in medicine due to age (I was only 15 instead of mandatory 16).

I did B.Sc (MPC) in Bhimavaram, my aunt's place, far away from where my parents stayed –Tirupati. I got first class marks in I B.Sc. but since my 12th class marks held good for a seat in MBBS at S.V.M.C. Tirupati, the next year I opted for a medical course but I was not as studious as I had been in my secondary and tertiary schooling. I was only average in terms of ranks. But I used to be friendly with my fellow students and I utilized my house surgeonship (internship-one year compulsory) to the maximum which enabled me to make up for whatever I had lost in theory during the learning period.

I undertook three months of general practice in a small town near Tirupati with which I wasn't happy though monetarily it was okay. I tried to go to the USA which didn't materialize. Then I shifted to Madras, my birthplace and started my stint as a junior to a very popular cardiologist in his private practice and did senior-internship of two years in a Government Hospital.

'I was introduced to a famous physician by my brother-in-law, also a doctor. Dr. R.S.R. who asked me to join immediately in 1976 but because I went to Kualalumpur to write for ECFMG for foreign studies, there was some delay in joining RSR clinic. The vacancy was filled by another 'smart' competitor to my utter disappointment.

In spite of the fact I was hard pressed for money I accepted an honorary position as a house-surgeon in the ICCU of Government Hospital where RSR was the chief physician. I worked there for two years without pay; it turned out to be a challenging assignment. I was hurt because of being let down I was determined to do well and win the admiration of my boss and others. I also took up a part-time job in St.Isabel Hospital. These two years of practical experience gave good opportunity to me to learn 'total medicine' at an early age. It was a blessing in disguise that I was not favoured for paid assistantship under my boss RSR. But as soon as my lucky predecessor left, I was taken in by 'RSR'. The initial disappointment provoked me to do well and there was no looking back. I got all the time admiration of my boss to the extent that my successor envied me and even commented that the boss did not deserve such loyalty. It was not loyalty that drove to me to work hard but my desire to learn from direct clinical experience.

My relationship with my boss was such that he never praised my work for he believed that's praise might spoil my learning process. But I knew that he valued my commitment to my profession. Nor did I show off before my juniors. I enjoyed the confidence of the boss. The good relationship with my juniors as well as my superior is, I think, the secret of my success in the most important initial years of my career.

Later RSR, used to refer me as a role model to my successors and how I was 'holding the fort' well. There are bosses who never admit your good work to you but hold you in high esteem. I believe that no boss can ignore good work done by you.

One instance comes to my mind. A well-to-do patient had a problem and I asked the nurse to give a particular injection, oxygen, etc., when the patient's attendant wanted to stall the treatment and phoned to my boss who admonished the attendant saying, 'my assistant knows his job' and hung up. From then onwards the attitude of people changed totally and they started to admire me. My confidence in my job and my work load started increasing. Those were the days when I was unmarried.

Then I got married to my childhood friend who is not a doctor and who has been waiting for me to decide.

In a doctor's life support from wife and children is crucial for the success in career. I was not lucky for my daughter was frequently falling sick for about 6 years, I was passing through tension. My wife used to be nervous. I must mention here, I played cricket and Sachin Tendulkar was my role model. He used to say he was successful because he had no problems on the home front.

After initial hiccups I settled down in my career and it proceeded in top gear as I have total support from my family and my daughter who is in 3rd year engineering in biotechnology. She is also an accomplished artist who takes part in extra-curricular activities.

I must mention my situation in Sri Ramachandra Medical college Teaching—Assistant. Professor—1986-1990 from where I resigned to set up full time private practice for the sake of my patients. In the college I enjoyed clinical teaching more than classroom lecturers which require ten minutes preparation for an hours lecture. Within the department of internal medicine I was known as 'ECG man' as seniors referred to me and discussed complicated ECGs. Friendly, with students on duty and off duty, respect for my seniors, I enjoyed playing cricket with hostel students whenever I was free.

I was sincere, loyal, duty-bound in my work which made me to learn a lot of practical medicine faster than what one would have learnt in a PG course. Meanwhile, after about four years I got PG seat (internal medicine) and pursued it in Kilpauk

Medical College. I completed my MS degree after a few attempts for want of theory skills. *But my work experience had set such sound platform that I could begin independent practice very confidently.* I was a total physician from the word go and was able to handle simple a well as complicated issues very well.

As I grew in my practice, I developed my own style without being a stereotype of my boss. I would like to acknowledge my gratitude to him and thank God to work with such an eminent clinician in my early career and I owe a lot to him. My mother, Dr. Yasoda Devi, historian was a great source of inspiration to me in whatever I did. I was very fortunate in that respect. Although I literally lived in intensive care units of a Government hospital and St. Isabel's hospital at the beginning of my career, I got exposed to aggressive medicine very early in life. I cultivated the art of looking at a sick person as a whole rather than confining myself to the disease. As my practice picked up, I had more of geriatric patients who looked for compassion, encouragement rather than the technicalities of diagnosis and treatment, I mean a bit of holistic treatment. I am sure you must have seen the movie "Munnabhai-MBBS" a fantastic one where a layman could make sick happy. I am sure and I believe that science and solace can be synchronized and correct and optimum treatment can be administered without compromising on scientific protocols. Sometimes I pray to God to guarantee good health to some patients which makes them live happily with the problem.

For many problems it's only control, no care, then why not give them some confidence, that is controlling their mental process which we may fail to address in our busy workaday schedule. Hence I believe with good rapport with client and proper communication, one can convince and make a patient compliant to get good results.

By this one can give optimum treatment without prohibitively expensive tests and drugs.

So I believe apart from skills and knowledge, with experience, conviction, self belief and positive gut feeling one can do wonders in administering right treatment for the right person. This helps in cost cutting, unnecessary hospital occupancy etc. Ofcourse you cannot do this without right rapport and total trust from the client.

Queer litter twists and quirks go into the making of an individual

A Beautiful mind

Comment

How come a medical doctor is having a sport person as role-model? He even derives meanings from movies.

There are number of pointers to mangers and juniors in every field for soft skills.

Case 13

My experiences in the Banking Sector

I started my Banking career as a clerk in a metropolitan branch under private sector. We enjoyed a close relationship with our superior officers who used to extend a helping hand whenever required. We had also some hard task masters who used to nag for every type of work done by us. During those days the Manager was all powerful, having the power to appoint or dismiss the staff. If one was sincere in his work, he would be in their good books and could hope to be rewarded at an opportune moment. Otherwise, he had to face the music almost on a daily basis. Thus in the private sector as long as one enjoyed the confidence of the superiors, he would receive the reward and enjoyed a lot of liberty in his work also. Those were the good old days.

Where I had worked under three managers as the second officers things were different. One was very conservative and invariably drove away the clients, while another was very liberal in sanctioning loans to a certain category of borrowers. After nationalization the Banks were required to implement various schemes formulated by the Government. As against this under private sector the Bank Managements had their choice of borrowers. The urban branch where I was working started lending to agricultural operations and gave financial assistance to small scale Industry and small Business under Self–Employment schemes which was totally a new area for the banks and the bank Staff. We were required to adapt ourselves quickly to the changed situation. We slowly started getting into the rural places for extending our lending to various Agriculture and other sectors. We were also required to open rural branches for this purpose. We studied various schemes and learned the ropes quickly as was expected of us. As a second man in the branch I was training people to come up to the expectations of the management. Encouraging them in keeping things up to date and making my staff adapt themselves with new skills which I had learnt during my career. They also cooperated with me in keeping the branch up-to-date as I was carrying them with me all along putting myself as a buffer between them and the management.

From the urban branch I was posted as in-charge of a rural branch which was predominantly an agriculture based branch. Till then I never lived or worked in a village. I had to adapt myself to this new situation in my life as well as in my career.

The village where I was posted had two political factions. One party till then stayed away from the branch. I studied the situation and started lending helping hand to the people in the group to become customers of the branch and over a period they stated feeling as one group in the village and helped the branch with fresh business. They used to tell that once the branch developed they could also develop with it. Instead of telling them in words, I showed them in action and made them realize the utility of the bank for their progress. I should say I enjoyed their confidence, love and affection which I cherish even to this date. I was looked as their friend, philosopher and guide not only in this village but in about 40 villages around the area.

During my stay there we were required to implement a number of Government schemes under 20 point economic programme and other schemes of the Government and improve the standard of living of the rural poor (who are below poverty line). Under nationalization the personal touch we were enjoying in the private sector started slowly diluted and the gap between the bosses and others started widening. So, if one had committed a small error however much sincere he was, he was being punished mainly due to this lack of personal knowledge of the persons concerned. Apart from the schemes formulated by the Government, we were also introducing certain schemes suitable to people of a particular area, person or situation.

The government departments used to dump huge number of applications on us without taking into consideration the staff position. But as a manager it was my duty to work within certain parameters. But in the process, we used to get threats from various quarters and we were pressurized to lend to certain people without looking into the norms. As a lender I was to have full knowledge of the borrowers, their capacity to implement the scheme and their capacity to repay the loan. Some of the schemes were politically motivated, but as manager one should not go beyond the norms or set rules to safeguard bank's funds and our position, as we were accountable to our higher authorities. The post nationalization scenario left everyone in a situation that though you are a non entity so far as the higher authorities are concerned you have to deliver the goods working for the Government as well to as the management. Of course, the higher authorities are also answerable to Government. This is the peculiar situation of the nationalization. I had to show lot of flexibility and adapt myself to the hostile environment but there is a silver lining.

The village folks regard you not only as a Branch Manager but seek guidance in their daily affairs like their children's education, marriage, property matters, family affairs, and what not. They used to seek my advice wherever they required. But once you enjoy their confidence you are not dragged into their disputes. Even today if I go to their village I get the same amount of affection they were giving me when I had been the Branch Manager.

I was the Secretary of the Lions Club of that rural area and I was adjuged, the Best Secretary. During my tenure the club has undertaken a number of useful schemes to help the people in general and the villagers around in particular. I motivated people in the club to help the needy.

During that period the area had the worst cyclone. The club helped the cyclone victims with medicines, blankets and clothes and food material under my guidance. When the trees on the roads leading to bigger towns were uprooted by the cyclone we took people to clear the roads and helped the people to reach the towns for their daily requirements. I was also involved in getting sanction for protected water to the village through the club's good offices from the concerned Government departments. I was also involved in getting land allotment to the Montesorrie school sponsored by the club during my tenure as Manager. We had also sponsored bright students for higher studies with financial assistance and some of them are in the US now.

Thus, even though that was my first experience, I quickly adapted myself to the situation and made a mark for me as well as for the branch by maintaining cordial relationship with the people. In the process I could develop the branch business also.

When the area was devastated by cyclone, I surveyed the crops in all the 40 and odd villages and submitted my views for extending further help to the affected people, which further enhanced the reputation of the bank in the area and this has laid the foundation for further growth of business in the following years.

Notwithstanding the personal difficulties I had during my stay in the village my stay there had given me a very good experience as to how bank's business could be developed once you come to enjoy the confidence of the people in and around the place. I am still cherishing the moments I spent in the company of those good souls.

Sarma

Comment

Sarma's Checkered Career

I have known him throughout our careers. Having worked in city branches of a public sector bank, he developed expertise in credit proposals and day to day bank activities. He showed leadership qualities. Thus he had both hard and soft skills.

Then came the bank nationalization; he was required to serve in a rural branch which had seen two outstanding managers who had exemplary soft skills required to serve the rural community.

Sarma knew he had to meet the expectation of the already well served rural people. But his hard skill—viz. credit appraisal, technical skill could not make him compromise. By then there was too much interferences from the Block Development Officers who dumped large number of applications and brought pressure to fulfil the targets.

As he visited village for obtaining firsthand information on the viability and feasibility of the credit proposals, he faced a new problem: a section of people in each village complained that their needs were not met by the previous manager. These complaints, he realized arose because of politics.

Hard skills are the same, but environments differ, the scale of operations are enormous-politics too.

He served in such difficult situations developing or honing up his soft skills consisting mainly on balancing relationships, combining firmness with humaneness. He had to be not only honest but must appear honest. He served and survived for 4½ years and then he was transferred from a village in A.P. to the city of Kolkatta on promotion where he had to head small scale industries and small business division. It was child's play for him where he had more satisfactory period. It was to his liking and he received praise not only from the bank but even the Government.

After some transfers and promotions he retired and settled down to a retired life. He still remembered the two tenures and reminisce in them.

The case illustrates a point, the diversity of cultures not only among people within the organization, more importantly the diversity of cultures of the place of posting demands high degree of flexibility and adaptability, although the soft skills are transferable.

These profiles illustrate the experience of many different people pursuing many different career paths. From those narratives you can infer the need for soft skills, SOFT ness of soft skills which are learnt more often than not on the job. Flexibility is key note of these transferable skills–transferred in a copy book style.

Case 14

Experience is the best teacher

Personality Development and career both are interlinked. My own experience in my professional career explains this aspect.

My personality development started very early in my childhood, learning lot from my father's influence. I had strong desire to study engineering but domestic compulsions forced me to become a Chemistry graduate. Even after my graduation I had a strong inclination to take up a marketing career as a medical representative. But here I was rejected for lack of right aptitude! I had to settle for a technical job (analytical chemist) in an engineering concern. Years later circumstances forced me to take up a marketing career. I considered it not only as an opportunity but a challenge to fulfill my ambition. I accepted the new career. My success in marketing revolved round sheer *hard work* and *practical approach* by trial and error method. It was a do or die situation for me. I had to work and show results in marketing career through *hard work* and *application of mind.* It involved a lot of *self-learning.* Some of the marketing strategies that I was forced to follow may not match with theory.

As a case study I can give an example: During my marketing promotional tour I had to meet a prospective customer, aged 75, along with my dealer. The meeting was arranged at his house (in a remote village), as it was his lunchtime. When my dealer apprised me of some of the facts I could not believe. I was told that he would be taking lunch almost naked, except for a loin cloth and that I should not feel delicate. Even entering his house itself was a pleasant surprise, as we had to brush past a person obstructing our entry. (Later on I came to know that this person was the son of our customer who managed the theatre where we were supposed to sell our product). Exactly as I was told, my customer was taking lunch, on seeing me he felt shy and rushed inside to dress up. We discussed our offer and finalized the deal.

I am not only astonished to meet such a customer, I had great experience of understanding customer requirements. To know the exact amount of intake of food he takes his weight before and after taking his lunch using only an *imported* weighing machine as he has strong belief that made in USA products only are of best quality. This notion only made him to use an American company product rejecting our product. Before accepting our product he had asked us to meet him at the theatre to personally check the performance of our product. If one has to follow only the standard marketing concepts of customer contact, I would not have met him at all. My IIM colleagues consider it below dignity and prestige while contacting customers. You should have a *flexible approach* if you want to be successful.

While we acquire knowledge to become full fledged qualified professional, practical experience converts knowledge into reality of execution. It is just like a qualified electrical engineer knows much more than an ordinary fuse carrier, but at the same time ignorant of how to fix a fuse. My son, who is an engineer, called a neighbour to put the fuse in our house!

There is no substitute for wisdom gained through practical experience.

V.G.

Comment

There are things *what they don't teach in Harvard*

Case 15

An Intrepreneural Journey

I worked as a lecturer after my post-graduation in Agricultural Economics. I enjoyed teaching and I thought I would get opportunity to go to the US for doctoral qualification. That was in 1970. Bank Nationalization in 1969 changed the scenario with more and more agricultural graduates were taken into Bank Service as direct recruit officers. The job in the bank was both challenging and prestigious where my specialized knowledge was put to use with enough freedom and independence at the gras-roots level. At the same time I had the opportunity to learning agricultural banking. The agricultural professional must work with the farmers and the 'lab—to—land' concept must be made a reality. I was fascinated at the prospects.

Entry: The job selection process was tough. A private agency conducted the test and selected candidates were interviewed next day. There was a final interview conducted by a panel of senior executives in the bank. One of them an economist later became CMD of the bank.

I joined the bank in 1973 and never looked back and retired from the same bank as a DGM one year before superannuation when I fell foal with the then CMD. I knew I would not become GM which was my goal in my life, because ED & CMD posts were filled by the Government which was not what I aspired for.

I have no regrets because of my experience at the bank. I am able to pursue my consultancy service in microfinance to leading world class enterprises.

Let me list below the variety of experiences I had in Bank Service.

1. Entry point: My anchor had been my technical competence as an agricultural scientist. At the branch level I was granted special increment for adapting banking principles to produce quality loans. Soon I was aspiring to become a complete banker.
2. I got converted as a generalist and became a manager I had to pass through a tough interview for it.
3. Because I was interested in teaching I applied for the post of a trainer in 1987 and got selected after another interview and GD and aptitude test. Eventually I became head of training system at the apex staff college as DGM.
4. Before that when I was Chief Manager I underwent another exercise for selection of officers on fast track. Out of a batch of 50 people I was one among the 10 selected.
5. In 1990 I had overseas assignment at Dubai which was again through interview process. I was no.1 in deposit mobilization attracting large number of Indian expatriates. The branch was bankers to the Indian consulate and many Indian public sector undertakings. I was officially designated as Treasurer of the Bank in UAE and looked after dealings with the central bank of UAE. Many more. To sum up the tenure was highly satisfying and the international exposure benefited me in my career.
6. I was on a committee on Bank Reorganization, a feather in my cap before the overseas assignment.

I was fortunate to have joined a progressive and leading bank which had man-power planning and succession plan. I was spotted and groomed for higher positions and the bank gave this much variety of experiences for it.

Yet, it ended on a sad note for I had to quit my extended 'family' with a hitch on a flimsy issue.

Reflecting on the career I must say I am grateful to the bank as an institution that supported and shaped my growth. Yet interpersonal problems can come to everyone in the career as aberrations to an otherwise wonderful life in work.

Most satisfying Assignment: I would consider my tenure as Regional Head of Surat Region as the most satisfying assignment in my entire career in the bank.

This was due to:

1. The expertise I had developed as a bank officer/executive over a period of 29 years was put to use. What I wanted to do earlier for the development of the bank in many areas, I could implement with excellent results.
2. With 94 branch heads and more than 1200 staff, I had the opportunity to utilize my skills—(both soft and hard skills). During my stewardship, the cost of deposits was brought down to a ridiculously low level, and at the same time increased yield on advances, no other region had achieved (2003). This had even led to doubts in the minds of the top management about the varacity of figures and prompted them to go in for verification by the GM (insp). But I got a clean chit, and my efforts were recognized and appreciated.

K.K.

Comment

His choice and control of career are an example. There have been some specialists who even became ED and CMDs of PSUs. They are examples of intrapreneurs. But K.K. who aspired for GM's position had to content with one level too low. Never mind he is doing extremely well after leaving the bank.

Case 16

Steering through in top Gear

Divine Grace

I was born in a poor family in a village of pre-independence India with no electricity and other amenities. My father was a teacher and a Gandhian in every sense of the term–truth, non-violence, simple living, working for the uplift of the poor villagers. He would petition to the people in power and authority for railway station, post office, drinking water etc. He did not ask for wealth but just enough to feed and educate wife, four daughters and three sons.

Like most others in the village we lived in a house with a thatched roof. I remember as a child that every summer there used to be a fire accident destroying more or less the whole village, except our house. You may call it a miracle or a result of my mother's prayers. No wonder I grew as a child full of faith in Almighty. I believe and even to this day that I succeeded in my career due to a divine intervention. My value system in my life never changed. Hope, faith, light beauty, God, nature, miracles, honesty, hard work remained with me till now and shall ever remain.

Walking three miles to the station to catch a train to go to school ten miles away returning in the night in darkness was my daily routine which shaped my career in the bank. It was a matter of anxiety, no fear, because of hope. Reaching home safe without being bitten by a snake, a common occurance in our village, were part of my day's tension and relief. Probably I could steer through my career in bank where daily tensions and relaxation at the end of the day are common.

Being the first male child in the family I was showered with greatest affection by my parents. So my focus was studies so that I could be of some financial help to my family as quickly as possible. My hobby was writing poetry in praise of God. This was in consonance with my father's dream of educating me beyond school. I was the first graduate from our village.

My studies were not free of hassles. I was married at 16 to a girl aged 9. I was so shy even to distribute the invitation cards to my teachers and other students. My focus on studies was shattered. All the same I secured 1st rank in English and Telugu. The next two years I spent in Kakinada and completed my degree in Mathematics and Statistics with distinction. I got into bank in 1960 with the help of my brother-in-law as an apprentice for 6 months before I was appointed as a clerk in the bank.

I had a clear vision—I must work hard and work my way up in the bank. In 1965 I was promoted to officer cadre at the age of 24. There was no looking back on my career from then on. I had to compete with specialist officers and direct recruitees belonging to officer cadre and I found no problem.

My capacity to learn quickly and acquire the new skills and knowledge coupled with the background and family values stood me in good stead in my career. Being a story writer and poet in Telugu language, creativity and innovation came to me naturally.

I could stand out heads and shoulders above others whose experience taught them, 'see backwards and go forward'. There is a statement made in Alice in Wonderland: If you want to remain at one place, you have to run; if you want to go somewhere you have to run twice as fast; It is true of me in bank career. Ultimately I achieved something which was impossible for any one who joined as a clerk in any bank. I received many awards and rewards, elevations and special increments and the like.

In 1969, which is the year when my bank was nationalized, I read the future of banking in India, made a rough sketch of my career path which I showed to my wife. I set myself the position of Deputy General Manager by the time of my superannuation, but I retired as General Manager on a foreign soil, a special favour. This once again reinforced my belief in divine intervention.

My potential for innovation came into full play when I served for four years as Regional Training Officer—incharge of the Regional Training Centre at Chennai. I could catch the eye and imagination of the big bosses and the remaining career was cakewalk because I was one of the few most accepted persons in the bank. My knowledge of Tamil and Carnatic Music helped me in my public relations. Many of the top officials in south were lovers of music. The 'Power of positive thinking' by Norman Vincent Peal influenced me. Already a believer in divine grace, the book influenced further and reinforced my positive thinking.

For the first time my financial status improved when I was posted to Dubai. I could educate my children without great difficulty unlike my father. Apart from monetary benefit the Dubai posting boosted my contacts with the top management and I had accelerated promotions without extra effort. I was already groomed by the bank to become G.M., thanks to the succession planning in this progressive bank.

In this process I was posted to head the experimental corporate banking branch. I had to compete with many stars of the bank. That was divine intervention I have been harping upon! It was bank management's pet experiment, success or failure would have affected my career, either way. There was tension and pressure, but my God helped me steer through and I came off with flying colours.

In the penultimate phase of my career, I was posted as CEO of South African operations, which brought me international recognition. The branch at Durban was inaugurated as a part of 2500th branch in the Golden Jubilee Year of Indian Independence. It was inaugurated by no less a person than Sri Gopala Krishna Gandhi, Mahatma's grandson on 15th August 1997, Durban was the place where Gandhiji had spent 22 years as a lawyer. It was a historic day both for me and my bank. The preparations for opening were done in record time of three months which paved my way to become G.M-CEO of European Operations in London.

1. I was one of the very few in my bank to get overseas assignments 3 times.
2. Probably I was first clerk to become a G.M in the South.
3. My association with AWARE, an NGO, in Hyderabad which exposed me to the poverty of tribals and their struggle for survival which is worse than what I had experienced as a child in my village.

Now I am focusing my attention on my village—my Janmabhoomi—in the form of education, employment, and integrated personality development of the rural youth, to give back a part of what I had got from it.

D.S.M.

Here is an example of a man who steered well on the superhighway but attributes his success to divine intervention. With this faith, probably, he allowed his life run its natural course-the successful career. Fulfillment is flowing in utility to society. His 'role model', is legacy, he will leave. The two above profiles can be compared.

K.K. wanted to become G.M but ended up as D.G.M. DSM wanted to become D.G.M. but became G.M. Both of them did not aspire for the top position. They knew that that requires political support.

In my view faith in almighty is faith in oneself. Both lead to positive thinking and positive effort.

2
Swerve and Sever

Swerve and Sever

How do you know when you have reached the dead-end? There can be lots of signs; at the end of the day you feel dull. You engage in loose talk and office politics. You grow cynical and critical of every minute thing. May be you are continuously passed over or not even considered for promotion. At such an impasse there is likelihood of getting along and easygoing stages mentioned before. The need to summon your soft skills is of utmost importance. Decision- making, problem solving, heart-to-heart (tete-a-tete) talk with family, friends, colleagues, mentors, and any one who matters to verify the gut feelings.

Weigh the options. Sever – leave the organization, swerve–turn to alternate courses within the organization. Seek financial, moral, and other tangible support, last but not the least, emotional support. Leaving an organization you served so long, is not easy. Practical considerations outweigh the emotions. You are 'setting forth' again: *positive attitude* and *goal setting skills* are the immediate requirements to battle the crisis.

Swerve

If the company does not encourage, then they look for avenues to *swerve* and start own. As the word swerve suggests, sudden deviation, with skills—actual and potential—both hard and soft, they make new career even after 40 or 50 years of age. They change the course. Others may struggle a little longer and sever the long connection with the company towards which they would have developed attachment. The result is voluntary retirement or premature retirement out of frustration. Such people with skill, energy and capacity to learn must 'set forth' and find a new career with some gestation period to take off a bright career. In a large organization one can change the course by changing the function. We have a case discussed at the end of the chapter. He had a career change, virtually, when he became a barefoot banker. Later, even this he had to change by opting for faculty position in the staff college.

There are some who, after nationalization of banks, found the seat hot and quit abruptly and paid for their hasty decision. It is a lack of soft skills—the critical thinking, problem solving, and decision making, and networking. That does not mean they are failures. They did find their own paths and remained contented. We cannot prescribe to them any course. They have to find. The choice is made and they don't blame anyone else. Nor do they go into depression, again a soft skill of managing self. There is a person, whose case is not included here, who chose C.A even though his parents wanted him to become an engineer. He got into the private firm to become its partner. He specialized in income tax laws and appeared before the tribunal on behalf of his clients. He wanted to gain experience on the other side and applied for National Tribunal Direct Recruitment Board. He got selected and worked as judge and gained new experience. Our skills both hard and soft can get blunt and ineffective. A sabbatical leave is like taking off time from work to sharpen our 'saw', so that we can work more efficiently and effectively after the return. There are professionals who after several years in private practice accept government employment or public sector employment to gain experience which helps them later when they come back for private practice.

A company secretary or chartered accountant or lawyer or doctor with good private practice may accept corporate job, judicial post, advisor to government, administrator and may return to private practice. All these people believe there is no substitute to direct experience. If you want to become versatile, multi–skilled, multi–faceted personality you need to take a short term stint. It is similar to functional transfer in corporate and civil services.

Ex–service men with OLQ (officer like qualities) fit in a variety jobs after retirement from military service.

Steering through has a new dimension in the recession and financial crisis the world has been facing now-a-days. One HR professional has this to say:

> Jobs for life were a thing of the past long before the global recession came on. So getting the pink slip does not signify the end of the world.

But if you would hold on to your job till the market regains buoyancy, you will have to become proactive about your *commitment* to the job and the organization. Commitment, courage, control, and competence are all part of value-skills complex.

Case 17

Life Planning and Career Planning of Couples

The career path trod by "VV" is more by accident than by design.

His schooling has been completed in modules at different places of Andhra Pradesh because of the frequent transfers of his father who worked with a nationalized bank. His higher education too similarly affected.

While schooling and intermediate board studies are not much to write about, the turning point came when the family shifted to Chennai following yet another transfer. After an unsuccessful attempt at the engineering entrance exam conducted by the Osmania and JNTU universities as the intermediate marks were not sufficient to get him admission in any of the R.E.Cs , "VV" has taken up promising course in corporate secretaryship in a degree college at Meenambakkam, Chennai.

The real upshot has come when he received all the encouragement from parents to pursue a string of degrees in the areas of law, company secretaryship & costing at Ahmedabadwhere his father was posted for 10 years.

After undergoing professional training prescribed by the ICSI, "VV" has initially worked as a company secretary in a wireless communication industry, then switched over to soft drinks, hotel and finally a blade manufacturing industry at Hyderabad. The desire to stay closer to parents in their retired life has restricted the career path to Hyderabad.

In the last 15 plus years of service with the blade manufacturing industry, the job description and responsibilities varied from legal to finance to costing with the basic responsibility being that of a company secretary. During this period, he added yet another feather to his cap, by acquiring an MBA in finance from Osmania University.

From the cosy corridors of legal and company secretarial cabins to the rough and tumble of shop floor dynamics of production at factory premises meant a continuous process of reinvention of skills, style of functioning, adaptation to the differing needs of the employer, while deriving sustenance from the enriched academic background; and this more than anything has punctuated and else enriched the career learning curve of "VV".

Work experience in his own words!

As a company secretary with 23 years' experience, I had to interact with top management on one hand and various departments, both at the registered office and the factory on the other, ensuring compliance with corporate laws and economic legislation, tax and labour laws. The mother of all corporate legislation is the "companies act" which coupled with allied legislation encompasses most of the work of a company secretary. While holding board meetings, convening general meetings, filing returns/forms/documents constitutes the routine work, co-ordinating the different organs of a body corporate forms an integral part of a company secretary's job. Good corporate governance, effective communication with shareholders, government agencies and market players forms the benchmark(s) for evaluation of performance.

As a member of the legal profession with 12 years of corporate experience, my work involved briefing the advocates about the cases, drafting of various agreements, powers of attorney, deeds, bonds and representing the company for deposition before courts of law in chief and cross examination for evidence.

As a member of the Institute of Cost and Works Accountants of India with 5 years of costing in the manufacturing units of the company, I had to develop a costing system for the cost of production of various brands, products of different divisions. The tools for development of a viable costing system involved compiling of data from all the cost centers, preparation of raw data for developing consumption patterns of various items of cost, collection of data relating to closing floor stocks, percentage of rejection, maintenance scheduling for break-downs and utilisation of manpower, machines and utilities.

As a management student from 1996, I realised that qualities of an individual are far more relevant and determinant than qualifications. If qualifications give a platform for performance, qualities of leadership, integrity, industry and commitment take one up the ladder in his career.

I shall narrate a very recent, rich experience I had in a span of three months from March to May 2008:

A group of foreign citizens from the US and local representative consulted me for incorporation of a company for carrying out their mission of conducting educational programme for secondary and higher school students from the US in India, in the shortest possible time with money for the project coming from abroad. Drawing strengths from the academic background in different disciplines and work experience so far, I have successfully implemented the project within the timeframe allotted to me. From this I have come to the following conclusions:

1. It is the knowledge of companies act, which made it easier for me to suggest solutions for the *modus operandi* to be followed in incorporation of the company.
2. It is the experience to work with teams that enabled me to coordinate and correspond with newly appointed auditors, legal counsel and the local representative apart from plethora of emails to foreign nationals for the purpose of culling personal and official data required for the formation of the company.
3. It is the knowledge of various corporate and foreign exchange legislation that helped me in complying with the

statutory formalities for foreign direct investment in India through the Reserve Bank of India.

4. It is the network of contacts in the professional circles that made it possible to complete certain certification and authentication work in the course of implementation.
5. It is in this assignment that I realised about my abilities to independently handle complex situations on my own.
6. It has given me an opportunity to relook at my career plans for switching over from service in an organisation to service to an organisation as a full time practising company secretary.
7. As a consultant, one may diversify the range of services depending upon one's qualifications, qualities, contacts and stamina.
8. It is a case of networking of career growth and growth through networking for which there is no superannuation.

Wife's Career

A qualified pharmacist graduate, got married to VV in November 1989. Her career commenced in the year 1988 shortly after her graduation from M.S.University, Baroda. She worked in a private company in Navsari, Gujarat in production (parenterals division) and received recognition as approved pharmacist from Foods and Drugs Administration, Gujarat.

She moved to Visakhapatnam in the year 1990 to join her husband who had taken up a job in a soft drinks company. Keeping abreast with the modern times, she also has taken up a job in the quality control department of a manufacturing company, dealing with formulations.

After shifting to Hyderabad a year and a half later, she continued her yearning for working by joining another pharmaceutical company within the city. She worked for one and a half years in production (parenterals division) under stringent working atmosphere. Her boss, the Production Manager turned out to be a hard task master, despite that she maintained composure and competence at all points of time. She felt happy when she came to know that her work was recognized not only by her boss but also the Managing Director of the company. The best compliment came when she had to resign under compelling circumstances to attend to domestic duties. The Production Manager commented that he was losing his right hand signifying the important role she played in the department.

Keeping in tune with the times, at the next working opportunity in the year 1999, she joined a training organization for getting first-hand experience in the field of medical transcription. Since then, she switched a couple of jobs in the same line in search of newer and better prospects. Her work involved transcription of files received from foreign companies with accuracy and efficiency. In this phase, she got acclimatized with the integrated chain of activities like, editing, collection work and billing. Currently she is associated with a private company formed by a group of professionals engaged in all the value added services of medical transcription. The proximity to the top management enriched her inherent qualities and gave her exposure to technology and techniques of management. Her pharmacy background coupled with rich experience gel well for a successful career in the profession of her choice.

The career planning without sacrificing her domestic responsibilities within the self-imposed constraint of restricting to Hyderabad for staying closer to parents and parents-in-law has been the hallmark of her professional pursuit thus far.

Formula for Success – Hard + Soft

Reading between the lines the profile of V.V. as it is emerging proves the formula S = H + S, Success is a function of the combination of hard skills and soft skills.

V.V. resigned from the private manufacturing company after nearly 20 years of service after dilly-dally, in spite of his recognizing that his talents and qualifications are not being fully utilized.

He set up an independent practice as a practicing company secretary. In about 3 months time he earned as much as he was getting in the employment. More than earning he is learning a great deal. He is very much conscious of his learning and articulates it. This enhances the very learning. He learned that he has more talents than he imagined. His soft skills are fully utilized in dealing with clients. His 'reporting and rapporting' are extraordinary, a rare combination.

His communication skills both oral and written are put to best use in helping the client in drafting the resolutions and building rapport which seem to come naturally. What is more important is that his hard skills – use of computers are improving which are vital for his efficiency in the profession.

He is understanding the dynamics of business growth and development, the secret of which lies in networking. There is synergy and the results are enhancing his confidence levels which is the key to success in private practice. He is a professional and he knows the difference between a professional and employee. But he now deals with clients who are entrepreneurs who belong to a different species. He is demonstrating the meaning of empathy–stepping into the shoes of the other persons and understanding his fears, anxieties, and doubts. His knowledge, his skills, and his values have to be harnessed. Though late he is re-inventing himself. To realize one's true potential one must first discover it.

Shifting focus at will is a soft skill

While he was in company service, much of his work was determined by the routine and higher ups. He was not fully occupied in the factory either. Both at home and in office he was able to find lot of spare time when he was reading material relating to the profession of company secretary. He was compiling various amendments and legal information. All that knowledge is coming in good stead now. But he is unable to find time to read. *Economic Times* his favourte source of information in private practice. Nevertheless he carries the paper in his brief and reades whenever he finds time.

Case 19

A case of Changing Careers - Life Long Learning

As a young boy, I desired to study Engineering. However, I had to satisfy myself with a Degree in Science. The financial cumpulsion at that time made me to join a sales job in a multinational tea company even though I was never interested in a selling career.

I changed my career thereafter to ***banking*** because it afforded an opportunity to add to my qualifications. Punctuality, commitment and dedication to work earned me a good name as a bank employee.

With an in-built interest in learning continuously, I studied, in my spare hours, to appear for the professional examination conducted by the Indian Institute of Bankers. I came out with a distinction in that examination and soon after was promoted to officer cadre.

My father never approved these changes, but he did not object to my doing what I liked. My aversion for selling was probably because I saw my father struggling to sell Insurance policies.

After assuming my duties as an officer. which involved supervising and approving others' work, I realised that my job role was getting quite routine and boring, as it simply, at that time, involved a pen-pushing activity, passing umpteen number of vouchers and transactions.

Regular income and job security made me stick to the banking career even though my heart was not with it cent per cent, so my life became routine and mechanical, without any challenge element.

In the year 1969, fourteen commercial banks including the one in which I was working, were nationalised and taken over by the Central Government. The purpose was to make banking facilities accesible to people in the rural and semi urban areas which were neglected by the private banks until that time. The emphasis after nationalisation was branch expansion and rural development including upliftment of the neglected sectors of the society. This sudden change in the working style of the bank made my career much more interesting for me.

During my stint as a sales person with the tea company, I had some exposure to the rural India. Dealing with the rural folk was not new to me. As against a selling experience in rural areas while I was with the tea company, the rural experience in a bank was more laudable and challenging.

In the year 1970, I was fortunate enough to be one of the 28 people in the country in our Bank to be trained at Pune on "Agriculture Finance". The training programme was spread over a period of 10 weeks.

Many eminent personalities addressed the trainees on the problems of rural credit. I always enjoyed reading books as my first hobby, irrespective of the job I was doing , I continued my reading habit and read several books on a, variety of subjects. I realised later, that this was my strongest quality compared to many others and this made me to stand in good stead whenever there was a Group Discussion or a Seminar on any important subject.

Reading the Reports on All India Rural Credit and the writings of Mahatma Gandhi made a deep impact and established in me. So my vision about a banking career went through a metamorphosis, thanks to the Banks Nationalisation in 1969. There was no need to quit bank for changing careers.

The free self was restless and itching for practical experience in the rural development, particularly the small and marginal farmers. The transformation from a ***"class banking"*** **to "mass** ***banking"*** kindled new interest in me in taking my banking career to new heights.

I had to wait for 3 years after receiving the training in rural credit, to get my chance to be posted in a backward district as a Branch Manager. I was the first manager of the branch, and I had the freedom to experiment and experience.

I toured villages, identified the felt needs of the villagers, formulated schemes for lending and deliver credit at the grass roots level, to later earn the name as a "Bare-Foot Banker". I earned the respect as a "pioneer" and an "example" in the credit delivery system in rural areas.

It was amusing for me to discover that I inherited the "trait of village trotting" from my father who had toured villages to propagate wearing of khadi and discarding the habit of drinking-during the Pre-Independence period as a part of the satyagraha movementin 1928/29.

I started liking my job and took it as a ***"movement".*** I won the laurels more from the public and the government authorities than the remote Bank Management, who were more concerned about the numbers and figures and not the quality of change and impact of my work in the areas served by my branch. My self-confidence and popularity in the rural areas were not liked by my bosses who, as a result, transferred me to many other places in quick succession. I was overlooked for promotions and other incentives which went to people close to the big bosses, rather than to people who struggled to traslate national goals into action.

My newfound enthusiasm started dwindling. I started looking for new opportunities, within the constraints I had. As a matter of divine intervention, I got an opportunity to apply for a faculty position at the Bank's apex training establishment. It was here that 1 went through a rigorous process of selection through Group Discussion and a panel interview. I was chosen at once to be a senior faculty. I had had no teaching experience until then. But the skills of communication which were inherent in me coupled with the experience gained from the "Faculty Development programme" for which I was nominated (I came out as an outstanding trainee) made me to establish myself as an important faculty member at the staff college.

My yearning for learning at the age of 50, earned appreciation from my other professional faculty members who were much younger in age to me.

Class-room affords excellent opportunity to learn if some one is ready to ask questions and challenge the precepts presented in the class. I was discovering that I was an 'ace learner'.

The staff college had directly recruited core faculty, all Doctorates in different disciplines. Besides, the faculty from IIM Ahmedabad was visiting the college as guest faculty. I networked with all of them who wondered at my enthusiasm and appreciated my energy to learn. They gave me all encouragement which served as an external motivation to excel in teaching.

During this period I learnt to write cases, notes, articles to journals, attended seminars, presented papers besides designing and conducting training programmes. Thousands of trainees were exposed to my classes and were thrilled. Many of them became my fans who demanded my sessions in every programme. After 10 eventful years at the college, I retired and returned to Hyderabad. That was in 1992.

After retirement from the Bank, I started another career as Trainer and Writer both of which I enjoyed. Rewards and recognition by others was never my priority-Recognition by my own "self" was what was important to me. Deep down in my heart, I derive the satisfaction today for serving different segments of the society, in my own humble way. I feel I am a fully satisfied person with a case of challenging careers and with a yearning for life long learning.

Case 18

My profile- My identity

I like to introduce myself as an engineer by qualification and a salesman by accident. In fact, my association with engineering was itself an accident – both before and after. I was pressurised into joining engineering, much against my will because it was very difficult to get an engineering seat in those days, yet I managed to get one. Thereafter while I started working as a junior engineer at a project site in Andhra Pradesh, I met with a serious accident , which immobilised me for quite some time. Both these left an indelible influence in my mind that I should seek a change in profession.

When multi-national oil major offered me the change, after a series of tests and interviews, I jumped at it. When I joined the marketing side in this oil major-many were annoyed. It was a far cry from a four-year study of civil engineering to selling 'kerosene / petrol / diesel'. It involved a lot of travel, long hours of work. I was pleasant all the time. Being an extrovert was alien to my grain. As a child and later as a youth, I was a very standoffish person. I would always wait to be introduced. I was known for my short temper. But what gave me the courage to accept this challenge was that, not withstanding my reserved nature, I was a public speaker of some repute and was an actor to boot in my student days. I was said to have the gift of the gab.

First twelve years of my sales assignment were a tough. Composure and patience are essential for a market man. It needed constant review and revision of my attitude and behaviour. It demanded the need to reform my communication skills which I did, slowly and steadily.

After nationalisation the opportunities in the organisation were better. While the multi-national company provided a good job, the nationalised company offered growth prospects and a career. I moved up the ladder quite quickly. In a matter of 10 years I moved up 6 times- the growth was exponential and I was very proud of myself – I still am.

While this growth gave me pride and ego satisfaction, it added to my responsibilities and called for a thorough revision of my interpersonal relationship. It was at this time that I opted to undergo a series of 'person' oriented training programmes. The ISISD, ISABS. IIM (A).ASCI, were some of the organisations that took me under their fold and coached me. I was trained to be a trainer. I realised that training others is a very high degree of education in itself. This changed my entire outlook on life, its priorities and its demands.

Looking back I still think, the turning point on my life is the 'person' oriented programmes I underwent and the mentoring support I got. .

I am more than convinced that while most of us may have to do things, we may not fully like to, but the challenge lies in finding an opportunity in a calamity.

K.S

A retired General Manager of a Public Sector undertaking shares the importance and benefits of person growth labs—training.

Adaptability and Theory of Evolution

Darwin is remembered; a number of articles appeared in the Newspapers for tuning into breakfast information time series – titbits.

The oft quoted phrase, 'Survival of the fittest' is not what Darwin said: His mechanism for survival and reproduction is natural selection. It is defined by different people differently:

> 'The phrase *Natural Selection* means that there is a continual struggle going on among animals and plants (and humans) to survive, and those that *vary* from others in a *useful* way will tend to survive and reproduce (produce young) that will also have these variations'.

A *natural process* that results in *survival* and *reproductive success* of individual or groups best *adjusted* in their *environment* and that leads to *perpetuation* of genetic qualities best suited to that particular environment.'

'Useful variations' is a useful concept. Change within, to adapt to changes without. It is 'reactive' theory. Sri Aurobindo and Mother of Pondicherry think differently. There is a second factor – 'will' to change to evolve into a higher order, newer, not gradual, sudden, swift and with synergy.

Synergy is *collective effort* of most of the members of the species. When there is, critical mass change there is sudden change of state. Boiling water is an example. When water is heated then bubbles formed which burst and become water molecules again. As the heat is on, as more and more bubbles form and interact, then there is steam emanating. Water changes into vapour. There is a change of state.

When a critical mass of people or members of a species 'will' to change, there is then sudden, swift and sweeping change; no resemblance to the earlier state. But change of state is reversible; but evolution is irreversible, I believe. Probably so, I have no idea. I only wish it that way.

'Man's qualities are monkey's weaknesses' Satprem, author of 'Mind of Cells', an inmate of Pondicherry Ashram.

Let us take the second definition quoted above.

It is worth examining, with its integrated concepts relevant to our topic of soft skills. We said that adaptability is a soft skill. Darwin's reference was to the species, not individuals or man made organizations. Still we frequently refer to the concept, *survival of the fittest* in respect to competition in the market place.

Natural selection is the mechanism for survival and reproduction in the altered environment; and perpetuation. It is an adjustment vis-à-vis environment. This means if there is no change in the environment there won't be adjustment. It is a consequence of changes in the environment. The species will perpetuate without need for adjustment and have no adjustment necessary in the shorter periods. Let us look at another meaning, 'natural selection means that there is continuous struggle (going on among plants and animals) to survive and 'those that *vary* from others in a useful way will tend to survive and produce young that they will also have these useful *variations'*.

The adjustment is in the useful variations. That is how diversity is taking place. There is proliferation of diversity as a mechanism of survival and reproduction to perpetuate.

The proliferation of the soft skills is similar. The mechanism is natural selection of useful variations, (vary from others).

Satprem, disciple of Mother of Pondicherry, wrote,

> 'There exists in fact a real need for a new scientific approach that the world consider the part played by the creature in its own evolution, that would stop looking at evolution as a one-sided – environmental – affair and welcome the admission of the second player'.

'Modern sciences' view that the adding up of mutations (relatively permanent changes), the modifications of DNA in the germ cells, is what creates a new species in the course of time, may be quite right, but what triggers those mutations in the first place? Mutations 'seem to us in our ignorance to arise spontaneously' (Darwin)...

> 'Could it be that, at least partially, it *wills* its own mutations, its own mutations, it aspires for a change of air because of its own suffocation or *growing sense of inadequacy in the milieu*'.

He suggests: there exists, in fact, a real need – second player. The second player is the 'free will' – will to change for better, more adequate to survive and revive... From macro-level to micro level the phenomenon is true.

Variations and Natural selection of Soft skills

Darwin's life itself was a struggle against ill-health; yet he survived upto the age of 73 and went on studying living things and collected massive data so as to make him write,

> 'My mind seems to have became a kind of machine for grinding laws out of large collection of fact, but why this should have caused the atrophy of that part of the brain on which the higher tastes depend, and may possibly be injurious to the intellect, and more probably to the moral character, by enfeebling the emotional part of nature'.

Had he revived the atrophied part of the brain by reviving his interest in Music, Art, and Poetry; had he re-invented himself, he would have lived full hundred years! (His interest in Music, Art, Poetry was already referred).

Long before Darwin, many thinkers had similar ideas on evolution. But it is Darwin who crystalised it from out of massive data he collected as a naturalist with 'steadfast patience of a growing crystal when crowded spheres are generated' (Stephan Zweing). That is the difference between 'invention' and 'innovation', one is abstract and the other is concrete. Innovation has bias for action, doing or a device, something new and better.

Unique path is similar to natural selection – the mechanism given to the world by Charles Darwin: from out of struggle to strive comes the natural selection of variations of characteristics in a useful way to survive and reproduce or replicate. Individuals and their ideas, skills, replicate and multiply. That explains the soft skills proliferation and re-production to leave a legacy.

Like all books, this book too has taken the route of evolution–natural selection, the mechanism identified by Charles Darwin because like all living things, it has to survive, and reproduce, through a process of adjustment and adaptation–

Natural selection which means 'that there is continual struggle that goes on... to survive and those that *vary* from others in a *useful* way.. will tend to survive... the progeny will have these variations.' I tried to make it different. It varies from the conventional text books. The variations lie in Cases, Acronyms & Anecdotes, Snippets, and Titbits all the components of the CAST are aimed at 'learning' – for survival and reproduction.

Multi Skills

Subtle variations, almost difficult to notice, is the hallmark of a flexible employee which makes him highly wanted, highly employable by selectors.

To understand the idea no better example comes than from the game of cricket. There is tremendous competition to be selected and re-selected to make a career in cricket. Survival of the fittest is true in this game.

"Amit Misra, a leggie, who took 5 crickets on his debut, was spotted by his coach 15 years back".

Long internship in domestic cricket before he got a chance in the test match.

> *sincere, hardworking, disciplined,* ever *willing to learn* and he just wants to bowl and bowl in the nets.... A wonderful wrist-spinner (a specialization) any captain would love to have... His *mentor* Bhardwaj, par excellence... was not only a coach, mentor, band ambassador...

You will be lucky to have one such mentor to 'fight' for you in your career progression. It is not luck; it is a work out, look out, for one such guru.

> "Misra rips the ball hard and the resolution caused it to dip. He used his crease and the angles intelligently with subtle changes in length and trajectory.

The fact that Dhoni (wicket-keeper captain) had a silly point and a short leg in position showed Misra was spinning the ball both ways."

Mark, the support system is in place.

"He used straight one—not quite the top-spinner or a flipper off full length trajectory.

'Watson's batting innings was eventually terminated by a delivery that pitched on leg and went through straight. The crowds were in raptures.

...he mixed them quite well, a short man who gets the ball come down in a parabola...he forces the batsmen use their feet".

Misra has the advantage of mixing his hard and soft skills.

SECTION - IV

FROM HERE TO ETERNITY

1
FITNESS

POST-RETIREMENT-A NEW BEGGING

The last the letters, initials FUL of the acronym SUCCESSFUL stand for fulfillment and also Fitness, Utility, and Leaving of legacy – the three elements of fulfilled life.

Fitness to survive long retirement, Utility – fitness to be of use by the society, Legacy – leaves an example for the progeny

> Fittest to survive and transmit to the progeny the characteristics that are survival worthy. (Darwin)
>
> Utility to the society (the environment) will ensure survival of the organism; it is an important characteristic the progeny learns.
>
> Legacy is what is transmitted.

Fulfilment

Life long employment in government or public sector or large scale private sector companies was what was preferred by people belonging to earlier generations. Their aspirations were limited to loyal, disciplined, service with own cherished values, knowledge, and skills, soft skills in particular. Many Indians from educated class served the British Government as teachers, clerks, accountants, stenographers confined to indoors. There were lawyers who opted for government service and rose to become District, High Court Judges; banks, insurance companies, and oil companies provided excellent avenues. This apart there are many who belonged to the same families and opted for civil services like their fathers and other relatives.

Some of them have many stories about their long careers to tell their grandchildren. Some of the first person accounts are similar to what the retired people share. When I was working in Kakinada, which was known as rendezvous of the retired, we had many savings accounts of retired people. Whenever they come to bank they *shared* with pride their exploits, -which they thought was their achievements, their principles, values, and troubles and struggles. If they find you too busy to listen, acknowledge, approve, compliment or praise, they get disappointed: considering their business value to the bank we were compelled to appear to be responding.

After their stories become stale and no longer exciting they may start talking about their health problems or pilgrimages 'sans eyes, sans ears, sans everything—add to it sans money, sans social support, the senility sets in.

There are few, very few, who are club birds whom I used to find in the tennis court or billiards room having a good laugh at their declining agility. What they really enjoy is the company of the other like-minded.

Fulfillment is the goal, the end; the means are *utilization* of god given gifts and acquired talents through diligent practice to *leave a legacy* to the progeny and posterity some intentional and some unintended.

We are born with certain inheritance over which we have no control–our parentage and patronage of cultural legacy. We are the beneficiaries of a legacy and transmitters of legacy. Born with a legacy, live and grow in it and bequeath it to the future generations collectively with others. Our contribution is our fulfilment.

Recluse, "*Vanaprasthya*' or secluded life in the forest is a stage preparatory to the final stage of renunciation. This life is characterized by severe discipline in matters of food, dress, and other physical comforts… has to worship his favourite gods and guests, and has to study and observe penance with perfect equanimity… transition from house holder to that of *sanyasin,* ascetic… probation entitling one to enter a state of complete renunciation.. *Sanyasin* transcends the bonds of the flesh and rises into the realm of the spirit…

> The scheme of *asramas* (student, house-holder, recluse, and ascetic) is based on the ethical principle that man should discharge his duties fully before aspiring for liberation from the bonds of the flesh and world… the way to glory.
>
> ***The Cultural Heritage of India Vol II***

Without retiring into forest, you can withdraw from material hankering and world comforts reduced to minimum. Regulated life with moderate activity, engagement in something beneficial to the society. What you actually withdraw from is the duty of a house-holder, hardest duties, leaving them to children. You can remain a 'witness' without interfering unless called upon. Even so, like a good manager you allow others to decide by supplying with information and analysis of the data. Like the traditional Guru-kulam style you can engage in *Samvad*, dialogue, not debates.

Fitness LIES[1] entirely in four factors

Longevity Identity Engagement Spirituality

Consider longevity of retired life. 25 to 30 years of extended life span, uncertainty of its tenure, and declining agility and health make it look like eternity, an endless phase. Hence the title, *from here to eternity.*

Eternity has another connotation, life beyond death.

> Ah, there is the rub…. To die, to sleep; perchance to dream… for in that sleep what dreams may come, when we have shuffled off the mortal coil, must give us pause. There's the respect, that makes calamity of so long life; for who would bear the whips and scorns of time… but that the dread of something after death, the undiscovered country from whose bourn, no traveler returns, puzzles the will, and makes us rather bear those ills we have, than fly to others we know not of?
>
> Thus conscience does make cowards of us all.
>
> ***Shakespeare (Hamlet, Prince of Denmark)***

[1] **LIES:** Longirity; Identity; Eangagement; Spiritnatity

Hamlet's dilemma may haunt us all and the conscience does make cowards of us all and make us misfits to bear the whips and scorns of so long life, unless we plan and prepare for the eventuality. At least remember and be with Henry Longfellow who gave us the *psalm of life:*

Trust no Future, howe'er pleasant!
Let the dead Past bury its dead!
Act, - act in the living Present!
Heart within, and God o'erhead!

To combat the calamity of so long life, treat it as opportunity to *engage* in some moderate activity that suits your *identity* acting in the living present. What about spirituality? You may include in your regular activities listening to religious discourses, take yoga courses, and attend meditation classes. But if you don't work on what you received you may get deceived. Self deception is the worst thing that can happen to you.

There is an alternative prescription, *Karma Yoga.* If what you engage in is not to be an escape, it should be an altruist action, selfless service, proximate or remote. That becomes a step in the long journey towards attaining *spirituality.*

Fitness (Dictionary Meanings)

Capacity of an organism to *survive* and *transmit* its genotype to reproductive offspring as compared to competing organisms… also the contribution of a genotype to gene pool of subsequent generations.

It is a quality of being *fit*, the broadest term here, means having the qualities or qualifications to meet the conditions, circumstance, purpose or demand.

Readiness and adaptability to meet the challenges, the situation demands.

Survive and transmit; be an example and leave a legacy to the progeny and posterity. At the more mundane level, the AIM[2] in retirement is threefold:

- Avoidance of sickness
- Involvement in some activity
- Maintaining identity

Avoidance of sickness is keeping good health, physical, mental, and social wellbeing, which is dependent on the other two aims.

Proneness to sickness has its roots in our genes. Knowing our physical constitution is one way to avoid harmful food, activities, climate both physical and social. Health has been defined as physical, mental, and social wellbeing, all of which you might have neglected due to career pressures. Busy executives have the knack of postponing acuteness through palliatives and ignoring the warning signals the body never fails to give. Involving in social activities has its problems, your lack of soft skills, inter-personal relations and lack of adaptability and flexibility. The last aim – maintaining identity is by far the most vexed problem post retirement. We may have to devote more space for it. Before that, let us go through the following reflections on an article written in 1979, the contents of which are valid even to day.

Identity

After severing connection with the organization on superannuation, highly successful people find themselves in a fix. I have passed through this for 17 years now. I can speak for myself and advice on planning for the eventuality. The text of this sort which is inevitably the outcome of a range of influences and previous work apart from my personal experience makes me quote from reprint of an article written 30 years ago, November-December 1979 issue of Harvard Business Review. As I was clearing my old papers from the shelfs I tumbled on this one

[2] **AIM:** Avoidance of sickness; Involvement in some activity; Maintaining identity

providentially. It reveals cultural differences of the West and the East. The author Leland P.Bradford wrote:

'I was the chief executive of an organization I had helped found, as well as a professional behavioral scientist, and I should have known better. But I didn't. After 25 yearts of working under the strain of building an organization, of interweaving the ideas and needs of the key staff with a multiplicity of outside forces, I was ready for the beautiful promised land of retirement. I persuaded my wife to leave our lovely George town home and move to North Carolina, where I could golf to my heart's content and enjoy relief from the stress of having to make daily decisions. I thought it would be just wonderful'

How wrong I was! The organization moved on without me. Important decision I had made were reversed.

No one called for advice. As far I could see, no one cared... it hurt'.

There is a case of BLs: his IT projects have not seen the light during his tenure, but they are being implemented much later. The organization might acknowledge the contributions made by the people who no longer connected to the organization.

He found that golf did *not fill a day*. How to 'fill the day' Fulfilment is missing now; it was there every day before retirement. Our ancestors knew the problem of the 'house holder' would face once he enters the '*Vanaprasta ashrama*'. The change is anticipated well in advance and the man is 'ready for the beautiful promised land of retirement' in the words of the author. Vanaprasta ashramite's day, the hermitage life, is filled fully, a completely fulfilled routine. Thoreau, an American naturalist showed a way but it has been ignored by the modern American. We too have become 'modern'. The problems we face today are similar.

The chief executive of a modern corporation has Goals, Routine, Achievements, Socialization and Power. The GRASP[3], that holds, for most fulfilling day, 18 hours a day.

---

[3] **GRASP:** Goals; Routine; Achievements; Socialization; Power

> 'Organizations provide *goals*...goals make *achievement* possible… Achievement brings in affirmation from others and from one's self. Without this periodic affirmation, self-esteem and self-worth diminish.'
>
> 'To be without goals is to be purposeless, to have no reason…to live'. If nothing else routine fills the time. The system moves on….
>
> 'The organization, for almost all positions, provides colleagues, workgroups, teams, committee, units or departments'.

Whenever there is a call the stock answer is Sir, is in the meeting. The Indian variation is when the boss is called at home, the stock answer is, 'Sir is in Puja'.

> 'Work provides the contacts vital for psychological well-being'.

Social contact is the most important loss after retirement. Any contacts you establish after retirement are not bound by common work goals. You withdraw because it lacks the kind of binding and mutuality.

Of course, power and influence for most employees the companies provide to some degree or other are now missing. *What is to be done?* Here is a couple of snippets from the article.

> *Routines and time:* The busy executive with wide-ranging interests and multifaceted decisions to make seldom realizes the stabilizing force of set routines – regular staff meetings, daily agendas on the desk each morning, planned luncheon engagements, organized trips, prearranged social events.

Routine is a stabilizing force. You need *Routine* even after retirement – regular moderate activities, rituals and pastimes.

Recent research on adult development stresses that growth and learning can continue throughout the life span. The tremendous increase in continuing education courses offered by colleges, community organizations, and high school is based on this premise. Acceptance of the concept of a new career, increasingly supported by organizational and societal careers change.

A career, lest the word seem pretentious, can be any sustained activity whose purpose or goal is meaningful to the person, where motivation is maintained, and where achievement brings affirmation from self or others.

The last section of the article is not very helpful except that he suggests attending to training programmes for employees due for retirement and planning for another career. He begins the last section with, 'There is no cook book recipe for retiring'. All are agreed on that. I have an 'acronym prescription': What the retiree has lost is GRASP, a hold. He has to GRASP[4] another, new *Goals; new Routine; new Achievements; Socialization; new Perspective* in place of power. It may not have the power in the sense it was used previously but has the power to influence, leaven with the fruits of knowledge, experience, values, professionalism. The entrepreneurial spirit, reservoir of soft skills. You may not demand company but it will come in the form of younger generation looking up to you.

Treat retirement as a career. **Set forth** on the journey; **Unique** to you; **Choosing** the right career; **control** it; make it **enterprising** and enjoyable based on your interests and personality type and anchors; **steady**; **stable**; engaging in **fringe work** (moderate, regular, activities), with **utility** to larger society directly or via; and Learning Life Long you will leave a **legacy** no doubt, an example for others. We explained the meaning of 'Control' doing things deeper to your heart, what you want to get out of life. Follow Deepak Chopras' LIFE LATEST presented in the appendix VI.

A Case of Dr. B.L.S

Because Dr.BLS did not show interest in hardcore banking operations, he could not move up faster than his junior colleague who could show concrete results in operational business. Business figures which show current performance get rewards much quicker than research and development work in departments like IT and Projects whose results accrue over a longer period. Nevertheless like Dr. BLs one can take pride in back-office far-reaching contribution. Success is not

---

[4] **GRASP:** Goals; Routine; Achievements; Socialization; Perspective

restricted to occupying top positions. It depends on one's choices. The so-called 'loop-line' careers come handy later after superannuation for their unique talents, orientations, and expertise for continuous engagement and utility.

There are people who have slipped into easy going stage (Refer to STAGES) think retirement is an *escape* and not to be engaged in any activity but to enjoy life with hard earned (or is it hardly earned?) terminal benefits in terms of money. ESCAPE[5]: Emotionally; Satisfying; Comforting Activities; Passage of time; Easy way. The last 'E' can stand for 'entertainment'. TV and movies have helped the aged in the passage of time. It is more passive viewing than active watching. These entertainment media claim that they are 'edutainment' moments. The soap opera with each episode leaving expectation to the next episode seem to increase life expectancy. Anticipation makes us live longer. There is something to live for, the next episode!

Soon they search for alternate ways to pass the time. Gandhiji found the villagers in British India needed 'Charkha' to fill the time with fulfillment. Are the retired in similar impasse? They need a 'Charkha', wheel, repeated productive activity, suitable to individual identity. They cannot compare themselves with Sri Aurobindo who escaped from jail and became a sage. Many successful retirees associate themselves with the ashram at Pondicherry for edification. Even there they are engaged in some constructive activity. You cannot escape from work. Do it with laudable intentions.

On identity I am impressed with Dr. Cynthia Barnett's 10 ways to finding 'Your true identity in retirement'.

10 ways to Finding Your True Identity in Retirement

by

Dr. Cynthia Barnett

---

[5] **ESCAPE:** Emotionally; Satisfying; Comforting: Activities; Passage of time; Easy way

There are definite benefits to having an identity in life. By knowing your identity, you are better able to accomplish your goals, whatever this may be. Well, this is especially true during your retirement years. By knowing who you are and what you need to accomplish in life, you'll gain a sense of confidence and pride and your life will have precise meaning. You won't feel as you are living an unfulfilled life. In this brief article, we'll discuss 10 ways to find your true identity. They are as follows:

I reduced the 10 ways into an acronym RETIREMENT[6]. What each letter stands for is discussed below.

1. **Refuse** to fade away: You have identity which found expression for four decades. Your career is central aspect of your identity. Through a variety of means, mainly, through work experience you have discovered who you are and what you want from life. Now there is a change in the situation. If you planned for the eventuality you have no problem. If you have not made any precise plans for the next 10,15, 20 years you can take up a SPAN[7] of jobs available to meet extended span of life:

Simple and undemanding Part-time employment Advisory or consultancy services Net work with some NGO etc

Or you can join the FRINGE workers

Read below: FRINGE benefits

Fringe is something marginal, additional or secondary to the main activity. There are many who John Lees, a career coach of the United Kingdom and author of the books, called them *Fringe workers*. Fringe workers are those who are neither employed on a permanent basis nor fully self-employed. The acronym FRINGE[8] has the list:

Free-Lance Workers- Journalists, Photographers, Artists, Singers, Writers etc. they advertise and seek to offer services. Free lance editors, proof readers, the number of people who

---

[6] **RETIRMENT:** Refuse to fade away; Enter; Treat it as a new beginning; Involve; Remain active; Ensure youthful attitude; Maintain positive attitude; Engage in productive work; Network for a cause; Try a hoby.

[7] **SPAN:** Simple; part-time; advisory; Net work

[8] **FRINGE:** Freelance; Retired; Interim manager; Need based; General; Employed on and off.

offer their services and products are increasing with change in technology and process. They are out-sourcing resources who enjoy freedom and independence and sell on the basis of their specialised skills and technical competence.

Retired and the Re-employed- Their experience and administrative skills helps them seek part-time employment. Accounts and office managements are some of the areas.

Interim Managers- Professionals who move from one employer to another without any written contract accepting a role or project for a few months with lumpsum arrangement.

Need—based voluntary workers. John Lees says 'increasingly sophisticated arrangements exist to connect volunteers with need-- based projects and organization. Placement is done not only in organized companies but by adhoc arrangements with individuals using advertising channel at the behest of the companies without any obligation.

General Job Sharers and part-time employment.

Employed on and off. They seem to combine conventional employment with consultancy freelance and a portfolio of employments and self employments.

You can choose any of the above immediately after superannuation.

2. **Enter** the job market with a new set of goals

If goals till superannuation were upwards mobility, to become CEO or CMD and succeeded, you have to revise your life plans with new set of goals. You had fulfilled your ambition and saved enough and on introspection you find the dreams you know, you suspect, or dreams that lie hidden surface more prominently. You may choose a second career more laudable than the positions of prestige and power you had enjoyed. (Read Kiran Bedi's profile). But choose a career that suits your genius, talents, interests, and personality etc.

Full many a gem of purest ray serene

The dark unfathomed caves of ocean bear

Thomas Gray

The 'gem' is inert. In the case of humans it is covert, hiding within every one. It has to be lifted up by oneself.

By one's self should one raise one self,
And not allow one self to fall;
For self alone is the friend of the self
And the self alone is the enemy.

Gita

Arise, Awake, stop not till the goal is reached

Swami Vivekananda

That is our legacy. Now look for opportunity 'mounted on yoga'. (yogarudhasya)

3. **Treat** it as a new beginning. Retiree gets terminal benefits in terms of money, pension, P.F, gratuity, or annuities, dividends, etc. There is another legacy in terms of terminal ailments – life style diseases which can limit your capacity and enthusiasm. Remember retirement is not a terminus *ad quem*, final limiting point of time. But it is only a terminus *a quo*, first limiting, point of time.

   Whether your first career choice(s) were right or not may be examined. You have another choice to work towards greater fulfillment.

4. **Involve** in some gainful employment. Continue to work is a choice. SPAN and FRINGE working have already been mentioned.
5. **Remain** active. Physically and mentally. Moderate regular activity that is interesting and fitting with your personality type. Will keep you in good health.
6. **Ensure** youthful attitude:

That ends this strange eventful history,
Second childishness and mere oblivion
Sans teeth, san eyes, sans taste, sans everything.

Shakespeare (As you like it)

> A 90 year old whose past-time is golf playing came home sad because he was unable to see how far the ball had gone. Next time he took his brother-in-law who was 105 but whose eye sight was intact to give him feed back on the ball-trajectory. But alas the 105 year old had poor memory to recall how far the ball had travelled!

If you believe retirement is the beginning of the last stage, the second childishness and mere oblivion sans everything, you will prove it. Beware of the negative attitude. It is far away and far from second childishness. Nor does it mean what Dr.Cynthia Barnett recommends. What is youthful in Dr. Cynthia Barnett's view?

> '60 bungee jumping, rock climbing, ice-skating, or simply travel. By acting like you feel, you will maintain a youthful attitude'.

It is a Western idea. We come across later in our discussion on 'Bucket List', a review of a movie by the same title. Behaviour determines the attitude. The suggestion is that converse is true, behaviour can change attitude. The last mentioned behaviour viz travel can be undertaken to watch the youthful doing rock climbing, ice-skating, horse-riding, and so on. But there are other ways to feel and act with youthful vigour. Join group of younger men and women and have fun. It is common for seniors mingling with seniors. But to mingle with juniors you need their acceptance. You begin to feel lack of youthfulness when the younger shun. Networking and interacting with welcoming youth depends on your soft skills, sense of humour, in particular. You can think of other ways. Tastes for modernity, new gadgets, computer savvyness can help. Don't be or behave as if you are old fashioned.

7. **Maintain** positive attitude: 'Be a beacon of light and shine'. You know your success so far is due to your positive outlook. You need to continue with it and not let it go.
8. **Engage** in productive work. Point no.4 speaks of gainful employment. Your aim there is to work for money. Do it for some productive purpose. The output must have some utility value, beneficial to the largest number. It should serve social purpose. It is not charity that you are seeking. It is well earned

work and not labour. We distinguished work from labour in the beginning.

9. **Network** for a worthy cause. Among SPAN of job 'N' stands for networking with NGO or some such organization. Point 4, point 8, and point 9 should be read together. In all these your identity must be visible and acknowledged by the society you are serving via another organization. There are many PPPs emerging (Public Private Partnership ventures). Your services will be readily taken by them.

   Networking in general satisfies one of the aims viz the social well-being. To the avoidance of sickness goal you may avoid 'sick' people who are cynical or gossipers. Avoid noise and noisy people. There are those whose social activity and any engagement is gossiping, derision, denigration.

'Distance yourself from people who use you to meet their needs. They drain your energy.

Dr.C.B.

They give their unsolicited advice discouraging you. To remain positive in your attitude you have to keep right company.

One worthy cause one can network with is adult education. Read sepeate discussion that follows.

10. **Try a hobby.** Everybody knows its value. If you had no hobby of your own till superannuation or you had postponed for this day, you can begin in right earnest.

In conclusion, retirement is not the end but the beginning. You can find purpose and meaning in your life. By refusing to fade away, maintaining a positive attitude, maintaining a youthful attitude, cultivating a hobby, joining a worthy cause, finding new goals, remaining active, continuing to work, changing your attitude, and being productive, you can retire successfully and you will have meaning and purpose in your life.

Dr. C.B

Reverting to ancient dharma of social order the four *ahramas* – Students, householder, recluse and ascetic. Recluse is retirement into forest working towards the next stage, ascetic, *sanyas.* Recluse or withdrawal from the worldly aspects of life leading to spiritual life for eternity or after life. Of the four factors, longevity, identity, engagement, and spirituality, the first three are not considered. Longevity does not bother them, identity is given up, free from any engagements other than spiritual pursuit in the company of Rishis.

Retirement in the modern context is extention of house-holder ship which entails responsibility, duties, not of rights and privileges. Present day society needs the services of the senior house-holders before they take up the recluse-ship. Recluse-ship is not literally retiring into forest but mentally and emotionally withdraw while living in midst of the world.

It is the attitude with which you perform that is important.

FITNESS - Utility

Stalling Senility: Some thinking and planning must go into what you intend to do beyond 60. For the self employed, business men, and entrepreneurs; many professionals like lawyers, doctors, and accountants 60 is not the age to think of what to do. Even they have to reduce their activity gradually and hand over to younger people their enterprises. May be beyond 70, 80 or 90, there must be a time when you have to call it a day and engage in service, spiritual activity with moderate, regular, and satisfying work to stop the aging process. Even if physically weak people can be active mentally and psychologically and for the people who are employed after the superannuation is a problem about which they may have to plan some what. It is here they must take stock of soft skills in which they are strong.

Every residential complex or local areas have associations or welfare societies in which you are asked to take some position—secretary, president or treasurer. After one or two terms most of them get fed up and refuse to take up responsibility. A careful examination will reveal that it is due to inadequate soft skills. While heading a beauracratic organization if you are able to get things done and derive a sense of achievement, it is more due to power and authority rather than because of soft skills—leadership, carrying people along, communicative competence, transparency, patience, empathy, articulating in one to one, small group, public address, logical presentation and so on. Organizing and mobilizing people, trusting and being trusted behaviour without the power and authority. You need political skills; influencing skills, inspiring confidence and the list is long.

If you have mastered all these soft skills while in service and produced results without using authority and power, then it will appear child's play to you in later years. May be drafting skills in the appeals you make to public authorities will come in handy.

Often in service most reading, writing and presenting is done by people much junior. After retirement you want to engage in writing a book or any other written work you find you have no inclination. You say you have no time. Writing is an engaging and satisfying work. As mentioned before that Damija wrote his first book at 88! Rajaji wrote Mahabharatha and Ramayana in simple English in 80s. All the writers are doing service that way and they leave a legacy. Paul Newman's foundation is a case in point. From the foregoing soft skills are needed not only in our active careers but even in the twilight years. They are in fact life skills.

Reading the case histories of those who retired from service in the private or public sector undertakings, you get an impression that all of them have had satisfactory career. Satisfaction is not the same thing as fulfillment. Among all the meanings of the word fulfillment, *'to develop the full potentialities'* is what accounts for the difference between the two terms. All of them are satisfied with what they accomplished under the circumstance of bureaucratic system in which the freedom is curtailed. They might have compromised or succumbed to pressures from above. When these people take up a career or job of their free choice, they would have found themselves in more productive and lucrative occupation. Only then they would have understood the true significance of freedom. They might realize that they had undersold themselves before superannuation.

2

UTILITY

First for the dictionary meaning: Noun **General**

- Fitness for some purpose or worth to some end.
- Something useful or designed for use.
- Greatest happiness of the greatest number.

Public Utility

- A service provided by a public utility
- A routine operations

Utility (adj)

- Capable of serving as a substitute in various roles or positions.
- Kept to provide a useful service, *not for show.*
- Serving primarily for utility rather than beautify: utilitarian.
- Designed or *adapted* for general use.

Utility is an aspect of fitness discussed in the previous chapter. Life after retirement must have utility value. The relationship between organism and the environment is reciprocal, interdependent. An individual must 'pay back" in whatever measure it might be. Collectively the contribution becomes enormous. Supportive environment will support you and everyone when you and everyone contributes public utility - greatest happiness of the greatest number. Squirrel's support to Sri Rama's cause in Ramayana illustrates the point. Squirrel gets the satisfaction when Rama accepts it for the larger cause.

A retiree must think and act in the manner of the squirrel's help to a worthy cause.

Networking with those engaged in a worthy cause.

There is one activity in which enterprising educators, professionals, activists, and entrepreneurs are engaged - adult education. Distance learning and continuing education have long been recognized as means to transform the society, bringing into the fold of adult learners all sections of society rural, urban and metropolitan. It is a movement. There are TRIBES[1]:

1. ***Traditional:*** who impart perennial knowledge, teacher in the classroom, in the village, in forests, mountains, islands; these men and women reach out to everyone who lacked it. Religious discourses can be included in it. (Fanatics and Fundamentalists are excluded).
2. ***Remedialists:*** They help correct the dysfunctional wrong habits forced on them because of birth, upbringing, and lack of formal education. Dropouts included. Social skills training is in this direction to make the backward fit for the modern requirements.
3. ***Inspirers:*** There is need to motivate some people. Men like Swami Vivekananda did it to instill confidence in every Indian to match the Westerner.
4. ***Builders of Institutions:*** These are entrepreneurs who start and build organisations to educate the adult learners. There are intrapreneurs within the existing institutions who turn them into institution of excellence. All students are truly adults in psychological sense whatever may be their age.
5. ***Emanicipators:*** They are change agents who mobilize people for self-rule and self-development adding scientific temper.
6. ***Self-actualisers:*** They know that every one has enormous potential which must be tapped. They combine all the above 5 categories of adult educators.

TRIBES: Traditional; Remedialist; Inspirers; Builders of Institutions; Emanicipators; Self-actualisers.

All have specialized skills in the soft skills arena: Collaborating, Re-educating, Diagnosis, Information purveying, Building teams, Leavening, Enthusing. They are a CREDIBLE lot.

These adult educators must consider themselves as CREDIBLE change agents displaying all 8 elements – sets of soft skills – in their behaviour.

At the same time the other side – the learners must display equally important characteristics. They are CASTES[2] unto themselves:

C – Commerce	-	not merely exchange of goods and services, but ideas, opinions, information; mutuality is the essence of commerce
A – Achievement	-	need for achievement is high
S – Self-control	-	take responsibility for achievement by self-control
T – Tenacity	-	hard work – ready to face obstacles
E – Enterprise	-	enterprise – DRIVE
S – Self-actualization	-	self-actualization – as goal

For others what lies ahead does not seem to matter. They have accumulated knowledge and soft skills, particularly networking skills. But their networking is with the 'birds of the same feather'. Their number is rather large. With no plans for future, no need for money and with extraordinary conversational skills, they do have their own ways of fulfilling their needs. Recall what Dr. Cynthia Brandett cautioned against. These people, make noise and encroach upon your time and energy. These are:

---

[2] **CASTES:** Commerce; Achievement; Self-control; Tenacity; Enterprise; Self-actualiztion.

- Critical, clinical, cynical Re-reporters, Entertainers Eavesdroppers Dubious, Doubtful, Denigrators, Sycophants

1. Critical, Clinical, and Cynical

They had acquired critical and analytical thinking in the long career before retirement. It paid them well. At times they showed clinical precision in examining the problems they encountered. So far so good. But the problem is now with their negative attitude and jealousy they do not know. They become cynical. They have sneering disbelief in sincerity and integrity of others who take up worthy social causes. They think it is all because of self interest and ulterior motives. Recently an intellectual joined a political party and became a member of the inner circle. He failed to win the elections on his own twice before. He was denied a ticket in the new party and had quit it. On his behaviour after leaving the party and denigrating the party promoter as 'owners' without scruples, a spokes person of the party made a comment that 'he was an intellectual with a stunted growth like *bonsai* plant'. *Bonsai* plant is a plotted plant cut and pruned to remain a dwarf – an artistic, decorative peace.

There are such intellectuals who 'cut and prune' themselves during active careers without normal growth and development now display most of the CREEDS[3] behaviour. They have two extreme behaviours – cynical and sycophancy. They look for reports, re-report, denigrator, and entertain others with such reports. 'Politics' in corporate world, political party level, university level, in the scientific field, name any field they are there to comment. What is this 'cutting' and 'pruning' about? They have the required talents which are skewed, absence of many soft skills – positive attitude and lack of flexibility in particular. Having chosen their path they should not become cynics which is self-hurting. This is my view.

---

[3] **CREEDS:** Critical; Re-reporters; Entertainers; Eavesdroppers; Dubious; Sycophants.

2. Re-Reporters

They report what is reported in media to those who already knew it. It is selective repeating. Media has its biases and prejudices. They take every thing they read as facts.

Based on the unverified 'facts' and unvalidated and unacceptable assumption, they express their opinion. Any denial is discounted with emphasis. It ends in futile defenses and unfruitful debates. If in the group there is ill informed, he gets 'educated' in the wrong. They do the opposite of adult education. When other like minded join, it becomes public opinion. It is how rumours spread and gossip gains.

3. Entertainers

These reportings have high entertainment value to the old, suffering old, who enjoy joke. Laughter being the best medicine, is blessing in disguise. They are good mimics bordering on buffoonery. They create noise in a situation where it is not called for.

4. Eavesdroppers and Enchroachers

These people who pry into private lives and enchroach on the time and energy of others to get the meat to meet their personal needs of filling time. (Dr. Cynthia Barnett)

5. Doubtful and Dubious

They don't believe anything or trust any one. They keep the company of 'the steady and the wise' and remain ever dubious. The others need them to nod their heads, even perfunctorily.

6. Sycophants

All people need them to boost up their ego. They are parasites who need others to admire and to look up. To keep company of those who are considered great and infallible gives them ego satisfaction and the company.

These are some of the ways they escape from work, labour, boredom, and loneliness.

Case 19

A case of an adult educator

Till 45 Prasad Rao could not find his ground in career selection and continuation. He discovered himself as he began teaching in the *gurukulam* style, the traditionalist style, imparting the perennial legal knowledge to students of higher education in Law.

He is now 70 going at his own pace and peace and rhythm. He has a hobby – writing poetry as a spiritual pursuit to occupy himself fully.

A gold medalist in economics in M.A, discontinued study of law, joined a bank for lucrative salary and perks and quits after 13 'long' years. Long because he never liked the bank job. He hated frequent transfers which every upward mobile welcomes for quicker promotion – 'Motion is a must for promotions'. Had he continued he would have become CMD of some bank. During this time he completed law. Now he enrolled himself for legal practice and struggled for ten years because he could not compromise with the dishonest means that accompanied success in lower courts. Yet his dream was to become Supreme Court Judge which remained unfulfilled. Had he taken up career in Judiciary he would have realized his dream. There was a legacy – his maternal grandfather was a High Court Judge and his father was a brilliant teacher and scholar in law and Sanskrit. It was the latter's legacy, that he seemed to have inherited.

He presented me with two of his books of prosody and also quoted to me a *Sanskrit sloka* the meaning of which is:

Work in youth for old age;

Work throughout life for after life.

I read between the lines to derive meaning in support of my theme in this book. Choose and pursue a career in keeping with your genius so that you can choose another meaningful career in retirement. The career in retirement shall be of fulfillment, utility, and leaving a legacy that lives after the final departure.

I found a line (English translation) in one of the poems which reads:

> Faith is stepping out on to nothing and landing on something.

I titled the section I as 'from nowhere to somewhere'; and the Section IV as 'from here to eternity'.

'Set forth' on a journey is stepping out on nothing. Throughout the journey you are trying to discover yourself – a little each time.

His dream of becoming Supreme Court Judge remained a dream; He keeps working – teaching – may be one of his disciples will become one. Every teacher has this vicarious satisfaction of one of his students reaching to the top.

Teaching adults is truly a worthy cause. He has another dream. He wants to acquire another doctorate in law from a foreign university. Every teacher must develop himself – keep learning lifelong because knowledge is escalating; he knows he must be on board the escalator. He combines traits of two types of adult educators – Traditionalists and Inspirers. He is not interested as 'builders of Institutions' or 'emanicipators'. To some extent he is a 'self-actualizer' helping students realize their full potential.

He told me with pride that he produces 15 Ph.ds in a year as an unofficial guide and coach. His main contribution is in the form of notes on variety of topics obtained through desk research. These notes are published as books through which he gets royalty besides 'gurudakshina' – an altruistic work.

Living in the present means burying the past which he did. Continue to do what he now enjoys, teaching and preparing young aspirants to get their Ph.ds, thereby increasing population of Ph.ds, is serving society of legal professionals who may improve the condition of the general public through research and enhancement of legal knowledge.

I have two contrasting examples of my two grandfathers. Paternal grandfather had a very successful career. Hailing from a poor family, studying under the street lights, became first B.A., B.L., in composite Madras state, left lucrative practice as leader of the bar, joined Government service rose to become first ever Indian District and Session's Judge, earned the title Divan Bahadur on retirement and drew pension for longer period than the actual number of years of service. But his life in retirement was a miserable 20 years and finally died an unhappy man.

One reason was his blindness coupled with the Great Depression and lavish spending before the depression. He lost everything of his amassed wealth in British service.

He had career that gave him fulfillment; he had no need to work. He did not involve himself in any social activity. He remained blind literally and figuratively to the surroundings. His visits outside his house was confined to visit to the physician. He did not leave any property; but he did leave a legacy to his progeny, one role-model of a man who rose from humble beginning to high status man by hard work, values, and skills and knowledge. His long-life after retirement was not worth emulating. No doubt two economic set backs, one in 1906 when a joint stock company failed in which he saved all his savings. Another, the Great Depression when he lost landed property including his house. He took retirement for granted and lack of the financial planning and lack of frugal living, two negative values that doomed his later life. Particularly it is relevant in the present day's economic crisis globally.

On the other hand my maternal grandfather who served a Zamindar as Estate Manager, having stared as a Tahasildar, till his death. He had to continue work because of two reasons. To ekeout livelihood and to serve loyally the Zamindar after the Zamindari system was abolished. He rarely fell sick having scrupulously avoiding sickness through diet and long walk to the estate office. He practiced what Gandhi preached and practiced. My grandfather showed by example and had no need to preach or promote. Simple, truthful, non-violent, authentic and not authoritative.

Faced death with dignity

I saw him bed-ridden first time, his kidneys having failed. He refused to be admitted to a hospital. He said, 'my time has come, I want to die peacefully in my own house. I must die before *Amavasya'*. he died on 'MahaSivaratri day which preceded *Amavasya.*

This man did not amass wealth to lose any. He left the house and no debts. But he left a rich legacy to us, a complete man, lived and died with dignity. He had no intermediate stop of retirement. He worked till last with loyalty, commitment, and competence.

By serving the estate he served the society in his own way. He had fulfillment, utility to society, and left a legacy to his progeny. That was the life he chose and lived with full control with no hiatus.

Both of them belong to earlier generations. But their lives have lessons to the present generation as well.

- There are some who dread retirement, since they miss the sense of order in their day from employment; those who have no hobbies or interest to pursue.

Case 20
Case of BVS

I retired from a Bank after 34 years of satisfactory service. When I was looking for a job I got an opportunity to work in a reputed hospital as an administrative officer. I chose this job for two reasons. One, when I retired I was heading administration in the regional office of the bank for about 6 years. I developed the necessary skills in administration. The second reason was I thought through service in a hospital I could serve society. But alas I had to quit the job within two months because I was asked to pass false bills which, I learnt was the culture of the hospital. It shattered me and I never thought of another job because there was no need for money for a living. However, I confined my social activities to being president, secretary, or treasure of our residential complex and by being secretary of Retired Officers' Association.

The strong resentment to corrupt practices was on account of my up-bringing and in my service in the bank, I had been tempted on a few occasions but I resisted. Once the staff and the clients knew that I was honest, they stopped offering any bribes or favours and their respect for me grew. Whenever I was transferred from one branch to another, this reputation travelled faster and reached the branch to which I was transferred before I reached it.

To explain my steadfast adherence to honesty I must go back to the time when I was 14 and studying in 9th class. I was poor in mathematics and science and therefore I told my father that I did not want to study further. Instead I go back to village and engage in farming or alternately join the army.

My father, was highly qualified chartered engineer who excelled in his work and won the title Rao sahib and Rao Bahadur from the British, was surprised at my sudden outburst. Then he gave a sermon:

You are too small to think of such things. Don't compare yourself with others. You can study well and pass examinations. But what is more important in life to succeed is honesty. Keep good friends who can give you good advice. Work with faith in god. Think that you are far better than crores of people in the world. You are fortunate to be born in this family. Think positively.'

He continued:

Always be grateful to your employer. If you make him happy he will make you happy. Live within your salary. Don't do wrong things for earning more money.

Although young in age these words were arrows that hit the bull's eye. Till to-day they ring in my ears. That was the reason why I could quit the hospital job without any hesitation.

I passed B.Com and joined LLB when I casually applied for DRO (Direct Recruit Officer) post in a Karnataka Bank and got appointment after an interview. I think I was selected because of my extra curricular activities in school and college. I was in Boy Scouts in school, into N.S.S and N.C.C. in college as group leader.

I worked in Udipi and Mangalore. My father wanted me to be with him in Chennai and therefore I had to change the bank accepting a clerical post. But I was posted to Kakinada, in this bank. I was fortunate to work under two good bankers and served the branch from its inception. Being a small branch trying to establish itself I could learn all the work in all the departments. Soon I discovered that I was good at *relationships*. The branch progressed rapidly and within 3 years I was promoted to the officer cadre. I was sent to Vizag to assist in the organizing of a new branch there. From that time onwards I was identified as an expert in making arrangements for a new branch. On a number of occasions I was deputed to the branch opening. The Gujrati bank systematically expanded their branch network in A.P.

My first posting as manager in rural branch came as a boon in 1968. It was an experimental one-man branch. I was given a servant allowance of Rs.50/- and my residence and the branch were one and the same, My wife became the Bank's unpaid 'employee'. Though she was not doing any writing work, she accompanied me in outdoor work for deposits mobilization! It was women folk, the decision makers, observing *purda* that made my wife's contribution significant. Thanks to the quick growth the branch became a full-fledged branch. This experiment was most rewarding experience in my early career.

Awarded for work in service, loan recovery, and public relation. I was instrumental in getting telephone and tar road for the village.

I spent money from my pocket on the domestic servant more than what bank allowed because of my natural disposition.

The village life is different from the urban life. I had to change myself to the new situation. As I was manager of a bank who commanded a special place in the village I must meet their expectation in my conduct. I went beyond their expectations by organizing picnics, tournaments in badminton, volleyball and elocution contests on topics like 'savings'. I influenced the influential land lord to donate money for the improvements of the infrastructure for the school from a thatched shed to tiled roof. I derived pleasure in the community service. Branch had no strict timing. It was like day and night bank. Recalling those wonderful days itself is an elixir to me.

From the village branch. I was transferred to Hyderabad to a new branch to be opened as second man to work under another senior. By then, Branch opening was Childs's play for me. For the next six years I was part of the rapidly growing branch maintaining as usual excellent relations and also good house-keeping and maintaining records. Many branches in AP used to refer to me for any doubts or procedures or information instead of regional office which was situated in Chennai.

In 1978 yet again I had to go to Kadipikonda, near Kazipet for opening new branch and worked there till 1982.

I was sent to Visakhapatnam on a new mission, to put a derailed branch on track. There was no progress in deposits. The customers were unhappy. I took it a challenge and I had the support of the regional management. There is enough potential in a place like that and at one time the branch did excellent work. I knew where things would have gone wrong. Bad relations. Good relations had been my forte. Where should I begin? I asked myself. I must ensure the support of my staff. I conducted staff meetings, not one several. I invited the union leaders for discussions. I knew the best way is to keep them on my side. They should convince the staff which they did. You may ask, why? They helped me because of previous record of good relations with all the stake holders. Once I established this the other things began to fall into place. The staff served the customers and satisfied customers gave business. Our chairman attended a customers meet, rare opportunity for any branch. Eventually the branch won 'Best performance' award in the region. And I was promoted to scale III (Senior Manager) position and transferred to Vijayawada, a large—sized branch in 1984. Here I improved the infrastructure. I got the branch fully air-conditioned. I arranged picnics and entertainment programme for the staff and family members. My strategies varied from branch to branch. I was very happy and contended. There was one experience which I was missing viz. service in a controlling office. I asked for transfer and was awaiting orders. Then some thing tested my ethics again. The zonal manager has asked me to do something improper. There was credit proposal pending which was beyond my powers and was pending with the zonal office. On his visit to the branch the zonal manager asked to split the loan amount and grant three loans under my discretion.

I avoided doing it on the pretext of the orders of transfer. Next thing that happened was that I missed my promotion to scale IV, a coveted post! I took it in the right spirit. The next six years I spent in the Regional Office as head of administration under different Regional Managers all of whom did not change me from the responsibility because all the managers in the region were happy and approached me for advice and for access to regional managers. I was deputed for making arrangement for branch opening and inauguration.

I retired in 1994 with a grand farewell—When all categories of staff, officers, and executives showered encomiums on me which made me emotional. I settled down in Hyderabad. Many of my former colleagues keep in touch with me. More over I have been representing the Retired Officers and I am invited to attend conferences and meetings throughout the country.

I am now a technical adviser on banking to ALEAP, Association for Lady Entrepreneurs A.P. They refer credit proposals to me before they are approved and submitted to banks. I appraise them and advise them the degree of care they have to take using my technical knowledge as an experienced banker. For the service I render and the competences for it I owe it to the bank.

A Second Career

When you retire and look back on your past, you FIND[4] a new mission-Follow The Inner Promptings, Notions and Drive.

Here is an example of how mission crystallized for a police officer of outstanding career, Kiran Bedi, the super cop's post-retirement strategy speaks for itself. She says,

"*Remember one Gandhi and team of dedicated workers had given the freedom movement a decisive direction*".

She is doing the same thing as a one woman army! This is freedom of a different kind:

'Life has really opened up', she asserts after retirement. Earlier it was professional and personal commitments. Now it is just personal. *I make my own choices*'.

Free and independent to do any challenging work with what she accumulated and internalized–knowledge, skills, and values. What choices she has made now? She earns from Radio, T.V, and newspaper columns to serve the nation through her NGOs. What skills, knowledge, and values made her to make these choices?

Soft Skills Repertoire

She can communicate with competence, both in writing and orally, one to one, one to many, and many to many. Her interventions in big debates on the small screen are excellent, she has been excellent presenter of view points. You even find her listening eagerly to what others have to say. That she is a bold woman cop everybody knows. A complete woman! What is her strategic plan? P.P.P. Police Public Partnership. She believes that there is greater intention from the common man to trust and work with the police. Hence her value is PPP. The common man is extending his helping hand to reach out to the police as the recent Jamia Nagar has shown. She, however, regrets that the political agenda, lack of integrity, and absence of trust among the police come in the way. She feels it is a communication gap where her NGO, a website can help. She has two sites. One is

---

[4] **FIND:** Follow; Inner; Promptings; Notions; Drive.

www.safeindia.com. People can register their complaints which she passes on to DGP of the concerned state with a copy marked to the complainant. There is a follow up to keep track of action being taken. Then there is site, www.indiapolice, where complaints from a policeman are registered. It is sent to DG withholding the identity of the complainant.

When did she plan her mission PPP and strategy of websites?

She must have entertained these ideas long before retirement because of knowledge and values and confidence in her own *motivated skills*. The skills which she enjoys showing. She can do absorbing, altruistic work.

She got other ideas: I was working on a plan where one lakh youth of the civil defence would work with the 55,000 men of Delhi Police, situations like that of Jamia nagar where the people exposed and detected early.

She says, 'I could sense things in advance'. How is she so confident? 'I had inkling that the powers don't make me Delhi Police Commissioner. I had told them I wont hang on to it. They asked me to write mission reports. I asked what about implementing past mission reports that are gathering dust?

'Policing is the easiest to do if you follow the rules'. Once she got Indira Gandhi's car lifted by a crane from the no-parking zone and refused to suspend the sub-inspector. It had a trickledown effect.

She believes that in most cases of dispute between landlord and tenants, it is the communication gap that is coming in the way. She is playing the role of social adjudicator calling it *'Aap Ki Kachehri'* where the cases are not sub-judice, like the panchayats which have become castiest, communal, and political, an alternative to panchayats.

The students must read such accounts of eminent, truly eminent that regularly appear on the media, *reflectively* to get the inspiration they need in their youth. They can transform some people. Bedis and the like have been exposed to such literature in their early life.

More Titbits from media

Kiran Bedi launches Nomark's new range. Nomark's products include Green, Blue, and Pink range of anti-marks fairness creams, suitable for below 25 years, above 25 years, and all other age groups respectively. Dr.Bedi, touted as the Police Officer with a human face said that the products are designed to give women confidence. Ms. Bedi who is into brand motion activity for the first time, will divert her honorarium to her three NGOs (mentioned above) working in the area of rehabilitation of drug-abused children, prison reforms, and cultural development of under privileged.

Examples of Utility: fitness for some purpose or worth to some end; something useful or designed for use.

Capable of serving as a substitute in various roles or position, stand by... useful.

Here are tidbits that serves as an examples of senior citizens utility.

A hobby from youth becomes a passionate profession in old age with social service in mind. Old age is an advantage for 60-year-old Lakshmi Anjaneyulu to turn her hobby of making idols into a profession that earns.

"I always wanted to make idols but never had the time. With children well settled.... Thankfully a husband who is very supportive, I have time on my hands.

It was passion held back by responsibilities–space for family–and when she was free of the shackles, she unleashed it with nimble fingers'.

She sculpted around 1000 plaster of paris (POP) figurines of traditional music composers. (Vaggeyakarulu) and gods and goddesses in the last four years.

"The other day a couple of idols got noticed in *bommala koluvu* on *Sankranti*", brought me to limelight. I want them to reach music lovers. They are rare idols. 'I sell my idols for anything between Rs.200 and Rs.275. I had not signed agreement with any emporiums because it would cost the music lovers more than Rs.1200/- which they may not afford'

She has re-invented herself. Besides passion, talent and interest merging, it has become a mission in the old age.

3
LEGACY

A Role Model

A relative of mine died in the year 2000 of liver cancer. It was not a sudden end. There was period of anxiety and painful adjustment to the reality. All his children were abroad.

After his demise his wife decided to publish a book consisting of all his stories published in magazines from time to time. His children and nephews were asked to write their memories of the departed soul to be put in the book. These men and women are all making successful careers in India and abroad. What they wrote is very revealing.

Case 21

Two things that I would like to remember about Prakasa Rao uncle.

'The first is his reader hat. He was a voracious reader – practically everything under the sun, books, periodicals, magazines, advertising blurbs – were grist to his reading mill. But he particularly loved reading books by P.G.Wodehouse and Agatha Christie, and greatly enjoyed Sherlock Holmes and Perry Mason. He owned a great number of books and one of my earliest memories of mamaiah is the multi-volume Encyclopedia set in his Bangalore residence. His book collection was just the perfect icing on the tempting cake of mamaiah's company when we used to go to Bangalore for summer vacations in the 1970s'.

Let us then trun to the world of PGW, Mamaiah is nor any single persona – he is not a Jeeves, nor is he Lord Ickenham, Galahad, Emsworth, or any of the host of other characters. He is a combination of the best in them all.

All his nephews inherited one common characteristic – his love of reading, and that too PGW, Sherlock Holmes, Perry Mason, and Agatha Christie.

'It is to mamaiah's credit that he did not use his honed cultural, linguistic and verbal savvy to become a smooth-talking salesperson that not only sells a refrigerator to Eskimos but gains repeat orders from them, or a lawyer, let alone to seek wider employment for it by crossroads of his career, asking himself, *"Have I got it in me to rake in the big bucks by becoming a Winston Churchill of India? No? Very well, then I will bring sunshine into the lives of everyone I meet".* We can only be grateful for the choice he made."

Nephew: A Professor in Hyderabad University.

His children wrote:

"Mr. Prakasa Rao started writing short stories in Telugu at the young age of 18, and had his first story *Nalupu* printed in *Vinodini in 1947.* He wrote numerous stories before and after, and this collection is a sample of his work, spanning the five decades that he wrote stories. Most of these stories were published in general interest, and literary magazines in Andhra Pradesh and in the USA.

Prakasa Rao was born in 1929, and lived in Rajahmundry, Bombay, Pune, Hyderabad, and Bangalore. While he changed several professional hats from weatherman to public relations officer to advertising executive he was always an active and enthusiastic proponent of literature and culture, especially Telugu literature and culture. In recent years, he also became interested in classical dance and music and started studying the theory behind Bharata Natyam.

After retirement in the early '90s, he spent a large part of his time in the *US* and Germany, where he was able to find time again for his first love – writing. He had begun translating the Natya Shastra into English a few years ago, which he had intended to be the magnum opus of his literary career. However, he could not complete this project because of his demise on February 21, 2000.

Simultaneously, he wrote several Telugu short stories in the last 4-5 years. He has left us this legacy of stories which while seemingly humorous and light-hearted, pose profound questions and offer commentary on our lives and times".

What were his talents, interest, and personality type?

Talent for writing, creative artist, his interests are, art, music, dance, literature, his personality is a combination of social, artist, enterprising traits. He had a sense of humour nurtured by 'P.G.Wodehouse'. he is personification of Gita concept as defined in verse 15, Chapter 17: *words that are not hurting, that are truthful, loving* and *helpful* and *spiritual self study, constitute* tapas of the speech.

He did not seek power, prestige, and possessions. He did not leave any property worth mentioning to his children. What he left for his children is visible in what his kith and kin said. An active Rotarian who could have become Governor had he tried. He rejected the offer. He made his choices according to his inner prompting but not for external consideration.

His brother-in-law wrote:

PRAKASA RAO, A ROLE-MODEL, PAR EXCELLENCE

He was on PAR with himself - true to his self.

Psychologists tell us that many people make false assertions of self and put up futile defenses when others do not accept the falsity. In the end they make a mess of their lives. There are three positive ways to live with self-esteem and self satisfaction. I call them PAR values, PAR[1] being an acronym standing for:

Pursuing what interests us
Accepting others as they are
Refining every role we play.

Prakasa Rao did all the three. He pursued public relations and advertising in occupational life and creative writing and study of Natya Sastra in leisure time.

He looked for strengths in others leaving weakness as potential for development and growth. With this outlook he had

[1] **PAR:** Pursuing; Accepting; Refining.

no difficulty with people who differed from him or who are not up to the mark. He gave love and received it in equal measure.

Finally he played multiple roles, excelled in all of them. He managed and balanced the conflicting demands of the different roles cast on him. Son, brother, husband, father, and so on. He volunteered community roles like that of Rotarian which he chose not for prestige and position but to express solidarity with service minded people. He kept his role as a story writer in abeyance for 30 years only to take up with greater vigour late in life. He would have continued had cancer not taken him away from us. Even during the illness he pursued the role of the writer. He began writing on Natya Sastra which he could not complete. He played the role of a patient admirably. He won the admiration of his doctors, nurses and others who attended on him. He appeared to me as a man who knows that the life is a drama and that all of us play our parts in it. We have our entries and exits, appearances, behaviour and costumes, and above all, we must get our lines right. He wore his costumes and said his lines according to a pre-determined script. The story writer in him was very conscious of these details. On 10th February 2000, he attended all the functions in the wedding of his nephew. Inspite of advanced stage of cancer he arrived in time in right costume, dhoti and kurta or full suit, and blessed the couple according to the tradition and ritual, put up a cheerful face at times and solemn look at other times everything appeared according to the script he himself had determined.

He played every role as an enactment with all sincerity and sense of purpose. Behind all these performances there are certain innate qualities, sanguine temperament, ability to change moods without being moody, with ease and at will. Above all stable emotions. There is nothing make believe about his performance in every role that he played.

BUCKET LIST

Leaving a Legacy

Movies can be sources of information and inspiration particularly in youth, middle age, and even old age if we can make sense of the subtle message they suggest. Different audiences can draw different meanings depending on the creative depiction of the makers. It is a powerful mode of learning. I have made reference to another poignant movie 'Awakenings' already. I have snippets for you from another movie I was shown by my grand daughters on a laptop computer with subtitles. One an engineering student, the older of the two, thought or drew her own conclusion as a story in which the two old men, the only main characters did not want to leave any legacy which is what I wanted to draw from the story. Let me put before you my inferences as a senior citizen. I had earlier discussed Malcolm Gladwell's book *Outliers* which highlighted *opportunity* and *legacy*, two influencing external factors that greatly help a man or woman *do things that are out of the ordinary.*

Legacy itself is an opportunity. That is how positive thinkers see.

> 'Two cancer–ward roommates, an irascible billionaire (Edward Cole) and scholarly mechanic (Carter Chambers), decide, when they get the bad news, to compose a bucket list–*things to do* before you kick off the bucket–and head for an around–the–world adventure of their lives'.
>
> 'Skydive–power a Shelby Mustang around a race track–gaze at the Great pyramid of Khufu–discover the joy in their lives before it is too late.
>
> ***BLURB***

How did they get cancer? Crisp opening scenes depict the causes: coffee addiction and addiction to smoking cigarettes respectively.

Edward Cole, the coffee addict, is the big boss of the hospital who laid a rule that 'two patients in one room with no exception'. When he fell sick for the first time, as a patient he became victim of his own rule when the administration, (his own) refused to accede to his frantic commands for an exclusive room. He was reminded that several earlier requests had been rejected by him and if they do now there would be an enormous PR problem.

Edward lacked the soft skill, *empathy*–vicariously experiencing the feelings and concerns of others (patients) although as an entrepreneur it was an essential trait. Now he has learnt through direct experience as a patient. This was Edwards Cole's chief problem in his entire life which rendered him homeless–he has only a house–no family space. He has only space for work life. Even here he has no space for his associates. He makes it known to the viewer when he makes an emphatic statement, to his board, '*you need me; I do not need you;* That explains everything. Applying CREAMS of personality types Edward has entrepreneurial qualities, meticulous, and realistic, but non– social, non– conventional, and non–artistic. He started making money from the age of 16 and is in 80s now–most successful in terms of wealth, power, and prestige as a most influential person. An irascible person he blurts out when he felt that the Chambers his companion was trying to reform him.

"Just because I told you my story doesn't invite you to be part of it. You have no idea who I am. I build a billion dollar business up from nothing. Presidents asked for advice, I have dined with Royalty... This trip around–the world was meant 'to be fun for us, not meant to change me".

It was his companion Carter Chamber's plan to change him to allow space for his family that irritated him. Edward earlier shared during an intimate conversation with Carter that he had no one except his daughter with whom he severed the relationship, the only family member. On their return from the trip, Carter deliberately arranged a detour and left Edward at the door of his daughter and expected him to *knock at the door.* At this he was hurt and blurts out the above tirade.

Legacy

Carter is a black–an African American from a working class having moved up from his class in one generation. It is Carter who made it possible. He wanted to become a History Professor but ended up as a mechanic because of legacy of poverty. He married a nurse and had three children, two sons and a daughter all of them had better careers. Carter sacrificed his own ambition for the sake of family. An engineer, a tax–consultant and vocal musician, a strong family unit. Carter's cultural legacy he leaves is family relationship; career progression is at the family level, not at self, individual level. The tradition will be continued by his children into future generations who would remember their ancestor having turned the tide. The family culture of Carters is similar to what is obtaining in India where millions of working class people aspiring and sending their children to universities for higher education.

Edward had a different legacy–affluence and influence. His becoming superboss, a most successful business tycoon because of his legacy which was denied to Carter. Edward is personification of greed, avarice, power, possession, prestige, and physical stamina till he was afflicted with cancer. When he was diagnosed as terminally ill with cancer, he was shaken. He makes tantrums while the other patient Carter was cool and suffering silently. The two personalities are result of heredity, genes, endowment, unique, distinct and different. How do they face impending death?

When Edward's desire to be alone, solitary, he was compelled to be with another similarly placed but different in many respects; the companionship does change us. Carter was superior in experience having undergone the dreaded chemotherapy before Edward. Edward suppressing his ego of omniscience, asks Carter how painful was chemo. Carter uses his power by refusing to oblige. He says, 'you will know it soon'.

The companions discuss many things. Edward who is accustomed to 'command and control' was compelled or made to talk on equal terms. Suicide. A survey on whether people want to know the date of death before hand; 96 percent of the respondents do not want to know. But Carter belongs to the 4 percent and prepares the 'bucket–list' and throws. Edward picks it up. Together they prepare the list. Edward wants to 'kiss the most beautiful girl in the world'. Ironically, Carter makes him realize toward the end of 90 minute movie that the most beautiful girl was his estranged daughter! Edward had no space in his life for his daughter, the only member of the family left. Reason: she married a man against his wish. That was sufficient for the man to alienate her. All his space is swallowed by his career–'work' towards making himself the richest and powerful man on earth! Greedy men have no space for anything else. Although 'they *dig their own graves*, they forget they need someone else to sod them'. (James Joyce)

Opportunity

Here is a real opportunity–a few months to live. Edward is not new to planning, preparing and performing. He has all the money to go on the round–the–world trip. They go to pyramids, African Safari, Taj Mahal, and finally they come to the Himalayas. But alas the weather does not permit. They can only make it next spring, which they do not have. They think of alternate plans. But Carter suddenly becomes home sick and calls off the tour much against the wish of Edward who has no home to feel home sick.

Let us go back to the hospital before they escaped on the around–the world trip. Carter's wife wanted her husband to shift to a better hospital. He does not agree. She complains that he was not a fighter. 'What happened to the fighter? Are you waiting for a miracle to happen?' she asks. He had been a fighter. Now he knew it was no use fighting. Instead of fighting in the hospital let him do something before it is too late. That's the cultural legacy of Carter which is similar to Indian traditional culture. Carter's wife and three children visit him in the hospital. His wife even quarrels with him. That is a sign of concern and not sign of unhappiness, although they tell each other, 'I hate you', typical of any culture in which marriage is sacred as is in ours.

Mrs. Chambers, Virginia, contacts on phone Mr. Edward Cole and tells him at the top of her voice; while they were on their trip around-the-world.

> 'I am a nurse all my life; I have seen human tragedy all my career–I am prepared for my husband's death. I want him back. I don't want to miss him any longer while he is alive'.

That speaks volumes of their family culture so different from that of Edward, both of which belong to one America of Obama! On the return at the insistence of Carter, when the plane is about to land, they gracefully say 'America'. A feeling for motherland–

sense of belonging to a nation. There can be several cultures in one nation. This is echoed by Obama–there are no different Americas, there is only one "United Stated of America". Call it patriotism or sense of belonging, it is a wonderful sentiment–call it soft or hard, that perception is called for, in every Indian.

Sitting on the top of the pyramid the scholar mechanic asks two questions:

Carter	:	Have you found joy in your life?
Edward	:	Yes.
Carter	:	Have you brought joy to others in your life?
Edward	:	You ask them.
Carter	:	The question is put to you. Let me put it this way. After breakup with your daughter.
Edward	:	(No answer)

When they reached the foot of Himalayas and found they could not make it to the peak because of bad weather Carter says:

The mountain is telling us something. 'It is time to go home' Alas! Edward had no home to go.

So, he had no where to go. Eternity is waiting for him.

Carter goes back, spends the last couple of days with wife, children, and grandchildren before collapsing.

Edward was shown knocking at his daughter's door and remembers her childhood kissing her fondly 'the most beautiful girl'. He is also shown asking his colleagues whether they had read Divine comedy! They put blank faces.

> "The subject of Divine Comedy is a great one, for it pictures the poet (Dante) penetrating to the depths of hell; then passing up into purgatory, the realm where sinners are purified before they can enter heaven and finally mounting to highest heaven (paradise). Dante, the poet, was led by his dead sweetheart. Beatrice became his guide and leads him through nine spheres of paradise to the heaven where God himself dwells."
>
> ***Children's Britannica***

Edward Cole was guided by Carter Chambers in the last months before he himself died. At Carter's funeral Edwards makes a speech by which the viewer finds Edward transformed. Before that happened Carter leaves a letter addressed to Edward.

'I have gone back and forth in the last few days, trying to decide whether or not I should write this. In the end I realized I would have regretted if I didn't. I know, the last time, we saw each other we weren't hitting the sweetest notes. It certainly was not the way, I wanted our trip to end. I suppose I am responsible, and for that I am sorry. But in all honesty, if I had the chance, I'd do it again...

...find joy in your life. You once said you are not like everyone. Well that is true, you are certainly not everyone. But every one is everyone. Our lives are streams–flowing like a river–towards whatever heaven lays in the midst beyond the falls. Find joy in your life, Edward. Kiss the most beautiful girl in the world... (your daughter)

Close your eyes, let the waters take you home.

Edward died in May–eyes closed and heart open' voice over says.

Now read the funeral speech of Edward:

'Good afternoon. My name is Edward Cole. I do not know what most people say on these occasions. In all honesty I have *tried to avoid* them. The simplest thing is, *I loved him and I miss him.*

Carter and I saw the world together. It is amazing, when you think that only three months ago we were strangers. I hope it doesn't sound selfish of me. But the last months of his life were the best months of mine. He *saved my life;* he knew it before I did. I am deeply proud that the man found it worth his while to know me. In the end I think it is safest to say that *we brought some joy to one another's life.*

So, one day when I go to final resting place and I happen to wake up next to certain wall, a gate I hope that Carter is there to vouch for me and show the ropes on the other side.... (to come up from the depths into the purgatory)

Do they leave a legacy? What legacy? Find joy. Bring joy to one another. That way we can all help each other realize our potential as much as possible in one life.

EPILOGUE

Set forth, from unclear position – no where – I just started with what I knew from own experiences. Then the experiences of others came in handy. There is diversity. Then I read couple of books from the Western authors.. then I knew I am in the right direction but no precise goal. I proceeded cautiously. I re-discovered my own *unique* style. I wanted to stick to it. It is free-writing allowing for brain storming along. Then I made my *choice* to put the soft skill in the perspective of careers and personal development. I avoided diversions. I began reading the profiles from the angle of soft skills. I made imaginative derivation. I *controlled* the direction of my journey by sticking to the definition of success. I first made SUCCESS as an acronym that defines success. Setforth, unique path, choice of career, control, enterprise and enjoyability (ethics) steady, satisfying. As I began reflecting on the profiles of senior citizens continuing with some sort of satisfying (to them) activity or other I extended the concept to include old age occupation to push senility farther into 90s or even more.

Eventually I found my acronym SUCCESSFUL–setforth; unique path; choice; control of careers; enterprising; ethics and enjoyable; steering through soaring high; swerving or severing or superannuation; fitness; utility; and leaving a legacy.

Yes I *steered* through it, overcoming obstacles, *soaring* in spirits whenever I found a tidbit from daily news paper. I think this book will have the *utility* to the largest numbers, may be I will leave a *legacy* as a worthy writer.

APPENDIX-I

Repertory Grid Exercise, an instrument that helps in fathoming deep into one self

'psychometric instruments with phenomenological orientation...

Phenomenon means observable fact or event, something known through our senses. We observe people in a situation or event and draw conclusions about them and give a 'construct' or an attribute to describe. We shall call them 'constructs'.

Repertory Grid exercise is a method to pull out these constructs from our brain and put them on paper. We have a model or a map in our head which represents the outside world. Our attempt through this exercise is to draw that map or model out from inside. That is a process of probing into our inner mechanism the way a psychiatrist does. Here we are our own psychiatrist.

In this 'game' there are *elements*, objects of study survey, things, ideas, and people (TIP). Then there are *constructs* attributes attached to the *elements*. The language used is significant. They reveal your concepts (theory) as also fears, doubts, emotions. It is a small group activity meeting in a quiet place. You and your close friends or relatives constitute the group engaged in an activity to help each other probe the internal.

Elements: Objects of study, objects are observed facts. For the purpose of your study you can select 6 career paths of persons known to each individual. Alternately you can select the elements from out of case histories presented in this book. For this you must read all the cases histories at least once. These historical facts can be taken as phenomena. Keeping soft skills, that paved the careers of individuals in the cases you have to take a triad—three cases—and focus your attention and find out the 'odd man'. Think of something similar to two of them, but different from the third. You know 'odd man out' game. Here is an example. Delhi, Pune, Chennai, depending on which 'construct' you produce. Suppose your construct is 'sea shore', Delhi and Pune are similar, 'Not a sea shore'. If you produce 'national capital' as construct then Pune and Chennai are similar but different from Delhi which is national capital. What is critical is the constructs you produce looking at a phenomenon.

Taking three of the cases—Michael Faraday, Doctor in 'Awakenings, Venkat your construct in finding something similar to two of them, you may use 'passion' as construct and find this similarity in Faraday and Venkat. You will produce 'passion' if you believe that it is a soft skill. This is your unique production, the other members in the group have their own elements and constructs. You may only state the construct and nothing else. There is at this stage only sharing and pooling constructs and put off the discussion for a little later.

What the members are interested in is the maximization of constructs which are the list of soft skills. You leave the elements and focus on the constructs. But if your colleagues in the group object to the construct or ask how you have come to such a conclusion, you may refer to the information the case, the actual words or statements made. From facts you move to the concept, a backward integration.

REPERTORY GRID EXERCISE

Theory	:	Kelly's theory of Personal Constructs
Elements	:	Objects of study/Survey: Things, ideas and people
Constructs	:	Attributes attached to elements Language expressed by participants revealing their fears, anxieties, doubts, concepts, etc.
Place	:	A quiet place where small group activity is possible
Equipment	:	Grid forms, small size cards, pencils with erasers (enclosed)

Method : Steps:

1. Elements are chosen and written on cards
2. Grid form filled
3. ODD MAN OUT technique to produce constructs
4. Constructs written on the grid form
5. Exercise repeated till sufficient constructs are produced
6. Discussion in small groups and presentation
7. Facilitator summarizes learning
8. Abstract conceptualization
9. Action plan for Experimentation

Advantages

1. Participation of every person
2. Probing into own models
3. Drawing upon own concrete experiences
4. Focus on specific examples
5. Framework for discussion
6. Data used is undisputed
7. Learning takes place silently
8. Learner to based instruction

Sum up

A A Awareness of own model

B B Beware of other models

C C Compare own model with others

D D Develop common models

E E Elaborate own models

REPERTORY GRID

Elements Attributes	1	2	3	4	5	6	7	8	9	10	11	
1												
2												
3												
4												
5												
6												
7												
8												
9												
10												
11 Total												
12 Average												
13 OVERALL VIEW												
14 Difference between overall view & average												

APPENDIX-II

BE ARMED NOT ALARMED

This is the slogan I gave in my earlier book, 'Personal and Emotional Competence' to deal with our emotions. Be ARMED not alarmed.

Awareness

Regulation

Motivation

Empathy

Deft handling

The focus was on the individual. What is true of individual could be true of collectivity, groups, and country as well. Let us try to apply the above step by step approach to the country's approach to 26/11 Mumbai attack in 2008.

Awareness

The country became aware of the terror within hours thanks to media coverage. We became angry. Angry with whom? For what?

'We were inundated with expressions of aggression often born out of *ignorance...* People to whom we listened are people who have rarely engaged with the issues that confront the Indian society' one columnist wrote a fortnight later. She added, 'much of it is manufactured consent'—'enough is enough' '9/11 of India, suggesting action similar to that of US for 9/11 attacks in Newyork. The consent of the urban educated middle class as the consent of the whole country to retaliate with aggression calling for the next step.

Regulation

While the electronic media was escalating the angry mood into one of rage through its coverage and reporting, it was the slower medium, the print media that regulated the emotion by asking more questions. Regulation means 'to allow the flow of emotion to required strength, not allow it to overwhelm us'. Aristotle wrote,

'Anyone can become angry. That is easy, but to be angry with the right person, to the right degree, at the right time for the right purpose and in the right way, this is not easy.'

Mark the difference between suppression and regulation. Where there is disturbance to the equilibrium state, as in the case of India during that fateful 60 hours, all living systems return to its original state as it did really happen to us in this country. The evidence of return can be seen from the utterances of men in power. The Prime Minister, inaugurating an international conference of jurists on 'Terrorism, Rule of Law and Human Rights' on December 13, 2008, said,

'The threat of terrorism is not divisible. The fight against it is also not divisible. The defence of freedom and peace is also not divisible... the target, our cities, is also target on our economy... our democracy... the fight against terrorism should not result in brutalization of our society.. we must demonstrate our faith in the Rule of Law...'

In the same session the Chief Justice of India cautioned:
'One of the ill effects of unrestrained coverage is that of provoking anger amongst the masses.. there is also a possibility of such resentment turning into an *irrational desire for retribution...* may be used as justification for undue curtailment of individual rights and liberties.'

It happened in Andhra Pradesh at the same time when in an acid attack on two girl students, the 'public' anger invoked 'eye for eye, tooth for tooth' savage law, an example of *irrational* desire for *retribution*! Again the media played an unrestrained part. Regulation is to keep emotions with in limit so that there is further debate within.

Motivation

Having regulated the emotion to keep it within limits, we must take the next step motivation. Emotion is energy. Suppression leads to depression and no action. Awareness, regulation and motivation are one process, simultaneous. Again media help us, it did allow the flow to channelise towards constructive thinking. It made us read world opinion. Their sympathy and caution towards us. It showed we are not alone in the counter terrorism measures.

Empathy

We must listen to others including Pakistan media and government. We need more information. There are other countries who are sailing in the same boat, counter terror groups. They are asking a different set of questions than what our media have raised:

1. What does this dramatic shift in terror tactics represent for counter terror planning world wide?
2. Can we participate—contribute to the answer and take lessons from their efforts?
3. Can we network with them—taking allies? Can we see the attack not on Mumbai but on the entire world? This critical thinking is in the domain of soft skills. Calm contemplation, *upanisad*; sit in a group and repeat, that is what our ancient sages did.
4. What actions will an inflamed and political India take, both at home and against the hostile neighbour?
5. How will these affect the current strategic situation?
6. What will be the follow-up on implications for counter terror in the militants' heart land Afghanistan, Pakistan border?
7. What is new about Mumbai attack?

It represents a complete change from traditional terrorist operations, mobile, trained, and well prepared terrorist units engaged on suicide missions outside conflict zones–a new phenomenon.

They take credit for engaging police, the air force, N.S.A. for 60 hours by a handful of terrorists and get inspired to repeat the exploits.

Thinking, reflecting, understanding and expressing our soft skills by 'upgrading global natural security systems to deal with centrally coordinated suicide terror squads'. We should become part of the solution internationally, not become part of the problem. It is a case of soft skills preceding hard skills. But all these depend upon the assumption that we have necessary hard skills which can be summoned at will at any time—the military option.

I think Indians demand for action against Jehadi groups is entirely legitimate.' Dr. Hoodbhoy comments, 'but this must be done through international pressure upon Pakistan'. A few more excerpts from the interview for a German Magazine.

LeT was supported by the Pakistani military and ISI because it focused on fighting Indian rule in Muslim Kashmir,... (any serious move against LeT) will make military and ISI earn the bitter enmity between them (They dread this enmity)...

'The real power lies with the Pakistan Army which has yet to decide who the real enemy is [The Islamists who offer nothing positive: They are 'against population planning, educating females, tolerating other sects etc'... 'All they know—and know well—is how to make war.. most Pakistanis do not want to live under these *fanatics'*

That's *empathy* for the Indian urban middle class citizen who is angry. 'Most Pakistanis are against/Islamists who offer nothing positive... they know how to make war and they don't want to know anything outside their fanaticism. The military which is 'no longer being called upon to fight India which is what they were trained for', is 'confused, demoralized, practically, zero public understanding or support'

Final word from the distinguished scientist, from Pervez Hoodbhoy.

'India should not attack Pakistan. Instead it should work for stronger Pakistan.... 'We Pakistanis have to realize that this is war for our survival as a civilized nation, an one that we must win... the state could disintegrate else where quite rapidly leaving the fanatics in charge.

Deft handling—Assertiveness

So much for empathy. What is left is 'deft handling'—summoning all the soft skills—courage, conviction, building relationship between the civil societies of the two nations and put a stop to warmongering.

As Sartre said, 'emotion is a social act requiring social skills.' Today we call them soft skills. Tomorrow we may call them life skills—survival skills. One of the most important skills is *assertiveness* and the next is *negotiation* skills. An assertive person, group, or country recognizes the rights of others while asserting their own. They give respect and thus guard their self respect. India's self respect is hurt. That is the underlying course of anger and unity. We must be *firm.* We must not respond *too quickly* but not too slow in our response. We must be moderate in our speed of response. These are the attributes assertiveness. Our stand and our communication must be firm and fair.

The whole management of emotional upsurge lies in deft handling in the use of soft skills of those who represent India.

It is essentially in communication between the two nations the language we speak: Zardari said quoting his wife Benazir Bhutto before the attack, 'there is a little bit of India in every Pakistani', and a vendor in Delhi told Sarfaraz Manzoor, a Pakistani, in respond to his saying, 'I am a Pakistani, Pakistan and India are one.'

Promoting these social exchanges between the citizens of both nations will be a lasting solution.

Sarfaraz Manzoor wrote, I was born in India, Lahore which became Pakistan 14 years later. I love India but I don't hate Pakistan...can only begin healing wounds of Partition) when we acknowledge the personal and political tragedy of Partition.

Zardari, let me keep saying what he said before 26/11; Both the countries have one common enemy—poverty of millions...terrorism is probably off shoot of poverty and lack of education among the masses'

Tolerance and freedom from prejudices and bias can be ranked high on soft skills.

'The recent barbaric act in Mumbai is the outcome of failure of government, opposition, and democracy. On the other hand, globally people are surprised at the maturity of India's reaction. Post Mumbai crisis, despite anger at administration, lack of security, the public at large is not asking for waging war on Pakistan'.. said Dr.Amartya Sen.

'The importance of India's soft power can hardly be over—estimated. L but at the same time economic diplomacy is equally very important. What we need is right mix of both said Mr.S.K.Lambah, Special envoy to Prime Minister.

They both spoke at an event of the Aspen Institute India (AII), an international organization whose *'mission is to internationalize India's business, political and cultural leadership'*.

Does that include Pakistan whose terrorists want to destabilize India economically and politically?

APPENDIX-III

READING MAKETH A FULLMAN

'Reading maketh a fullman, conference a ready man and writing an exactman'. These words written four centuries ago by Francis Bacon are apt to this day – the most vital soft skills in my view for these lead a man or woman towards personality development and realisatioin of full potential.

Baconian octrins. 'RAW'

It is derived from Francis Bacon's doctrines Francis Bacon (1561-1626) was a statesman, philosopher, and an essayist who wrote many books in Latin. But he was more known for his book in English 'Of proficience and Advancement of Learning'. In the story, New Atlantis Bacon described what he thinks and a collage should be like. The advice he gives in his *essays* often quoted: reading maketh a fullman; conference a ready man and writing an exact man. It is an inspiration to me to write my first book RAW skills. Raw is at once, an acronym and an idiom.

Acronymically RAW stands for Reading, Articulating (speaking and listening, substitutes for conference in Bacconian doctrin) and writing skills. It was knack to create acronyms that made me attempt writing a book. I have used acronyms in the class-room to catch the eye of the learners. In my later book 'Communicative Competence' (2006) I had included everything from RAW skills except 'Reading maketh a fullman' which is what I included in this.

There is an idiomatic use of bacon–bring home bacon–which means 'succeed', 'win', make a living. You need to 'bring home the bacon', bacon literally means a salted or smoked pig's meat, inferring, eke a livelihood; you must get a job and succeed in your career.

You can bring home baconian doctrine to bring home bacon!

For if you want to succeed remember always about RAW skills, quiet essentially soft skills. Coming to English language proficiency, you need to read a lot, speak and listen a lot, and write a lot, the only way to master it. In this monograph my emphasis is on Reading English Advancing Day by day – (READ).

Bacon's Beacon beckons you to take up the study of English language earnestly reading more and more English literature.

MBA syllabus includes Business English in Soft Skills. Reading regularly English literature, fiction or non-fiction or professional journals, magazines, even News Dailies can enhance your proficiency in English language as well as knowledge and wisdom. There is a proliferation of written material and to atleast with the ever escalating knowledge, one cannot but strive to improve his efficiency in reading English material.

It is ironical that reading is not included in the long list of soft skills. Even under English language skills only speaking, listening, and writing are mentioned under oral and written communication.

It is ironical because, reading, writing, speaking and listening are like four wheels of the communication automobile. Any one wheel missing, the vehicle would not move forward. In this section I wish to present all about efficient reading.

The attributes of a Full Man are integrity and wholeness, *integrity* within and *wholeness* without. His calm and composed integrity within is because he 'sees' the outside word with BIFOCAL spectacles.

- Big Picture
- Immediate
- Future
- Open Mind
- Combines
- Accommodates
- Logical

Big Picture: Sometimes referred as Helicopter view, his focus is on relationships between parts not on parts per se.

Immediate: His concern, however, is immediate present. He acts in 'living present'

Future : Still, he peeps into the future with an OPEN MIND and COMBINES the short term goals with the long term objectives. He ACCOMMODATES Opposite views. He has the ability to reconcile the seemingly opposite view points. LOGICAL He has the ability to present his view points logically. He is lucid in his expression.

Versatile Reading Paves the way.

1. ***Reflective reading for Insights*** (e.g. reading poetry, You recall and 'chew' the 'cud').
2. ***Responsive reading for Enjoyment*** (e.g. reading a novel. You follow the footsteps of the author)
3. ***Receptive reading for information*** (e.g. reading articles)

READ TO

- **RAISE** brain Power
- **ENHANCE** experience
- **ADAPT** to Changes
- **DEVELOP** database

Read to Raise Brain Power

You do physical exercise to build your muscles so that they become strong and enduring. You need mental exercise to build the big muscle inside the head – Brain. The brain consists of billions of cells – the neurons; they die in thousands per day. Yet you don't lose your ability to comprehend and retain. The brain power is in the inter-connections that the neurons make and not in their number! The neuron is designed to receive information, like a green leaf is designed to receive sunlight. Brain is designed to thrive on : *Stimulation, Change & Challenge, Ambiguity, Novelty,* Reading provides ***stimulation*** and prepares you for ***change*** and without difficulty; you can find ***novelty*** in what you read. The neuron collects information by its ***dendrites*** which is processed in the ***cell body*** and transmitted to the other neurons via its ***axon***. The neurons 'talk' to each other and establish pathways like the beaten tracks in a village.

Read to enhance your own Experience besides knowledge

Experience is the best teacher is an old adage. It is true, provided you are attentive and reflective to your own experience and that of others. Books contain others' experiences. Sometimes reading a book is like looking into a mirror. From books you can find logic for your own experience, and intuitive learning. You gain self-confidence and conviction. In the 21st century when knowledge is continually escalation it imperative to read 'online'.

Read to Adapt to Changes

"You have to run to remain in place; if you want to go somewhere, you have to run twice as fast." *Alice in wonderland.*

To adapt to changes in a fast moving world you have to think ahead. Reading helps. Books contain *Future Shocks.* Reading such books prepare you mentally to face 'shocks' lightly.

Read to Develop Database

Brain stores information in its neural networks. Reading

(a) develops database

(b) increase storage capacity

They are mutually reinforcing. The more you read, the more you want to read, the more is the increased capacity of the brain to retain and retrieve.

Information is for widening the base-***broad basing*** not for ***broad-casting*** above.

Read the titbits 'Read More for better English' and 'Ladies and Gentlemen'. Narayan Kurup the author of 'Ladies and Gentlemen' proves 'Reading Maketh a Fulman'.

Don't pull is the first requirement for cultivating healthy reading habit.

Don't ***proof read***: Proof reading is a specialized skill meant for a special purpose. People who proof read can not tell what they have read. They can only correct letters and spelling and punctuate. Normal reading is for receiving the meaning not for correcting the mistakes.

Don't ***under score*** : If you have a tendency to use a pencil or finger to guide your reading, it should be got rid of; when you underscore, your focus is on words and not meaning.

Don't do ***loud reading or lip movement:*** Both of which make you focus on words and not on meaning. There are occasions and purposes when one may have to read aloud. Except for those occasions and purposes when one may have to read aloud, moving lips slows down the reading speed.

DON'T PULL

- Proof Reading
- Underscoring
- Lip Movement
- Loud Reading

Reading is MINDSACT

Reading is not a physical activity. No doubt the eyes must get sensitized to the printed matter. Regular reading will train the eye to scan and increase the span of vision. The eye can scan the object with 1/20 of a second. It has a span of about four words. Thus theoretically it can capture 4800 words per minute. That may be possible. But what we are concerned with is comprehension of what the printed material contains.

Remember reading is a '**mindsact**'

* **Material:** Our ability to comprehend the content depends on several factors. First the material should be physically attractive: the size, shape, colour, texture and layout influence our reading. Old dusty files to beautifully bound brand new books come to us for our use. Whether it is shabbily written document or a boldly printed material it has a bearing on our inclination to read.
* **Inclination:** The inclination also depends on our mood and readiness to pay attention to the material at hand. It is

better to postpone reading than struggle with the material comprehending little.

* **Need & Decision making style :** Our inclination to read, again, depends on the need – the importance and the urgency. Often in life both in private life and work life there is need to gather information to take right decisions. Such information is available in newspapers, journals, magazines, books or old files. There may be some whose style is to take decisions on the basis of hunches and *guesstimates*. These persons may not be inclined to read the written material. Others must quickly tease out information from variety of printed sources. For them the need to read becomes both important and urgent.

Reading Styles

The reading styles vary according to importance or urgency or both. The matrix below summaries the different styles that might be used.

	Urgent	**Not Urgent**
Important	Rapid Reading	Reflective Reading
Not important	Random Reading	Responsive Reading

"some books have to be tasted, others swallowed and very few have to be chewed and digested"; that is some books are to be read only in parts, others, to be read but not curiously and some, very few to be read wholly and with diligence and attention. Francis Bacon.

Random reading is for swallowing, reflective reading for chewing and digesting. In the days of Francis Bacon, there was probably no need for rapid reading, the phenomenon of the rapidly changing information age! Today's busy manager has to taste and swallow lot of information to take decision. In fact ***flexibility* is the hallmark of the skilful reader, a soft skill.**

Regurgitate Reading: Extending the metaphor to 'Chewing the cud by the cattle', the manager might taste all serious stuff to allow 'saliva to ooze' and then swallow rapidly at first. Later he might regurgitate, surge back to mouth, the partly digested matter for second munching an ideal combination of rapid reading and reflective reading which makes comprehension complete and insightful. This may be called Regurgitate Reading. You read *to lead by the nose!*

* **Surroundings:** That reading requires quiet surroundings is self evident, although there are rare people who can concentrate on reading inspite of noises around and noise in the context.
* **Acquaintance:** Familiarity with the subject matter helps in reading and comprehending quickly. Every profession has its own jargon which the professional can read and comprehend with ease. It is easier to read one's own professional journals than alien journals and magazines.
* **Concentration:** Concentration is more a habit than a skill. If you allow your mind to wander most of the time, you cannot concentrate on a particular occasion. It is necessary to cultivate the habit of doing things one at a time. Listen to radio, watching T.V., reading a letter, listening to a friend, writing a note, or meditating on a deity, be it for a minute or an hour, all demand concentration, a habit one must cultivate.

  I repeat, if you have the habit of concentrating one thing at a time and also have the ability to shift the focus from one to another, then, you will be able to read without losing concentration.

  Concentration on one means closing the mind for all the rest at that moment.
* **Time**: Time is an important factor. Our brain has a biological clock. It has it's peak time and low time. There are some who are a.m. type and those who are p.m. type. The a.m type prefer early hours for serious reading. The p.m. type read when everybody goes to bed. Whatever time you choose remember that you do reading awake and active and not for dozing off and going to sleep, then there is a danger of your going to sleep every time you read even in day time.

MINDSACT

- Material
- Inclination
- Need
- Decision
- Surroundings
- Acquaintance
- Concentration
- Time

Reading has two elements:

(a) Comprehension

(b) Time

What is important is not speed per se, but speed of comprehension. It is like typing. When you learn to type scientifically, you will improve speed with practice. So when you learn to read effectively, you will improve your speed with practice.

Do this exercise.

Select a good article (or any expository writing, a report) ***you can only read well what is well written !***

Read the text for 5 minutes as per your present habit. Count the number of words, read, and calculate the words per minute. If you have comprehended the text well and your speed is less than 200 words per minute, then you need to improve.

Reflective Reading

"Where the mind is without fear and the head is held high;

Where knowledge is free;

Where the world has not been broken up into fragments by narrow domestic walls;

Where words come out from the depth of truth;

Where tireless striving stretches its arms towards perfection;

Where the clear stream of reason has not lost its way into the dreary desert sand of dead habit;

Where the mind is led forward by Thee into ever widening thought and action –

Into that heaven of freedom, my Father, let my country awake."

As I sat down to write this essay intuitively I recalled Rabindranath Tagore's invocation. I wrote it down and began to underscore certain words. These words provoked certain thoughts, TRUTH IS ONENESS. We see it as fragments because of domestic walls built by us, the barriers of communication – not sharing knowledge and information – a thoughtless inaction. Why? Because I am possessive? Or I do not know how to share? Lack of soft skills?

This presentation is about the skills one must acquire and perfect to receive, assimilate and share our knowledge and information with others to make this world, the Heaven of Freedom. People of the world like billions of neurons in one brain must interact to enhance the brain's and the world's capacity. Reading, Auditory – Ariticulatory and writing skills have such profound significance. This is reflective reading, for INSIGHTS of knowledge, and accumulate stock of ideas.

Responsive Reading

Here is a piece of narrative which should be read responsively, following the footsteps of the writer and enjoy the sheer beauty of expression. You can even enjoy reciting such passages to others.

The Decisive Hour at Waterloo June 18, 1815.

"FATE is prone to reserve her smiles for the mighty and for those who do great deeds. She will remain faithful for years to one man, will be the devoted slave of a Caesar, an Alexander, or a Napoleon, she has a liking for primitive natures, akin to herself – incomprehensible, unfathomable.

Yet occasionally, at very rare intervals, she sets her cap at some inconspicuous mortal, placing in his hands threads of doom, the clumsy weaving of which may change the course of history. The poor fellows on whom destiny thus bestows her favours are alarmed rather than delighted; they are overwhelmed by the torrent of responsibility which sweeps them into the mighty river of world happenings. For the most part, therefore, they allow the threads to slip from their tremulous fingers. Seldom indeed do events prove so cogent that even the weakling is carried upward to soaring heights. The great moment passes swiftly, and he who fails to grasp his opportunity will never be vouchsafed another". Stephan Zwig.

Receptive Reading for Information

What is Receptive Reading? Receptive Reading is TRANSDUCTION not transfer. It is like drawing water from a well, not opening a tap to drink water.

The writer persuades; the reader transduces. The reader decodes what the writer encodes. There is infact, conversion of one from of energy – the words – into another from – the ideas.

Receptive Reading involves Filtering

There is simultaneous amplification and attenuation. It's like crossing a busy road or recognizing a face in the crowd. Amplification means reading, paying more attention to certain details, and attenuation means paying less or no attention to other details. You concentrate on the traffic to your right and traffic to the left for the purpose of crossing the road; you ignore the rest. You recognize your friend with the mental picture stored in the brain and you don't 'see' other faces. You have filtered.

STRATEGIES FOR RAPID READING

Scan, Select, and Skim

Improving efficiency in reading is essentially a strategic change of HABIT. When you go to a Library or Book Stall you really scan. Scanning an article involves reading the title, a few lines of the introduction in and concluding para. You can also casually look at the section headings, if there are any. With your purpose clearly in your mind you can now decide whether you should read through the article or not. If you are really interested in reading the article, but don't have the time to do so, you can skim through the article.

Skimming is something like looking for a face in a crowd. You take – in a number of faces before you fix your gaze on the one you are looking for. Similarly you skim through a para to find the topic sentence.

Which sentence or sentences?

It depends on the style of the writer – he may use inductive principle or deductive principle or any other method of reasoning.

Induction consists of enumeration of facts and individual cases and conclusions based on them. It proceeds from specifies to the general, whereas deduction proceeds from statement or conclusion from which particular instances are drawn.

This way you can comprehend 70%, if you are still interested you can come back to it later.

Even if you have time it is better to skim before you read responsively from the beginning of the article to the end. Both comprehension and speed will be better. More importantly you have less strain comprehending it.

The formula is **rapid reading + responsive reading.**

As I already mentioned it's a matter of change of habit. Changing habit is not easy. It requires commitment and patience. Atleast you can experiment with a new idea and reap the benefits. I have been a regular reader since my school days. But it is only much later that I cultivated the habit of scanning and skimming before reading responsively. I am happy it has become a regular habit with me. There is no reason, why you should not develop a habit of scanning and skimming and reap the benefits.

Skip words Skip sentences and Skip even paras.

Words are vehicles of thoughts. You are interested in ideas and thoughts not words or sentences. You may wonder how it is possible to take ideas and leave words. A little reflection will make the point clear. Every writer has ideas which he converts into words and sentences. Bt he is bound by conventions of grammar and syntax, and has to necessarily complete each sentence. The reader however is not, and hence, you are free to skip not only words but also sentences and paras.

Skip the words but take the ideas.

Self-Appraisal of Reading Habits

		V Good	Good	Average	Poor	Bad
1.	When you consider yourself as a reader, under which category that, follow would you place yourself?	1	2	3	4	5
		Always	**Generally**	**Some times**	**Rarely**	**Never**
2.	Do you enjoy the 'process' or act of reading?	1	2	3	4	5
3.	Do you scrutinize your reading material first, before reading it thoroughly?	1	2	3	4	5
4.	Are you able to locate the main ideas easily?	1	2	3	4	5
5.	While reading do you move your lips, feel vibrations at your throat?	1	2	3	4	5
6.	Do you vary your speed and method with the difficulty of the material and your purpose for reading it?	1	2	3	4	5
7.	While reading do you find it difficult to keep your mind from wandering?	1	2	3	4	5
8.	Do you often "doze off" or find your eyes tiring ?	1	2	3	4	5
9.	Do you prefer t read in bed?	1	2	3	4	5

APPENDIX-IV

ON SAYING 'PLEASE'

—A. G. Gardincr

1. The young lift-man in a City office who threw a passenger out of his lift the other morning and was fined for the offence was undoubtedly wrong. It was a question of "Please". The complainant entering the lift, said, "Top". The lift-man demanded "Top please", and the concession being refused, he not only declined to comply with the instruction, but hurled the passenger out of the lift. This, of course, was carrying a comment on the manners too far. *Discourtesy is not a legal offence and this does not excuse assault and battery.* If a burglar breaks into my house and I knock him down, the law will acquit me7and if I am physically assaulted, it will permit me to retaliate with reasonable violence. It does this because the burglar and my assailant have broken quiet definite commands of the law. *But no legal system could attempt to legislate against bad manners, or could sanction the use of violence against something which it does not itself recognise as a legally punishable offence.* And whatever sympathy with the lift-man, we must admit that the law is reasonable. It would never do if we were at liberty to box people's ears because we did not like their behaviour, or the tone of their voices, or the scowl on their faces. Our fists would never be idle, and the gutters of the City would run with blood all day.

2. I may be as uncivil as I may please and the law will protect me against violent retaliation. I may be haughty or boorish and there is no penalty to pay except the penalty of being written down an ill-mannered fellow. The law does not compel me to say "Please" or to attune my voice to other people's sensibilities any more than it says that I shall not wax my moustache or dye my hair or wear ringlets down my back. It does not recognize the laceration of our feelings as a case for compensation. There is no allowance for moral and intellectual damages in these matters.

3. This does not mean that the damages are negligible. It is probable that the lift-man was much more acutely hurt by what he regarded as a slur upon his social standing that he would have been if he had a kick on the shins, for which he could have got a legal redress.

   The pain of a kick on the shins soon passes away but the pain of a wound to our self-respect or our vanity may poison a whole day. I can imagine that lift-man, denied the relief of throwing the author of his wound out of the lift, brooding over the insult by the hour, and visiting it on his wife in the evening as the only was of restoring his equilibrium. For there are few things more catching than bad temper and bad manners. Probably the man who said "Top" to the lift man was really only getting back on his employer who had not said "Good morning" to him because he himself had been henpecked at breakfast by his wife, to whom the cook had been insollent because the housemaid had "answered her back." We infect the world with our ill-humour. Bad manners probably do more to poison the stream of general life than all the crimes in the calendar. For one wife who gets a black eye from an otherwise good-natured husband there are a hundred who live a life of martyrdom under the shadow of a morose temper. *But all the same the law cannot become the guardian of our private manners.* No Decalogue could cover the vast area of offences and no court could administer a law which governed our social civilities, our speech, the tilt of our eyebrows and all our moods and manners.

4. But though we are bound to endorse the verdict against the lift-man, most people will have a certain sympathy with him. *While it is true that there is no law that compels us to say "Please", there is a social practice much older and much sacred than any law which enjoins us to be civil. And the first requirement of civility is that we should acknowledged service. "Please" and "Thank you" are the small change with which we pay our way as social beings.* They are the little courtesies by which we keep the machine of life oiled and running sweetly. They put our intercourse upon the basis of a friendly co-operation, an easy give-and -take, instead of on the basis of superiors dictating to inferiors. It is a very vulgar mind that would wish to command where he can have the service for asking, and have it with willingness and good-feeling instead of resentment. Excerpts from A.G.G.Gardiner's On Saying 'Please'

5. I should like to "feature" in this connection my friend, the polite conductor. By this discriminating title I do not intend to suggest a rebuke to conductors generally. On the contrary, I am disposed to think that there are few classes of men who come through the ordeal of a very trying calling better than bus conductors do. Here and there you will meet an unpleasant specimen who regards the passengers as his natural enemies-as creatures whose chief purpose on the bus is to cheat him, and who can only be kept reasonably honest by a loud voice and an aggressive manner. But this type is are-rarer than it used to be. I fancy the public owes much to the Underground

Railway Company, which also runs the buses, for insisting on a certain standard of civility in its servants and taking care that standard is observed. In doing this it not only makes things pleasant for the travelling public, but performs important social service.

6. It is not, therefore, with any feeling of unfriendliness to conductors as a class that I pay tribute to a particular member of that class. I first became conscious of his existence one day when I jumped on to a bus and found that I had left home without any money in my pocket. Everyone has had the experience and knows the feeling the mixed feeling, which the discovery arouses. You are annoyed because you look like a fool at the best and like a knave" at the worst. You would not be at all surprised if the conductor eyed you coldly as much as to say, "Yes, I know that stale old trick. Now then, off you get." And even if tin-conductor is a good fellow and lets you down easily, you are faced with the necessity of going back, and the incovenience, perhaps, of missing your train or your engagement.

7. Having searched my pockets in vain for stray coppers, and having found I was utterly penniless, I told the conductor with as honest a face as I could assume that I couldn't pay the fare, and must go back for money. "Oh, you needn't get off that's all right," said he. "All right," said I, "but I haven't a copper on me." "Oh, I'll book you through," he replied. "Where do you want to go?" and he handled his bundle of tickets with the air of a man who has prepared to give me a ticket for anywhere from the bank to Hong Kong. I said it was very kind of him, and told him where I wanted to go and as he gave me the ticket, I said, "But where shall I send the fare?" "Oh, you'll see me some day all right," he said cheerfully, as In-turned to go. And then, luckily, my

fingers, still wandering the corners of my pockets, lighted on a shilling, and the account was squared. But that fact did not lessen the glow of pleasure which so good-natured an action had given me.

8. A few days after, my most sensitive toe was trampled on rather heavily as I sat reading on the top of a bus. I looked up with some anger and more agony, and saw my friend of tin-cheerful countenance. "Sorry, Sir," he said. I know these are heavy boots. Got'em because my own feet get trod on so much, and now I'm treading on other people's. Hope I didn't hurt you, sir". He had hurt me but he was so nice about it that I assured him he hadn't. After this I began to observe him whenever I boarded his bus, and found a curious pleasure in the constant good nature of his bearing. He seemed to have an inexhaustible fund of patience and a gift for making his passengers comfortable. I noticed that if it was raining he would run up the stairs to give someone the tip that there was "room inside". With old people he was as considerate as a son, and with children as solicitous as a father. He had evidently a peculiarly warm place in his heart for young people, and always indulged in some merry jest with them. If he had a blind man on board, it was not enough to set him down safely on the pavement. He would call to Bill in front to wait while he took him across the road or round the corner, or otherwise safely on his way. In short, I found that he irradiated such an atmosphere of good-tempered and kindness that a journey with him was a lesson in natural courtesy and good manners.

   What struck me particularly was the ease with which he got through his work. If bail manners are infectious so also are good manners. If we encounter incivility, most of us are apt to become uncivil, but it is an unusually uncouth

> person who can be disagreeable with sunny people. It is with manners as with the weather.... A cheerful person descends on even the gloomiest of us with something of the benediction of a fine day. And so it was always fine weather on the polite conductor's bus, and his own civility, his conciliatory address and good humoured bearing infected his passengers. In lightening their spirits he lightened his own task. His gaiety was not a wasteful luxury, but a sound investment.

I have missed him from my bus route of late; but I hope that only means that he has carried his sunshine on to another road. It cannot be too widely diffused in a rather drab world. And I make no apologies for writing a panegyric on an unknown bus conductor.

APPENDIX-V

A NEW MODEL FOR INDIAN ENTREPENEURSHIP

Varanasi Bhaskara Rao

Sri Narayana Murthy of Infosys won the Ernst and Young world Entrepreneur award, The first Indian to win it. It was given 'for intellectually, philosophically, ethically, and spiritually driven entrepreneurship and his company's outstanding financial performance and global impact in a dynamic and volatile Industry'. That was how the citation read. This is the model we may consider to promote in the training for entrepreneurship programmes.

It applies to all categories of entrepreneurs drawn from cities to villages.

The creation of awareness is the main thing. It should become & mass movement. There are a few self-made persons driven by achievement-motivation. They learn vicariously through observation and imitation of role models. There are others who need to be shown the path to entrepreneurship through training in achievement motivation.

The thumb rule for motivation is the fifty-fifty rule. In the case of entrepreneurs it has to be eighty-twenty. Eighty being internal and twenty external. The twenty comes from external rewards, recognition and support from Government. Achievement motivation may lie dormant in many people. It must be fostered by presentation of case studies. McClelland and his coworkers set about the task of designing a training course to increase achievement motivation. Their prepositions were summarized under four major headings : Goal-Setting, Motive Syndrome, Cognitive Support and Group Support.

Civil Disobedience Movement

Gandhiji brought out the latent achievement motivation among the masses. He became a role model to hundreds and thousands of Satyagrahis. They were all entrepreneurs par excellence. They might not have created wealth; they paved the way for self-reliance, hard work and achievement motivation in the society. What is not stressed in the present education of entrepreneurship was stressed by Gandhian path to growth. He believed in the dictum 'there is enough for everybody's need; not enough for everybody's greed!' Entrepreneur must be free from greed model of Keynesian economics. It is not greed that should drive the Indian but nationalism with in globalism. First let us solve the problem of hunger in our own country. Let us release the human resources - production by the masses -even the most unlikely resources in terms of their present capacities, city to village. This was how Gandhi transformed freedom struggle into a mass-movement. Reading *"who's who of freedom struggle in Andhra Pradesh',* I found there were many, who contributed their ??? but with a missionary zeal and *sense of sacrifice*. If we carefully analyse their life sketches we see all the qualities and activities of an entrepreneur.

Dr Pattabhi Seetharamaiah, who founded Andhra Bank, Andhra Insurance Co., Bharat Lakshmi Bank, Hindustan Ideal Insurance Co. etc., with a view to rehabilitate the freedom fighters after their return to normal life, was an entrepreneur. Desodharaka Kasinathuni Nageswara Rao Pantulu, who was in the forefront of the freedom movements was also business entrepreneur, having founded *Amritanjan* and *Andhra Patrika.* There have been many who worked in the enterprises with the same zeal and achievement motivation. Their patriotism to the country was transferred to the loyalty to the company and commitment to the profession without giving up patriotism.

The chief quality that is missing in the present model and which is central to the new model suggested is *altruism*, self-less service. This is an Indian value. It is essentially based on the core-principles of truth, nonviolence, simple living and fearlessness.

Fostering of these qualities

'Group discussions of achievement in relation to the folk lore ... and expressed values of the culture' (Kolb, 1974) will foster the ooornotivatioh. The civil disobedience movement in 1930s is more than folk-lore. It has been documented, recorded history. Many of these freedom fighters displayed entrepreneurial behaviours later in their lives. The 'western model based on greed, avarice, hard work, self-reliance etc must be replaced with a new model based on nationalism and absence of greed and avarice and vulgar display of riches, retaining hard work and self-reliance. The environment, the external motivation, was shaped by Gandhiji and a climate was created by educating the masses through his example. But to-day's entrepreneur suffers from the lack of supportive environment. In spite of it there are people like Narayana Murthy who have earned awards at the international level.

Applying the major propositions under broad four-heads referred above Goal-Setting, Motive Syndrome, Cognitive Supports and Group Support to the freedom struggle, we have the following :

Civil disobedience movement had clear goals. Each group of volunteers had set their own realistic but challenging goals and achieved them through self-monitoring. They had the motive syndrome which is defined as *integration of thoughts, actions* and *contexts,* There was clarity of purpose among all, clear guidelines coming from the Congress working Committee. Their nationalism was based on principles of Truth, Non-violence, Fearlessness, simple living (Khadi), self-reliance.

The cognitive supports came from discussion and dialogues and resolutions and communication. Sharing vision and unified action were essential ingredients of their success. There were group supports in the form of local discussions, direction and mutual support. There were *sibirams* and *ashrams* from where groups of volunteers led by one designated as the *dictator* to go out to offer satyagraha, boycott of foreign goods, picketing at the liquor shop and promotion of Khadi.

The Indian society has always been an achieving society in spite of several invasions. It is said in 18th century India there were cities comparable to London of that time. That accounts for the material success. But philosophically intellectually, ethically and spiritually we have always been superior and second to none at any point of time in our history. Therefore there is no need to look at western models. Through study of civil disobedience movement and example set by many entrepreneurs we can find entrepreneurship models in our native rocks.

APPENDIX-VI

TEMPERAMENT

Long-term emotions management

-Varanasi Bhaskara Rao

Awareness, regulation, motivation, empathy and deft handling are ideas imported from the West. What the West is gradually realizing is what we had from time immemorial, the philosophical outlook. Greed, Pride, Passion, Prejudice, Competition and Selfishness are at the root of emotional disturbances. Unless we are ready to examine and reorient our life-styles we may continue to resort to short-term, temporary measures to alleviate distress caused by emotions.

Doctors advise their heart patients to change their lifestyle, which they do not heed. They are the people who would like to have the cake and eat it too. They pay the price. Some say they are willing to take the risk rather than lead dull and unexciting life. Well, every individual has his choice. For those who wish to examine their life styles here are ten keys of Dr. Deepak Chopra for active mastery.

The following are not his exact words or statements, but I have tried to retain the original meaning.

Ten Keys to Active mastery : LIFE LATEST

1. Live in the present
2. Identify the intelligence beneath the physical.
3. Fear not, love!
4. Escape from defence, anger etc.
5. Listen to your body.

6. Avoid judging others, their opinions.
7. Take time for meditation.
8. Eschew approval from others.
9. See "outside" as reflection of "in here"
10. Touch not the toxic.

*Inspiration : Ageless Body, Timeless Mind by Deepak Chopra

1. Live in the Present:

19th Century American poet H.W. Long Fellow wrote

Trust no future however pleasant,

Let the dead past bury its dead;

Act, act in the living present,

Heart within and God overhead;

Weep not over spilt milk. Chronic remorse over past misfortunes is an unwanted sentiment. Looking ahead may be necessary. Future plans are a must; induced anxiety or fear of future should not lead to neglect of the present.

2. Identifying the intelligence beneth the physical

Heart within and God overhead is a good emotion. Faith in the divine grace without which things may not happen. When they do happen to arrogate the success to one self may make one 'proud' of himself. When things do not happen one may blame others.

3. Fear not, Love

Fear is a basic emotion. Fear of others taking away something from us may distance us from others. To love people and to be with people seeking the social support will drive away the fear. 'Love cannot be cultivated by thoughts. Love can come where there is complete silence.'

4. Escape from defence, anger etc. (Read appendix – Be Armed not Alarmed)

Do not make false assertions of self and make futile defenses when others do not accept the falsity. These defences may lead to frustration, aggression, withdrawal or hatred for others.

5. **Listen to your body**

   Body signals both positive and negative sensations. Some of the signals are pronounced and others hardly discernible. One has to practise self observation first at the body level and then at mind's level. Listening to sensations, feelings and intuitions enables you to regulate through conscious I effort. As a rule this can be practised along with meditation, before it.

6. **Avoid judging others and their opinions**

   We've a tendency to measure others behaviour with our own yardstick. Each person is unique; he or she has his or her strengths and weaknesses. Some have high intelligence, others are intuitive. Yet others imaginative, some are calm and controlled, others highly strung, outgoing and dynamic. The very same people will carry with them some weaknessess which must be allowed.

   You may belong to one type and have difficulty to tolerate people who are of opposite types. Opposite of toleration is prejudice, a negative and painful emotion. Prejudice and Pride may give rise to other emotions like irritation, frustration, and even anger when working with others who ire not like you.

7. **Take time for meditation**

   There are many versions of meditations and initiation methods. All of them may be good. Choose the one that suits you and stick to it. Wavering or changing either methods or techniques may lead to frustrating experience. What is important perhaps is the regularity and persistence. Even in meditating what is your goal or desire? Calm and composed state or levitation or some such powers used for material gains? If the goal is the latter then there is failure awaiting you accompanied by emotional disturbances.

8. **Eschew approval from others**

   Give up seeking approval of others for everything that you say or do or think. It creates anxiety in doing and living in the present. You may talk in careful and calculated manner. It can affect even your thinking. You think of results and consequences than the actions that need to be done. This leads to lack of confidence and indecision. This quality is opposite of item no. 6, judging others.

Judging others and seeking approval are like two sides of the same coin. They lead to defensive behaviour and emotional disturbance. When we insist on others approving our ideas, actions and decisions we resent them when they question, comment or accuse us and defend, deny, or evade. We begin to judge them and even attribute mala fides in .their intentions In the end we are either hijacked into a guilty state or go into depressed state. We may become angry or even breakdown and continue with chronic remorse.

A better course is to remain calm and readily admit mistakes, if any, to ourselves and look ahead with "heart within and God overhead."

9. **See 'outside' as reflection of 'in-here'**

People whom you love or hate most are projections of your inner world. What you most hate is what you most deny. What you love most is what you most want in yourself You can learn more about yourself through using the relationship with others as mirrors.

Projection according to one definition is a process of attributing one's own quality to others. According to Freud projection is a process attributing one's own baser qualities to others as a defence against acknowledging them as one's own.

10. **Touch not toxins**

Food, drink and tobacco as well as negative feelings hurt the body. Knowing fully well the fact people consume foods that are harmful. People smoke and drink for relaxation which is purely temporary. They know it that it is harmful in the long run. If they ignore the early warning signals, negative signals in the form of major ailments will arrive. The same is the case with negative emotions like anger and too much anxiety can lead to ulcers.

PART – B

BUSINESS ENGLISH

BRITISH LEGACY-USE OF ENGLISH

Out of the blue, as a nation, we inherited and continued with English language. For the past 60 years a fortunate few have been making best use of the legacy. Gradually more and more people are learning the language as a part of improving communications in English, what has come to be known as Soft Skill No. 1.

The education policy which is based on the principles of expansion, inclusion, and excellence, invariably - encourages learning English for higher education and better job opportunities.

This Part B of the work is co-authored by Ms. Y. Kameshwari, a retired English teacher from Kendriya Vidyalaya.

BLUE: British; Legacy; Use of; English

Where Does Indian English Stand?

Y. Kameswari

English enjoys a unique position in India and its use is considered a status symbol, a sign of modernity and the privilege of the elite. The seeds for this language were sown in 1600, with the advent of the East India Company and the Christian Missionaries. English became prevalent by 1800 through the English medium schools and convents. {#Thomas Babington MACAULAY'S "MINUTE ON INDIAN EDUCATION"}. LORD Macaulay's dream of creating a group of bilinguals in India, " A class who may be interpreters between us and the millions whom we govern – a class of persons, Indians in blood and colour, but English in taste, in opinion, in morals and in intellect," did not fully materialize as the curtain dropped on the British Raj in India. The British left, but their rich legacy– The English language, remains even to this day – 60 years after independence. It is a great advantage to us in this country in the context of globalised economy.

Post-Colonial India evolved a new language called Indian English. The Indian speaker who is not born to this language thinks in his own mother tongue – Hindi, Bengali, Marathi, Kannada, Tamil, Telugu and so on and tries to translate his thoughts directly into English. The English thus moulded, modified and evolved, is tinted with the vibrant hues of his socio cultural background and flavoured with the regional tones and accents. It is heterogeneous and innovative, but it is also amusing and some times puzzling to the English. The term "*Indian English*" is used derogatively and the 'elitists', the old timers who take pride in using standard British English, raise eye brows and display 'Smirks of disdain' when they hear the Indian

English. How does one define this language? It is English spoken, written and used by the common Indian, who takes liberty with the syntax, semantics and etymology of the language.

COMMON ERRORS IN ENGLISH

The native speaker of Indian languages commits errors in almost all areas of English, like grammar, usage, syntax etc.

In Grammar the tenses add to the tension, the prepositions run helter skelter in search of their proper positions but mostly in vain. The articles come and go as they please. The adverbs add to the confusion.

The usage of English (Indian English) is very interesting. Certain words wear a new garb and are used in a different sense. The English prefixes / suffixes hug the Indian words, and new expressions are born. Indian words enter the English dictionaries.

Tautology, repetition, malapropism, truncation -all contribute their humble mite to increase the ambiguity of Indian English.

Syntax

Webster's Ninth New Collegiate dictionary defines Syntax as, ' a connected or orderly system; harmonious arrangement of parts or elements; the way in which words are put together to form phrases, clauses or sentences; the part of grammar dealing with this'

Grammar decides the accuracy of a language and a sound grammatical knowledge is essential for well structured sentences. The Indians commit errors while using verbs, adding question tags, answering yes or no questions, using articles, prepositions etc.

Tense – using progressive tense for static verbs

Wrong usage	**Correct usage**
• *I am loving the entire experience of writing*	- I love the entire experience of writing.
• *She is knowing the answer*	- She knows the answer

The native speaker of Indian languages may not find the following expression odd.

Wrong	Correct
He is having very much property	- He has a lot of property.
The food is tasting very good	- The food tastes good.

As per the grammar rules, words of perception, possession and emotions / feelings do not take the progressive tense.

Tensions or tenses?

Wrong usage	Correct usage
I did not went there	I did not go there
I did not cried when I saw the movie.	I did not cry when I saw the movie

Did never takes the past tense

Skipping of verbs

People often say - What I did?

Where he went?

Instead of –

What did I do? Where did he go?

Sometimes we find the following word order in questions. What you would like to eat? Where you would be going in holidays?

Instead of –

What would you like to eat?

Where would you be going in holidays?

The inversion that should take place has not taken place

In a statement subject precedes the verb. In an interrogative statement subject and verbs are inverted

Eg: You went there? (is wrong structure).

Instead to be separated from Did you go there?

(is structurally correct.)

Questions

Tag Questions

Tag question consists of two words, a tensed and an auxiliary verb and a personal pronoun. The verb is basically a copy of the host's root verb. But typically n't is either added or deleted.

Eg: It was raining, was n't. It?

He did not complete the work, did he?

He completed the work, did n't he?

Most of the time Instead of using the proper question tags – Is n't, it? -no? etc., are used

Indian usage-

She sings very melodiously, is n't it?

He is very lazy, no?

She completed the work, did she?

Correct usage:

She sings very melodiously, does n't she?

He is very lazy, is n't he?

She completed the work, did n't she?

Answer to the Question content -

yes, I did /

no, I did n't

Look at the following examples:

Do you mind closing the window? Yes, I do

The speaker means that he does n't mind and he will close the window.

A question like – "Did you go on leave?" may sometimes elicit a response like – "yes, I did n't ; instead of "no I didn't

Nouns – Number

Certain nouns are always to be used as plural and some always as singular. The following nouns do not take the plural number.

- He has lots of <u>luggages</u>
- His <u>hairs</u> are standing out

I have many works to do

He gives many advices

Expression like the following are common in India

His poetries have a depth

The sceneries of Kodaikanal are breath taking

The machineries are rusted

Grammatically the following usage is correct

Scenery	-	or some scenes
Poetry	-	or a collection of poems
Machinery	-	or many machines

Expressions like :patience,
stuff,
wine

are not prefixed by many, few, some etc.

words like much, a lot of,
little, a little, some etc.

are to be prefixed to these uncountable nouns.

Singular nouns are used for objects/ subjects which are always to be referred in plural by some Indians

Social studies becomes: Social Study

Mathematics becomes math/maths/max

Articles

Omitting the articles or using them where they are not required is a common error in Indian English.

Eg: I went to village or I went to temple instead of – I went to the village

Using 'one' in place of 'a' is also common

Let me tell you one story

One kind lady came to me

Indians sometimes use the following expressions

Wrong usage	**Correct usage**
A honest man	an honest man
An European	a European
An University	a University
An one eyed man	a one eyed man

See appendix

FOLLOWING SENTENCES CONTAIN ERRORS

He is more taller than his brother

He is awarded Padmashri for his most excellent Contribution to tribal welfare

There are many unique instances of the same kind.

Of the two brothers, he is the best.

These are some of the expressions in English Language as it is spoken in India.

Grammarians insist that two comparatives and two superlatives should not be used in the same sentence.

Eg: more taller

In the same way words like unique, excellent, rare, universal, perfect etc. do not take any other degree of the adjective

But writers take liberties with grammar and we come across expressions like rarest of the rare. Well Known writers like Shakespeare used the expression, "This is the most unkindest cut of all", two superlatives"

(Julius ceasar – Mark Antony's speech)

Prepositions

Three types of errors occur while using the preposition, - using a wrong preposition, using a preposition where it is not required, not using a preposition where it is necessary. Following are a few examples of these.

Let us discuss about the issue

He grieved the death of his friend

Pay attention on my words

Correct usage

Let us discuss the issue

He grieved over the death of his friend

Pay attention to my words

when the part of speech changes, the prepositions change

a person may order (verb) a cup of tea

But

He may place an order (noun) for a cup of tea

Discuss: to talk in detail about something – the preposition is not required.

Grieve is always followed by over

Pay attention is followed by standard preposition to

Usage

A native speaker of English may feel lost when he comes across an expression like

I cannot able to do the work

Please, on the Light, T.V., Fan

Please close the Light T.V., Fan

Current went, Current came, (instead of power)

In the above sentences the influence of mother tongue/regional language can clearly be seen. However, a direct translation or a one to one translation is not always possible and a language has to be learned as the native speaker uses it.

But and also have a different usage and placement in Indian English

I was just joking but, instead of but I was joking

I did not go only – instead of "I did not go"

There is an overuse of words like actually, seriously, obviously, generally etc

Eg: seriously, she is a good person

Actually, I am not feeling well

Truncations: Certain words are abbreviated by truncating a part of the word

Look at the following sentence

I am going native tomorrow

Instead of saying

I am going to my native place tomorrow

Jason Baldridge points out not only to the abbreviations but also to the extended meaning of particular expressions

He says, "Indians also shorten many words to create commonly used words. Enthusiasm is called enthu: as such it can be used in new ways. One can say "That guy has a lot of enthu". While this is simply an abbreviation enthu can also be used as an adjective where enthusiasm cannot, as in, "He is a real enthu guy". Same applies for fundamentals, which is shortend as fundas, 'she knows her fundas". What is interesting about fundas is that when the 'as' ending is dropped and 'U' is added it takes on a new meaning and can be used in a new way. Fundu basically means, wonderful or brilliant. One can say, "he is a fundu person" or even "he is fundu"

Compound words

Indian innovation is clearly seen in coining compound words, where the native English speaker uses only one word.

Some of the compound words created are

Cousin Brother } in place of cousin
Cousin Sister }

Key bunch, age barred, pin drop silence, time pass etc.

Quirky but Quite India

In south India one comes across expressions like that and all, this and all, to convey the meaning all of that or regarding that

Q. Can I return your book tomorrow? I am going out now

A. That and all I do not know. I need it urgently now

just & simply are expressions used in a typically Indian Way

a. why did you do it?

b. Simply

or

A. Just I was telling him

Tautology: effective or emphatic usage of English for many Indians means using two similar words to convey the same meaning. Standard English requires only one word.

Eg: the true facts are

A fact cannot be false

The following expressions are typically Indian

Eg: He committed a blunder mistake

a. blunder is a grave mistake; either it has to be a blunder or a mistake

I repeat my question once again

What does repeat mean?

He returned back my money

Return itself is sufficient

If suppose, a widow woman, reverted back are sometimes used.

However, tautology is not uncommon to the native English speakers/writers

HW and F G Fowler in "The king's English' points out such errors.

- Lord Rosebury has not budged from his position, splendid, no doubt – of (lonely) isolation (Times)
- If any real remedy is to be found, we must first diagnose the true nature of disease, (see Appendix) however, is not hard.

Repeat, Repeat!

To stress the general idea and express its intensity the same word is repeated

Q: Did you finish reading the book?

A: Yes, yes! (accompanied by an emphatic shake of the head)

A hearty welcome

Come,come! sit,sit!

Following expressions appear quite normal to the Indian.

- He worries about small, small things
- He visited different, different places last month
- She has curly, curly hair.

Ambiguity

Wrong word order, contraption of a sentence or clause, malapropism, confused thinking all these may result in ambiguous expression.

Word order

Wrong word order can send wrong connotations. The following examples from Wren and Martins High School Grammar and composition illustrate this

In thirty-seven wrecks only five lives were **Fortunately lost:** (keep fortunately at the beginning of the sentence)

For, sale of piano, the property of a musician with carved legs (carved legs belong to the piano)

A nurse maid is wanted for a baby about twenty years old (who is twenty years old?)

'The Right word at the Right Time" Readers Digest Publication, gives beautiful examples of the importance of word order and the ambiguity created by not following it. *(See the appendix)*

Right word at the Right time page 42. – gives

The machinery only seems to go wrong when Jessie is operating it.

Does the machinery go wrong when Jessie is operating or does it only seem to go wrong? Where should the *only* be put?

Visiting aunts can be a bore

What is boring? Is it going and visiting or the aunts who are visiting you.

Removers of distinction (a display outside a transportation place)

Are they reputed people of distinction to transport the furniture

or

Do they remove distinction?

If the baby does not thrive on fresh milk, boil it (grammatically "it" refers to the baby)

Icelandic fish talks

Talks on Icelandic fish is probably a better title

Even the phrases have to follow certain order

We may refer to M.S. Subbalakshmi "as a famous carnatic singer", not "a carnatic famous singer"

A black, leather bag, not a leather black bag

Paying more attention to reordering and restructuring the words makes the sentence more meaningful and leads to better understanding of your speech or writing.

IDIOMATIC DISTORTIONS

The word idiom comes from the Greek 'idioma' private property, Every language pulsates with a life and individuality of its own because of the idiomatic expression that comes naturally to the native speaker of that language.

An idiom can be defined as a sequence of words whose combined meaning does not follow regularly from the meaning of individual words.

It is raining cats and dogs (heavy rain)

I always looked up to him (respected)

Not only the idiomatic expressions are distorted expressions, but some of the words and phrases have acquired a meaning of their own in Indian English.

Mrs/Mr. indicate the marital status of a woman or a man. But in Indian English it is quite common to say – My Mrs. Went out. Her Mr comes home very late – instead of saying my wife / her husband, etc.

Mrs. is also added to proper names. Mrs. Geeta instead of Mrs. Geeta Iyer or Mrs. Iyer.

The word funny originally means odd, amusing but in the modern parlance it has become an equivalent of rude, aggressive. That man was acting very funny after returning from states. (showing off)

She started acting funny after getting the lottery (Proud / aggressive)

High tech relates to technology but acquired the additional meaning – incredible.

He is wearing a high tech outfit.

Freak,

Dictionary gives the meaning – a person, animal or plant which is abnormal or deformed.

But the modern Indian may mean by this expression 'having a good time'.

Eve teasing is another word coined to indicate 'sexual harassment'.

'I got a firing' – may not mean you are thrown out of job but you are scolded, you got an oral dressing down.

Thumbs up: an illeterate person may be called a thumbs up because he puts his thumb impression instead of signature.

On the anvil: The Indian press uses this to say that something is about to appear or happen.

A mountain resort is referred to as a hill station

Hotel, A restaurant or a specially big hotel

Lodge, A small hotel

Sometimes, lodge is where you stay and hotel is where you eat.

He is having blood pressure normally means he is having high blood pressure

A diabetic is said to have sugar complaint.

Boss

Not necessarily one's senior official, the word can be used for a friend, a porter, a waiter or for just anyone.

Eg: glad to see you boss!

Look at the following

In the face of it, the rule appears a most advisable one. Correction. On the face of it, the rule appears a most advisable one.

On the face of it, is prima facie; the other means in spite of it.

She retained her calm in the face of many difficulties

The following expression is an idiomatic exp with something omitted.

If you repeat your teacher, you can learn the tables faster.

Repeat after: means say what she says and is the correct usage.

'I pay my pocket, sir', an irate subordinate tells his boss; he means-.

I will pay from my pocket

Many a questions are raised regarding the honesty of the minister

It is either many a question is raised or many questions are raised.

He waited behind the wings and allowed things to go wrong.

In the wings is the correct usage

It was a fatal day when I met her!

Does he want to say fateful? Or his marriage proved fatal to his happiness?

I tried to personally persuade him to pursue higher studies. But my words proved to be water on duck's back.

Water off a duck's back is the correct idiom which means have no effect.

The high incidents of dowry deaths;

Incidence is frequency; incident an event

Here the writer wants to say incidence.

Some more examples:

I want two Xeroxes of this card.

Xerox is the name of a company that supplies photocopies. The correct usage is 'I want two photocopies of this card.'

Maximum, worst are used differently in Indian English; the former for most; the latter for something very bad. In the same way slow and soft are swapped.

"I shall speak slower for your" meaning I will speak softly. "Make the fan softer means, make the fan go slow"

Using "as" where it is not required Mahatma Gandhi is regarded as the father of nation.

A warehouse is called a godown

Ten millions is referred to as a crore

Hundred thousand is a lakh

Himalayan blunder, nose screw (a woman's nose ornament) are some of the Indian expressions.

Rhyming words: Indians, especially the Hindi-speaking belt use rhyming words. The second word does not have any meaning.

chai, vai, mall shall

Ice cream vice cream

Prefixes / suffixes

Adding English prefixes and suffixes to regional words is a common practice in India

Maskafy: maska is buttering in Hindi; flattering some one.

Dom and- ism are generously added to Indian words

Cooliedom

Goondaism

Use of bazi / baji or – giri

Business bazi, dadagiri, cheating giri

Wallah

Taxiwallah, cooliwallah, music wallah

Use of ji or saheb to name (sometimes both)

Welcome to India Smith saheb!

Call Guptaji immediately

Sabji or sirji is also heard in many places;

what's you good name? a direct translation from Hindi is slowly becoming a relic of the past. Still people introduce themselves in the following way

My good self so and so

My self so and so

MATRIMONIAL ENGLISH

English used in matrimonial columns of India.

The matrimonial columns of a newspaper are abuzz with expressions which may not be understood by the native speaker of English

An unmarried person of any age is a boy or girl; B.A. pass / B.A. fail; wheatish complexion etc. or some examples of Indian English

All is not lost

The flexibility and adaptability of the English language allows the inflow of words and expressions from all the other languages enriching itself with subtle nuances and imperceptible shades of meaning and usage. But equal credit must be given to the ever increasing socio - cultural impact of India on the west, and in the process on the English language. The adherents of standard / British English may look down upon Indian English, but many words of Indian origin have found their way into English and have been accepted.

According to Chillibreze writer, Mahalakshmi Radhakrishnan (http//www.chillibreze.com/articles/Indian contributions to the oxford dictionary.asp) many words associated with spirituality, have made their way into English languages.

Eg: Yoga, Mantra, Guru, Pundit, Karma, Dharma, Nirvana etc.

Among the 80 new words in the lexicon, are words as varied as – badmash, bandh, dhaba, bhelpuri and chamcha

She says, "Even some other trendy Indo English words like eveninger, bifurcate, prepone, Gymkhana, buck, corporator, tank, bogie and day wise have been incorporated in the new edition (11th edition of concise dictionary oxford) catamaran and curry have their origin in Tamil"

words related to Indian cuisine are chutney, tandoor, etc.

Richard Garner, Education editor points out the contribution of sports world to create new words

(http/w.w.w.independent.co.uk/news/uk/this-britian/ hinglish-makes-its-debut-in English-dict).

The sporting world also brought new entries to the dictionary. The crystal palace manager lain Dowie is credited with bouncebackability 'the ability to recover after a set back, especially in sport". Tapping up makes its debut – after the illegal approach by Chelsea to. Arsenals' Ashyley cole it is defined as "the illicit practice of attempting to recruit a player while he is still bound by contract to another team"

"Chin music – "bowling or pitching aimed at the batsman or batter's head" is a contribution of cricket. Certain on the street words make interesting reading-cyberathlete = a professional player of computer games.

Mother-out-law – the mother of one's ex-husband or ex-wife

asymmetrical warfare – warfare between a powerful military force and a weak guerilla force.

Not only do Indian words make their debut in the English Dictionary, but the Indian writers also have been winning accolades in the literary world. Indians have been recipients of the coveted, prestigious, Booker, Man Booker and Best of Booker prizes, the Pulitzer etc. Old literary giants like Radhakrishnam, Jawaharlal Nehru, Ravindranath Tagore, Vivekananda – to name just a few-are acknowledged best writers in English and have been acclaimed for their linguistic proficiency and literary fervour. Yes. All is not lost! But in spite of the bright spots, the basic structure of a language cannot be twisted and turned out of shape so that it becomes unrecognisable. A global language is preferable to a local / national language, for global dealings.

FROM LOCAL TO GLOBAL

The Need for Global English

As the individual nations merge into a global village and become interdependent for trade and commerce, for information transfer in science and technology, for their very survival – a common, standardized language, which can be understood and used by every one, a global language is required. English has the flexibility and potential to be understood by the majority of the world. In the words of Vimala S, Chillibreeze writer – "The British Council reports that nearly 375 million people speak English as a second language and 750 million speak it as a foreign language........Statistics show that three quarters of the world's mail is in English, four fifth of electronic information is stored in English". Global English is inevitable because information transfer across the world is continuous. Translation of the entire information into English is very cumbersome and economically not viable.

What is Global English?

Global English is a denationalized and simplified variety of English, not different from basic English language. It is different from "Englishes[1]' and transcends the local, regional and national boundaries.

It is standardized English which can be understood by all the countries.

Mechanics of Global English

Global English has to keep the target readership in mind. Clear, simple and terse expressions which can be understood by the target group are to be used. Too formal or overtly stiff, stilted expressions are to be avoided as also jargon and slang. Following tips can be helpful.

---

[1] The word Englishes is used by David Crystal. (English as a Global language. Cambridge U.P. 1997) Vimala. S. Says Global English is a short hand for English in and around the world in the latter half of the 20th C. (He does write about the new technology, with a particular acknowledgement of local dialects (Englishes)

General Sentence Structure

Short, simple sentences are preferable to long complex sentences. If a complex sentence is used, the subordinate clauses should be used. The sentence must be well sequenced and logical so that it can be read, understood and translated properly into the required language "The King's English" gives the following examples of unnecessarily complex sentences which are verbose.

An elementary condition of a sound discussion is a frank recognition of the gulf severing two sets of facts. (Times)

A simpler expression is

There can be no sound discussion where the gulf severing two sets of facts is not frankly recognized.

- The sign of the times point to the necessity of the modification of the system of administration. (Times) A simpler expression.

It is becoming clear that the administrative system must be modified.

Words: familiar, short words are preferable to long unfamiliar words.

Will you permit me to homologate all you say today regarding the selfish minority of motorists who ...(Times) homologate means agree with;

envisage, visualize terminate, utilize, emblemed can easily be replaced by faced, see, end, and use. A person who has a limited vocabulary and uses this language for trade will be less perplexed.

Long Phrases: can be replaced by one word. Or verbs can be used in place of nouns

At a later date: later

To the fullest of my knowledge
According to my understanding } As I understand.

The purpose of this report, memo, letter - for, I write this to use of verb in place of noun is preferable.

In anticipation of - I anticipate

In expectation of - I expect

Make a decision - decide

Submit a proposal - propose

Extend a hearty welcome - welcome

Punctuation: "The work of punctuation is mainly to show or hint at, the grammatical relation between words, phrases, clauses and sentences". Punctuation marks, properly and accurately used give a significance, stress and decide the tone of the writer. However, punctuation has become the biggest casualty in modern times. Wrong punctuation marks, omission or use of too many punctuation marks send wrong signals to the target reader group and the very purpose of the communication is lost. Instead of establishing understanding, it may offend the reader.

Dealing with each punctuation mark is not possible. The function of a.,? and! are self – explanatory. Let's take a look at apostrophe, comma and semicolon.

The comma, (,) if placed wrongly may completely alter the meaning of what is written.

Lynne stress, in her book "eats, shoots and leaves" gives beautiful illustrations of this;

Leonara walked on her head, a little higher than usual.

The comma is misplaced.

Read the sentence as-Leonara walked on, her head a little higher than usual.

The convict said, the judge is mad -

The convict, said the judge, is mad.

The comma does the magic and makes the sense clear.

Commas are used to fill gaps

Annie had dark hair; sally, white.

The expression sally had white hair <u>or</u> but sally had white hair – is included in the comma.

But using a comma where it is not required also leads to problem.

Don't guess, use a timer or watch

The sentence implies, don't guess or use a timer or watch.

A semicolon or full stop is required after guess and gives the meaning "better use....

Like comma, the 'S creates chaos and confusion in most cases of wrong usage.

Possessive pronouns and possessive determiners do not require an apostrophe.

Your's faithfully or your's sincerely is not

grammatically acceptable however popular it may be

An apostrophe indicates omission of figures or letters;

'09 - for 2009

He hasn't done it - for has not

I'am - for - I am

I'll - for - I will and so on

'It is' can be written as it's; but the possessive pronoun its does not require an apostrophe.

A contraption of 'it is' requires an apostrophe 'S

It's your turn means – it is your turn.

The organization at its best – however does not require an apostrophe since its reefers to the organization and is not a contraption of it is.

The apostrophe also indicates plurals of words-what are the do's and don't's?

Current guides to punctuation, including FOWLER'S Modern English Usage state that with modern names ending in "s" and any foreign names with an unpronounced final s, the apostrophe 'S is required.

Keats's poems not Keats' poems.

Alexander Dumas's The Testament

However,

Jesus' disciples

Conscience' sake do not require's but only the sign of - apostrophe

One may talk about a bird's nest or birds' nests as the case may be.

However Teacher's Day

Or

Boy's Hostel

Indicate one teacher and one boy. They have to be written as Teachers' Day; Boys' Hostel.

The semicolon is almost like a full stop but the pause is for a lesser duration

Sentence linkers: Linkers are cohesive devices and support the coherence of thought. But, however, yet, further, therefore – are some of the linkers.

Again, a wrong linker may send a wrong connotation.

My uncle had been sick for a long time; I served him day and night. Therefore he died.

The linker implies the service is responsible for the death of his / her uncle.

A Linker gives a clue to what is going to come in the next sent, paragraph etc.,

Stilted/formal tone: very stilted formal language should give way to informal, natural language. Can the following sentence be altered for better understanding?

The DICHOTOMY between what you quoted and what you scripted in your bill has sent waves of shock across the company. We can visualize a contiguity of such event which may dissuade us to continue future dealings with you.

Don't send the READER RUNNING to a dictionary. Use simpler words. To quote Mathew Parris, "we, English have a habit of playing things by ear. We distrust the resort to a single, final, timeless arbitration"

CONCLUSION

The English Language is – in a flux and cannot be confined to rules of grammar, vocabulary, semantics etc. New words are accepted, existing words change their meaning and significance, innovations are allowed. However, for trade and commerce, for information transfer in science and technology – a standardized simplified, grammatically correct English called Global English is to be used.

APPENDIX – 1

1. VERBS

The following verbs cannot be used in Progressive Tense

Words of perception: See, hear, smell, notice, taste, recognize.

'I am seeing a beautiful picture,' is grammatically wrong. But when you say, ' I am seeing my friends in the evening', you mean to say, you are going to visit your friend. The second sentence is grammatically correct.

Words of perception, when used in a different sense, can take the progressive verbs.

Verbs of emotions Do not take the verb in the progressive tense.

Want, wish, desire, feel, like, love, hate, hope, refuse, prefer, etc.

I am hating her
I am loving it
} are grammatically wrong

Verbs of thinking-(do not take the progressive tense.)

Think, suppose, believe, understand, agree, consider, trust, remember, forget, know, imagine, etc.

Verbs indicating possession (have = possess)

Have, own, possess, contain, consist of etc.

I am having a house is grammatically wrong.

But

"I am having breakfast", is acceptable because he is having meals – taking

He is having a tough time – indicates he is going through a tough time – not that he is the owner of the tough time

APPENDIX – 2

2. NOUNS

Classified as countables and uncountable. Uncountables do not take plural number.

Eg: Water, Sand, Gold, Wood etc.,
Some words are always used in plural.

Eg: spectacles, tongs, pliers, socks, trousers, alms, obsequies etc, thanks (noun)

Some words are always used in singular and the verb that governs them is in singular

Aircraft, sheep

Names of subjects: Mathematics, Physics, Statistics etc

APPENDIX – 3

3. ARTICLES

An is used before a word that begins with a vowel or vowel sound

Vowels are – a, e, i, o, u

All the other letters are consonants

However, it is grammatically correct to say an honest man instead of a honest man – because 'h' is silent in this word

In the same way

European
Or
University } begin with vowels but they are pronounced as Y'. Hence,

the correct usage is – a European. Not an European similarly in a University – not an University. In one-eyed man the word one begins with a V sound. Hence it is correct to say a one-eyed man not an one-eyed man.

APPENDIX - 4

4. PREPOSITIONS

A preposition indicates place, time, or direction

Following words do not require a preposition

Despite	means	in spite of
Await	means	wait for
Discuss	means	talk at length about some thing

Describe – give a detailed description of

Fear
Order } Verbs

Accompany

Flee

Some words require a prepostion

What are you looking? Is a meaningless question. It should be what are you looking for? at?.

Standard Preposition

Some words take only one preposition congratulate on, famous for, conducive to etc.

Some words take different prepositions, but the meaning changes with each preposition

He is cut out to be an artist (exhibited traits of)

Cut down your expenditure (reduce)

She is cut up with grief (qrief stricken)

Look: Look after, look into, look down upon,

look upto – all convey different meanings

when the part of speech changes, a different preposition is required

I order a cup of tea

I placed an order for a cup of tea

She is fond of children

She has a fondness for children

He is charged with murders.

He is arrested on charges of murder.

APPENDIX – 5

5. BE A GOOD WRITER – (TAUTOLOGY)

So you have always wanted to learn how to write something with a bit more zip than a grocery list. Look no further; here are some valuable tips, courtesy of plain language, gov.

- Avoid clichés like plague : they're old hat.
- Parenthetical remarks (however relevant) are unnecessary
- Do not use a foreign word when there is an adequate English equivalent quid pro quo
- Exaggeration is a billion times worse than understatement
- Don't repeat yourself, or say again what you have already said.
- Be more or less specific
- Proof read carefully to see if you left any words out

Reader's Digest – January, 2009

APPENDIX – 6

6. INTERNET

- REAL BUT IMPERFECT ENGLISH FOUND AROUND THE WORLD SOURCE – http//www.world-english.org /globalenglish.htm
- Doctor's surgery, India: SPECIALIST IN WOMEN AND OTHER DISEASES
- Zoo, India, PLEASE DO NOT FEED THE ANIMALS, IF YOU HAVE ANY SUITABLE FOOD, GIVE IT TO THE GUARD ON DUTY
- Restaurant, India, OPEN SEVEN DAYS AND WEEKENDS TOO
- CEMETERY, India: PERSONS ARE PROHIBITED FROM PICKING FLOWERS FROM ANY BUT THEIR OWN GRAVES
- TEMPLE, India, IT IS FORBIDDEN TO ENTER A WOMAN EVEN A FOREIGNER IF DRESSED AS A MAN
- Hotel broucher, India: THIS HOTEL IS RENOWNED FOR ITS PEACE AND SOLITUDE IN FACT, LARGE CROWDS FROM ALL OVER THE WORLD FLOCK HERETO ENJOY IT.

APPENDIX – 7

7. INTERNET

Here is a list of some common English language sentence errors that we, in our daily lives, make

Incorrect: it was so late there was no taxi
Correct: it was so late that there was no taxi available

Incorrect: It's seven twenty o'clock
Correct: It's seven twenty

Incorrect: Your coat is broken
Correct: Your coat is torn.

Incorrect: let me help you todo your work
Correct: Let me help you with your work

Incorrect: Susan didn't make a fault anyway
Correct: Susan didn't make a mistake anyway

Incorrect: may I borrow your phone
Correct: May I use your phone

Incorrect: Would you mind posting this letter for me? Yes, certainly
Correct: would you mind posting this letter for me?Of course not.

Incorrect: He becomes better
Correct: He got better

Incorrect: We'll have a hearing test tomorrow
Correct: We'll have a listening test tommorrow

Incorrect: I recommend you to take a long vacation
Correct: I recommend that you take a long vacation

Incorrect: The last bus leaves at eleven o'clock. It's about eleven now, Hurry up!
Correct: The last bus leaves at eleven o'clock. it's nearly eleven now, Hurry up!

Incorrect: It was still bright outside
Correct: it was still light outside

Incorrect: The hall can seat two hundred people
Correct: The hall seats two hundred people

Incorrect: anywhere will do
Correct: Any place will do

Incorrect: He is much interested in things Chinese
Correct: he is very interested in Chinese things

Incorrect: Wait here please, I'll come back in a minute
Correct: Wait here please, I'll be back in a minute

Incorrect: I am uncomfortable
Correct: I don't feel well

Incorrect: Come to here
Correct: Come here

Incorrect: Common students in US don't wear a uniform
Correct: The average students in US don't wear a uniform

Incorrect: who cooked this salad?
Correct: who made this salad?

Incorrect: His restaurant attracts lots of customers
Correct: his restaurant attracts lots of guests

Incorrect: My friend Tony died in a traffic accident
Correct: My friend Tony was killed in a traffic accident

Incorrect: Different from me, she is proficient in English
Correct: Unlike me, she is proficient in English

Incorrect: Little children are difficult to understand that
Correct: It is difficult for children to understand that

SOURCE: common mistakes in English vocabulary: http//w.w.w India study channel.com /resource /9610

6. Source

1. The King's English. H.W. And F.G Fowler (O.U.P.)
2. Eats, shoots and leaves. Lynne Truss
3. High School English Grammar & Composition by wren & Martin – revised by N.D.V. Prasada Rao (S.Chand & Co)
4. Words often confused – by Dr. B R Kishore (New light Publisher New Delhi)
5. Linguistic and Social Characteristic of Indian English (Jason Baldridge)
6. Hobson Jobson: by Col.Henry Yule.R.E.C.B. and A.C.Burnell; Ph.D.C.I.E. EDITED BY WILLIAM Crooke B.A. Rupa & Co. Internet.
7. The right word at the right TIME (Reader's Digest Publication)
8. The Internet.

COMMUNICATION - WRITTEN AND ORAL

Oral and Written Communications are distinct from each other, though both are strong props to success – in life as well as in business.

ORAL COMMUNICATION

Oral Communication requires clear articulation, a well modulated tone, a standard pronunciation, a grammatically correct language and effective expression. The pitch should be high enough to reach the audience. Since the speaker is face to face with his audience he can tune in his talk to the response and reaction of his audience. Sometimes, he can moderate or alternate his talk as he goes along. Body language, gestures and eye contact also help the speaker in emphasizing his words or conveying his message. To be effective, oral communication needs to be fluent, appropriate and accurate.

Fluency

Fluency may be defined as the ability to speak with ease and facility and convey one's thoughts, ideas and schemes to the audience. Clear thinking, logical analysis, apt expression, good mechanics of writing and wide reading help fluency. Exposure to heterogenous groups of audience and the ability to anticipate their response also help fluency in speaking. Bookish language and scholastic expressions occupy only a secondary place in speaking.

Appropriacy

Appropriacy is the ability to keep in mind the audience, the subject matter and the reason for the talk. The who, what and why should determine the tune and tone of a speaker. The discussions held with a group of scientists or a talk given to a group of academicians will be entirely different from a dialogue held with the union or with colleagues in language, style and tone.

Accuracy

Speech does not require too formal a tone or too official a language. Colloquial language may even create easy camaraderie in speech when used in a group of locals where everyone understands its meaning and significance. Scientific, medical or technical jargon may not baffle where the group follows it easily. However, spoken English does require grammatically correct language, proper usage of words, a style and tone suitable to the occasion.

Great orators and inspiring speakers have sprinkled their speeches with refined humour, interesting anecdotes and enlightening illustrations. They try to drive the point home with reiteration, exclamations and sometimes interrogation (voicing doubts, asking confirmation etc.). But the speaker should not deviate too far away from his topic.

To gain further in sight into oral communication in its various forms refer to – Communicative competence By Shri Varanasi Bhaskara Rao

WRITTEN COMMUNICATION

The written word has a greater permanence and a larger accountability than the spoken one. Written language has to be formal and official; its style, direct and simple and the expression – clear, brief and exact. Jargon and colloquialism are to be avoided. The intimacy enjoyed in oral communication – body language, gesture and facial expressions of the speaker and the response of the audience; their approval or disapproval – cannot be found in written communication. If the writing is woolly, the words-overloaded and the sentences lengthy and complex, the reader may misinterpret the text and draw inferences and conclusion which are not intended by the writer. Writing is a serious business that requires caution, prudence and communicative abilities.

BUSINESS ENGLISH Vs EFFECTIVE ENGLISH

Business English has to be effective English. It is neither antagonistic nor in contrast to standard English. But it has a restricted usage. As discussed in the other chapter of this book, Business English needs to be clear, accurate and simple. There should be a judicious balancing of active and passive voices. A short word for a long one, a familiar word for an unfamiliar one, a verb for a noun are preferable. Foreign phrases, abstract words, circumlocution which lead to ambiguity may be avoided. The format, either conventional or current should be followed. Basic knowledge of grammar and vocabulary are required. The tone has to be appropriate – neither servile, nor bullying. Effective English also requires most or all of the above but it goes beyond the laid down rules and regulations and has a wider, far reaching application.

WHAT MAKES ONE AN EFFECTIVE WRITER?

Reading

As listening precedes speaking, reading precedes writing. What an average reader knows is a pale blue patch of the sky. He has to experience the vastness of the blue expanse through wide, and varied reading which enriches his vocabulary, enhances his creativity and in general widens his horizons.

Reading can be intensive-an indepth study of structures, vocabulary, contents etc. study of textbooks and research material come under this category.

Reading can be extensive, reading for pleasure, independent reading with speed. Pleasure reading enhances receptive skills which in turn generate new ideas and thoughts and lead to productive skills. Absolute originality is a myth and one has to nurture the creative ability by constant reading. A good writer reads intensively as well as extensively.

Types of Reading

Reading can be done in Four different ways –

- Reading the lines
- Reading between lines
- Reading beyond lines
- Reading with involvement

Let's read the following extract from Time magazine, dated February 02, 2009, by Joe Klein in the four different ways mentioned here.

INAUGURATION IN THE ARENA

BY JOE KLEIN

TIME MAGAZINE, FEBRUARY 2, 2009

"I, BARACK HUSSEIN OBAMA, DO SOLEMNLY swear..." Well, nothing was more stunning and cathartic than those few words. Not the remarkable American diorama in all its polychromatic wonder – spread out for miles on the National Mall in Washington. Not the clear, sober cadences of the new President's Inaugural Address. Not the prayers and tears, the unstoppable smiles and barely controlled giddiness of what may have been the happiest crowd ever to grace the nation's capital. A man named Barack Husssein Obama is now the President of the United States. He came as the ultimate outsider in a nation of outsiders – the son of an African visitor and a white woman from Kansas – and he has turned the country inside out. That he leads now is a breathtaking statement of America's open-mindedness and, yes, its native liberality. Even before his first act as President, and no matter how he fares in the office, he stands as a singular event in American history.

Reading the Lines

When we read the lines, we understand the extract describes Barack Obama's inauguration. The crowd is overjoyed. His election is an evidence of America's open mindedness and liberalism.

Reading the lines, helps to grasp the general meaning, to pick out the theme, events or ideas.

Reading between lines

Reading between lines helps to understand the writer's purpose or attitude, to respond to figurative language, appreciate humour, pathos etc.; indirectly, to enrich vocabulary and improve and understand structures better.

The writer eulogises the innate liberality of America. A careful reading of the following lines makes us realize it –

"He came as the ultimate outsider in a nation of outsiders. The son of an African visitor and a White Woman from Kansas and he has turned the country inside out".

'He stands as a singular event in American history'

Figurative Language

"Not the prayers and tears, the unstoppable smiles and barely controlled giddiness", The emotionally swayed crowds are immediately visualized. The resplendence of the occasion is mirrored.

Vocabulary Enrichment

We come across at least three words which take us to the dictionary – Cathartic, diorama, Polychromatic.

Catharsis is a purification or purgation that brings about spiritual renewal or release from tension. Caught in the seizures of recession, economic instability and despondency, America looks at the new president with high hopes, great optimism and deep faith. The word Cathartic reflects all these emotions and more –

Diorama is a scenic representation in which a partly translucent painting is seen from distance through an opening.

The actual oath-taking ceremony which has all the magic and mesmerism of a faery tale, is witnessed by vast crowds spread out for miles and miles on the national mall. The word diorama brings out the picture perfect, vision like reality of the scene.

Polychromatic refers to something multicoloured, a radiation that is composed of more than one length. People gathered on the national mall are of different races, ages, nationalities and social status. Polychromatic reflects all these variations.

Reading between lines is critical and intensive reading. Though the vocabulary used here is unfamiliar and scholastic it is apt and reflects the glory and magnitude of the event.

Reading beyond the lines

Will the radiant hopes of the milling crowds be fulfilled? Will racial prejudices raise their ugly heads in future? Or the nations come together to make the world a truly global village? A heaven on earth?

We read beyond the lines to speculate consequences.

Reading with Involvement

As we read the extract, we become one with the crowd, we almost hear the "Clear, sober cadences of the new President's inaugural address", we experience the "barely controlled giddiness" of the happy crowds.

This is reading with involvement, we identify ourselves with the characters, agree or disagree with the writer.

However mere reading will not make one an effective writer though it may generate ideas and highlight hitherto unknown areas of thought. Along with wide reading, effective writing needs rich content, originality, appropriate language and good mechanics of writing. Each idea has to be linked to the second one, each sentence to the next one with proper linkers. One paragraph should logically follow the other. The entire piece of writing should be one unit.

'Enemies, People' from PRECOCIOUS AUTOBRIOGRAPHY by Yev geny Yev TUSHENKO. Stands in sharp contrast to the article by Joe Klein. The language is simple, devoid of all ornamentation. There are no scholastic, unfamiliar words. Yet, the poignancy and emotional drama of the incident cannot be missed. The simple act of an old woman, giving a crust of bread to one of the soldiers, who, she feels, is not an enemy but a fellow human being in need of help, teaches a profound lesson in compassion, sympathy and humane values.

ENEMIES, PEOPLE

In 41 Mama took me back to Moscow. There I saw our enemies for the first time. If my memory is right, nearly twenty thousands German war prisoners were to be marched in a single column through the streets of Moscow. The pavements swarmed with onlookers, cordoned off by soldiers and police. The crowds were mostly women – Russian women with hands roughened by hard work, lips untouched by lipstick and thin hunched shoulders which had borne half the burden of the war. Every one of them must have had a father or a husband, a brother or a son killed by the Germans. They gazed with hatred in the direction from which the coloumn was to appear.

At last we saw it. The generals marched at the head, massive chins stuck out, lips folded disdainfully, their whole demeanour meant to show superiority over their plebeian victors. The women were clenching their fists. It was all the soldiers and policemen could do to hold them back. They saw German soldiers, thin, unshaven, wearing dirty bloodstained bandages, hobbing on crutches or leaning on the shoulders of their comrades; the soldiers walked with their heads down.

The street became dead silent – the only sound was the shuffling of boots and the thumping of crutches. Then I saw an elderly woman in broken-down boots push herself forward and touch a policeman's shoulder, saying: 'Let me through'- There must have been something about her that made him step aside. She went to the column, took from inside her coat, something wrapped up in a coloured handkerchief and unfolded it. It was a crust of black bread. She pushed it awkwardly into the pocket of a soldier, so exhausted that he was tottering on his feet. And now suddenly from every side women were running towards the soldiers, pushing into their hands bread, cigarettes, whatever they had. The soldiers were no longer enemies.

They were people.

Here is rich content – magnificent in its simplicity, strikingly real and emerging from the depth of the writer's heart.

THE OTHER COMPLEMENTS

Wide reading, rich content, genuine emotion, ingenuous expression – all go into the making of effective writing. But the rich content and genuine emotions are conveyed through good mechanics of writing – vocabulary and grammar.

VOCABULARY: THE SUBTLE AND THE INTENSE

Vocabulary is vast and varied. Mastering it is an uphill task but appropriate usage of words is a must in writing.

The subtle: As there are myriad tints in nature, so alike, yet so varied,' there are many words which appear to be similar, near synonyms and belong to the same class but with subtle differences. Realisation of these differences, or lack of it, makes the language effective or ineffective.

For Example 'regal' and royal' are synonyms. But we cannot talk about 'the regal family' – The expression, 'furnishings of royal magificence' sounds odd and out of place.

'Illicit and Illegal' are near synonymous. But illicit refers to those actions which are performed without a licence. This word is more limited in usage than illegal.

In the same way Old, old fashioned, obsolete, antique etc. have different connotations.

When we talk of an old man, we refer to his age.

But an old fashioned person can be young in years.

Obsolete refers to something out of use, a kind or style, no longer in use.

Antique: Something that belongs to an earlier period -

an antique mirror

Antiquated ideas are old fashioned ideas that have no relevance to the present day.

The Intense: Certain words have a greater intensity over the others, though they belong to the same family. They can be used only in a particular context. The following series of words illustrate this –

jolly, happy, merry, buoyant, blissful, ecstatic, beatific etc.

important, significant, weighty, momentous, pivotal

plain, homely, ugly, hideous;

whirlwind, storm, hurricane, blizzard

Lonely or solitary?

Words may have overtones and emotional connotation which sometimes decide the usage of a word.

The word lonely means – solitary, desolate. A lonely man is a desolate man, he is all alone, never visited by any one.

A solitary man need not necessarily be sad. He may prefer to be solitary – someone who is unaccompanied or something which stands all by itself – is solitary.

What is the Area?

It is wrong to think that each word has one specific meaning. The meaning of a word may vary in different contexts. The word value means differently when I say

"what is the value of this ring?"

I am referring to the price.

But when I say

'He values his good name' – I mean to say that

he takes pride in his name and tries to keep up his reputation.

When a word has two or more area meanings it should not be used in close proximity, which leads to confusion.

Eg: The two girls took nearly twenty minutes to reach the pillar box – only to find, they could not reach it.

The first reach refers to arriving at the destination, whereas the second refers to the height of the pillar box.

Akin but not Exact

Some words appear to be similar in pronunciation and spelling but there is a subtle difference in spelling and this alters the meaning and calls for a different usage.

The following sentences highlight this –

He made a judicial decision

The judiciary can make a judicial decision. What do we want to say?

He made a judicious decision

Judicious is discrete, fit, apt etc.

It is an officious letter

Officious has the archaic meaning of being dutiful, kind or obliging.

In the modern parlance, it conveys a negative sense – bossy, dictatorial, impertinent etc.

The writer wants to say,

It is an official letter / document etc.

An official is one who holds an office or is invested with an office; an official document is one which comes from the office.

The following pairs of words, used indiscriminately may cause confusion or lead to trouble.

Requisition – requisite

Classical – classic

Childish – childlike

Imminent – immanent – eminent

Illusion – elusion, allusion

Draught – drought

One has to be extremely careful in using these words. If in doubt, please consult a dictionary.

Glossing: One cannot avoid using new words.

A longer word. Sometime, may be more apt and may express the meaning better. In such cases, a gloss is put in parenthesis, to make the meaning clear.

In general, they are extremely ductile – that is, they pull out very easily.

If any light metal is lightly attacked with acid – 'etched' – as it is called

This practice makes the writing clear.

NURTURE, NOURISH AND STRENGTHEN

The first step in picking up vocabulary is referring to a dictionary, knowing the pitfalls in the usage and avoiding them. This is passive learning. One has to make a conscientious effort to nurture, nourish and strengthen his vocabulary. But the words are too many, the meanings – too subtle, varied and variable. There is a continuous influx of new words. How does one remember and retain all these words, their meanings and the usage? How can one update one's linguistic skills?

few clues –

- Wide and intensive reading
- Learn the meanings -
- Infer the contextual meaning while reading. Underline the difficult words as you go along and refer the dictionary at a later stage. Check how far or how close you are from the actual meaning.
- Familiarise the unfamiliar word by association with names, places and people. A word like "pulchritude", rings no bells; but, beauty is a familiar word. Remember a beautiful face, name, person or experience.
- "Trifles make perfection, but perfection is no trifle" – remember the subtle and the intense.
- Make use of new, complex, unfamiliar words to remember them better.
- Use a Thesaurus to expand your vocabulary.
- Go beyond the word for its proper usage
- See the extended or secondary meanings.

See the root words and the derivatives. For eg.- 'Filius' is a Latin word meaning 'Son'; words like "filial", "filicide" – have this root. Is the word 'affiliated' also related to this root? Officially linked to a larger (parent) organization is affiliated – a branch and a parent organization that are linked together.

GRAMMAR

Grammar appears dry and tough to many, but it alone can guarantee accuracy. In oral communication, grammar is sometimes overlooked, but writing requires the basic knowledge of grammar. Some of the common pitfalls are discussed here.

THE PITFALLS

Error of parallelism

Parallel constructions add clarity, elegance and symmetry to writing. Words, phrases and statements are to be co-ordinated to be grammatically parallel; noun to be aligned with noun, verb with verb and phrase with phrase. Look at the following examples.

(a) It was both a long meeting and very tedious (Incorrect)
  a better structure is –

  The meeting was both long and tedious.

(b) To teach, to supervise and delegating work – are a few of the tasks our office manager performs.

  a better structure is -

  To teach, to supervise and to delegate work are a few of the tasks our office manager performs.

(c) Poor writing costs money, wastes time and customers feel alienated.

  a better structure is –

Poor writing costs money, wastes time and alienates customers.

The subject is poor writing – a second subject "customers" cannot be used.

Ambiguity created by Pronouns

Look at the following sentence.

John told Tom that he had passed the examination.

Does 'he' refer to John or Tom? It is not clear

The delicate Relatives

The relative pronouns sometimes cause problems.

The relative pronouns - who, whom, whose are used for persons

'Which' is used for things

'that' is used for both

Is it 'who' or 'whom'?

Normally who is used for persons in the nominative case and does the work of the subject of a sentence.

The boy who stood first in the class, is well known to me.

The boy stood first in the class

He is well known to me

The pronoun 'who' clearly refers to the boy

The pronoun 'whom' is said to be in the accusative case and is the object of a sentence.

The boy whom we all admired, disappointed us.

We all admired the boy – He disappointed us.

We is the subject and boy is the object. Though in the sentence 'the boy' appears to be the subject, it is not so. If the voice is changed, the relative pronoun changes.

The boy who is admired by all of us –

This is grammatically correct

Look at the following examples.

There are some who (not whom) I think are clever

They were a people whom (not who) it was not advisable to excite

It was not advisable to excite them.

They were such people

The relative pronoun -

'whom' takes the place of them in the first sentence.

Whose is used in speaking of persons, animals and also things without life

Eg.: The dog whose bark is so loud _ _ _ _ _

The tree whose branches are cut _ _ _ _ _

The relative pronoun 'that' is normally used for inanimate objects, trees etc; but it is preferred to who or which in the following sentences.

After adjectives in the superlative degree.

The wisest man that ever lived, made mistakes

After the words – same, any, all, none, nothing only.

Man is the only animal that can talk

All is well that ends well

After the interrogative pronouns – who, what;

Who am I that I should object?

What is there that he does not know?

The distributive pronouns

Each, every, any, either, neither – are distributive pronouns. They are followed by the verb in singular.

Eg.: Each one of you <u>is</u> capable of getting admitted to IIM's.

Neither of the brothers is disciplined.

The distributive pronouns are followed by the pronoun 'he' if the gender is not specified.

Each one has to carryout his duties.

It is grammatically wrong to say

One has to carryout his duties

This indefinite pronoun 'one' takes only 'one' and no other pronoun.

One has to carry out one's duties.

Though it sounds pedantic and artificial, grammarians insist on this usage.

Difference between –

Either -

Either - or

Either means one of the two. The verb that follows this is always in singular.

Either of the sisters is/has ______ is perfectly correct.

However, the correlative conjunction 'either – or' is governed by different rules –

Either he or his friends have to complete the assignment / have to give an explanation etc.

The second subject following '- or' decides the Verb.

In the same way, 'neither' refers to two people or things –

Eg.: Neither of the songs is to my liking.

In neither – nor, the subject following – 'nor' decides the verb.

Neither he nor his friends have attended the meeting.

With the first person 'I' – a different verb is used.

Neither he nor I am present

A better construction is –

Neither he is present nor I am

This / That

These / Those

Look at the following sentence.

The Literature of India is more ancient than America.

(This is incorrect)

We cannot compare the Literature of India with America. We have to compare it with the Literature of America.

The Literature of India is more ancient than that of America or, the Literature of India is more ancient than America's. The sentence is structurally correct.

Placement of Adverbs

The placement of adverbs is very essential.

Some of the common errors:

Interchange of very and too

Very and too are not interchangeable

'too' means "in excess of"

"I am very tired," is, preferable to

"I am too tired".

In the same way, the use of 'never' for 'not' is not acceptable. It is ridiculous to say

'Kipling was never born in London'

Adjectives and adverbs are not interchangeable. It is grammatically wrong to say –

He will pay dear

It should be –

He will pay dearly

It is wrong to say –

Always aim highly

It should be

Always aim high -

It is wrong to say –

"This hardly won liberty was not to be lightly abandoned".

'Hardly' is negative. The sentence implies that we did not win liberty.

It is correct to say –

"This hard won liberty was not to be lightly abandoned.

'Only' and 'Enough'

The adverb 'enough' is to be placed after the word it modifies.

The room is big enough to accommodate seventy students.

He is foolish enough to answer back his boss.

The adverb "only" should be placed before the word it modifies.

He has written only four books (not more than four)

Note how the meaning of a sentence changes with the placement of "only".

That student passed only in Economics (not in other subjects)

Only that student passed in Economics (others did not)

That student only passed in Economics (not a high score – just passed)

If a sentence contains an adverb of time, place and manner the sequence to be followed is –

Adverb of manner	- (melodiously, sweetly, angrily etc.)
Adverb of place	- (at the concert, here, outside)
Adverb of time	- (Yesterday, now etc.)

Wrong placement of an adverb sends unwanted connotations and creates chaos.

Some of the adverbs may appear similar but they can not be interchanged. The following are adverbs of degree

rather, fairly, barely, much, almost

rather and fairly mean moderately, but fairly is used with favourable adj. Thus, one can say –

I have done the exam fairly well

But one cannot say –

I have done the exam rather well

One cannot say –

It is fairly hot in Hyderabad

One has to say –

It is rather hot

In the same way

Whether cannot be interchanged For - <u>if</u>

Unless	"	"	until
Though	"	"	yet
Where	"	"	wherever

The Participle

The participle is a verb adjective and it must be attached to some noun or pronoun.

Eg.: A rolling stone gathers no moss

A lost opportunity never returns

Errors occur, if the participle is left without a proper subject reference. The following example creates confusion because of this error.

Standing on the bridge, the river flows away.

The participle "standing" cannot refer to the river. The sense becomes clear when we say -

standing on the bridge, I saw the river flowing away.

Another example:

Entering the room, the decorations were breath – taking

A clearer construction is –

Entering the room, I found the decorations (were) to be breath taking.

Where the participle is understood, there is no need of subject reference.

Sword in hand, he rushed on the jailor.

He held the sword in hand and he rushed out. The subject is he in both parts of the sentence.

Chaotic Correlatives

Conjunctions which are used in pairs are called correlative conjunctions. The function of a conjunction is to join two words or two sentences.

Some of the correlative conjunctions are –

Either	- or
Neither	- nor
Both	- and
Not only	- but also
As soon	- as
Scarcely	- when
No sooner	- than
Seldom or	- never

When the writer is confused and mixes two legitimate constructions in one sentence, a faulty construction emerges. The following sentence illustrates this –

No sooner had she reached the station when the train left.

No sooner is always followed by than –

No sooner had she reached the station than the train had left.

The following construction is wrong –

We were not only interested in his achievements but by his potential.

We were interested not only in his achievements but also by his potential.

(both followed by prepositions)

or

We were not only interested in his achievement but also impressed by his potential.

(both followed by a finite verb)

Seldom or never and 'seldom, if ever' – both are correct. The phrase 'seldom or ever' is meaningless.

We seldom or ever see those for saken who trust in God.

It should be 'seldom or never'

'Like' and 'as' are sometimes wrongly interchanged.

He dresses like his father.

or

He dresses as his father does

We cannot say 'he dresses like his father does'.

Eg.: I try to sing as my teacher, M.S.Subbalakshmi, sings

or

I try to sing like my teacher, M.S.Subbalakshmi

Both are correct.

CONCLUSION

It is said, "a botanist knows the Chemistry of a flower, not its poetry". Grammar, usage, vocabulary are the Chemistry of writing. No one can undermine their importance. But rich content, genuine emotions, innovative thinking, creative urge – these are the poetry of writing. Effective writing is a judicious combination of both.

ANNEXURE

EFFECTIVE AND IMMORTAL

A few examples of effective writing

Gandhiji's Talisman

"I will give you a talisman. Whenever you are in doubt, or when the self becomes too much with you, apply the following test. Recall the face of the poorest and the weakest man (woman) whom you may have seen, and ask yourself, if the step you contemplate is going to be of any use to him (her). Will he (she) gain anything by it? Will it restore him (her) to a control over his (her) own life and destiny? In other words, will it lead to swaraj (freedom) for the hungry and spiritually starving millions?

Then you will find your doubts and your self melt away".

- One of the last notes left behind by Gandhi in 1948, expressing his deepest social thought.

Source: Mahatma Gandhi [Lat Phase, Vol. II (1958), P.65]

The language is simple, the expression – direct, but the message is clear.

Note the expression, "hungry and spiritually starving" –

The hunger and starvation relate to the soul.

The last line –

"Then you will find your doubts and your self melt away".

Not only your doubts disappear, you also melt away – you lose your identity, you become one with the society, the nation; you understand the meaning of 'Swaraj'.

The simplicity and truthfulness of the man is reflected in his words.

Equally powerful are the words of Swami Vivekananda; but the style and language are entirely different.

"This is the great fact – strength is life, weakness is death; strength is felicity, life eternal, immortal; weakness is constant strain and misery; weakness is death".

There is repetition, there is reiteration – but there is inspiration.

He also says,

> "Feel, my children, feel. Feel for the poor, the ignorant, the downtrodden; feel till the heart stops and the brain reels and you think you will go mad; then pour the soul out at the feel of the Lord, and then will come power, help and indomitable energy."

The words are intoxicating and energizing and the mind reels under their impact. The high rhetoric gives strength and effect to the passage.

The Dreamer

MARTIN LUTHER KING JR: ON THE MALL IN WASHINGTON 1963

> I say to you today, my friends, that in spite of the difficulties and frustrations of the moment I still have a dream. It is a dream deeply rooted in the American Dream… I have a dream that one day on the red hills of Georgia the sons of former slaves and the sons of former slave owners will be able to sit down together at the table of brotherhood… I have a dream that my four little children will one day live in a nation where they will not be judged by the color of their skin but by the content of their character. I have a dream today…. And if America is to be a great nation this must become true. So let freedom ring from the prodigious hilltops of New Hampshire. Let freedom ring from the mighty mountains of New York. Let freedom ring from the heightening Alleghenies of Pennsylvania! From every mountainside, let freedom ring. When we let freedom ring, when we let it ring from every village and every hamlet, from every state and every city, we will be able to speed up that day when all God's children, black men and white men, Jews and Gentiles, Protestants and Catholics, will be able to join hands and sign in the words of the old Negro spiritual, "Free at last! At last ! Thank God Almighty, we are free at last"!

These are not words. These are visions of a Blackman whose soul cries out in anguish for freedom. He wants to cry out, "Free at last! at last!"

Almost four decades and a half later, his dreams come true. Barack H. Obama becomes the 44th President of America, a powerful speakes who wields the language most effectively.

From Obama's Inaugural Address

Extracts from Obama's inaugural speech

My fellow citizens: I stand here today humbled by the task before us, grateful for the trust you have bestowed, mindful of the sacrifices borne by our ancestors.

Forty-four Americans have now taken the presidential oath.

The words have been spoken during rising tides of prosperity and the still waters of peace.

Yet, every so often the oath is taken amidst gathering clouds and raging storms.

At these moments, America has carried on not simply because of the skill or vision of those in high office, but because we the people have remained faithful to the ideals of our forbearers, and true to our founding documents.

So it has been. So it must be with this generation of Americans.

The first sentence which is very compact is written in simple English. He is humbled at the immense task that lies a head of him, but grateful that the people have chosen him to carry out this task and aware of the sacrifices made by his predecessors. All his thoughts are expressed in concise but effective English.

"The rising tides of prosperity and still waters of peace" are apt metaphors,

"Gathering clouds and raging storms" symbolize the strenuous struggles the country has faced. The last sentence is appealing for its simplicity, effective for its sincerity.

For we know that our patchwork heritage is strength, not a weakness. We are a nation of Christians and Muslims, Jews and Hindus-and non-believers. We are shaped by every language and culture, drawn from every end of this Earth; and because we have tasted the bitter swill of civil war and segregation, and emerged from that dark chapter stronger and more united, we cannot help but believe that the old hatreds shall someday pass; that the lines of tribe shall soon dissolve; that as the world grows smaller, our common humanity shall reveal itself; and that America must play its role in ushering in a new era of peace.

The expression "Patchwork heritage" reflects the "Polychromatic wonder" of America. The tone is very positive. Obama talks of 'Common humanity' but also declares that America will play the leader in ushering in a new era of peace.

> This is the source of our confidence-the knowledge that god calls on us to shape an uncertain destiny. This is the meaning of our liberty and our creed-why men and women and children of every race and every faith can join in celebration across this magnificent mall, and why a man whose father less than 60 years ago might not have been served at a local restaurant can now stand before you to take a most sacred oath.

Obama describes the creed of America and defines liberty. This is also the vision of Martin Luther King Jr. come true; an answer to his anguished cry. Obama becoming the president proves "the patchwork of heritage is strength, not a weakness".

Source

Communication in Business by Peter Little.

Communicative competence by Varanasi Bhaskara Rao

High School English Grammar & Compositon by Wren and Martin

CONVERSATIONS IN WRITING

'Communication is an interchange of thoughts, opinions or information through speech, writing or signs.' Says Robert Handerson. Organizations thrive on communication _especially, written communication 'since everything cannot be informed or instructed. Written communication takes the form of Business Letters, Memos, Circulars, Reports, Fax, E-mails etc.

Good Business Letters 'will become excellent ambassadors for you and your organization,' and are the lifeline of any modern organization. But as you sit down at your desk with a serious intention of writing a letter, you suddenly find that the message or information you want to send is lost somewhere between the brain and the page. You know what you want to say but are not sure how to express it effectively. You feel the inadequacy of your linguistic skill, you are at a loss to distinguish relevant information from the irrelevant, and are not sure of the salutation or the conclusion of your letter. 'With doubt and dismay you are smitten'. You find you are fumbling, waffling. For most of us speaking comes naturally, but writing requires an effort. How can we overcome this apparently insurmountable hurdle?

We can --- by taking the props of practice and perseverance.

"True ease in writing comes from art, not chance,

As those move easiest who have learned to dance."

(Alexander Pope)

Effective writing is a skill which has to be learned and mastered over a period of time, to be practised persistently and pursued relentlessly.

THE SUBSTANCE---AND THE SPIRIT

A business letter, to be effective must take care of two areas----

- *The substance*
- *The spirit*

The substance------by substance I mean the lay out /structure of the letter, the formal language appropriate to the letter, division of paragraphs, length of paragraph, sub titling, numbering etc. A business letter with proper spacing, with proper punctuation marks, without grammatical errors creates a favourable impression and the recipient may pick it out of the pile of letters that he has to look into.

The Spirit—the lay out is only the skeleton. It has to be filled with flesh and blood. Life must be breathed into it so that it will achieve the purpose for which it is written "It will get things done for you". Soft skills acquired throughout your career and outside it, skills imbibed from the family, peer group and society play a vital role here. Courtesy, style of the letter, the tone, the mood – all contribute to the effectiveness of the letter. A good business letter must be a harmonious blend of substance and spirit

COMPETENCY IN COMMUNICATION

A business letter can be written to different people for different purposes. For it to be successful, you must **KNOW YOUR READER.**

You must know whether your reader is a

Layman, An expert, An executive, A user.

If you know your reader, you can tailor your message better---suitable to his experience, age, temperament, seniority etc.

KNOW THE PURPOSE OF YOUR LETTER.

A letter may convey information, carry instructions; it may persuade or apologize; it may be a letter of complaint, or an answer to a complaint. Depending on the purpose, write down your letter. If the letter has more than one purpose, concentrate on the most important one. One letter cannot have too many objectives.

PROCESSING-- It is the journey to the drafting of the letter, or the actual writing of the letter

CHARACTERISTICS OF A GOOD BUSINESS LETTER

Brevity, simplicity, precision, tone, culture, style of the letter, the language -- all go into the making of a good business letter.

Brevity-----A good business letter should be brief and to the point. As Joseph Priestlly says, "the more elaborate our means of communication, the less we communicate".

The business people are busy and have limited time to read letters. The busy executive would like to skim through it and get to the bottom line. Moreover the interest in the business letter goes as far as it affects the working world. However, brevity is not synonymous with rudeness .Precision is not being blunt or offending.

The following two different ways of conveying the same information clarify the difference between brevity and bluntness.

"After carefully reviewing the proposal ,we have decided to prioritize other projects in the quarter.."

"Nobody liked your project idea, so we are not going to give you any funding."

The second statement is brief and to the point, but here courtesy is made a casualty. The first expression, though indirect, is less offensive and more diplomatic and is preferrable to the second one .Be precise, clear, but courteous.

THE ROAD LESS TRAVELLED

Till Recently very formal expressions, stuffy language, long sentences are used in business letters.

The modern trend is a conversational tone, familiar words, known phrases, and shorter sentences. Active voice is preferred to passive voice and verbs to nouns. Let us remember, there is no business English, there is only standard English.

AVOID THESE PHRASES

According to the communication workshop in port Washington N.Y., and the secretary's letter we should avoid following phrases.

....To be perfectly honest

Needless to say

Enclosed herewith, please find

If you should have any further questions, please do not hesitate to call

For your perusal, review and kind consideration

We deem it advisable

It has come to my attention

The undersigned

Pursuant to your request

Transparent to the user

Under separate cover etc

OFFICIAL, NOT OFFICIOUS

In the same way, some of the sentences are verbose, officious and full of jargon and clichés. But they have been followed for a long time and some people still consider them to be business English

For example —

'I am in receipt of your esteemed favor'

Sounds very verbose. __ Esteemed favour is unnecessary, obsequious.

A sentence like

'Thank you for your letter of' is much better'.

An expression like

'We are endeavoring to procure' __ can be altered to "We are trying to get"

Another commonly used business expression is

'Kindly acknowledge receipt of the same.'

The use of 'the same' as a pronoun is not standard English.

'Kindly' is officious here. __'Please send us a receipt' is much better

Technical language must be avoided in a business letter unless you are writing to an expert. If it is absolutely necessary to use technical words define and explain the words.

> An environmental services brochure that was sent to purchasing managers used such language as "An aquifer characterization in situ volatilization to treat the vadose zone".

What does the recipient make out from this?

BE ACTIVE---

A balanced sentence makes use of active as well as passive voice.

However in business world passive voice is used more frequently than active voice; this makes the sentence vague. Sometimes it is difficult to fix up the responsibility.

Look at the following example

The net benefits of the shareholders are grossly overestimated.

Who overestimated? It is vague. If you are the team leader and do not want to draw attention to yourself you can resort to such language.

But it is not always possible to use active voice. Active voice is not necessary when the cause of action is of little importance.

News of the merger was reported this morning.

It is not important who reported the merger. The fact that a merger took place is important.

"Those terms are often misunderstood in business circles". There is no need to say by whom? It is implicit.

JARGON, CLICHES, TRITE PHRASES.

'---The word jargon is most useful if reserved for derogatory reference to the special language of a trade, profession or field of study', says Peter Little in the book, 'Communication in Business.'

Jargon is to be avoided as it may not be understood by an outsider .If you are in publishing house you may talk about ***'blue line', 'dummy', 'mechanical'*** etc Expressions like __

Terminate the illusion----for switch off the light

or

Revenue commitment-----for—tax increase, __Sound ludicrous.

Following examples focus on scientific jargon.

The biota exhibited hundred percent mortality response.
In simple English - All the fish died
The architect talks of fenestration
when he means the number of windows in a building
The hospital almoner uses 'domiciliary patients'
to refer to patients in their own homes
ambulants
to refer to those that can walk.

TRITE PHRASES-----

Trite phrases do not make the writing effective. They make your writing foggy and confuse the reader. An example,

In 'THE MANAGER'S GUIDE TO BUSINESS WRITING' Suzanne D .Sparks gives the following example of an application

My resume, though brief, and my little brochure pretty well tell my story. In a nutshell I tired of the rat race after over a quarter century and seven years, have been my own man .But as my free lancer knows ,things blow hot and cold, and I am certainly not booked to full capacity. A steady thing for a couple of days a week might be right down my alley.

What does the applicant really want ? He wants a part time job. But the receiver may not go beyond the first two lines and can never reach the focal point..

THE TONE

A business letter is a professional document. and requires professionalism. If you are out of tone and tune, it wastes the time of your recipient, kills contracts, turns your customers into foes.

According to Chrissie Wright, the tone must be positive, definite and sincere in a business letter

Be positive---

Avoid negative words and expressions. Do not mention what you cannot do or what the other person has not done.

Do not say __ 'Your failure to take action'.

Say __ 'We expect prompt action in future.'

Do not say __ 'We cannot supply your goods by first of June'.

Say __ 'We will definitely be able to supply your requirement by1st July.'

If the information is negative and you have to convey it, give a reason for what happened, soften the blow. If you are in the wrong, or, the company made a mistake, don't hesitate to apologize. Look at the following examples.

'It is essential that you comply with our request. We shall have to institute legal action against you if you do not remit the full amount of your liability by June 3rd.'

A better and a more diplomatic way of putting it is _"Please remit your payment by June 3rd to avoid legal action".

Look at this example

'Due to an error in processing your order, it was billed more than once to your account, credit has been issued and we hope you are not inconvenienced.'

Better admit the mistake at the outset and mention the action taken.

'We apologize for the inconvenience of our processing error. We have corrected your account'.

In the same way, do not postpone complimenting the other person, if he did something worth complimenting. If there is good news to convey, do it immediately A genuine written appreciation is a treasured memento. Your reader may go back to it again and again or show it to his friends

'Congratulations! You have done it again!

'Welcome to Neeraj Industries. You are a member of our family now' [offering a job)

'Here is good news for you.'[a promotion offer]

Be definite.

Avoid foggy expressions

Don't say,

'As soon as possible; mention the date or month,---by the end of June;

Don't say, 'As expressed in my previous letter-'say exactly what you have expressed ,then give the date and reference no. etc.

Instead of saying 'I will hold the tickets for you', 'say I'll hold the tickets for you for three days'. Say 'complete the work by December.' instead of saying, 'complete the work as soon as you can.'

AVOID INTENSIFIERS

Hyperbole and exaggeration have no place in business letters.. Your letter must convince your reader that you will carry out your promises. Though natural and appropriate in a casual conversation, intensifiers should be avoided in professional writing. Avoid expressions like---'extraordinary, literally, really, totally, absolutely, sensational, amazing, revolutionary"—etc.

A good letter captures the reader's attention immediately.

A complimentary, positive beginning sets the tone of your letter.

A positive tone---

It has always been my dream to-----

I have been a fan of your company ever since I set my eyes on your computer

A question

can arouse the interest of your reader-

Did you ever face the problem----?

Do you know that-------?

Would you like a steady supply of superior quality elements , for your popular electric heater, ovens, and toasters?

Introduce an element of surprise to grab the attention of your reader.

"In the last three years, I have tracked down and brought to justice eight of the FBI's ten most wanted criminals-"

"Latest Japanese machinery operated by a team and well trained work force has enabled us to supply elements that meet the exacting standards of leading firms such as Hot Pot, Super Heat, Vikram Lites. We will be happy to supply elements to you also".

CUSTOMER CARE

Though a business letter must be objective ,and cannot entertain any personal likes or dislikes, it need not be a series of brisk sentences. Your customer is, no doubt, a busy businessman, but he is also a human being. "Tickle his ego". Let him know that you care for him. Suzanne D. Sparks gives the following examples

Sample-A

This is to announce that as of June $18^{th,}$ Bagin Technology will begin manufacturing computerized controls for power lawn mowers in order to enter an expanding market that will allow the company to take advantage of its leading position in electronics controls

Sample-B

As one of our loyal customers you should be among the first to know our big news. As of June 18th Bagin Technology will begin manufacturing computerized controls for power lawn mowers. You have helped make us the leaders in the world of electronic controls, and we would like to show our appreciation for your trust by expanding to serve your needs for electronic controls,

Sample A conveys information but is too business like, whereas sample B has a pleasing personal touch and makes the customer continue to read.

PERSONAL BUT PROFESSIONAL----

Giving a personal touch does not mean crossing the line of control, forgetting the etiquette of business communication, forgetting professionalism.

PERSONAL BUT UNPROFESSIONAL

The following letter is personal but unprofessional and casual. The writer is in a real hurry.

LETTER – A

Fine Foods LTD.
10, Bridge street
London
S.W.105 TG

Hello Mr. ROGER Jones,

I got the letter you sent on 1st September and the stuff about the stock control system you made. It Sounds great for us, but I want to check something before I buy it. You said the system is bang up to date

But what happens if you update it again soon? Do we get money off the new one? You said it takes three weeks to install the system---that's too long. Can't you do it any quicker? Hope you can reply soon. We are in a bit of a hurry.

Thanks,
Janet Brown.

LETTER – B

Is professional following the etiquettes of Business Communications.

Fine Foods Ltd
10 Bridge Street
London
SW105TG

Mr. R. JONES
Sales Manager
Thames Software Systems
River Buildings
Stockwell Walk
London
SW17 5HG
12th September 2006

Dear Mr. Jones,

Stock Control Software System

Thank you for your letter of 1st September and the information you sent regarding the stock control system offered by your company I certainly feel the system will meet our requirements. However, there are some points which I would like clarified before we go ahead and order the system.

Firstly, although you mentioned that the system has recently been updated, I wonder whether we might be eligible for a discount on any future upgrades.

Secondly, the installation and Implementation period of three weeks, to which you refer in your letter, seems rather long. Is there any possibility of getting the stems up and running on a shorter timescale?

I would be very grateful for a swift response to these queries, in order that we can begin the process as soon as possible.

Thank you in advance for your assistance. I look forward to your reply.

Yours sincerely,

J. Brown

Ms J. Brown

Purchasing Manager

A Business Letter – Try activities C. B.B.C—British Council 2006

SHIFT OF EMPHASIS FROM I \WE -------- YOU

A successful businessman shifts the emphasis from I or WE to YOU. and thus makes it clear that his interest lies in the interest of his customer. Bill Scott in his 'The Skills Of Communication,' says, "any letter in which the first word is 'I' or 'WE 'carries with it an impression of an arrogant writer".

I, WE attitude---	You attitude
We have received your letter of June12	Thank you for your letter of June12
I am happy to report	You will be happy to know
My long experience as a sales person	Your company will reap the rich fruits of my experience
I have five years experience as a sales executive	My five years' experience as a sales executive will enable me
We have shipped the two dozen steel racks You Ordered	Your two dozen steel racks must reach you soon, with this Letter.

CARE FOR CULTURE

In International correspondence we have to be specially careful in choice of words. The receiver who may have an entirely different background, and whose culture may be at variance with yours, should not feel offended at your language .It is also advisable to avoid gender specific words. This is a matter of sensitivity and your recipient (a-she)may feel excluded if not properly addressed. Any unnecessary mention of physical appearance, race, and marital state should be avoided. Instead of saying 'a male nurse, a female engineer 'use gender neutral language.

Gender neutral	Gender specific.
Chair person	chairman.
Mechanic	repairman
Fire fighter	fireman
Work hours	man hours
Supervisor	foreman
Humankind / Humanity	Mankind

A conversation in writing is a skill that can be acquired only with great care and effort. It has a long lasting, far reaching effect and can make or mar your career. Let us remember, "communication works for those who work at it" and treat it with the necessary seriousness.

LAYOUT OF A BUSINESS LETTER

A business Letter can be either blocked or indented. Many companies choose their own layout, which is normally the established, conventional, British way of writing. The blocked form, which is of a later origin and is generally followed today, is more practical and is easier to handle .In the blocked form everything starts at the left margin; with open punctuation----- (all punctuation marks outside the main body of the letter are omitted.) Whether blocked or indented every letter must have a lay out or structure. The letterhead on which the letter is written contains the name of the firm or company and its address.

It also carries a column for reference number.

Then comes the date ---it is usually written on the right hand side, parallel to the reference number .It is not a standard practice to write the abbreviated form of the date like-----18-11-2008, or,11-18-2008;A much better and standard way of putting the date is

18 November 2008, or November 18, 2008.

INSIDE ADDRESS

It contains the name and address of the organisation or individual to whom the letter is being sent. It follows the reference number

Each and every business letter must contain the following----

- Salutation.
- Heading.
- Body of the letter
  Introduction,
  The Text
  Closing line and concluding remarks
- Signature Block
- Enclosures

SALUTATION

The formal style of salutation is:

Dear Mr .Freddie

Dear Mrs.Freddie (for married ladies).

Dear Miss. Freddie,--(for unmarried ladies)

However, Miss and Mrs are substituted by Ms in the modern day business world.

If the reader's name is not known you might use a job title like –

Dear Production Manager etc.

If the name is not known,

Dear Sir, Dear Madam,

Dear Sir, or Madam, can also be used. But it is always advisable to take some pains and find out the name of your reader .Even a business letter cannot afford to be so business like. The last form of address shows a lack of personal attention and should be avoided.

While addressing a partnership firm that contains personal name or names, use Messrs.

For example--- Messrs Bulchand &co

Messrs Johnson and sons

Messrs Kumar and Kumar

Messrs Johnson and Brothers

Titles or ranks are used in the following way.

Prof.S.K.Bhatia

Col S. R. Yogesh.

Capt. S.R. Sharma.

Dr. P. K. Vaid.

Rev .S .K. Moses.

Maj. Gen. D.K. Patnaik.

Flt .Lt .G. S Cheema.

Padmashri. R.S .Daruwallah.

Dr (Mrs.) S. Rawat.

The Lighter side

The journalist Frank Giles married Lady Catherine Sackville, who as the daughter of an earl retained her title, after her marriage. On a journey abroad, they received an invitation from the British Embassy, addressed to Mr. and Mrs. GILES. Concerned at the breach of protocol, Giles rang up the embassy and started to explain, 'she isn't exactly Mrs. Giles,' 'that's all right.' said the voice at the other end cheerily.' Bring her along, anyway. We are not at all stuffy here'

Los Angeles Times.Dec.15 1981 in F.S. Pepper 20th century anecdote, sphere 1990.

When a person is addressed by designation like, Secretary, youth Federation of India,

The prefixes like Mr.\ Mrs.\ Ms are not required.

'Your Excellency' is used while addressing the ambassador or high commissioner of a foreign country.

HEADING OR SUBJECT LINE

Immediately after the salutation must come the subject line or heading. The subject line should be brief and tell the busy executive what the letter is about. It need not include all the details.

Look at the following examples.

Supply of 20,000 L.P.G. gas cylinders.

Steel strips, delay in supply.

Instead of giving the invoice no. or reference no. mention the details.

Invoice no.28789 may not mean much to your reader or 'your order no. -------dated-----may not immediately remind him of the actual details.

'Installation of new kitchen units 'can be much better.

The subject line must be separated from the main body of the letter in the following ways—

- By leaving space before and after it.
- By writing it in italics
- By writing it in capital letters.
- By underlining it.

MAIN BODY OF THE LETTER:

The body of the letter contains

(a) Introduction
(b) The text and action point
(c) closing line \concluding remarks

INTRODUCTION

The first part of a letter should identify any previous communication with date, and reference number you should also keep in mind -

- Who the writer is
- The information that you would like to convey
- The action to be taken
- The opening lines of the letter too must point to the topic you are going to write about -

'Your Jan 10 order for--------

Your enquiry regarding -------

After seeing your advertisement in ------------dt--------

THE TEXT----ACTION POINT

This is the part wherein you actually give the necessary information, lodge a complaint, answer a query, apply for a job, ask for information etc. As such it is the most important part of the letter .Before you set out to write your letter go through the description of your task carefully----are you applying for a job? Are you seeking some information? Writing a letter of complaint? Based on the description task identify the requirements and list them. Put them in a language that is simple, conversational and courteous. If an action is required from your company mention clearly what action is proposed by the company, who will take it and when .If an action is required from your recipient, state it clearly, in a polite language.

The action point is to be isolated and highlighted. Place it in a separate paragraph. If necessary use bold letters or italics. Also ensure that all the information provided is relevant, accurate and logically sequenced. Also ensure that no relevant or necessary information is left out.

Closing line & concluding remarks

Taking leave is as important as introducing yourself. You establish or confirm your relationship to the reader, and point the way ahead. A closing line is used to make a reference to a future event, to repeat an apology, or to offer help

For example---

If you require any further information, feel free to contact me;

Once again I apologise for any inconvenience;

I would appreciate your immediate attention to this matter;

Please advise as necessary

As you come to the formal close, you start wondering------ Is it 'Yours faithfully'

or 'yours sincerely' ?Which is suitable and better? Which is inoffensive?

Conventionally, the formal close must match the salutation.

The salutations,

Sir,

Dear sir,

Dear Madam, are followed by Yours faithfully,

The salutations,

Dear Sheila,

Dear Mr. Smith,

Dear Mrs Johnson------are followed by Yours sincerely.

When addressing a good friend as 'Dear Jack',

Best Regards, Best wishes, precede your signature.

SIGNATURE BLOCK

After the complimentary close, the signature must be put and name typed below that.. The signature can be illegible, and the reader may have a difficulty in deciphering the name.

Signature

R.K.ARORA.

If the individual signs in his official capacity his designation should follow the typed name.

Signature

R.K.ARORA

SALES MANAGER

If he is signing on behalf of the company, he should write,

For Arora Associates,

Signature,

R.K.ARORA.

Followed by---partner, Managing trustee, Attorney holder etc.

ENCLOSURES

Important documents, certificates, testimonials, invoice etc are attached to the letter. They should be mentioned on the left hand side of the letter.

Enclosures --------- 3

1-------

2-------

3-------

If the letter is to be forwarded to any one mention it as "c.c. to"

Take care, to go through your letter for the last time, before you send it.

> In1919, the 17th earl of Derby wrote a letter to the foreign secretary beginning,
>
> "My dear Curzon,
>
> I have always known you to be a cad. I now know you to be a liar.'
>
> The letter did not go off in the night's bag from the Paris Embassy .The next morning, Derby looked at it again. 'Perhaps it's a bit too strong. I think I'll have another go. "This time the letter began, 'My Dear George, You and I have known each other too long to quarrel over so small a matter.
>
> Randolph S Churchill, Lord Derby1960in F.S Pepper20th century, anecdotes, Sphere1990

Take a long, hard look, before you put your signature as you are sealing whatever promises you made in the letter. you are committing yourself and your organisation to take certain actions; you are trying to expand the business, gain the goodwill of your customer. Also remember when you say ' I ' you are expressing your own opinion. When you say 'we' you are talking on behalf of your company.

The finest eloquence is that which gets things done.' If the objective of your letter is well understood by your reader, and sets the ball rolling, you have written a good business letter.

OTHER FORMS OF BUSINESS COMMUNICATIONS

CURRICULUM VITAE

'Curriculum Vitae' literally means, "COURSE OF ONE'S LIFE". It is a brochure on yourself and as such, is the first rung of the ladder to employment. A well written C.V, which is interesting and impressive, cajoles the employer to read it to the end and put it in the "possibilities" list, instead of throwing it into the dust. The C.V. should make the employer call you for an interview.

The Planning

Before you set out to write your C.V., look at the job description carefully. Do you have all the required details? Do you have the required qualification and possess the desired skills? If your skills are different from the employer's expectations, can you link and transfer them to the present job that you are applying for?

Think the other way- if you are employing some one, what do you look for in him?

Any employer would look for -

(a) mental caliber such as, academic proficiency, intelligence etc.

(b) Skills - Communication skills, written and oral; Languages known; analytical & research skills.*

(c) Personality: leadership qualities, adaptability, willingness to work, positive attitude, ability to take up responsibility etc.

Keeping in mind the job description and employer's expectations, proceed to write you C.V.

The Format

Though there is no fixed format for a resume, we find the following categories;

(a) Chronological

(b) Functional

(c) A combination of both.

---

* (Refer to communicative competence by Varanasi Bhaskar rao)

Chronological Resume

This is the easiest to prepare as the previous job details are given in a chronological order. There can be a straight chronological order wherein experience is listed in the order it occurred with the most recent employment or education listed last. However, reverse Chronological order is preferred, wherein, the most recent experience tops the list and any employer is genuinely interested in this. Personal details, educational qualifications, work experience etc are mentioned under different heads.

Functional

A functional resume stresses the applicant's areas of skill, personality and achievements instead of filling the application with personal details, academic excellence (achieved long back). An alert applicant, while preparing his resume, thinks through the necessary skills needed for the job and tailors his application to the needs. This is called targeting your C.V. your future employer's interest lies in you contribution to the profession and your achievements - not a long list of your previous jobs; and your academic pursuits. But, if you are applying for a job for the first time, without previous experience, then you have to talk about your academics and extra curricular activities. The job objective should be stated clearly in both types, in clear, precise language.

Skills

Under skills you can mention the languages you are proficient in, special course you have attended, your membership in a professional organization etc. A brief summary of any innovative practices which benefited your organization, the goals achieved and the targets reached - written at the beginning of the resume sets the tone and attracts the attention of your employer. (**See appendix I**)

Personal Details

Restrict your personal details to the bare essentials like - Name, Address, contact number-Telephone no, Mobile no, e-mail address etc. Don't clutter your resume by writing father's name, marital status, sex etc. unless you are specifically asked to mention them or, they add values to your resume.

Gaping Gaps:

Long gaps in your career may cause a concern to your prospective employer. If you hopped from job to job he may ear mark you as "a rolling stone". In both the cases it is better to mention clearly the reason for the gaps or shift in a Job- like, "pursued higher studies", "ill health of spouse", "shifted for availing better medical facilities" "shifted to this place as it is an education center", etc.

If you have worked in the same capacity in different organizations, club them under one head - "worked as a Sales Manager in Harris Teeter, J.C. Penny and Macy's". Avoid saying anything negative about your previous employer(s).

References

Minimum two names should be given as reference, along with their contact number and address, (if possible) courtesy demands that you take the permission of the people or at least inform them before giving their names as reference. It is preferrable to give the name of someone who can vouch for your professional performance, some one linked with your job and the name of your dean / professor etc., instead of a friend or a close relative who may talk about you in glowing terms but is unaware of your professional competency.

Language

Simple language and lucid expression are very essential for a resume. It is a pleasure to go though an application which is cliche /jargon free, with no spelling mistakes or grammatical errors and has a neat appearance. A good dictionary and grammar book should be your constant companions.

Instead of beginning every sentence with the first person, T it is better to use abbreviated language. "Introduced an innovated scheme", Represented my company in the World Trade Association" are much better expressions than "I have introduced an innovative scheme[1].....etc.

Tone

The tone has to be appropriate to the application - modest but not servile, confident and assertive, but not arrogant. Expressions like " I beg to inform you" I promise to make day and night one, if you are so kind as to take me in", etc. should be avoided. After all, you are offering you talents, experience and achievements to some one who needs them, for a price - your salary and perks. Your prospective employer should be eager and feel that he is a better beneficiary if he offers that job to a gifted, talented person like you. Your contribution to a voluntary organization, your activities in social service units, the awards/ merit certificates you have won - all speak for you. Do not hesitate to put them in your resume. If your employer has not heard about them, you have not mentioned them.

A Resume is a reflection of your self. It is 'SELF-ON-SALE', let it be genuine, lucid and original. But a word of caution here-do not brag about what you have done. Inflation of achievements and escalation of your contribution may put you in a tight corner when you are employed since the expectation of your employer are also inflated and escalated. The resume has to be truthful and genuine.

Your resume is an eloquent document of what you are and what you can do for the prospective company in the years ahead.

Appendix – I

(CV to be added)

The summary is given in brief. The skills, "under knowledge base" follow. Then comes experience in different organizations.

Address takes only one line.

The column 'Education' is filled briefly at the end. Both experience and education are given in the reverse chronological order, starting with the latest and going backwards in the resume, it is always good to begin with your strong points and then go to the others.

E-MAIL

The electronic mail has become a powerful device of communication in the Corporate World. The increasing complexity and competition of organizations calls for co-ordination through communication. Because of its speed and ease of use, E-mail has become a means of such communication.

Initially, the E-mail is used to send short messages. Today, it can be used to send messages and data that can range from pictures to animation to programmes. E-mail can broad cast messages to multiple receipents, read and discard messages, file and retrieve messages. Graphics and sound can be added to the messages.

On line business makes use of E-mail. The web-form and web-applications can automatically generate two kinds of E-mail. They are, acknowledgement E-mails and notification E-mails.

Acknowledgement E-mails may be sent on your behalf to users who submit a data page. Notification E-mails are sent to fixed E-mail addresses, normally within your organization to notify one or more people that a new, or updated submission is made. All the form fields are automatically included in the notification E-mail.

E-mail in a business world is a professional document as it can be written to a client, business partner, suppliers, staff or a board members. The rules that apply to any business letter apply to E-mail also and the E-mail should be composed with due thought, attention and care.

E-mail Etiqutte (a k a Netiquette)

According to Suzanne D.sparks following 'Netiquette' has to be followed.

Marjori Brody, President of Brody Communications Ltd offers the following tips on E.mail etiquettes.

- Watch your Words
- Be concise to eliminate follow up phone calls
- Don't make antagonizing or critical comments
- Few people like "Spam"- unsolicited E.mails
- Nothing is private; any body may read your message
- Keep attachments to a minimum; they can over load system and tax patience.
- Consider copying others in the office, using the F.Y.I or "for your information", designation
- Never assume anything: many users are n't familiar with the lingo, emoticons and E-mail acronyms that you may be using.

Try not to compress every thing into one E-mail. Select one topic for one E-mail. If there are three points of discussion, send three different E-mails, with three different headings. This way, your reader can read each E-mail and prioritize the tasks according to his convenience and urgency. E-mail does not require a signature. Write your name. Internal electronic mail can be formatted like a memo.

MEMORANDUM

A Memorandum, normally called a 'memo', is also a business communication, but it is communication within an institution or organization. It is shorter than a business letter and less formal. Memos act as a back up of inter office, oral communication. Though there is no fixed format for a memo, every memo should carry basic information like.

To,

From

Date

Subject. etc.

In memos we drop address, salutations, complimentary closes etc. Memos are written for various purpose. A memo can be written informing you about a meeting that you have to attend to; to furnish facts or details required by a senior officer; to ask a colleague requesting help or clarification of some information; short investigative reports also can take the form of a memo.

Language

The language to be used in a memo depends on the reader and the purpose. A memo which gives brief, factual status reports or instruction, may use dry, matter of fact language.

Following memo does not require high flown English language.

To Senior Manager (H.R.) — From – Sonali Mani

August,12,19....

Response to ad.in T.O.I.

Here is a summary of the responses so far to our ad in Times of India (Aug.2.) for management position

Position	Number of Application
Senior Manager, Marketing	17
Manager H.R.D.	28
Manager, Accounts	9
Assistant Manager Marketing	64

This is informative and no interpretation is required.

But, if you send a memo to a colleague, requesting his help or asking for some clarification the language can be more conversational without being excessively polite. If the memo is about a meeting that you have to attend, all the essentials like day, date, time, venue, subject to be discussed and names of other participants should also be mentioned, so that the participant can not only attend the meeting but also discuss and analyse; he can really participate in the meeting.

A Sales Manager asked his administrative Assistant to send memo (along with a copy of quarterly sales figures) to the sales staff asking them to meet with him on the following Friday. A sample of his memo

Memorandum

To : all salels Representatives.
From : Jim Martin
Date : July 15, 19.....
Sub : Sales Meeting

Please attend a sales meeting on Friday July, 18 at 3.00 P.M. in the regional Manager's office. We will discuss the attached quarterly sales totals.

This meeting is important be cause we may have to reduce dealerships and retail units

Susan L.Brock. Better Business Writing.

The date, time venue and purpose are clearly mentioned and the sales person can come prepared to the meeting. The purpose of sending the memo is fully served.

Short investigative reports written as memos may involve the writer's interpretation and some times his recommendations.

Memos may reach various destinations, for different purposes. But they are written documents and may be referred to for some purpose by someone in future. They also speak for you. As such, the language in any memo should be courteous and formal; free of slang, grammatical errors and should be gender neutral. Proof read you memos for style, mechanics and content so that you will not say anything embarrassing to yourself and your organization.

Most of the time the word memo carries a negative connotation – it may inform about laying off, a wage cut, a corrective measure to be implemented against an employee, turning down an employee's request for a transfer, or a change of department etc. Even in such memos, the tone should be human and courteous; positive but precise and direct. If the writer is too subtle and does not convey the bad news directly, the recipient may nurture hope where there is no hope.

A Memo with a ***Positive Tone***.

Memorandum

To : John Williams

From : Marsha Brown

Date : May 12, 19

Re : Response to transfer request

After we spoke last week, I checked into the possibility of your transferring to our San Francisco Office. Unfortunately, I learned a transfer is not currently possible for two reasons. First, our department needs your experience and skills for new product marketing. Second, this year, San Francisco is expanding its accounting department only.

I am sorry your proposed transfer did not work out. Please let me know, if I can assist you in any other way.

SUSAN L.BROCK. BETTER BUSINESS WRITING

Note the positive tone when he talks of the experience and skills of John Williams. He also gives a genuine reason why the transfer cannot take place. The last sentence adds the milk of human kindness offering assistance, if required.

Since a memo is a written communication, but within the company, it should be simple and informal Mr. Mathew M. Monippally says, “A memo is like a home meal. A home meal is n’t elaborate. It is simple and informal. There is little ceremony”.

FACSIMILE

Facsimile is a communicative device that transmits electronically an exact copy of a document from one location to another. Most of the offices are going for their fax machines for quick transmission of messages. Fax message is crisp and to the point. As the name of the sender and receiver appear in the message, there is no need of traditional greetings. Besides information, photographs, diagrams, illustrations can be easily and speedily transmitted through fax.

Following are a few samples of fax:

<table>
<tr><td rowspan="4">F A X

Company Name
Street Address
City, ST ZIP Code
Phone Number
Web Site
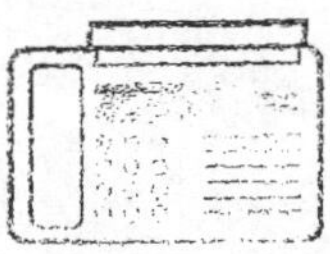</td><td>To: [Click here and type name]
Fax number: [Click here and type number]</td></tr>
<tr><td>From: [Click here and type name]
Fax number: [Click here and type number]</td></tr>
<tr><td>Date: 3/14/2009</td></tr>
<tr><td>Regarding:
[Click here and type subject]
Phone number for follow-up:
[Click here and type number]</td></tr>
<tr><td colspan="2">Comments:</td></tr>
</table>

FAX

To: From: jyadavaW

Fax: [555.555.555] Pages:

Phone: [555.555.555] Date: [Pick the date]

Re: CC:

Reason: [Select Reason for Fax]

Priority: [Select Priority for Fax]

Comments:

[**Address**]

Facsimile transmittal

To:	**[Name]**	Fax:	**[fax number]**
From:	**[Name]**	Date:	**3/14/2009**
Re:	**[subject of fax]**	Pages:	**[number of pages]**
Cc:	**[Name]**		

Urgent For review Please comment Please reply Please recycle

Notes: Select this text and then delete it or replace with your own. To save changes to this template for future use, choose **Save As** from the **File** menu. In the **Save as type** list, click **Document Template**. The next time you want to use this template, choose **New** from the **File** menu, and then double-click the template.

APPENDIX - A

WRITING BUSINESS LETTERS Useful phrases.	
Salutation	• Dear Mr. Brown Dear Ms White • Dear Sir • Dear Sirs • Dear Madam • Dear Sir or Madam • Gentlemen
Starting	• We are writing to inform you that- to confirm to request to enquire about .. • I am contacting you for the following reason. • I recently read/heard about ... and would like to know... • Having seen your advertisement in ... I would like to... • I would be interested in (obtaining/receiving) • I received your address from ... and would like to • I am writing to tell you about -
Referring to previous contact	• Thank you for your letter of March 15 • Thank you for contacting us. • In reply to your request • Thank you for your letter regarding • With reference to our telephone conversation yesterday • Further to our meeting last week ... • It was a pleasure meeting you in London last month • I enjoyed having lunch with you last week in Tokyo. • I would just like to confirm the main points we discussed on Tuesday...

Making a request	• We would appreciate it if you would • I would be grateful if you could... • Could you please send me.... • Could you possibly tell us/let us have... • In addition, I would like to receive • It would be helpful if you could send us ... • I am interested in (obtaining/receiving...) • I would appreciate your immediate attention to this matter. • Please let me know what action you propose to take.
offering help	• We would be happy to... • Would you like us to... • We are quite willing to... • Our company would be pleased to
Giving Good news	• We are pleased to announce that • I am delighted to inform you that • You will be pleased to learn that...
Giving Bad news	• We regret to inform you that... • I'm afraid it would not be possible to • Unfortunately we cannot/we are unable to • After careful consideration we have decided (not) to...
Complaining	• I am writing to express my dissatisfaction with... • I am writing to complain about/ Please note that the goods we ordered on (date) have not yet arrived. • We regret to inform you that our order n°— is now considerably overdue. • I would like to query the transport charges which seem unusually high.

Apologizing	• We are sorry for the delay in replying ... • I regret any inconvenience caused • I would like to apologize for (the delay/the inconvenience) ... • Once again, I apologise for any inconvenience.
Orders	• Thank you for your quotation of ... • We are pleased to place an order with your company for ... • We would like to cancel our order n°... • Please confirm receipt of our order. • I am pleased to acknowledge receipt of your order n°... • Your order will be processed as quickly as possible. • It will take about (three) weeks to process your order. • We can guarantee delivery before ... • Unfortunately these articles are no longer available/are out of stock.
Prices	• Please send us your price list. • You will find enclosed our most recent catalogue and price list. • Please note that our prices are subject to change without notice. • We have pleasure in enclosing a detailed quotation. • We can make you a firm offer of ... • Our terms of payment are as follows :
Referring to payment	• Our records show that we have not yet received payment of ... • According to our records ... • Please send payment as soon as possible. • You will receive a credit note for the sum of ...
Enclosing documents	• I am enclosing ... • Please find enclosed ... • You will find enclosed ...

Closing remarks	• If we can be of any further assistance, please let us know • If I can help in any way, please do not hesitate to contact me • If you require more information ... • For further details ... • Thank you for taking this into consideration • Thank you for your help. • We hope you are happy with this arrangement. • We hope you can settle this matter to our satisfaction.
Referring to future business	• We look forward to a successful working relationship in the future • We would be (very) pleased to do business with your company. • I would be happy to have an opportunity to work with your firm.
Referring to future contact	• I look forward to seeing you next week • Looking forward to hearing from you • Looking forward to receiving your comments • I look forward to meeting you on the 15th • I would appreciate a reply at your earliest convenience.
Ending business letters	• Sincerely, } • Yours sincerely, } (for all customers/clients) • Sincerely yours, } • Regards, (for those you already know and have a working relationship.)

Appendix - B

Resignation Letter

22 Tufton Street
London, SWIP 3TL
Tel: 020 75931760

November 1st 2007

Josie Waters
FieldersPharmacy
14, Broadway
London, SE 1 7 DG

Dear Mrs. Waters,

I am writing to provide formal notice of my resignation from fielders Pharmacy.
My last day will be November 14th 2007.

I trust that two weeks is sufficient notice for you to find a replacement for my position. I would be pleased to help train individual you choose to take my place. Thank you for employing me for the past three years. My experience as clerk, supervisor, and floor manager bas been very positive and I'm confident that I will use many of the skills I have learned at fielders in the future.

If you have any concerns, please contact me at my personal email address. All the best,

Appendix - C

Lay-off Letter

Pino's Plazzaria

Viale Silvani

10, 2345 Bologna, Italy
Tel: 051 52079

November 30th 20---

Joanne Montague

Via Belmeloro 18
40123 Bologna

Dear Ms. Montague

As you are probably aware, the recent smoking ban has a bad impact on our business. "Our sales have dropped 40 percent in the six months. Though we do not expect this to be a long-term condition of our business, we don't expect sales to return to normal until the summer when our patio opens for the tourist seasons.

Due to the loss in business we regret to inform you that we are off all of our hosts and hostesses for the winter and spring. With business being so slow our servers can handle the task of greet seating customers on their own.

You are entitled to two week's severance pay, which will be paid on you next paycheck. Please come in for any scheduled shifts week.

Thank you for your hard work and dedication at Pino's Pizzaria.

Apply again for our next summer seasons.

Sincerely,
Franco Bellini
Franco Bellini
Owner

APPENDIX - D

BUSINESS WRITING

This section contains actual writing, samples of letters and memos. All samples contain weaknesses and errors common in business writing. Some of the weaknesses are more subtle than others. Please read each sample carefully, and evaluate each stage: the "before" version, the "corrected" version, and the "improved" version.

WRITING SAMPLES

DESCRIPTION: John Freeman, President of ABC Enterprises, requested his accountant to explain why his accounting bill doubled since last year. Following.is the accountant's response.

BEFORE **APPENDIX – Dl**

XYZ ACCOUNTING CORPORATION
1420 Fremont Way
Oakdale, CA 95123
(805) 772-4322

July 2, 19XX

Mr. John Freeman
ABC Enterprises

Dear John:

In response to your letter of June 15, 19XX, enclosed please find Exhibit A. As you can see, the work performed for you this year is different than last year. In addition, the parameters of tasks increased since last year. Accordingly due to this fact and the fact that our billing rates were raised this year; it was necessary to increase our charges for professional services rendered. Hopefully, this letter offers some explanation as to the question you raised. If you require more additional information, please don't hesitate to contact us.

Sincerely,

XYZ Accounting Corporation

Better Business Writing Susan L Block

APPENDIX — D2

WRITING SAMPLES (continued)

CORRECTED

XYZ ACCOUNTING CORPORATION
1420 Fremont Way
Oakdale, CA 95123
(805) 772-4322

July 2, 19XX

Mr. John Freeman
ABC Enterprises
2027 Washington Blvd.
Oakdale, CA 95123

Dear John:

In response to your letter of June 15, 19XX, enclosed please find Exhibit A. As you can see, the work performed for you this year is different than last year. In addition, the parameters of tasks increased since last year. Accordingly due to this fact and the fact that our billing rates were raised this year; it was necessary to increase our charges for professional services rendered. Hopefully, this letter offers some explanation as to the question you raised. If you require more additional information, please don't hesitate to contact us.

Sincerely,

XYZ Accounting Corporation

TRITE · CONDESCENDING · CLICHE! · USE "FROM" · JARGON · OMIT · OMIT · PASSIVE · OMIT · USE "ANSWERS" · WORDY · REDUNDANT · WORDY

APPENDIX — D3

WRITING SAMPLES (continued)

CORRECTED

XYZ ACCOUNTING CORPORATION
1420 Fremont Way
Oakdale, CA 95123
(805) 772-4322

July 2, 19XX

Mr. John Freeman
ABC Enterprises
2027 Washington Blvd.
Oakdale, CA 95123

Dear John:

In response to your letter of June 15, 19XX, enclosed please find Exhibit A. As you can see, the work performed for you this year is different than last year. In addition, the parameters of tasks increased since last year. Accordingly due to this fact and the fact that our billing rates were raised this year; It was necessary to increase our charges for professional services rendered. Hopefully, this letter offers some explanation as to the question you raised. If you require more additional information, please don't hesitate to contact us.

Sincerely,

XYZ Accounting Corporation

TRITE
CONDESCENDING
CLICHE'
USE "FROM"
JARGON
OMIT
OMIT
PASSIVE
OMIT
USE "ANSWERS"
WORDY
REDUNDANT
WORDY

APPENDIX - El

WRITING SAMPLES (continued) S

EMPLOYMENT AGENCY COUNSELOR'S LETTR

Following is a letter from an employment agency counselor to businesses announcing a new telephone communication setup

BEFORE S

September 5, 19XX

Dear Employer:

We have established a special phone communication system to provide additional opportunities for your input. During this year we will give added emphasis to the goal of communication and utilize a variety of means to accomplish this goal. Your input, from the unique position of employer, will help us to plan and implement an effective plan that meets the staffing needs of your company. An open dialogue, feedback and sharing of information between employment counselors and employers will enable us to work with your staffing needs in the most effective manner.

Sincerely,

Ted F. Jones
Employment Counselor

APPENDIX - E2

WRITING SAMPLES (continued)

CORRECTED

September 5, 19XX

Dear Employer:

We have established a special phone communication system to provide additional opportunities for your input. During this year we will give added emphasis to the goal of communication and utilize a variety of means to accomplish this goal. Your input, from the unique position of employer, will help us to plan and implement an effective plan that meets the staffing needs of your company. An open dialogue, feedback and sharing of information between employment counselors and employers will enable us to work with your staffing needs in the most effective manner.

Sincerely,

Ted F. Jones
Employment Counselor

APPENDIX— E3

IMPROVED

September 5, 19XX

Dear Employer:

We have established a special phone system to improve the communication between employment counselors and employers. Please call our office any afternoon between 4:00-5:00 if you have questions about available applicants or if you'd just like to talk. We believe that if we encourage you to call, we can establish a closer relationship and better meet your staffing needs.

Sincerely,

Ted F. Jones
Employment Counselor

[This revised version of the letter sounds much more' human.]

APPENDIX - F

A VERY CONFUSING LETTER

To,

General Manager (Finance)

Sub: Servicing of Servo Amplifier Unit, Type : A06b-H109, Make: Max

Problem : RPM variation is coming and while stopping the motor more vibration is coming.

The above Servo Amplifier Unit send for servioing to M/s Max India, Mumbai vide: 139 dt 05.07.08 after service the above unit received vide : 636 dt 14.11.08 same time our machine (Mon Seiki CNC Lathe Machine) send for reconditioning work to M/s HMT India, Bangalore on 14.10.08 after reconditioning the above machine received on 26.12.08 and installed on 10.01.09.

After receiving servo amplifier unit it was not possible to check the unit immediately because machine was not available here. After receiver of machine checked servo amplifierunit found same problem is repeated and hence it was rejected and sent back to M/s Max India Vide : DC 234 dt 29.01.09 and for same item again we received invoice from Max India. We feel there is no payment involved now, as this unit is not at all working after repairs.

REFERENCES:

Better Business Writing - Susan L Brock

The Managers' Guide to Business writing - Suzanne -D Sparks

The craft of Business Letter writing - Mathew M Monippally

The skills of communicating - Bill Scott

Hand Book of Practical Communication Skills - Chrissie Wright

Business Communication - K K Sinha

Communicative Competence -Varanasi Bhaskara Rao

Internet.

REPORT-WRITING

Y.Kameswari

Effective Communication plays a vital role in the increasingly complex and competitive corporate world and has become "an undeniable strategic necessity". Communication can be either oral or written but the importance of the written word as an unavoidable "organizational structure" has to be taken note of. Written Communication has many advantages like permanence, legal validity, fixing accountability etc. It may take the form of a memo, reminder, manual, letter, periodical, in-house magazine, etc. One very important form of the Written Communication is writing a report. No doubt, an onerous and intimidating task for many, but is unavoidable.

What is a report ? What are the characteristics of a good report? What is the objective of a report ? What are the different types of reports ? What goes into the making of a good report ? What are the pitfalls to be avoided ?

A report, by definition, "is a statement describing what has happened", or, "describing a state of affairs". The report is expected to examine and analyse a particular situation or problem, give details of investigations made and actions taken. The reporter draws conclusion from the given facts and makes his recommendations.

What makes a good Report ?

Excellence in Report writing can be achieved by :

(a) Careful Planning and Preparation

(b) Structure of the Report

(c) Presentation

Planning & Preparation

Two important questions to be asked are Why ? Who ? The report must be appropriate to its purpose and reader. There are two types of readers - (1). Report Readers, (2). Report Users. Normally the report is prepared to bring certain information to the attention of the senior management, competent to take a decision. Full knowledge of the background of events, facts and consequences are required for this. Reports can be requests to senior management to initiate action. Sometimes colleagues and specialists may use these reports. They are report users.

Report readers may not be experts in the field but senior managers with control over budgets. A report with too many technical details may go above the head of report users and over explanation may offend an expert. The report should accommodate both the categories. Careful gathering of facts, as well as relevant and necessary information should be the first step. The facts gathered should be accurate. They should be analysed and presented in a well structured report.

Language

The French Philosopher Pascal once wrote a letter to a friend apologizing for its length. "I lack the time," he wrote, "to make it brief." This should not be the case with a report. The language should be simple and precise. There is no place for exhibition of erudition, flights of fancy, linguistic jugglery, tautology and jargon. The structure and vocabulary should befit the report.

Sections / Sub-Sections

The report is to be divided into Sections and Sub-Sections and each one is to be numbered. Notation helps in ready reference. Decimal numbering is the most forward method of Notation. Look at the following:

- Section - 1
- Sub-Section - 1.1
- Paragraph - 1. 1.1.1.
- Para -- 2. 1.1.2

The Notation 3.2.1 indicates first paragraph of the second sub-section and third section. Normally 3sub-divisions should be sufficient

Final Checking

Final Cheeking and Cross Cheeking is very essential as it ensures that the report conveys the required information in a lucid and the appropriate language. Final checking helps on the following ways

Repetition can be avoided

- Confirms the accuracy of facts and figures and supports to your conclusion.
- Helps you to check the recommendations made are realistic.
- Verifies the continuity of thought and logical sequencing
- Helps you to avoid using too many sub-headings and to club, some if necessary.
- Finally, it ascertains the material at hand is sufficient.

Structure of A Report

Reports are prepared on various occasions for various purposes. The reports can be classified as Laboratory Reports. Research Reports. Field study Reports, Feasibility Report, Financial Reports, Annual Reports and Technical Reports. The structure of a report may vary depending on the type of report.

The Annual Report

The Annual Report provides the vital information to the investment audience with a summary of the company's performance over the previous year and its outlook for the upcoming year. Besides the shareholders, customers, strategic partners, legislators and regulators, the financial community and the media rely on the Annual Report.

The Employee Annual Report highlights

(a) How did the contributions of employees affect the company's performance.

(b) What is expected of them in the years ahead.

"The Employee Report makes the link between employee efforts and the final outcome, adding context and meaning to the cold financial statement in the share holders' report".

Apart from the Employees Report, there can be (a). Letter Style Report, (b). a Schematic report (look for ex. In the appendix) K.K. Sinha, app. 1, 2, 3.

The Letter Style Report

It is normally written on the company memo used for internal communication. It carries no salutation and only a signature without any subscription.

Some times the report can have enumerated paragraphs. The numbered paragraphs add to the clarity and readability of the report.

The Schematic Report

The Schematic Reports are written to a specific scheme under headings like. . .

(a) Terms of Reference

(b) Action taken

(c) Findings

(d) Conclusion

(e) Recommendation

After giving a reference - exhibiting the products at New York International Fair, you may describe the action taken - how the stall was set up, what were the problems encountered and how they were solved etc.

The findings include about the actual stall, customer reaction, any important customers that you have come across, your action (inviting them to India etc.), the expenditure incurred, the difference between your stall and others, etc.

Conclusion may cover the impact of the stall and necessity of such stalls in future.

Recommendations may highlight the need of increase in financial sanctions, increase in sales persons, engaging a full time sales representative with knowledge of foreign languages etc.

Structure of Technical Report

Most formal Reports are technical and professional. They follow a specific structure and sequence. Chrissie Wright in his *practical communication skills* recommends the following:

- Title Page
- Acknowledgement
- Abstract
- Contents Page
- Introduction
- Findings
- Conclusion
- Recommendations
- Appendix
- References
- Bibliography

A report may not always have all the above. But it is better to keep the above in mind and follow the same sequence.

Title Page

Any, but the shortest reports should put the title on a separate page. The title itself should be the biggest, boldest and the most attractive.

- The author's name should be in smaller letters, followed by date, ref. no.
- Receiver's name / signature
- Company name, address and logo
- Confidentiality mark

Copy No. (For restricted reports).

The title must be precise but brief.

The main title can be followed by a longer, explanatory title.

E.g. BIGGER & BETTER
A strategy for growth in the next media.

Acknowledgements

Thanking a sponsor or those who helped in writing the report has a psychological impact and is best placed at or near the beginning of a report.

Abstract

The authority competent to take action, may not always find time to go through the report in its entirety. He would like to read the abstract and understand the report.

"An abstract should not be a mere recital of the subjects covered. Expression such as "is discussed" and "is described" should never be included. The abstract should be a condensation and concentration of the essential information in the paper"

An abstract is good if it

- Gives the background so that the reader can understand the context
- Gives all the essential points of the main report in a few sentences, laying special stress on conclusions, recommendations and action points.
- Avoids lists, minor details, examples, quotations, numbers
- If it is of appropriate length and language, informative, rather than descriptive language is to be used) the tone must be impersonal.
- Is clear, concise, complete and correct.

Contents

A table of contents should be prepared even before writing the actual report. It should include the title of every section and sub-section, including Appendices. If the illustrations are too many, a separate list can be provided for them.

The table of contents...

- Clarifies Thinking
- Allows for Flexibility
- Ensures a Logical Sequence

Findings

Facts are sacred. The information in any report must be scrupulously accurate. The facts themselves can be gathered from. ...

- Organised Surveys; Questionnaires, Interviews.
- In-house Documents, Minutes of Meetings.
- Technical Data, Past Reports
- Company literature, Publicity material, Computerised information.
- Newspapers, journals, books, thesis and articles.

While presenting facts, the writer has to be objective. The facts should be accurate.

Introduction

The introduction should clearly indicate

(a) The Subject / Topic of the Report;

(b) The Purpose of the Report;

(c) The Scope;

(d) The Shape

he subject of a report differs from the purpose. A report may talk of Wall Street Collapse, the frauds Committed by the financier Mad-off and the consequences. The purpose of the report can be to stall such frauds in future, to look into the legalities of the issue, to advise / bail out the investors.

Conclusion

A Conclusion is what the report arrives at after analyzing the facts. The report makers' understanding and analysing the facts are tested when he draws the conclusions.

Recommendations

A report's purpose is to persuade, to justify expenditure incurred or to recommend action or a series of actions to be taken. The recommendations just do that. Based on the conclusions drawn, the recommendations are to be made / while recommending, the reporter has to urge and sometimes advise. However, the recommendations should be specific, measurable and achievable.

Appendix

A voluminous report discourages the reader at the very outset and may never be read with interest. To avoid this, an appendix is to be prepared. Following are the different types of appendices.

(a) Detailed information required by a few / limited readers. Statements, which are too lengthy may not to be included in the main reports.

(b) **Tables and Figures** - Accuracy of figures is of the utmost importance. All tables should be numbered and titled. All columns should be clearly headed and units of measurement defined.

(c) **Diagram** - An appropriate diagram at the appropriate place is more eloquent than the most eloquent language. The diagram, however, should not be accompanied by too much information. Several simple, clear diagrams are preferrable to a single, cluttered one.

(d) Photographs and Maps - They should be presented on an extended page, so that the reader can see it open alongside the text, while reading.

References

By convention, references usually precede bibliography. References are made to materials specifically referred to or quoted in the report. Each reference will include author, title, place and date of publication.

Bibliography

It is a list of material useful and the same order author, title etc. should be followed as in references.

Presentation of a Report

Presentation of a Report is a Spoken Communication, a skill that can be developed, refined and perfected with meticulous planning and preparation. The following clues can be helpful.

- The presentation should give an overview of the report.
- The important aspects of the report like summary, conclusion, recommendations etc. should be highlighted. All the unnecessary details, explanations, examples, should be eliminated.
- A connection between the key concepts and the conclusion drawn should be established, so that the audience will have a clear understanding of the recommendations made.
- The audience have a right to ask questions when they need some clarification. The material / details / information required by them should be kept ready.
- The question can be answered as part of the presentation, unless it obstructs the logical flow of the presentation. If the answer involves a detailed explanation or lot of information, it can be done at the end of the presentation.
- There are no foolish questions. If they are tough or hard, do not feel agitated, angry or humiliated. Take a little time and answer them coolly.
- Take the help of an overhead projector; give a slide show etc. to make your presentation more colorful. However, the information displayed should be selective, important and relevant to your topic.
- Establish and keep eye contact with your audience.

Meticulous preparation, clear analytical thinking, adequate linguistic inputs turn this tedious, intimidating task of Report Writing/Presentation into a pleasurable and rewarding challenge.

Happy Report Writing!

References / Bibliography

Corporate Conversation by SHEL HOLTZ

Practical Communication Skills – Chrissie Wright

The Skills of Communicating – Bill Scott

Internet Business Communication – K.K. Sinha

Internet

Appendix

1. Examples of a bad write up – Richard Nilon

   Resumes for students and Professionals – www.psychpage.com

   Page 1 -3.
2. CSC 498/499

   Capstone Design Project

   Example of a Bad Report – Don't do this !
3. Examples of Good Report
4. Letter Style Report – Page – 499 Business Communication by K.K.Sinha

   Page – 500 " "
5. Schematic Report - Page 502